T0262306

Functions of Data Mining in Science, Technology and Medicine

Functions of Data Mining in Science, Technology and Medicine

Edited by **Mick Benson**

CLANRYE INTERNATIONAL

New Jersey

Published by Clanrye International,
55 Van Reypen Street,
Jersey City, NJ 07306, USA
www.clanryeinternational.com

Functions of Data Mining in Science, Technology and Medicine
Edited by Mick Benson

© 2015 Clanrye International

International Standard Book Number: 978-1-63240-242-4 (Hardback)

Contents

Preface

It is often said that books are a boon to humankind. They document every progress and pass on the knowledge from one generation to the other. They play a crucial role in our lives. Thus I was both excited and nervous while editing this book. I was pleased by the thought of being able to make a mark but I was also nervous to do it right because the future of students depends upon it. Hence, I took a few months to research further into the discipline, revise my knowledge and also explore some more aspects. Post this process, I begun with the editing of this book.

The aim of this book is to assist data miners who want to employ distinct data mining techniques. Data mining commonly encompasses areas of machine learning, pattern identification, statistics, data management and databases, artificial intelligence, etc. This book covers most of these areas by elucidating various applications. The readers will understand why and how data mining can also be employed for the enhancement of project management through this book. It will also serve as a great source of information and inspire readers to pursue education and research in this growing field; since the book also integrates extensive information concerning certain aspects and significance of data mining in various fields like pharmacovigilance, incorporating domain knowledge into medical image mining, electronic documentation of clinical pharmacy interventions in hospitals, etc.

I thank my publisher with all my heart for considering me worthy of this unparalleled opportunity and for showing unwavering faith in my skills. I would also like to thank the editorial team who worked closely with me at every step and contributed immensely towards the successful completion of this book. Last but not the least, I wish to thank my friends and colleagues for their support.

Editor

Data Mining Applications

Survey of Data Mining and Applications (Review from 1996 to Now)

Adem Karahoca, Dilek Karahoca and Mert Şanver

Additional information is available at the end of the chapter

1. Introduction

The science of extracting useful information from large data sets or databases is named as data mining. Though data mining concepts have an extensive history, the term "Data Mining", is introduced relatively new, in mid 90's. Data mining covers areas of statistics, machine learning, data management and databases, pattern recognition, artificial intelligence, and other areas. All of these are concerned with certain aspects of data analysis, so they have much in common but each also has its own distinct problems and types of solution. The fundamental motivation behind data mining is autonomously extracting useful information or knowledge from large data stores or sets. The goal of building computer systems that can adapt to special situations and learn from their experience has attracted researchers from many fields, including computer science, engineering, mathematics, physics, neuroscience and cognitive science.

As opposed to most of statistics, data mining typically deals with data that have already been collected for some purpose other than the data mining analysis. Majority of the applications presented in this book chapter uses data formerly collected for any other purposes. Out of data mining research, has come a wide variety of learning techniques that have the potential to renovate many scientific and industrial fields.

This book chapter surveys the development of Data Mining through review and classification of journal articles between years 1996-now. The basis for choosing this period is that, the comparatively new concept of data mining become widely accepted and used during that period. The literature survey is based on keyword search through online journal databases on Science Direct, EBSCO, IEEE, Taylor Francis, Thomson Gale, and Scopus. A total of 1218 articles are reviewed and 174 of them found to be including data mining methodologies as primary method used. Some of the articles include more than one data mining methodologies used in conjunction with each other.

The concept of data mining can be divided into two broad areas as predictive methods and descriptive methods. Predictive methods include Classification, Regression, and Time Series Analysis. Predictive methods aim to project future status before they occur.

Section 2 includes definition of algorithms and the applications using these algorithms. Discussion of trends throughout the last decade is also presented in this section. Section 3 introduces Descriptive methods in four major parts; Clustering, Summarization, Association Rules and Sequence Discovery. The objective of descriptive methods is describing phenomena, evaluating characteristics of the dataset or summarizing a series of data. The application areas of each algorithm are documented in this part with discussion of the trend in descriptive methods. Section 4 describes data warehouses and lists their applications involving data mining techniques. Section 5 gives a summarization of the study and discusses future trends in data mining and contains a brief conclusion.

2. Predictive methods and applications

A predictive model makes a prediction about values of data using known results found from different data sets. Predictive modeling may be made based on the use of other historical data. Predictive model data mining tasks include classification, regression, time series analysis, and prediction (Dunham, 2003).

2.1. Classification methods

Classification maps data into predefined groups or classes. It is often referred to as supervised learning. Classification algorithms require that the classes be defined based on data attribute values. Pattern recognition is a type of classification where an input pattern is classified into one of several classes based on its similarity to these predefined classes (Dunham, 2003). In this section; decision trees, neural networks, Bayesian classifiers and support vector machines related applications are considered.

2.1.1. Decision trees

Decision trees can be construct recursively. Firstly, an attribute is selected to place at root node to make one branch for each possible value. This splits up the example set into subsets, one for every value of the attribute (Witten, Frank; 2000).

The basic principle of tree models is to partition the space spanned by the input variables to maximize a score of class purity that the majority of points in each cell of the partition belong to one class. They are mappings of observations to conclusions (target values). Each inner node corresponds to variable; an arc to a child represents a possible value of that variable. A leaf represents the predicted value of target variable given the values of the variables represented by the path from the root (T. Menzies, Y. Hu, 2003).

Information entropy is used to measure the amount of uncertainty or randomness in a set of data. Gini index also used to determine the best splitting for a decision tree.

Decision trees can be divided into two types as regression trees and classification trees. The trend is towards the regression trees as they provide real valued functions instead of classification tasks. Applications include; Remote Sensing, Database Theory, Chemical engineering, Mobile communications, Image processing, Soil map modeling, Radiology, Web traffic prediction, Speech Recognition, Risk assessment, Geo information, Operations Research, Agriculture, Computer Organization, Marketing, Geographical Information Systems. Decision trees are growing more popular among other methods of classifying data. C5.0 algorithm by R.J. Quinlan is very commonly used in latest applications.

Decision tree applications	Authors
2006 – Geographical Information Systems	Baisen Zhang, Ian Valentine, Peter Kemp and Greg Lambert
2005 – Marketing	Sven F. Crone, Stefan Lessmann and Robert Stahlbock
2005 – Computer Organization	Xiao-Bai Li
2005 - Agriculture	Baisen Zhang, Ian Valentine and Peter D. Kemp
2004 – Operations Research	Nabil Belacel, Hiral Bhasker Raval and Abraham P. Punnen
2004 – Geoinformation	Luis M. T. de Carvalho, Jan G. P. W. Clevers, Andrew K. Skidmore
2004 – Risk assessment	Christophe Mues, Bart Baesens, Craig M. Files and Jan Vanthienen
2003 – Speech Recognition	Oudeyer Pierre-Yves
2003 – Web traffic prediction	Selwyn Piramuthu
2002 – Radiology	Wen-Jia Kuo, Ruey-Feng Chang, Woo Kyung Moon, Cheng Chun Lee
2002 – Soil map modelling	Christopher J. Moran and Elisabeth N. Bui
2002 – Image processing	Petra Perner
2001 – Mobile communications	Patrick Piras, Christian Roussel and Johanna Pierrot-Sanders
2000 – Chemical engineering	Yoshiyuki Yamashita
2000 – Geoscience	Simard, M.; Saatchi, S.S.; De Grandi
2000 – Medical Systems	Zorman, M.; Podgorelec, V.; Kokol, P.; Peterson, M.; Lane, J
1999 – Database Theory	Mauro Sérgio R. de Sousa, Marta Mattoso and Nelson F. F. Ebecken
1999 – Speech Processing	Padmanabhan, M.; Bahl, L.R.; Nahamoo, D
1998 – Remote Sensing	R. S. De Fries M. Hansen J. R. G. Townshend R. Sohlberg

Table 1. Decision Tree Applications

2.1.2. Neural networks

An artificial neural network is an interconnected group of artificial neurons that uses a mathematical or computational model for information processing based on a connectionist approach to computation (Freeman et al., 1991). Formally the field started when neurophysiologist Warren McCulloch and mathematician Walter Pitts wrote a paper on how neurons might work in 1943. They modeled a simple neural network using electrical circuits. In 1949, Donald Hebb pointed out the fact that neural pathways are strengthened each time they are used, a concept fundamentally essential to the ways in which humans learn. If two nerves fire at the same time, he argued, the connection between them is enhanced.

In 1982, interest in the field was renewed. John Hopfield of Caltech presented a paper to the National Academy of Sciences. His approach was to create more useful machines by using bidirectional lines. In 1986, with multiple layered neural networks appeared, the problem was how to extend the Widrow-Hoff rule to multiple layers. Three independent groups of researchers, one of which included David Rumelhart, a former member of Stanford's psychology department, came up with similar ideas which are now called back propagation networks because it distributes pattern recognition errors throughout the network. Hybrid networks used just two layers, these back-propagation networks use many. Neural networks are applied to data mining in Craven and Sahvlik (1997).

Neural Networks Applications	Authors
2006 – Banking	Tian-Shyug Lee, Chih-Chou Chiu, Yu-Chao Chou and Chi-Jie Lu
2005 – Stock market	J.V. Healy, M. Dixon, B.J. Read and F.F. Cai
2005 – Financial Forecast	Kyoung-jae Kim
2005 – Mobile Communications	Shin-Yuan Hung, David C. Yen and Hsiu-Yu Wang
2005 – Oncology	Ta-Cheng Chen and Tung-Chou Hsu
2005 – Credit risk assessment	Yueh-Min Huang, Chun-Min Hung and Hewijin Christine Jiau
2005 – Enviromental Modelling	Uwe Schlink, Olf Herbarth, Matthias Richter, Stephen Dorling
2005 – Cybernetics	Jiang Chang; Yan Peng
2004 – Biometrics	Marie-Noëlle Pons, Sébastien Le Bonté and Olivier Potier
2004 – Heat Transfer Engineering	R. S. De Fries M. Hansen J. R. G. Townshend R. Sohlberg
2004 – Marketing	YongSeog Kim and W. Nick Street
2004 – Industrial Processes	X. Shi, P. Schillings, D. Boyd
2004 – Economics	Tae Yoon Kim, Kyong Joo Oh, Insuk Sohn and Changha Hwang
2003 – Crime analysis	Giles C. Oatley and Brian W. Ewart
2003 – Medicine	Álvaro Silva, Paulo Cortez, Manuel Filipe Santos, Lopes Gomes and José Neves
2003 – Production economy	Paul F. Schikora and Michael R. Godfrey
2001 – Image Recognation	Kondo, T.; Pandya, A.S

Table 2. Neural Networks Applications

The research in theory has been slowed down; however applications continue to increase popularity. Artificial neural networks are one of a class of highly parameterized statistical models that have attracted considerable attention in recent years. Since the artificial neural networks are highly parameterized, they can easily model small irregularities in functions however this may lead to over fitting in some conditions. Applications of neural networks include; Production economy, Medicine, Crime analysis, Economics, Industrial Processes, Marketing, Heat Transfer Engineering, Biometrics, Environmental Modeling, Credit risk assessment, Oncology, Mobile Communications, Financial Forecast, Stock market, Banking.

2.1.3. Bayesian classifiers

Bayesian classification is based on Bayes Theorem. In particular, naive Bayes is a special case of a Bayesian network, and learning the structure and parameters of an unrestricted Bayesian network would appear to be a logical means of improvement.

However, Friedman (1997) found that naive Bayes easily outperforms such unrestricted Bayesian network classifiers on a large sample of benchmark datasets. Bayesian classifiers are useful in predicting the probability that a sample belongs to a particular class or grouping. This technique tends to be highly accurate and fast, making it useful on large databases. Model is simple and intuitive. Error level is low when independence of attributes and distribution model is robust. Some often perceived disadvantages of Bayesian analysis are really not problems in practice. Any ambiguities in choosing a prior are generally not serious, since the various possible convenient priors usually do not disagree strongly within the regions of interest. Bayesian analysis is not limited to what is traditionally considered statistical data, but can be applied to any space of models (Hanson, 1996).

Application areas include; Geographical Information Systems, Database Management, Web services, Neuroscience. In application areas which large amount of data needed to be processed, technique is useful. The assumption of normal distribution of patterns is the toughest shortcoming of the model.

Bayessian Classifiers	Authors
2005 – Neuroscience	Pablo Valenti, Enrique Cazamajou, Marcelo Scarpettini
2003 – Web services	Dunja Mladeni and Marko Grobelnik
1999 – Database Management	S. Lavington, N. Dewhurst, E. Wilkins and A. Freitas
1998 – Geographical Information Systems	A. Stassopoulou, M. Petrou J. Kittler

Table 3. Bayesian Classifiers

2.1.4. Support Vector Machines

Support Vector Machines are a method for creating functions from a set of labeled training data. The original optimal hyper plane algorithm proposed by Vladimir Vapnik in 1963 was a linear classifier. However, in 1992, Boser, Guyon and Vapnik suggested a way to create non-linear classifiers by applying the kernel trick to maximum-margin hyper planes. The resulting algorithm is formally similar, except that every dot product is replaced by a non-linear kernel function. This allows the algorithm to fit the maximum-margin hyper plane in the transformed feature space. The transformation may be non-linear and the transformed space high dimensional; thus though the classifier is a hyper plane in the high-dimensional feature space it may be non-linear in the original input space.

In 1995, Cortes and Vapnik suggested a modified maximum margin idea that allows for mislabeled examples. If there exists no hyper plane that can split the binary examples, the Soft Margin method will choose a hyper plane that splits the examples as cleanly as possible, while still maximizing the distance to the nearest cleanly split examples.

A version of a SVM for regression was proposed in 1997 by Vapnik, Golowich, and Smola. This method is called SVM regression. The model produced by classification only depends on a subset of the training data, because the cost function for building the model does not care about training points that lie beyond the margin. Analogously, the model produced by SVR only depends on a subset of the training data, because the cost function for building the model ignores any training data that is close (within a threshold ε) to the model prediction. The function can be a classification function or the function can be a general regression function. A detailed tutorial can be found in Burges (1998).

For classification they operate by finding a hyper surface in the space of possible inputs. Applications of Support Vector Machines include; Industrial Engineering, Medical Informatics, Genetics, Medicine, Marketing.

Support Vector Mechanism	Authors
2005 – Marketing	Sven F. Crone, Stefan Lessmann and Robert Stahlbock
2004 – Medicine	Lihua Li, Hong Tang, Zuobao Wu, Jianli Gong, Michael Gruidl
2004 – Genetics	Fei Pan, Baoying Wang, Xin Hu and William Perrizo
2003 – Medical Informatics	I Kalatzis, D Pappas, N Piliouras, D Cavouras
2002 – Industrial Engineering	Mehmed Kantardzic, Benjamin Djulbegovic and Hazem Hamdan

Table 4. Support Vector Machines

2.2. Time series analysis and prediction applications

Time series clustering has been shown effective in providing useful information in various domains. There seems to be an increased interest in time series clustering as part of the effort in temporal data mining research (Liao, 2003). Unvariate and multivariate time series explained respectively.

2.2.1. Univariate time series

The expression "univariate time series" refers to a time series that consists of particular observations recorded sequentially over equal time increments. Although a univariate time series data set is usually given as a single column of numbers, time is in fact an implicit variable in the time series. If the data are equi-spaced, the time variable, or index, does not need to be explicitly given. The time variable may sometimes be explicitly used for plotting the series. However, it is not used in the time series model itself. Triple exponential smoothing is an example of this approach. Another example, called seasonal loses, is based on locally weighted least squares and is discussed by Cleveland (1993). Another approach, commonly used in scientific and engineering applications, is to analyze the series in the frequency domain. The spectral plot is the primary tool for the frequency analysis of time series. Application areas includes financial forecasting, management, energy, economics, zoology, industrial engineering, emergency services, biomedicine, networks.

Univariate Time Series Applications	Authors
2005 – Financial Forecasting	James W. Taylor and Roberto Buizza
2005 – Enviromental Management	Peter Romilly
2004 – Energy	Jesús Crespo Cuaresma, Jaroslava Hlouskova, Stephan Kossmeier
2003 – Crime Rates Forecasting	Wilpen Gorr, Andreas Olligschlaeger and Yvonne Thompson
2002 – Financial Economics	Per Bjarte Solibakke
2001 – Unemployment Rates	Bradley T. Ewing and Phanindra V. Wunnava
2001 – Forecasting	Juha Junttila
2000 – Zoology	Christian H. Reick and Bernd Page
1998 – Industrial Engineering	Gerhard Thury and Stephen F. Witt
1998 – Emergency Medicine	Kenneth E Bizovi, Jerrold B Leikin, Daniel O Hryhorczuk and Lawrence J Frateschi
1998 – Biomedicine	R. E. Abdel-Aal and A. M. Mangoud
1997 – Economics	Hahn Shik Lee and Pierre L. Siklos
1996 – Sensors	Stefanos Manganaris
1996 – Economics	Apostolos Serletis and David Krause

Table 5. Univariate Time Series Applications

2.2.2. Multivariate time series

Multivariate time series may arise in a number of ways. The time series are measuring the same quantity or time series depending on some fundamental quantity leads to multivariate series. The multivariate form of the Box-Jenkins univariate models is frequently used in applications. The multivariate form of the Box-Jenkins univariate models is sometimes called the ARMAV model, for AutoRegressive Moving Average Vector or simply vector ARMA process. Also, Friedman worked multivariate adaptive regression splines in 1991.

The application areas of the method include neurology, hydrology, finance, medicine, chemistry, environmental science, biology.

Multivariate Time Series Applications	Authors
2006 – Neurology	Björn Schelter, Matthias Winterhalder, Bernhard Hellwig, Brigitte Guschlbauer
2005 – Neurobiology	Ernesto Pereda, Rodrigo Quian Quiroga and Joydeep Bhattacharya
2005 – Hydrology	R. Muñoz-Carpena, A. Ritter and Y.C. Li
2005 – Neuroscience	Andy Müller, Hannes Osterhage, Robert Sowa
2004 – Market analysis	Bernd Vindevogel, Dirk Van den Poel and Geert Wets
2004 – Policy Modelling	Wankeun Oh and Kihoon Lee
2004 – Medicine	Fumikazu Miwakeichi, Andreas Galka, Sunao Uchida, Hiroshi Arakaki
2004 – Economics	Morten Ørregaard Nielsen
2003 – Labor Force Forecasting	Edward W. Frees
2003 – Statistical Planning	Hamparsum Bozdogan and Peter Bearse
2002 – Chemistry	Jan H. Christensen
2002 – Biomedicine	Stephen Swift and Xiaohui Liu
2001 – Marine Sciences	Ransom A. Myers
2001 – Reliability Engineering	S. Lu, H. Lu and W. J. Kolarik
2000 – Environmental Science	Zuotao Li and Menas Kafatos

Table 6. Multivariate Time Series Applications

2.3. Regression methods

Regression is generally used to predict future values base on past values by fitting a set of points to a curve. Linear regression assumes that a linear relationship exists between the input data and the output data. The common formula for a linear relationship;

$$y = c_0 + c_1 x_1 + \ldots + c_n x_n \tag{1}$$

Here there are n input variables, that are called predictors or regressors; one output variable, that is called response and n + 1 constants which are chosen during the modeling process to match the input examples. This is sometimes called multiple linear regression because there is more than one predictor (Dunham, 2003).

Following subsections give explanations about non parametric, robust, ridge and nonlinear regressions.

2.3.1. Nonparametric regression

Nonparametric regression analysis is regression without an assumption of linearity. The scope of nonparametric regression is very broad, ranging from smoothing the relationship between two variables in a scatter plot to multiple-regression analysis and generalized regression models. Methods of nonparametric-regression analysis have been rendered practical by advances in statistics and computing, and are now a serious alternative to more traditional parametric-regression modeling. Non-parametric regression is a type of regression analysis in which the functional form of the relationship between the response variable and the associated predictor variables does not to be specified in order to fit a model to a set of data. The applications are mostly in fields of medicine and biology. Also applications in economics and geography exist.

Non parametric Regression Applications	Authors
2005 – Medicine	Hiroyuki Watanabe and Hiroyasu Miyazaki
2005 – Veterinery	A.B. Lawson and H. Zhou
2004 – Economics	Insik Min and Inchul Kim
2004 – Geography	Caroline Rinaldi and Theodore M. Cole, III
2004 – Biosystems	Sunyong Kim, Seiya Imoto and Satoru Miyano
2003 – Surgery	David Wypij, Jane W. Newburger, Leonard A. Rappaport
2002 – Environmental Science	Ronald C. Henry, Yu-Shuo Chang and Clifford H. Spiegelman
2001 – Econometrics	Pedro L. Gozalo and Oliver B. Linton
1999 – Econometrics	Yoon-Jae Whang and Oliver Linton

Table 7. Non parametric Regression Applications

2.3.2. Robust regression

Robust regression in another approach, used to set a fitting criterion which is not vulnerable as other regression methods like linear regression. Robust regression analysis provides an alternative to a least squares regression model when fundamental assumptions are unfulfilled by the nature of the data (Yaffee, 2002) . When the analyst estimates his statistical regression models and tests his assumptions, he frequently finds that the assumptions are substantially violated. Sometimes the analyst can transform his variables to conform to those assumptions. Often, however, a transformation will not eliminate or attenuate the leverage of influential outliers that bias the prediction and distort the significance of parameter estimates. Under these circumstances, robust regression that is resistant to the influence of outliers may be the only reasonable resource. The most common method is M-estimation introduced by Huber in 1964. Application areas varies as epidemiology, remote sensing, bio systems, oceanology, computer vision and chemistry.

Non parametric Regression Applications	Authors
2005 – Epidemiology	Andy H. Lee, Michael Gracey, Kui Wang and Kelvin K.W. Yau
2005 – Remote Sensing	Ian Olthof, Darren Pouliot, Richard Fernandes and Rasim Latifovic
2004 – Biosystems	Federico Hahn
2002 – Oceanology	C. Waelbroeck, L. Labeyrie, E. Michel, J. C. Duplessy, J. F. McManus
2001 – Policy Modeling	Bradley J. Bowland and John C. Beghin
1999 – Biochemistry	V. Diez, P. A. García and F. Fdz-Polanco
1998 – Computer vision	Menashe Soffer and Nahum Kiryati
1997 – Chemistry	Dragan A. Cirovic

Table 8. Non parametric Regression Applications

2.3.3. Ridge Regression

Ridge regression, also known as Tikhonoy regularization, is the most commonly used method of regularization of ill-posed problems. A frequent obstacle is that several of the explanatory variables will vary in rather similar ways. As result, their collective power of explanation is considerably less than the sum of their individual powers. The phenomenon is known as near collinearity. Data mining application areas are frequently related with chemistry and chemometrics. Also applications in organizational studies and environmental science are listed in table.

Ridge regression Applications	Authors
2005 – Atmospheric Environment	Steven Roberts and Michael Martin
2005 – Epidemology	L.M. Grosso, E.W. Triche, K. Belanger, N.L. Benowitz
2004 – Chemical Engineering	Jeffrey Dean Kelly
2002 – Chemistry	Marla L. Frank, Matthew D. Fulkerson, Bruce R. Patton and Prabir K. Dutta
2002 – Chemometrics	J. Huang, D. Brennan, L. Sattler, J. Alderman
2001 – Laboratory Chemometrics	Kwang-Su Park, Hyeseon Lee, Chi-Hyuck Jun, Kwang-Hyun Park, Jae-Won Jung
2000 – Food Industry	Rolf Sundberg
1996 – Organizational Behaviour	R. James Holzworth

Table 9. Ridge Regression Applications

2.3.4. Nonlinear regression

Almost any function that can be written in closed form can be incorporated in a nonlinear regression model. Unlike linear regression, there are very few limitations on the way parameters can be used in the functional part of a nonlinear regression model. Nonlinear least squares regression extends linear least squares regression for use with a much larger and more general class of functions. Almost any function that can be written in closed form can be incorporated in a nonlinear regression model. Unlike linear regression, there are very few limitations on the way parameters can be used in the functional part of a nonlinear regression model. The way in which the unknown parameters in the function are estimated, however, is conceptually the same as it is in linear least squares regression. Application areas include Chromatography, urology, ecology and chemistry.

Nonlinear Regressin Applications	Authors
2005 – Chromatography	Fabrice Gritti and Georges Guiochon
2005 – Urology	Alexander M. Truskinovsky, Alan W. Partin and Martin H. Kroll
2005 – Ecology	Yonghe Wang, Frédéric Raulier and Chhun-Huor Ung
2005 – Soil Research	M. Mohanty, D.K. Painuli, A.K. Misra, K.K. Bandyopadhyaya and P.K. Ghosh
2005 – Chemical Engineering	Vadim Mamleev and Serge Bourbigot
2004 – Dental Materials	Paul H. DeHoff and Kenneth J. Anusavice
2004 – Metabolism Studies	Lars Erichsen, Olorunsola F. Agbaje, Stephen D. Luzio, David R. Owens
2004 – Biology	David D'Haese, Karine Vandermeiren, Roland Julien Caubergs, Yves Guisez
2003 – Hydrology	Xunhong Chen and Xi Chen
2003 – Chemo metrics	Igor G. Zenkevich and Balázs Kránicz
2003 – Production Economics	Paul F. Schikora and Michael R. Godfrey
2002 – Quality Management	Shueh-Chin Ting and Cheng-Nan Chen
2001 – Agriculture	Eva Falge, Dennis Baldocchi, Richard Olson, Peter Anthoni
2000 – Medicine	Marya G. Zlatnik, John A. Copland
1999 – Pharmacology	Johan L. Gabrielsson and Daniel L. Weiner

Table 10. Nonlinear Regression Applications

3. Descriptive methods and applications

The goal of a descriptive model is describe all of the data (or the process generating the data). Examples of such descriptions include models for the overall probability distribution of the data (density estimation), partitioning of the p-dimensional space into groups (cluster analysis and segmentation), and models describing the relationship between variables (dependency modeling). In segmentation analysis, for example, the aim is to group together similar records, as in market segmentation of commercial databases (Hand, et al., 2001).

3.1. Clustering methods and its applications

Clustering is similar to classification except that the groups are not predefined, but rather defined by the data alone. Clustering is alternatively referred to as unsupervised learning or segmentation. It can be thought of as partitioning or segmenting the data into groups that might or might not be disjointed, clustering is usually accomplished by determining the similarity among the data on predefined attributes (Dunham, 2003).

3.1.1. K-means clustering

The k-means algorithm (MacQueen, 1967) is an algorithm to cluster objects based on attributes into k partitions. It is a variant of the expectation-maximization algorithm in which the goal is to determine the k means of data generated from Gaussian distributions. K-means is one of the simplest unsupervised learning algorithms that solve the well known clustering problem. The procedure follows a simple and easy way to classify a given data set through a certain number of clusters fixed a priori. The main idea is to define k centroids, one for each cluster. These centroids shoud be placed in a cunning way because of different location causes different result. So, the better choice is to place them as much as possible far away from each other. The next step is to take each point belonging to a given data set and associate it to the nearest centroid. When no point is pending, the first step is completed and an early groupage is done. At this point we need to re-calculate k new centroids as bar centers of the clusters resulting from the previous step. After we have these k new centroids, a new binding has to be done between the same data set points and the nearest new centroid. A loop has been generated. As a result of this loop we may notice that the k centroids change their location step by step until no more changes are done. In other words centroids do not move any more. It assumes that the object attributes form a vector space. Application areas include sensor networks, web technologies, cybernetics.

K-means Clustering Applications	Authors
2005 – E-commerce	R. J. Kuo, J. L. Liao and C. Tu
2005 – Text clustering	Shi Zhong
2005 – Peer to peer data streams	Sanghamitra Bandyopadhyay, Chris Giannella, Ujjwal Maulik, Hillol Kargupta
2005 – Bioscience	Wei Zhong; Altun, G.; Harrison, R
2004 – Image Processing	Mantao Xu; Franti, P
2003 – Cybernetics	Yu-Fang Zhang; Jia-Li Mao
2000- Adaptive Web	Mike Perkowitz and Oren Etzioni

Table 11. K-means Clustering Applications

3.1.2. Fuzzy c-means clustering

Fuzzy c-means is a method of clustering which allows one piece of data to belong to two or more clusters. This method (developed by Dunn in 1973 and improved by Bezdek in 1981) is frequently used in pattern recognition. It is based on minimization of the following objective function. The method is frequently used in pattern recognition. Application areas include ergonomics, acoustics, and manufacturing. Widely used in image processing.

C-means clustering Applications	Authors
2006 – Ergonomics	Stéphane Armand, Eric Watelain, Moïse Mercier, Ghislaine Lensel
2005 – Neurocomputing	Antonino Staiano, Roberto Tagliaferri and Witold Pedrycz
2004 – Acoustics	Nitanda, N.; Haseyama, M.; Kitajima, H
2001 – Manufacturing	Y. M. Sebzalli and X. Z. Wang
2000 – Image Processing	Rezaee, M.R.; van der Zwet, P.M.J.; Lelieveldt, B.P.E.; van der Geest, R.J.; Reiber, J.H.C
2000 – Signal Processing	Zhe-Ming Lu; Jeng-Shyang Pan; Sheng-He Sun
2000 – Remote Sensing	Chumsamrong, W.; Thitimajshima, P.; Rangsanseri, Y
1999 – Machine Vision	Gil, M.; Sarabia, E.G.; Llata, J.R.; Oria, J.P
1998 – Bioelectronics	Da-Chuan Cheng; Kuo-Sheng Cheng

Table 12. C-means Clustering Applications

3.2. Summarization

Summarization involves methods for finding a compact description for a subset of data. A simple example would be tabulating the mean and standard deviations for all fields (Bao, 2000). More sophisticated methods involve the derivation of summary rules, multivariate visualization techniques, and the discovery of functional relationships between variables. Summarization techniques are often applied to interactive exploratory data analysis and automated report generation.

Summarization applications	Authors
2005 – Genetics	Howard J. Hamilton, Liqiang Geng, Leah Findlater
2005 – Linguistics	Janusz Kacprzyk and Sławomir Zadrożny
2003 – Decision Support Systems	Dmitri Roussinov and J. Leon Zhao

Table 13. Summarization Applications

3.3. Association rules

Association rule mining searches for interesting relationships among items in a given data set. This section provides an introduction to association rule mining introduction to association rule mining.

Let I={i1, i2,...,im} be a set of items. Let D, the task relevant data, be a set of database transactions where each transaction T is a set of items such that $T \subseteq I$. Each transaction is associated with an identifer, called TID. Let A be a set of items. A transaction T is said to contain A if and only if $A \subseteq T$. An association rule is an implication of the form $A \Rightarrow B$, where $A \subset I$, $B \subset I$ and $A \cap B = \emptyset$. The rule $A \Rightarrow B$ holds in the transaction set D with support s, where s is the percentage of transactions in D that contain $A \cup B$. The rule $A \Rightarrow B$ has confidence c in the transaction set D if c is the percentage of transactions in D containing A which also contain B. That is,

$$\text{support}(A \Rightarrow B) = \text{Prob}\{A \cup B\}$$
$$\text{confidence}(A \Rightarrow B) = \text{Prob}\{B \mid A\}$$

(2)

Rules that satisfy both a minimum support threshold (min_sup) and a minimum confidence threshold (min_conf) are called strong (Han and Kamber, 2000).

3.3.1. The Apriori algorithm

Apriori employs breadth-first search and uses a hash tree structure to count candidate item sets efficiently. The algorithm generates candidate item sets (patterns) of length k from k − 1 length item sets. Then, the patterns which have an infrequent sub pattern are pruned. If an item set is frequent, then all of its subsets must also be frequent. Apriori principle holds due to the following property of the support measure; support of an item set never exceeds the support of its subsets.

Apriori algorithm Applications	Authors
2004 – MIS	Ya-Han Hu and Yen-Liang Chen
2004 – CRM	Tzung-Pei Hong, Chan-Sheng Kuo and Shyue-Liang Wang
2004 – Banking	Nan-Chen Hsieh
2004 – Methods Engineering	Shichao Zhang, Jingli Lu and Chengqi Zhang
2002 – Thermodynamics	K. T. Andrews, K. L. Kuttler, M. Rochdi

Table 14. Apriori Algorithm Applications

3.3.2. Multidimensional association rules

A top-down strategy is to be used for multi-level association rules considering more than one dimension of the data.

Multi Dimensional Association Rule Applications	Authors
2003 – Behavioral Science	Ronald R. Holden and Daryl G. Kroner
2003 – Health Care	Joseph L. Breault, Colin R. Goodall and Peter J. Fos

Table 15. Multi Dimensional Association Rule Applications

3.3.3. Quantitative association rules

In practice most databases contain quantitative data and are not limited to categorical items only. Unfortunately, the definition of categorical association rules does not translate directly to the quantitative case. It is therefore necessary to provide a definition of association rules for the case of a database containing quantitative attributes. Srikant and Agrawal (1996) extended the categorical definition to include quantitative data. The basis for their definition is to map quantitative values into categorical events by considering intervals of the numeric values. Thus, each basic event is either a categorical item or a range of numerical values.

Quantitive Association Rule Applications	Authors
2001 – Cybernetics	Ng, V.; Lee, J
2001 – Database Management	Shragai, A.; Schneider, M
2002 – Control and Automation	Tian Yongqing; Weng Yingjun

Table 16. Quantitative Association Rule Applications

3.3.4. Distance-based association rules

Distance Based Association Rule Mining can be applied in data mining and knowledge discovery from genetic, financial, retail, time sequence data or any domain which distance information between items is of importance.

Distance Based Association Rule Applications	Authors
2004 – Cardiology	Jeptha P. Curtis, Saif S. Rathore, Yongfei Wang and Harlan M. Krumholz
2003 – Computational Statistics	Thomas Brendan Murphy
1999 – Decision Support Systems	Daniel Boley, Maria Gini, Robert Gross

Table 17. Distance Based Association Rule Applications

3.4. Sequence discovery

Sequence discovery is similar to association analysis, except that the relationships among items are spread over time. In fact, most data mining products treat sequences simply as associations in which the events are linked by time (Edelstein, 1997) In order to find these sequences, not only the details of each transaction should be captured, but also actors are needed to be identified. Sequence discovery can also take advantage of the elapsed time between transactions that make up the event.

Sequence Discovery Applications	Authors
2003 – Cellular Networks	Haghighat, A.; Soleymani, M.R
2003 – System Sciences	Ming-Yen Lin; Suh-Yin Lee
2002 – Biochemistry	Gilles Labesse, Dominique Douguet, Liliane Assairi and Anne-Marie Gilles
1998 – Chemical Biology	Molly B Schmid

Table 18. Sequence Discovery Applications

4. Data mining and data warehouses

A data warehouse is an integrated collection of data derived from operational data and primarily used in strategic decision making by means of online analytical processing techniques (Husemann and et al., 2000) The data mining database may be a logical rather than a physical subset of your data warehouse, provided that the data warehouse DBMS can

Data Mining in Data Warehouses	Authors
2006 – Production Technologies	Pach, F.P.; Feil, B.; Nemeth, S.; Arva, P.; Abonyi, J.
2005 – Supply Chain Management	Mu-Chen Chen and Hsiao-Pin Wu
2005 – Business Management	Nenad Jukić and Svetlozar Nestorov
2005 – CRM	Bart Larivière and Dirk Van den Poel
2005 – Stock Market	Adam Fadlalla
2005 – Computer Integrated Manufactoring	Ruey-Shun Chen; Ruey-Chyi Wu; Chang, C.C
2005 – Customer Analysis	Wencai Liu; Yu Luo
2005 – Power Engineering	Cheng-Lin Niu; Xi-Ning Yu; Jian-Qiang Li; Wei Sun
2004 – Web Management	Sandro Araya, Mariano Silva and Richard Weber
2004 – Biology	Junior Barrera, Roberto M Cesar-, Jr, João E. Ferreira and M.D.Marco D. Gubitoso
2004 – Oil refinery	A. A. Musaev
2004 – Real Estates	Wedyawati, W.; Lu, M.;
2004 – Electrical Insulation	Jian Ou; Cai-xin Sun; Bide Zhang
2004 – Electrical Engineering	Wang, Z
2003 – Management	Qi-Yuan Lin, Yen-Liang Chen, Jiah-Shing Chen and Yu-Chen Chen
2003 – Corporate Databases	Nestorov, S. Jukic, N.
2002 – Oceanography	Nicolas Dittert, Lydie Corrin, Michael Diepenbroek, Hannes Grobe, Christoph Heinze and Olivier Ragueneau
2002 – Financial Services	Zhongxing Ye; Xiaojun Liu; Yi Yao; Jun Wang; Xu Zhou; Peili Lu; Junmin Yao
2002 – Corporate Databases	Hameurlain, A.; Morvan, F.
2002 – Human Resources	Xiao Hairong; Zhang Huiying; Li Minqiang;
2002 – Medical Databases	Miquel, M.; Tchounikine, A
2002 – Machinery Fault Diagnosis	Dong Jiang; Shi-Tao Huang; Wen-Ping Lei; Jin-Yan Shi
2000 – Biomonitoring	A. Viarengo, B. Burlando, A. Giordana, C. Bolognesi and G. P. Gabrielides
1999 – Banking	Gerritsen, R

Table 19. Data Mining in Data Warehouses

support the additional resource demands of data mining. If it cannot, then you will be better off with a separate data mining database. Data warehouses were emerged from the need to analyze large amount of data together. In the 1990's as organizations of scale began to need more timely data about their business, they found that traditional information systems technology was simply too cumbersome to provide relevant data efficiently and quickly. From this idea, the data warehouse was born as a place where relevant data could be held for completing strategic reports for management. As with all technologic development, over the last half of the 20th century, increased numbers and types of databases were seen. Many large businesses found themselves with data scattered across multiple platforms and variations of technology, making it almost impossible for any one individual to use data from multiple sources. A key idea within data warehousing is to take data from multiple platforms and place them in a common location that uses a common querying tool. In this way operational databases could be held on whatever system was most efficient for the operational business, while the reporting / strategic information could be held in a common location using a common language. Data Warehouses take this even a step farther by giving the data itself commonality by defining what each term means and keeping it standard. All of this was designed to make decision support more readily available and without affecting day to day operations. One aspect of a data warehouse that should be stressed is that it is not a location for all of a businesses data, but rather a location for data that is subject to research. In last few years, corporate database producers adopted data mining techniques for use on customer data. It is an important part of CRM services today. Some other application areas include; Production Technologies, Supply Chain Management, Business Management, Computer Integrated Manufacturing, Power Engineering, Web Management, Biology, Oceanography Financial Services Human Resources Machinery Fault Diagnosis, Bio monitoring, Banking.

5. Conclusion

The purpose of data mining techniques is discovering meaningful correlations and formulations from previously collected data. Many different application areas utilize data mining as a means to achieve effective usage of internal information. Data mining is becoming progressively more widespread in both the private and public sectors. Industries such as banking, insurance, medicine, and retailing commonly use data mining to reduce costs, enhance research, and increase sales. In the public sector, data mining applications initially were used as a means to detect fraud and waste, but have grown to also be used for purposes such as measuring and improving program performance.

Sort of the techniques like decision tree models, time series analysis and regression were in use before the term data mining became popular in the computer science society. However, there are also techniques found by data mining practitioners in the last decade; Support Vector Machines, c-means clustering, Apriori algorithm, etc.

Many application areas of predictive methods are related with medicine fields and became increasingly popular with the rise of biotechnology in the last decade. Most of the genetics research depends heavily on data mining technology, therefore neural networks, classifiers and support vector machines will continue to increase their popularity in near future.

Descriptive methods are frequently used in finance, banking and social sciences to describe a certain population such as clients of a bank, respondents of a questionnaire, etc. Most common technique used for description is clustering; in the last decade k-means method has lost popularity against c-means algorithm. Another common method is association rules where Apriori is the most preferred method by far. By increasing importance of corporate databases and information centered production phenomena association rules continue to increase their growth. Sequence discovery is also a growing field nowadays.

Another aspect of subject discussed in this paper was exploiting data warehouses in conjunction with techniques listed. It is expected that data warehousing and usage of data mining techniques will become customary among corporate world in following years. Data warehouses are regularly used by banks, financial institutions and large corporations. It is unsurprising that they will spread through industries and will be adopted by also intermediate sized firms.

Author details

Adem Karahoca
Bahçeşehir University Software Engineering Department, Turkey

Dilek Karahoca
Bahçeşehir University Software Engineering Department, Turkey
Near East University Computer Technology and Instructional Design PhD Program Department, TRNC

Mert Şanver
Google USA, USA

6. References

Abdel-Aal, R. E. and Mangoud, A. M. (1998), Modeling and forecasting monthly patient volume at a primary health care clinic using univariate time-series analysis, Computer Methods and Programs in Biomedicine, 56, 235-247

Agrawal, R. and Imielinski, T. and Swami, A.N. Mining Association Rules between Sets of Items in Large Databases, Proceedings of the 1993 ACM SIGMOD International Conference on Management of Data.

Agrawal, R. and Srikant, R.(1994), Fast Algorithms for Mining Association Rules, Proc. 20th Int. Conf. Very Large Data Bases (VLDB)

Andrews, K.T.; Kuttler, K.L.; Rochdi, M. and Shillor, M. (2002), One-dimensional dynamic thermoviscoelastic contact with damage, Journal of Mathematical Analysis and Applications, Volume 272, 249-275

Araya, S.; Silva, M. and Weber, R. (2004), A methodology for web usage mining and its application to target group identification, Fuzzy Sets and Systems, 148, 139-152

Armand, S. ; Watelain, E. ; Mercier, M. ; Lensel, G. and Lepoutre, F. X. (2006), Identification and classification of toe-walkers based on ankle kinematics, using a data-mining method, Gait & Posture, 23, 240-248

Bandyopadhyay, S. ; Giannella,C. ; Maulik, U. ; Kargupta, H. ; Liu, K. and Datta, S. (2005), Clustering distributed data streams in peer-to-peer environments, Information Sciences, In Press, Corrected Proof

Bao, H. T. (2000), Knowledge Discovery and Data Mining Techniques and Practice, Department of Pattern Recognition and Knowledge Engineering Institute of Information Technology, Hanoi, Vietnam

Belacel, N. ; Raval, H.B. and Punnen, A.P. (2005), Learning multicriteria fuzzy classification method PROAFTN from data, Computers & Operations Research, In Press, Corrected Proof

Bensaid, A.M.; Hall, L.O.; Bezdek, J.C.; Clarke, L.P.; Silbiger, M.L.; Arrington, J.A.; Murtagh, R.F. (1996), Validity-guided (re)clustering with applications to image segmentation, IEEE Transactions on Fuzzy Systems, 4,112 – 123

Bizovi, K. E. ; Leikin, J. B. ; Hryhorczuk, D. O. and Frateschi, L. J. (1998), Night of the Sirens: Analysis of Carbon Monoxide-Detector Experience in Suburban Chicago, Annals of Emergency Medicine, 31, 737-740

Body, M. ; Miquel, M. ; Bedard, Y. ; Tchounikine, A. (2003), Handling evolutions in multidimensional structures, 19th International Conference Proceedings, 581- 591

Boley, D.; Gini, M.; Gross, R.; (Sam) Han, E.H.; Hastings, K.; Karypis, G.; Kumar, V.; Mobasher, B. and Moore, J. (1999), Partitioning-based clustering for Web document categorization, Decision Support Systems, 27, 329-341

Boser, B. E. ; Guyon, I. M. ; Vapnik, V. N. (1992), A training algorithm for optimal margin classifiers, Proceedings of the fifth annual workshop on Computational learning theory, p.144-152, July 27-29,, Pittsburgh, Pennsylvania, United States

Bowland, B. J. and Beghin, J. C. (2001), Robust estimates of value of a statistical life for developing economies, Journal of Policy Modeling, 23, 385-396

Box, G.; Jenkins, G. and Reinsel, G. (1994) Time Series Analysis, 3rd ed., Prentice Hall

Box, G.E.P. and Jenkins, G.M. (1976) Time series analysis forecasting and control. Prentice Hall, Englewood Cliffs, New Jersey.

Bozdogan, H. and Bearse, P. (2003), Information complexity criteria for detecting influential observations in dynamic multivariate linear models using the genetic algorithm, Journal of Statistical Planning and Inference, 114, 31-44

Breault, J.L.; Goodall, C.R. and Fos, P.J. (2003), Data mining a diabetic data warehouse, Artificial Intelligence in Medicine, 27, 227

Bui, E. N. and Moran, C. J. (2001), Disaggregation of polygons of surficial geology and soil maps using spatial modeling and legacy data, Geoderma, 103, 79-94

Burges, C. J. C. (1998) "A Tutorial on Support Vector Machines for Pattern Recognition". Data Mining and Knowledge Discovery 2:121 - 167

Carpena, R. M. ; Ritter, A. and Li, Y.C. (2005), Dynamic factor analysis of groundwater quality trends in an agricultural area adjacent to Everglades National Park, Journal of Contaminant Hydrology, 80, 49-70

Carvalho, L.M. T. ; Clevers, J. G. P. W. ; Skidmore, A.K. and Jong, S.M. (2004), Selection of imagery data and classifiers for mapping Brazilian semideciduous Atlantic forests, International Journal of Applied Earth Observation and Geoinformation, 5,173-186

Chang, J. ; Peng, P. (2005) Decision-Making and Operation of OTDAS, Journal of Automation, 1, 102- 107

Chen, M.C. and Wu, H.P. (2005), An association-based clustering approach to order batching considering customer demand patterns, Omega, 33, 333-343

Chen, O. ; Zhao, P. ; Massaro, D. ; Clerch, L. B. ; Almon, R. R. ; DuBois, D. C: ; Jusko, W. J. and Hoffman, E. P. (2004), The PEPR GeneChip data warehouse, and implementation of a dynamic time series query tool (SGQT) with graphical interface, Nucleic Acids Research, 32, 578-581

Chen, R.S.; Wu, R.C.; Chang, C.C. (2005), Using Data Mining Technology to Design an Intelligent CIM System for IC Manufacturing, SNPD 2005: 70-75

Chen, T. C. and Hsu, T. C. (2006), A Gas based approach for mining breast cancer pattern, Expert Systems with Applications, 30, 674-681

Chen, X. and Chen, X. (2005), Reply to Comment on "Sensitivity analysis and determination of streambed leakance and aquifer hydraulic properties" by S. Christensen, Journal of Hydrology, 303, 322-327

Chen, Y.L. and Hu, Y.H. (2005), Constraint-based sequential pattern mining: The consideration of recency and compactness, Decision Support Systems, In Press, Corrected Proof

Cheng, D.C.; Schmidt-Trucksäss, A.; Cheng, K.S. and Burkhardt, H. (2002), Using snakes to detect the intimal and adventitial layers of the common carotid artery wall in sonographic images, Computer Methods and Programs in Biomedicine, 67, 27-37

Christensen, J. H.; Hansen, A. B.; Karlson, U. ; Mortensen, J. and Andersen, O. (2005), Multivariate statistical methods for evaluating biodegradation of mineral oil, Journal of Chromatography, 1090, 133-145

Chumsamrong, W. ; Thitimajshima, P. ; Rangsanseri, Y. (1999), Wavelet-based texture analysis for SAR image classification, Geoscience and Remote Sensing Symposium (IGARSS '99), 3, 1564-1566

Cirovic, D. A. (1997), Feed-forward artificial neural networks: applications to spectroscopy, Trends in Analytical Chemistry, 16, 148-155

Cortes, C. and Vapnik, V. (1995) Support vector networks. Machine Learning, 20:273–297.

Craven and Shavlik (1997) Using Neural Networks for Data Mining, Future Generation Computer Systems, 13, pp.211-229.

Crone, S. F. ; Lessmann, S. and Stahlbock, R. (2005), The impact of preprocessing on data mining, An evaluation of classifier sensitivity in direct marketing, European Journal of Operational Research, In Press, Corrected Proof

Crone, S.F. ; Lessmann, S. and Stahlbock, R. (2005), The impact of preprocessing on data mining: An evaluation of classifier sensitivity in direct marketing, European Journal of Operational Research, In Press, Corrected Proof

Cuaresma, J. C. ; Hlouskova, J. ; Kossmeier, S. and Obersteiner, M. (2004), Forecasting electricity spot-prices using linear univariate time-series models, Applied Energy, 77, 87-106

Curtis, P.; Rathore, S.S.; Wang, Y.; Krumholz, H.M. (2004), The association of 6-minute walk performance and outcomes in stable outpatients with heart failure, J Card Fail

Data Mining and Knowledge Discovery, 2(2), pp.955-974

DeHoff, P. H. and Anusavice, K. J. (2004), Shear stress relaxation of dental ceramics determined from creep behavior, Dental Materials, 20, 717-725

Delgado, M.; Sánchez, D.; Martín-Bautista, M.J. and Vila, M.A. (2001), Mining association rules with improved semantics in medical databases, Artificial Intelligence in Medicine, 21, 241-245

D'Haese, D. ; Vandermeiren, K. ; Caubergs, R. J. ; Guisez, Y. ; Temmerman, L. ; Horemans, N. (2004), Non-photochemical quenching kinetics during the dark to light transition in relation to the formation of antheraxanthin and zeaxanthin. Journal of Theoretical Biology, 227, 175-186.

Diez, V. ; García, P. A. and Fdz-Polanco F. (1999), Evaluation of methanogenic kinetics in an anaerobic fluidized bed reactor, Process Biochemistry, 34, 213-219

Dittert, N.; Corrin, L.; Diepenbroek, M.; Grobe, H.; Heinze, C. and Ragueneau, O. (2002), Management of (pale-)oceanographic data sets using the PANGAEA information system: the SINOPS example, Computers & Geosciences, 28, 789-798

Dunham, M. (2003) Data Mining: Introductory and advanced topics, New Jersey: Prentice Hall

Edelstein, H. (1997), Mining for Gold, Information Week: April 21, 1997

Erichsen, L. ; Agbaje, O. F. ; Luzio, S. D. ; Owens, D. R. and Hovorka, R. (2004), Population and individual minimal modeling of the frequently sampled insulin-modified intravenous glucose tolerance test, Metabolism, 53, 1349-1354

Ewing, B. T. and Wunnava, P. V. (2001), Unit roots and structural breaks in North American unemployment rates, The North American Journal of Economics and Finance, 12, 273-282

Fadlalla, A. (2005), An experimental investigation of the impact of aggregation on the performance of data mining with logistic regression, Information & Management, 42, 695-707

Falge, E. ; Baldocchi, D. ; Olson, R. ; Anthoni, P. ; Aubinet, M. ; Bernhofer, C. ; Burba, G. ; Ceulemans, R. ; Clement, R. ; Dolman, H.(2001), Gap filling strategies for defensible annual sums of net ecosystem exchange, Agricultural and Forest Meteorology, 107, 43-69

Frank, M. L. ; Fulkerson, M. D. ; Patton, B. R. and Dutta, P. K. (2002), TiO2-based sensor arrays modeled with nonlinear regression analysis for simultaneously determining CO and O2 concentrations at high temperatures, Sensors and Actuators B: Chemical, 87, 471-479

Freeman, J. A. and Skapura, D. M. (1991). Neural Networks: Algorithms, Applications, and Programming Techniques, Addison-Wesley, Reading, MA.

Frees, E. W. (2003), Stochastic forecasting of labor force participation rates, Insurance: Mathematics and Economics, 33, 317-336

Friedman, J. H. (1991). Multivariate adaptive regression splines. The Annals of Statistics, 19:1--141.

Fries, R. S. ; Hansen, M. ; Townshend, J. R. G. And Sohlberg, R.(1998), Global land cover classifications at 8 km spatial resolution: the use of training data derived from Landsat imagery in decision tree classifiers, International Journal of Remote Sensing, 19, 3141-3168

Gabrielsson, J. L. and Weiner, D. L. (1999), Methodology for pharmacokinetic/ pharmacodynamic data analysis, Pharmaceutical Science & Technology Today, 2, 244-252

Gerritsen, R. (1999), Assessing loan risks: a data mining case study, IT Professional, 1, 16-21

Gil, M. ; Sarabia, E.G. ; Llata, J.R. ; Oria, J.P. (1999), Fuzzy c-means clustering for noise reduction, enhancement and reconstruction of 3D ultrasonic images, Emerging Technologies and Factory Automation, 1, 465-472

Gorr, W. ; Olligschlaeger, A. ; Thompson, Y. - International Journal of Forecasting (2003), Short-term forecasting of crime. International Journal of Forecasting 19:44, 579-594

Gozalo, P. L. and Linton, O. B. (2001), Testing additivity in generalized nonparametric regression models with estimated parameters, Journal of Econometrics, Volume 104, 1-48

Gritti, F. and Guiochon, G. (2005), Critical contribution of nonlinear chromatography to the understanding of retention mechanism in reversed-phase liquid chromatography, Journal of Chromatography, 1099, 1-42

Grosso, L.M. ; Triche, E.W. ; Belanger, K. ; Benowitz, N.L. ; Holford, T.R. and Bracken, M.B. (2005), Association of caffeine metabolites in umbilical cord blood with IUGR and preterm delivery: A prospective cohort study of 1609 pregnancies, Annals of Epidemiology, 15, 659-660

Haghighat, A.; Soleymani, M.R. (2003), A Subspace Scheme for Blind User Identification in Multiuser DS-CDMA, IEEE Wireless Communications and Networking Conference

Hahn, F. (2005), Novel Valve for Automatic Calibration of a Chloride Sensor for River Monitoring, Biosystems Engineering, 92, 275-284

Hairong,X. ; Huiying,Z. ; Minqiang, L. (2002), Regional human resource management decision support system based on data warehouse, Proceedings of the 4th World Congress on Intelligent Control and Automation, 3,2118- 212

Hameurlain, A.; Morvan, F. (1995), Scheduling and mapping for parallel execution of extended SQL queries, Proceedings of the fourth international conference on Information and knowledge management, 197 – 204

Hamilton, H.J.; Geng, L.; Findlater, L. and Randall, D.J. (2005), Efficient spatio-temporal data mining with GenSpace graphs, Journal of Applied Logic, In Press, Corrected Proof

Han, J. and Kamber, M.(2000) Data Mining: Concepts and Techniques. Morgan Kaufmann.

Hand, D.; Mannila, H. and Smyth, P. (2001), Principles of Data Mining, The MIT Press.

Hansen, M.C. ; DeFries, R.S. ; Townshend J.R.G. ; Sohlberg, R. ; Dimiceli, C. ; Carroll, M. (2002), Towards an operational MODIS continuous field of percent tree cover algorithm: examples using AVHRR and MODIS data, Remote Sensing of Environment, 83, 303–319

Hanson, R. ; Stutz, J. ; Cheeseman, P. (1990) "Bayesian Classification Theory", Technical Report FIA-90-12-7-01

Hanson, R.D. (1996) Consensus by Identifying Extremists, Theory and Decision, Vol. 44(3), Springer.

Healy, J.V. ; Dixon, M. ; Read, B.J. and Cai, F.F. (2004), Confidence limits for data mining models of options prices, Physica A: Statistical Mechanics and its Applications,344, 162-167

Henry, R. C. ; Chang, Y. S. and Spiegelman, C. H. (2003), Locating nearby sources of air pollution by nonparametric regression of atmospheric concentrations on wind direction, Atmospheric Environment, 36, 2237-2244

Holden, R.R. and Kroner, D.G. (2003), Differentiating Suicidal Motivations and Manifestations in a Forensic Sample, Canadian Journal of Behavioural Science, 35, 35-44

Holzworth, R. J. (1996), Policy Capturing with Ridge Regression, Organizational Behavior and Human Decision Processes, 68, 171-179

Hong, T.P.; Kuo, C.S. and Wang, S.L. (2005), A fuzzy AprioriTid mining algorithm with reduced computational time, Applied Soft Computing, 5, 1-10,

Hsieh, N.C. (2005), Hybrid mining approach in the design of credit scoring models, Expert Systems with Applications, 28, 655-665

Huang, H. C. ; Pan, J. S. ; Lu, Z. M. ; Sun, S. H. ; and Hang, H. M. (2001), Vector quantization based on genetic simulated annealing, Signal Processing, 81, 1513-1523

Huang, J. ; Brennan, D. ; Sattler, L. ; Alderman, J. ; Lane, B. and O'Mathuna, C. (2002), A comparison of calibration methods based on calibration data size and robustness, Chemometrics and Intelligent Laboratory Systems, 62, 25-35

Huang, Y. M. ; Hung, C. M. and Jiau, H. C. (2005), Evaluation of neural networks and data mining methods on a credit assessment task for class imbalance problem, Nonlinear Analysis: Real World Applications, In Press, Corrected Proof

Hung, S. Y. ; Yen, D.C. and Wang, H. S. (2005), Applying data mining to telecom churn management, Expert Systems with Applications, In Press, Corrected Proof

Husemann, B.; Lechtenborger, J.; Vossen, G. (2000) Conceptual Data Warehouse Design, Institut f¨ur Wirtschaftsinformatik

Jiang, D. ; Huang, S.T. ; Lei, W.P. ; Shi, J.Y. (2002), Study of data mining based machinery fault diagnosis, Conference on Machine Learning and Cybernetics, 1, 536- 539

Jukić, N. and Nestorov, S. (2005), Comprehensive data warehouse exploration with qualified association-rule mining, Decision Support Systems, In Press, Corrected Proof

Junior Barrera, R M Roberto M Cesar, J E João E Ferreira, M D Marco D Gubitoso, Roberto M Cesar, João E Ferreira, Marco D Gubitoso (2004), An environment for knowledge discovery in biology, Comput Biol Med, 34(5), 427-47. ???

Junttila, J. (2001), Structural breaks, ARIMA model and Finnish inflation forecasts, International Journal of Forecasting, 17, 203-230

Kacprzyk, J. and Zadrożny, S. (2005), Linguistic database summaries and their protoforms: towards natural language based knowledge discovery tools, Information Sciences, 173, 281-304

Kantardzic, M. ; Djulbegovic, B. and Hamdan, H.(2002), A data-mining approach to improving Polycythemia Vera diagnosis, Computers & Industrial Engineering, 43, 765-773

Kecman, V. (2001). Learning and Soft Computing - Support Vector Machines, Neural Networks, Fuzzy Logic Systems, The MIT Press, Cambridge, MA.

Kelly, J. D. (2004), Formulating large-scale quantity–quality bilinear data reconciliation problems, Computers & Chemical Engineering (2004), 28, 357-362

Kim, K. J. (2006), Artificial neural networks with evolutionary instance selection for financial forecasting, Expert Systems with Applications, 30, 519 526

Kim, S. ; Imoto, S. and Miyano, S. (2004), Dynamic Bayesian network and nonparametric regression for nonlinear modeling of gene networks from time series gene expression data, Biosystems, 75, 57-65

Kim, T. Y. ; Joo, K. ; Sohn, O. I. and Hwang, C. (2004), Usefulness of artificial neural networks for early warning system of economic crisis, Expert Systems with Applications, 26, 583-590

Kim, Y. S. and Street, W. N. (2004), An intelligent system for customer targeting: a data mining approach, Decision Support Systems, 37, 215-228

Kondo, T. ; Pandya, A. S. ; Zurada, J. M. (1999), GMDH-type neural networks and their application to the medical image recognition of the lungs, 38th Annual Conference Proceedings of the SICE

Kuo, R. J. ; Liao J. L. and Tu C. (2005), Integration of ART2 neural network and genetic K-means algorithm for analyzing Web browsing paths in electronic commerce, Decision Support Systems, 40, 355-374

Kuo, W. J. ; Chang, R. F. ; Moon, W. M. ; Lee, C. C: and Chen, D. R. (2002), Computer-Aided Diagnosis of Breast Tumors with Different US Systems, Academic Radiology, Volume 9, 793-799

Labesse, G.; Douguet, D.; Assairi, L. and Gilles, A.M. (2002), Diacylglyceride kinases, sphingosine kinases and NAD kinases: distant relatives of 6-phosphofructokinases, Trends in Biochemical Sciences, 27, Pages 273-275

Larivière, B. and Van den Poel, D. (2005), Predicting customer retention and profitability by using random forests and regression forests techniques, Expert Systems with Applications, 29, 472-484

Lavington, S. ; Dewhurst, N. ; Wilkins, E. and Freitas, A. (1999), Interfacing knowledge discovery algorithms to large database management systems, Information and Software Technology,41, 605-617

Lawson, A.B. and Zhou, H. (2001), Spatial statistical modeling of disease outbreaks with particular reference to the UK foot and mouth disease (FMD) epidemic of 2001, Preventive Veterinary Medicine, 71, 141-156

Lee, A. H.; Gracey, M. ; Wang, K. and Yau, K. K.W. (2005), A Robustified Modeling Approach to Analyze Pediatric Length of Stay, Annals of Epidemiology, 15, 673-677

Lee, H. S. and Siklos, P. L. (1997), The role of seasonality in economic time series reinterpreting money-output causality in U.S. data, International Journal of Forecasting, 13, 381-391

Lee, T. S. ; Chiu, C. C. ; Chou, Y. C. and Lu, C. J. (2006), Mining the customer credit using classification and regression tree and multivariate adaptive regression splines, Computational Statistics & Data Analysis, 50, 1113-1130

Li, Z. and Kafatos, M. (2000), Interannual Variability of Vegetation in the United States and Its Relation to El Niño/Southern Oscillation, Remote Sensing of Environment, 71, 239-247

Li, L. ; Tang, H. ; Wu, Z. ; Gong, J., Gruidl, M. ; Zou, J. ; Tockman, M. and Clark, R. A. (2004), Data mining techniques for cancer detection using serum proteomic profiling, Artificial Intelligence in Medicine, 32, 71-83

Li, X.B. (2005), A scalable decision tree system and its application in pattern recognition and intrusion detection, Decision Support Systems, Volume 41, 112-130

Liao, T. W. (2003), Clustering of time series data—a survey, Pattern Recognation, 38, 1857-18

Lin, M.Y.; Lee, S.Y. (1998), Incremental update on sequential patterns in large databases, Proc Int Conf Tools Artif Intell., 24-31

Lin, Q.Y.; Chen, Y.L.; Chen, J.S. and Chen, Y.C. (2003), Mining inter-organizational retailing knowledge for an alliance formed by competitive firms, Information & Management, 40, 431-442

Lu, S. ; Lu, H. and Kolarik, W. J. (2001), Multivariate performance reliability prediction in real-time, Reliability Engineering & System Safety, 72, 39-45

MacQueen J., (1967) Some methods for classification and analysis of multivariate observations, Proceedings of the 5th Berkeley Symposium on Mathematical Statistics

Mamleev, V. and Bourbigot, S.(2005), Modulated thermogravimetry in analysis of decomposition kinetics, Chemical Engineering Science, 60, 747-766

Manganaris, S. (1996), Classifying sensor data with CALCHAS, Engineering Applications of Artificial Intelligence, 9, 639-644

McQueen, J. B. (1967): "Some Methods for classification and Analysis of Multivariate Observations, Proceedings of 5-th Berkeley Symposium on Mathematical Statistics and Probability", Berkeley, University of California Press, 1:281-297

Min, I. ; Kim, I. (2004), A Monte Carlo comparison of parametric and nonparametric quantile regressions, Applied Economics Letters

Miwakeichi, F. ; Galka, A. ; Uchida, S. ; Arakaki, H. ; Hirai, N. ; Nishida, M. ; Maehara, T. ; Kawai, K. ; Sunaga, S. and Shimizu, H. (2004), Impulse response function based on multivariate AR model can differentiate focal hemisphere in temporal lobe epilepsy, Epilepsy Research, 61, 73-87

Mladenic, D. ; Grobelnik, M. (1999), Feature selection for unbalanced class distribution and Naive Bayes, Machine Learning-International Workshop Then Conference

Mohanty, M. ; Painuli, D.K. ; Misra, A.K. ; Bandyopadhyaya, K.K. and Ghosh, P.K. (2006), Estimating impact of puddling, tillage and residue management on wheat (Triticum aestivum, L.) seedling emergence and growth in a rice–wheat system using nonlinear regression models, Soil and Tillage Research, 87, 119-130

Mues, C. ; Baesens, B. ; Files, C.M. and Vanthienen, J. (2004), Decision diagrams in machine learning: an empirical study on real-life credit-risk data, Expert Systems with Applications, 27, 257-264

Müller, A. ; Osterhage, H; Sowa, R. ; Andrzejak, R. G. ; Mormann, F. and Lehnertz, K (2005), A distributed computing system for multivariate time series analyses of multichannel neurophysiological data, Journal of Neuroscience Methods, In Press, Corrected Proof

Murphy, T.B. and Martin, D. (2003), Mixtures of distance-based models for ranking data, Computational Statistics & Data Analysis, 41, 645-655

Musaev, A.A. (2004), Analytic information technologies in oil refinery, Expert Systems with Applications, 26, 81-85

Myers, R. A. (2001), Stock and recruitment: generalizations about maximum reproductive rate, density dependence, and variability using meta analytic approaches, ICES Journal of Marine Science58, 937-951

Nestorov, S.; Jukic, N. (2003), Ad-Hoc Association-Rule Mining within the Data Warehouse, HICSS

Nielsen, M. O. (2004), Local empirical spectral measure of multivariate processes with long range dependence, Stochastic Processes and their Applications, 109, 145-166

NIST/SEMATECH e-Handbook of Statistical Methods, http://www.itl.nist.gov/div898/handbook

Nitanda, N. ; Haseyama, M. ; Kitajima, H. (2004), An Audio Signal Segmentation and Classification Using Fuzzy c-means Clustering, Proceedings of the 2nd International Conference on Information Technology for Application

Niu, C.L.; Yu, X.N.; Li, J.Q.; Sun, W. (2005), The application of operation optimization decision support system based on data mining in power plant, International Conference on Machine Learning and Cybernetics, 3, 1830 - 1834

Oatley, G. C. and Ewart, B.W. (2003), Crimes analysis software: 'pins in maps', clustering and Bayes net prediction, Expert Systems with Applications, 25, 569-588

Oh, W. and Lee, K. (2004), Energy consumption and economic growth in Korea: testing the causality relation, Journal of Policy Modeling, 26, 973-981

Olthof, I. ; Pouliot, D. ; Fernandes, R. and Latifovic, R. (2005), Landsat-7 ETM+ radiometric normalization comparison for northern mapping applications, Remote Sensing of Environment, 95, 388-398

Ou, J.; Sun, C.X.; Zhang, B. (2004), Design and building of data warehouse for steam turbine-generator set, Electrical Insulation, Conference Record of the 2004 IEEE International Symposium on, 12-14

Pach, F.P.; Feil, B.; Nemeth, S.; Arva, P.; Abonyi, J. (2006), Process-Data-Warehousing-Based Operator Support System for Complex Production Technologies Systems, Man and Cybernetics,36, 136 – 153

Padmanabhan, M. ; Bahl, L. R. ; Nahamoo, D.(1999), Partitioning the Feature Space of a Classifier with Linear Hyperplanes, IEEE TRANSACTIONS ON SPEECH AND AUDIO PROCESSING, 7-3, 282-287

Pan, F. ; Wang, B ; Hu, X. and Perrizo, W. (2004), Comprehensive vertical sample-based KNN/LSVM classification for gene expression analysis, Journal of Biomedical Informatics, 37, 240-248

Pappas, D. ; Piliouras, N. ; Cavouras, D. (2003), Support vector machines based analysis of brain SPECT images for determining cerebral abnormalities in asymptomatic diabetic patientsI Kalatzis, Medical Informatics and the Internet in Medicine, 28, 221 – 230

Park, K. S. ; Lee, H. ; Jun, C. H. ; Park, K. H. ; Jung, J. W. and Kim, S. B. (2000), Rapid determination of FeO content in sinter ores using DRIFT spectra and multivariate calibrations, Chemometrics and Intelligent Laboratory Systems, 51, 163-173

Pereda, E. ; Quiroga, R. O. and Bhattacharya, J. (2005), Nonlinear multivariate analysis of neurophysiological signals, Progress in Neurobiology, 77, 1-37

Perkowitz, M. and Etzioni, O. (2000), Towards adaptive Web sites: Conceptual framework and case study, Artificial Intelligence, 118, 245-275

Perner, P. (2002) Image mining: issues, framework, a generic tool and its application to medical-image diagnosis, Engineering Applications of Artificial Intelligence, 15, 205-216

Piramuthu, S. On learning to predict Web traffic, Decision Support Systems, 35, 213-229

Piras, P. ; Roussel, C. and Pierrot-Sanders, J. (2001), Reviewing mobile phases used on Chiralcel OD through an application of data mining tools to CHIRBASE database, Journal of Chromatography, 906, 443-458

Pons, M. N. ; Bonté, S. B. and Potier, O. (2004), Spectral analysis and fingerprinting for biomedia characterization, Journal of Biotechnology, 113, 211-230

Quinlan, J. R. (1993) C.4.5: Programs for machine learning, San Francisco: Morgan Kaufmann.

Reick, C. H. and Page, B. (1998), Time series prediction by multivariate next neighbor methods with application to zooplankton forecasts, Mathematics and Computers in Simulation, 52, 289-310

Rinaldi, C. and Cole, T. M. (2004), Environmental seasonality and incremental growth rates of beaver (Castor canadensis) incisors: implications for palaeobiology Palaeogeography, Palaeoclimatology, Palaeoecology, 206, 289-301

Roberts, S. and Martin, M. (2005), A critical assessment of shrinkage-based regression approaches for estimating the adverse health effects of multiple air pollutants, Atmospheric Environment, 39, 6223-6230

Romilly, P. (2005), Time series modelling of global mean temperature for managerial decision-making, Journal of Environmental Management, 76, 61-70

Roussinov, D. and Zhao, J.L. (2003), Automatic discovery of similarity relationships through Web mining, Decision Support Systems, 35, 149-166

Schelter, B. ; Winterhalder, M. ; Hellwig, B. ; Guschlbauer, B. ; Lücking, C. M. and Timmer, J. (2006), Direct or indirect? Graphical models for neural oscillators, Journal of Physiology, 99, 37-46

Schikora, P.F. and Godfrey, M. R. (2003), Efficacy of end-user neural network and data mining software for predicting complex system performance, International Journal of Production Economics, 84, 231-253

Schikora, P. F. and Godfrey, M. R. (2003), Efficacy of end-user neural network and data mining software for predicting complex system performance, International Journal of Production Economics, 84, 231-253

Schlink, U. ; Herbarth, O. ; Richter, M. ; Dorling, S. ; Nunnari, G. ; Cawley, G. and Pelikan, E. (2006),Statistical models to assess the health effects and to forecast ground-level ozone, Environmental Modelling & Software, 21, 547-558

Schmid, M.B. (1998), Novel approaches to the discovery of antimicrobial agents, Current Opinion in Chemical Biology, 2, 529-534

Sebzalli, Y. M. and Wang, X. Z. (2001), Knowledge discovery from process operational data using PCA and fuzzy clustering, Engineering Applications of Artificial Intelligence, Volume 14, 607-616

Serletis, A.and Krause, D. (1996), Empirical evidence on the long run neutrality hypothesis using low-frequency international data, Economics Letters, 50, 323-327

Shi,X. ; Schillings, P. Boyd, D. (2004), Applying artificial neural networks and virtual experimental design to quality improvement of two industrial processes, International Journal of Production Research, 42, 101–118

Shragai, A.; Schneider, M. (2001), Discovering quantitative associations in databases, IFSA World Congress and 20th NAFIPS International Conference, 1, 423-428

Silva, A. ; Cortez, P. ; Santos, M. F. ; Gomes, L. and Neves, J. (2005), Mortality assessment in intensive care units via adverse events using artificial neural networks, Artificial Intelligence in Medicine, In Press, Corrected Proof

Soffer, M. and Kiryati, N. (1998), Guaranteed Convergence of the Hough Transform, Computer Vision and Image Understanding, 69, 119-134

Solibakke, P. B. (2001), A stochastic volatility model specification with diagnostics for thinly traded equity markets, Journal of Multinational Financial Management, 11, 385-406

Sousa, M. S. R. ; Mattoso, M. and Ebecken, N. F. F. (1999), Mining a large database with a parallel database server, Intelligent Data Analysis, 3, 437-451

Srikant, R., & Agrawal, R. (1996). Mining sequential patterns: Generalizations and performance improvements, . Proc. of the Fifth Int'l Conference on Extending Database Technology (EDBT). Avignon, France

Stassopoulou, A. ; Petrou, M. and Kittler, J. (1996), Bayesian and neural networks for geographic information processing, Pattern Recognition Letters, 17, 1325-1330

Sundberg, R. (2000), Aspects of statistical regression in sensometrics, Food Quality and Preference, 11, 17-26

Swift, S. and Liu, X. (2002), Predicting glaucomatous visual field deterioration through short multivariate time series modeling, Artificial Intelligence in Medicine, 24, 5-24

T. Menzies, Y. Hu, (2003) Data Mining For Very Busy People. IEEE Computer, October 2003. 18-25

Tagliaferri, R. and Pedrycz, W. (2005), Improving RBF networks performance in regression tasks by means of a supervised fuzzy clustering, Neurocomputing, In Press, Corrected Proof

Taylor, J. W. and Buizza, R. (2006), Density forecasting for weather derivative pricing, International Journal of Forecasting, 22, 29-42

Thury, G. and Witt, S. F. (1998), Forecasting industrial production using structural time series models, Omega, 26, 751-767

Ting, S. C. and Chen, C. N. (2002), The asymmetrical and non-linear effects of store quality attributes on customer satisfaction,Total Quality Management, 13, 547 - 569

Truskinovsky, A. M. ; Partin, A. W. and Kroll, M. H.(2005), Kinetics of tumor growth of prostate carcinoma estimated using prostate-specific antigen, Urology, 66,577-581

Valenti, P. ; Cazamajou, E. ; Scarpettini, M. ; Aizemberg, A. ; Silva, W. and Kochen, S. (2006), Automatic detection of interictal spikes using data mining models, Journal of Neuroscience Methods, 150, 105-110

Vapnik, V. ; Golowich, S. and Smola, A. (1997) "Support Vector Method for Function Approximation, Regression Estimation and Signal Processing," Advances in Neural Information Processing Systems, vol. 9, Cambridge, Mass.: MIT Press.

Vapnik, V.N. (1995) The nature of statistical learning theory, Springer-Verlag New York, Inc., New York, NY,

Viarengo, A. ; Burlando, B.; Giordana, A. ; Bolognesi, C. and Gabrielides, G. P. (2000), Networking and expert-system analysis: next frontier in biomonitoring, Marine Environmental Research, 49, 483-486

Vindevogel, B. ; Poel, D. V. and Wets, G. (2005), Why promotion strategies based on market basket analysis do not work, Expert Systems with Applications, 28, 583-590

Waelbroeck, C. ; Labeyrie, L. ; Michel, E. ; Duplessy, J. C. ; McManus, J. F.; Lambeck, K. ; Balbon, E. and M. Labracherie (2002), Sea-level and deep water temperature changes derived from benthic foraminifera isotopic records, Quaternary Science Reviews, 21, 295-305

Wang, Y. ; Raulier, F. and Ung, C. H. (2005), Evaluation of spatial predictions of site index obtained by parametric and nonparametric methods—A case study of lodgepole pine productivity, Forest Ecology and Management, 214, 201-211

Watanabe, H. and Miyazaki, H. (2005), A new approach to correct the QT interval for changes in heart rate using a nonparametric regression model in beagle dogs, Journal of Pharmacological and Toxicological Methods, In Press, Corrected Proof

Wedyawati, W. and Lu, M. (2004), Mining Real Estate Listings Using ORACLE Data Warehousing and Predictive Regression, Proc. of IEEE IRI 2004.

Whang, Y. J. and Linton, O. (1999), The asymptotic distribution of nonparametric estimates of the Lyapunov exponent for stochastic time series, Journal of Econometrics, Volume 91, 1-42

Witten, I..E. ; Frank, E. (200) Data Mining: Practical Machine Learning tools and Techniques with Java Implementations, San Francisco: Morgan Kaufmann.

Wypij, D. ; Newburger, J. W. ; Rappaport, L. A. ; duPlessis, A. J. ; Jonas, R. A. ; Wernovsky, G. ; Lin, M. and Bellinger, D. C. (2003), The effect of duration of deep hypothermic circulatory arrest in infant heart surgery on late neurodevelopment: The Boston Circulatory Arrest Trial, Journal of Thoracic and Cardiovascular Surgery, Volume 126, 1397-1403

Xu, M. and Franti, P (2004) Context clustering in lossless compression of gray-scale image, 13th Scandinavian Conf. on Image Analysis

Yaffee, Robert A. (2002), "Robust Regression Analysis:Some Popular Statistical Package Options", Statistics, Social Science, and Mapping Group Academic Computing Services Information Technology Services

Yamashita, Y. (2000), Supervised learning for the analysis of process operational data, Computers & Chemical Engineering, 24, 471-474

Ye, Z.; Liu, X.; Yao, Y.; Wang, J.; Zhou, X.; Lu, P.; Yao, J. (2002), An intelligent system for personal and family financial service, Neural Information Processing, ICONIP'02

Yongqing, T.; Yingjun, W.; Zhongying, Z. (2002), Proceedings of the 4th World Congress on Intelligent Control and Automation, 3, 2203- 2207

Yves, Q. P. (2003), The production and recognition of emotions in speech: features and algorithms, International Journal of Human-Computer Studies, 59,157-183

Zenkevich, I. G. and Kránicz, B. (2003), Choice of nonlinear regression functions for various physicochemical constants within series of homologues, Chemometrics and Intelligent Laboratory Systems, 67, 51-57

Zhang, B. ; Valentine, I. ; Kemp, P. and Lambert, G. (2006), Predictive modelling of hill-pasture productivity: integration of a decision tree and a geographical information system Agricultural Systems, Volume 87, 1-17

Zhang, B. ; Valentine, I. and Kemp, P.D. (2005), A decision tree approach modelling functional group abundance in a pasture ecosystem, Agriculture, Ecosystems & Environment, Volume 110, 279-288

Zhang, S.; Lu, J. and Zhang, C. (2004), A fuzzy logic based method to acquire user threshold of minimum-support for mining association rules, Information Sciences, 164, 1-16

Zhang, Y.F. ; Mao, J. L. ; Xiong, Z. Y. (2003), An efficient clustering algorithm, Machine Learning and Cybernetics, 2003 International Conference

Zhong, S.(2005), Efficient streaming text clustering, Neural Networks, 18, 790-798

Zhong, W. ; Altun, G ; Harrison, R. ; Tai, P. C. ; Pan, Y. (2005), Improved K-means clustering algorithm for exploring local protein sequence motifs, IEEE Transactions On Nanobioscience, Vol. 4, No. 3, September 2005, 255

Zlatnik, M. G. ; Copland, J. A. ; Ives, K. and Soloff, M. S. (2000), Functional oxytocin receptors in a human endometrial cell line, American Journal of Obstetrics and Gynecology, 182, 850-855

Zorman, M. ; Podgorelec, V. ; Kokol, P. ; Peterson, M. ; Lane, J. (2000), Decision tree's induction strategies evaluated on a hard real world problem, 13th IEEE Symposium on Computer-Based Medical Systems, 19-24

Chapter 2

Data Mining Applied to the Improvement of Project Management

Joaquin Villanueva Balsera, Vicente Rodriguez Montequin,
Francisco Ortega Fernandez and Carlos Alba González-Fanjul

Additional information is available at the end of the chapter

1. Introduction

Most of the professional activities are developed as projects. Project management is a complex process involving many elements interrelated and dependent on external agents that may complicate its control. Projects, as defined by PMBOK of Project Management Institute (PMI, 2009), are designed to solve a problem or need, have a temporary effect and is unique in time and not repeatable in the same circumstances. Uncertainty is a key factor associated with project management. This factor affects the consumption of resources, the estimation of time and money as well as the impact of risk and quality.

In fact, risks, uncertainty or estimation are the key words to pursue for a project-oriented organization. And its complexity and difficulty are so significant that the deliveries are clearly unacceptable. CHAOS and other independent reports show success rates under 32% with a deviation in time and cost several times higher than initial estimation (Standish Group, 2010).

Traditional project management, regardless of sector, identifies a series of phases such as:

1. Initiation, where needs are identified and evaluated to know whether it is possible to carry out the project at this stage. Uncertainty is very high due to lack of accurate information, which means that the possibility of error in the estimate is high.
2. Planning, this aims to develop a solution in greater detail, by breaking down the problem into more detailed activities. This reduces uncertainty and makes estimates and forecasts. You must also define the tasks and calendar and estimate the time and money needed to undertake the project.
3. Execution. Once tasks are clearly defined, the implementation phase of the project can begin with the use of monitoring techniques and adjustments to planning, in order to

maintain control on the project. At this stage reducing uncertainty is critical, the risk of an incorrect estimate and the impact of this is much higher because there is no time to solve the deviations.

4.   Closure. Finally there is the closing stage of the project in which results are checked to determine if the project satisfies the needs for which arose, as well as collecting information on the problems detected, weakness or strength of the team. This is called lessons learned and has to be a source of information that is stored to be the basis on which decisions are made in future projects.

Project managers have to deal with those problems with a limited set of tools but it has been proven that better estimation levels at any stage and correct post-mortem analysis are the most influencing techniques for a continuous improvement. And that is only possible using analysis of data from previous projects. During the development of projects, very different sources of data can provide information about what is happening, including delays, overloads, etc. That data could be used for immediate analysis and correction but it can be extraordinarily useful for a global better performance of the rest of projects in which the organization is involved. A structured repository of the data will be an optimal source of key information for future success. The dataset is a snapshot that defines the behavior of the portfolio to be used for postmortem analysis to analyze trends and generate models that define the behavior of certain critical factors in the projects as estimating the expected risk or effort.

The information to be collected must come from every phase in the project: initiation, planning, execution and closure. Some problems may arise in the data collection phase since every project is unique by definition, therefore the types of data, fields or indicators to be stored may be different depending on the project, thus generating a very heterogeneous but less constant data set.

However, the phase which will benefit more from the implementation of data mining techniques is the initial planning phase. Since at this stage there is not much detailed information on the outcome of the project, the project manager may make bigger mistakes in the estimations about costs, efforts, time or risk probability.

All these issues are common to every type of projects; however they have a greater impact on software projects, since they possess several components which influence directly on estimation problems. These projects are developed in a constantly-changing technological environment. Cost estimation is linked directly to resources effort, which entails that proper budget estimation depends on the effort estimation measured in person-hour necessary to develop a product. Another determining factor in software projects is meeting the requirements with a series of quality assurances, to avoid nonconformities or defects.

Unfortunately those data cannot be easily processed manually due to their heterogeneity and that is the perfect environment for Data Mining, which performs the processing of information extraction from raw data in order to extract useful conclusions. Data mining is capable of examining the data creating rules or conclusions providing the organization with tools devoted to decrease the risks and uncertainty in the decision making process.

Data mining can be helpful in all stages and fields: estimating better costs, optimizing the bids, evaluating the risks, decreasing the uncertainty in the duration of tasks, etc.

The chapter presents in a learn-by examples way how data mining is contributing to improve the field of project management, including also guides and tips about how to approach your own problem.

When the organization has not enough information from its own data it can collect information from external databases. Currently there are databases that collect information from the project closure. For the analysis of these cases we used International Software Benchmarking Standards Group (ISBSG, 2012), which is a dataset that includes data compiled from information extracted from the implementation of projects of different nationalities and sizes.

This dataset consists of information systems projects. Such projects are characterized by the deliverable is a product with no physical existence itself and whose main cost lies in the development or design (not materials), it is logical to assume the cost of production is dominated by personnel costs, measured so their effort in person-months or man-hours. Here it highlights the importance of a good estimate of the effort since it is the main cost factor.

One of the most important objectives in the management of information technology projects has been focused on the correct estimation of effort and risk detection of defects or quality nonconformities in the implementation of the system.

There are many empirical models, which are conventional methods that are commonly used, based on a formula that fits the physical behavior of this attribute, but information systems evolve very quickly and are much better to have a method that allows us to adjust the model to the way we work and the technological environment for projects that develop our organization.

This need arises to model for effort and the risk impact measured as defects in the project. Procedure must be considered as a data mining project, for which it has been followed the phases given by CRISP-DM methodology (Chapman *et al.*, 2000). The major steps to be followed begin by data understanding; this stage is a study of available data. The next step is to perform the data preparation to modeling, since each technique needs a particular type of data.

After the application of the data mining analysis described, it can be obtained a reduction of uncertainty implicit in the projects, particularly in information technology systems. In addition, you can get more results as, for instance, relationships between attributes, identification of variables that provide information or are more meaningful to estimate the effort or to identify the level of risk o quality assurance.

2. Understanding the software project environment

As a case study, it has been chosen the information technology projects and it has been considered the need to identify, from the initial phase of a project, the estimation of effort and risk in a software project taking as reference a dataset compiled from previous projects within an organization. Therefore, first it must be learned the generic and common process of effort estimation and the significance of classification of potential risk of product development.

Ever since the beginning of information technology projects was first developed back in 1968, serious problems have been detected when it comes to fulfill the main premises of a project: meet the quality goals within a predefined time and cost, as well as it occurs in any other sector. This is commonly known as "software crisis", and it is defined as the existing complexity in building error-free programs. The reasons that provoke a software crisis may be, among others, the complexity of programming and the constant process of changing that an application must endure in order to be adapted to users' requirements.

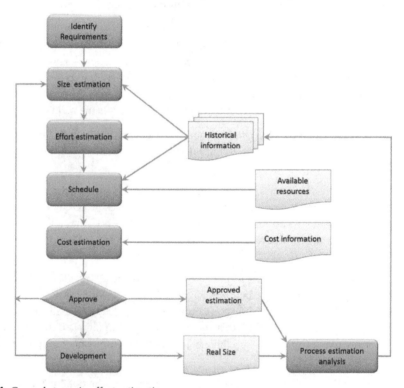

Figure 1. General stages in effort estimation.

Effort estimation is characterized by its complexity and its lack of reliability and high failure levels. (Lock, 2007), given that:

- Estimations *per se* require a great amount of time effort,
- Estimations are hastily performed,
- Previous experience is required,
- Experts' estimations are subjective,
- Information from previous projects is not stored as it is not time and cost efficient,

- Estimations are adjusted to available resources, it is known as "Parkinson's law"(Parkinson, 1955),
- Other characteristics of these projects are: the difficulty in finding similar projects, vague and changing requirements, etc.

The four basic steps to perform a more plausible estimation of a information technology project (Chemuturi, 2009) are the following ones:

1. Estimate the product development size.
2. Estimate effort in person-months.
3. Estimate total time.
4. Estimate final cost.

The first step in any estimation is the understanding and defining of the system to estimate. Software projects are intangible, thus the difficulty in understanding a product which cannot be seen or touched. Size estimation can be based on source lines of code or function points. (Albrecht & Gaffney, 1983). In order to estimate the schedule with resources, there are a series of rules depending on the type of project to perform, and they may be of help in a first estimation, although this process keeps improving as it is adjusted to a more detailed schedule. From this schedule, a distribution of necessary resources is extracted, which will have to be adjusted to the available resources to, eventually, provide the final schedule.

In this phase all the aspects of an initial estimation are considered, even calculating the project cost in terms of effort. Nevertheless, this value clearly will not be the final effort of the project, since there will be a series of efforts or costs to add, which stem from the needs and interests of the organization, such as general costs, profits, risks, technological environment, etc.

In 1986, Alfred Spector, president of Transarc Corporation and vice president of research and special initiatives at Google since 2007, published a paper comparing bridge building with software development; he reasoned that unlike the software, the bridges are built on budget, on time and do not fall, and if something is wrong it must analyzed why it happened (Spector & Gifford, 1986). The reason for such difference is an extremely detailed design. The design of a bridge stays permanent and admits no alteration; therefore the building contractor has little or no chance at all to modify the specifications. Another difference lies in the fact that, when a bridge collapses, causes are investigated and gathered as feedback to apply in future constructions, whereas in software development failures are hidden, so the benefits of lessons learned are not obtained.

After this first approach, a more rigorous study of problems and solutions was undergone. A number of institutions emerged, producing reports and statistical analysis, such as GAO (Government Account Office) – analyzing software development projects for the American Government, or ESPITI, studying the main problems of software development on European scale, which results are quite similar to the obtained in one of the more accepted reports, CHAOS (Standish Group, 1995), which indicates that most of the problems are related to specifications, management and documentation of projects.

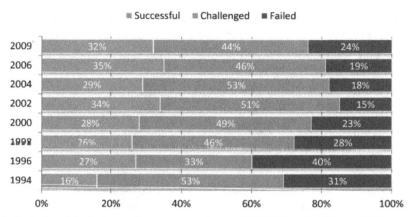

Figure 2. Evolution of the Software Project success. Source CHAOS (Standish Group, 2010)

The report shows that in 2009 software projects were 32% successful, thus a reduction as compared to 2006. 24% of the rest of projects have failed, understanding "fail" as cancelled or never used, and 44% of projects were changed, that is, delayed, over-budgeted or with less functionalities than the required.

From the previous considerations it is inferred that the complexity and variety of agents that affect correct effort estimation, illustrate the need to develop analytic methods which consider every agent which influence the development of the project and product, with specifications to be applied in an organization.

Besides, knowing, preventing and trying to mitigate any risk that a software project may be subjected to is a complex task, mainly as a result of the large amount of threats of diverse nature which are present since the beginning of the project.

The estimation of level risk is another key factor. Risk is reflected upon every main target of a project: time, cost and quality. Regarding time and cost, one could perform an assessment of the grade of certainty with which the models provide their previsions and, as a consequence, extend this time and cost. As regards the quality variable, specific models can be developed using similar data mining as the one used for time and cost estimation but to predict this resulting quality, which in the case of software projects it is usually related to the number of defects. Therefore, risk level can be estimated through the prediction of defects to be produced in the project.

Making a model or knowing the agents influencing the risk, as well as their severity, will allow the managers of software projects to facilitate project management starting process.

So far, the models have improved the effort estimation process; however they have not met the demands of software projects.

Given the high nonlinearity of the process and its dependence on non-quantifiable parameters, the case study is framed within the problems in which the application of intelligent data mining techniques has given successful results, with the introduction of significant control advances.

Therefore, when it comes to developing the models, the main target will be the estimation of risk and effort needed to develop the product, taking the available information on size, resources and other variables that may affect the development environment as a starting point.

3. Related works and assess situation

Software estimation process foundations were first established by Putnam (Putnam LH & Ann Fitzsimmons, 1979), who also developed another reputed method, Software Lifecycle Model (SLIM) (Putnam, 1978), based on Rayleigh curve adjusted to empiric results.

The most representative model of effort estimation is COCOMO (B. W. Boehm, 1981), developed by Barry W. Boehm. These types of models have their estimation based on a general equation as:

$$E = a \cdot S^b \tag{1}$$

where E stands for *effort*, S stands for the software size measured in source lines of code or function points, a and b are factors adjusted according to the type of project. One of the problems of these methods is their use of parameters such as source lines of code. It is quite complex to estimate the values of those variables before the beginning of the project, therefore, these models are difficult to apply before considering the requirements and design of the project. Afterwards, this method was revised to be adapted to the new software characteristics (B. Boehm *et al.*, 1995).

One of the key advances was undergone by Allan Albrecht and John Gaffney, who developed the Function Point Analysis (FPA) (Albrecht & Gaffney, 1983) as a method to estimate the functional size of an information system software.

This method meant a substantial progress if compared to the traditional kilo-Source lines of code (KSLOC); it abandoned size-oriented metrics, to start using functionality-oriented metrics. First, the system components are identified, quantified and classified as inputs, outputs, inquiries, logical internal files and external interface files. Once the unadjusted function points are calculated using a weighting table, it is adjusted with a complexity adjustment factor. This factor is calculated by the weighting of the influence of environmental agents on the project, which is: data communications, distributed processing, complex processing, end-user and configuration load among others. The development team productivity is then calculated in a more aseptic way, by using Function Points per Person-Month.

Different surveys as (B. Boehm *et al.*, 2000), compile the different traditional software estimation techniques.

Recently, it has been noted a trend to use computational intelligence techniques based on data to project management problems and these techniques were proved able to detect complex relationships. Classic approaches, which have been shown above, involve analytical or statistical equations (B. Boehm *et al.*, 2000). Usually, intelligent models utilize neural networks (Tadayon, 2005), fuzzy logic (Xu & Khoshgoftaar, 2004), tree decision (Andreou & Papatheocharous, 2008) and evolutionary algorithms (Dolado, 2001) for performing improved effort estimations.

In addition, research studies propose various data mining techniques to extract knowledge. Authors such as,(Briand *et al.*, 1992) utilized regression-based models combined with classification trees techniques applied on historical datasets in order to estimate the project cost.

Other techniques have used the concept of fuzzy logic; it was used to integrate the concept of risk uncertainty using fuzzy decision trees (Huang *et al.*, n.d.).

4. Application process and guidelines

Given the case of study is presented as a data mining application process, it has been considered the use of one of the more wide-spread methodologies: Cross Industry Standard Process for Data Mining CRISP-DM (Chapman *et al.*, 2000). This has already been used in order to solve similar problems (Montequín *et al.*, 2005).

This methodology defines the data mining life cycle process; it consists of 6 phases, this is a global process which is performed by process iterations, in addition, the phases interact with each other throughout the development process.

The initial phase is defined as Business Understanding and aims to identify the objective, which will be defined from a business perspective, which also has to assess the situation and design a plan of data mining project.

The next step is defined as Data Understanding and its aims are to collect and review data; this begins with an initial dataset that is processed to get familiar with the data, performing the first contact with the problem, discovering data quality problems, identifying the first hypothesis and defining initial relationships.

When the Understanding step is complete, CRISP-DM proposes a new step for preparing data for subsequent modeling. The data preparation phase has all the activities necessary for building the final dataset, its goal is to select and clean the data. This phase can be performed several times. This task includes the selection of rows and attributes and data cleaning to conform to requirements of used modeling tools. It should be borne in mind that each modeling technique requires a particular data type or a preparation adapted to its needs. Therefore it has to perform transformations on the attributes, such as converting numerical values to nominal or otherwise, processing missing values, identifying outliers, reducing the size of variables or samples, etc. This phase is closely related to the following modeling and there is much interaction between them

The next phase is the modeling, at this stage the modeling technique that best fits to study requirements should be selected and its parameters are calibrated to optimal value. Therefore, stepping back to the data preparation stage could be often necessary.

After the modeling phase, it has to perform the evaluation phase. The confidence degree that ensure as valid model has been set from the beginning. It must determine whether the business issue has been sufficiently resolved.

A data mining study is not completed in the evaluation phase, but it has to continue with a deployment plan and subsequent monitoring and maintenance of model results.

This whole process is iterative, since it generates a cycle that is repeated until the criteria of success is met, i.e. if the objectives are not met at the evaluation phase, it has to do another cycle, for which you have to develop a new data set or to define new initial objectives.

In the methodology phase, targets and strategies of data collection must be fixed. It has been chosen to use an existing dataset, whose collection is approved by an international prestigious organization as ISBSG, International Software Benchmarking Standards Group. Release 10 has been used as case of study.

5. Application case

To achieve the fixed objectives and analyzing the available attributes of the dataset, it is considered as target a set of models which predict the development effort and three predictive models capable of estimate the number of potential defects that will be included in the information system to be developed (minor, major and extreme). Once the models are developed, one can analyze which parameters provide more information and are more sensitive to changes in the problem to be predicted.

Once the targets are defined, the following phases of the methodology are applied, which entails data examination.

5.1. Data understanding

This section has examined the data to identify quality and relationships that define a first hypothesis. ISBSG database contains information recorded on the projects, which is what an organization wants to record its own repository.

The dataset is formed by variables such as:

- Rating (associated with data quality as rated by ISBSG organization),
- Size measurement metrics (Function points, SLOC: Source Lines of Code),
- Product environment and architecture (development, documents, language, hardware, operating system, methodology),
- Quality (number of minor, major and extreme defects).

The amount of information that will be used is 4106 projects and 106 attributes. Data is collected from projects that come from different countries, as well as a large number of different types of organizations. It can be seen in the attribute "Organization type" that has projects in the following sectors: Engineering (38%), Services (21%), Insurance (17%), Public (12%) and Banking (10%).

In order to analyze the data quality for modeling, some basic statistics are performed to identify ranges in which numeric variables move and the dispersion of the cases of categorical variables.

After an initial analysis of the dataset, the first observed characteristics are that there are a lot of categorical variables, which complicates their use by some methods that do not support these types of variables.

As projects are heterogeneous, the cases do not collect information on all attributes, therefore there are plenty of missing values (Acock, 2005).

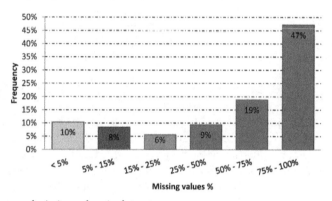

Figure 3. Frequency of missing values in dataset

Only 10% of the attributes have an amount of missing values below 5%; depending on the importance of some of the variables, it could be used up to 18% of the attributes of the dataset. However, as the figure shows, more than 75% of the dataset variables have missed over 75% of information, this means that, at the most, only 25% of the projects would have information available in these variables, which implies a great reduction of the dataset to be used for modeling. As a result, over 80% of the attributes of the dataset would not be used for modeling.

In order to identify the first hypothesis and check the consistency of the data, linear correlations have been searched.

As regards the attributes that are the targets for this study, you can choose between the three variables that reflect effort and productivity (as measured by effort per functional size) which have a strong linear relationship, so the study will take one of each as a representative. There is also a relationship between "Summary Work Effort" and variables that represent the breakdown effort into phases, especially between Specify, Build and Test phases. In the figure, one also can observe a direct linear relationship between planning and design phase, and between specify and test phase. It follows a trend that projects with much effort in the planning phase also make great efforts in the design phase, and those with great effort in the specify phase, do also have it in the test phase.

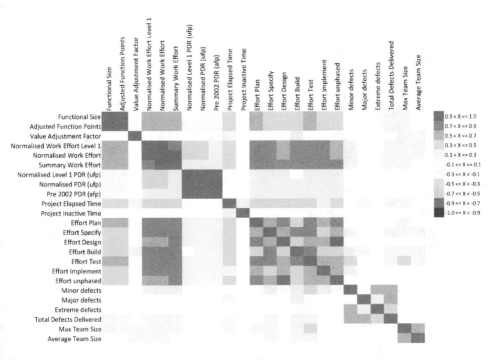

Figure 4. Linear correlations between numerical variables

In the case of defects, it is observed a direct linear relationship between the "Minor defects" and "Extreme defects"; it also appears a slight direct trend with the effort, thus it can be deduced that the high number of defects is associated with projects with strong development effort.

Another preliminary study which can be done is the multidimensional data visualization for which they have used self-organizing maps SOM (MacDonell, 2005). This visualization method allows us to identify groups of data for similar projects and to find nonlinear relationships within the variables set in exploration.

The SOM map shows the previously identified linear relationships between "Summary Work Effort" and the variables that break down the effort into phases, since high values of each of the variables are distributed in the same area of the map.

The extensive blue areas show the great amount of missing values identified above, in order to extract more information with this technique, the data should be filtered and the missing values be processed.

As a conclusion of this initial data exploration phase, it is observed that a high percentage of the dataset attributes will not be used due to the large amount of missing values; it also must be selected which categorical attributes can be transformed to obtain predictive models. This is a usual situation in this kind of environment.

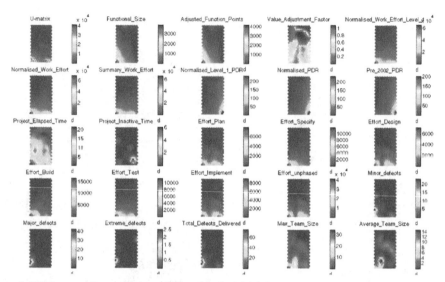

Figure 5. SOM map of the problem variables with the initial dataset

5.2. Data preparation

Next step is the preparation the data to be used for modeling technique; for this particular case it has been considered the use of predictive algorithm to generate models. To do so, the data are first prepared, filtering cases to form a homogeneous group, and clearing cases with low quality or that are outliers, but it has to preserve the cases that remain extreme but belong to a wider group.

Attributes that have a high percentage of missing values are removed from the study dataset, since they will not be able to be used.

"Normalized Work Effort Level" and "Level 1 Normalized PDR" variables have been selected as candidates for the target of effort estimation model, since they are two ways of expressing the effort, either through the reported effort by the team or the hours needed to develop a function point.

To ensure the reliability of the data that form the modeling dataset, projects that have a quality rating with little credibility are removed. Dataset will consist only of projects that have collected data about development team effort (e.g., project team, project management, project administration).

As seen in the introduction section, size estimation is a prerequisite for effort estimation, so this is an attribute that has to take part in the dataset used to generate the model. In the ISBSG repository "Count Approach" attribute is available, this is the functional size measurement method (FSM Method) used to measure the functional size (e.g. IFPUG (ISO/IEC 20926, 2003), MARK II (ISO/IEC 20968, 2002), NESMA (ISO/IEC 24750, 2005), FiSMA (ISO/IEC 29881, 2008), COSMIC-FFP (ISO/IEC 19761, 2003), etc.).

Group	Attribute	Type	Acronym	Effort M.	Defect M.
	Functional Size	Numeric	FS	In	In
Size	Adjusted Function Points	Numeric	AFP	In	In
	Value Adjustment Factor	Numeric	VAF	In	In
Effort	Normalized Work Effort Level 1	Numeric	NWE	Out	In
Productivity	Normalized Level 1 PDR	Numeric	PDR	-	In
	Project Elapsed Time	Numeric	PET	In	In
	Project Inactive Time	Numeric	PIT	In	In
	Effort Plan	Numeric	EP	-	In
Schedule	Effort Specify	Numeric	ES	-	In
	Effort Design	Numeric	ED	-	In
	Effort Build	Numeric	EB	-	In
	Effort Test	Numeric	ET	-	In
	Effort Implement	Numeric	EI	-	In
	Minor defects	Numeric	MiD	-	Out
Defects	Major defects	Numeric	MaD	-	Out
	Extreme defects	Numeric	ExD	-	Out
	Total Defects Delivered	Numeric	TD	-	Out
	Development Type	Categorical	DT	In	In
	Package Customization	Categorical	PC	In	In
Project	Language Type	Categorical	LT	In	In
	Programming Language	Categorical	PL	In	In
	CASE Tool Used	Categorical	CTU	In	In
	Used Methodology	Categorical	UM	In	In
Team	Max Team Size	Numeric	MaT	In	In
	Average Team Size	Numeric	AvT	In	In

Table 1. Data dictionary of candidate attributes for both modeling

Since the measurements performed with different methods are not comparable (Cuadrado-Gallego et al., 2010), the dataset is filtered by "Count Approach" to provide uniformity with the measurements taken for functional size, in this case the projects that use IFPUG are taken, as this is the most used. This situation does not apply for an organization, as it will only use one type of measurement.

For the effort model there are certain attributes, such as the breakdown of effort phase (EP, ES, ED, EB, ET, EI and EU), that cannot be used because they are another way of expressing the effort. Other attributes are not known at the time of estimating the effort, as is the case of defects, which can only have that information after the product is developed. Other variables may be taken as model inputs to know its influence and then, if they are relevant, they can be estimated to predict the effort depending on its variation, as is the case of PET and PIT.

As the elements that cannot be involved in the effort model present a high number of missing values, it was decided to perform two separate datasets, one for each model.

Then, it is decided to take NWE "Normalized Work Effort" as target, because the productivity (PDR) is calculated as the ratio between NWE and FS. PDR was discarded since the use of normalized effort for development team only and unadjusted functional count should render the most comparable rates, but excludes the adjustment factor (VAF) that, in contrast, it does affect the effort.

For the processing of nominal variables two possible encodings have been considered, depending on the number of different values the variable may take.

In the case that a variable may take a low number of categories, as is the case of PC, CTU and UM, it has been created a number of dummy variables equal to the number of categories as shown in the table below. In this case, although the variables may take three categories, it was encoded as two new variables, and with the code "0 0" is represented no information as a state.

Package Customization (PC)	PC_Y	PC_N
No	0	1
Yes	1	0
Empty (missing value)	0	0

Table 2. Process de nominal variable PC for two binary variables

For variables that take a larger number of categories, as is the case LT, DT and PL, it has been transformed into a single numerical variable, so as not to generate so many binary variables. Since it cannot be assumed that there is the same distance among categories, therefore it cannot generate an encoding in consecutive numbers because the algorithm based on data could be misleading. For encoding these variables, each category has been replaced by the average effort associated with each category; thereby the distance between categories is preserved

Using techniques such as box-plots and percentile thresholds to remove outliers, cases that seem extreme in one variable can be lost, however they can coincide with the values taken in the other project attributes. Therefore, it was decided to make a projection of the n-dimensional space to identify those that are located far away from the rest.

There has been a data projection using the Principal Component Analysis PCA technique (Pearson, 1901), it allows us to pass from an n-dimensions space to two dimensions in this case by analyzing the principal components.

The figure shows a bubble chart with the dataset projection for which it has been used functional size (FS) as bubble size and effort (NWE) as fill color.

There is a series of clusters that appear due to the addition of nominal variables to the dataset, which generates layers in the projection. In this case, the group at the bottom of the chart is associated with "Yes" values in the package customization variable (PC).

Three projects associated with medium and high values of effort (NWE) are identified and located far from the normal behavior of the other variables in the group, especially the red point to the right that corresponds to very high values of effort (NWE) and associated with a low value of the functional size variable (FS), which would be associated with low functional complexity projects, but with an stronger effort (NWE) than the rest. It can also be remarked, that the red point is associated a value "Yes" in PC variable, which means it should be closer to the group at the bottom.

For all these reasons, it can be deduced that this project is an outlier in the dataset.

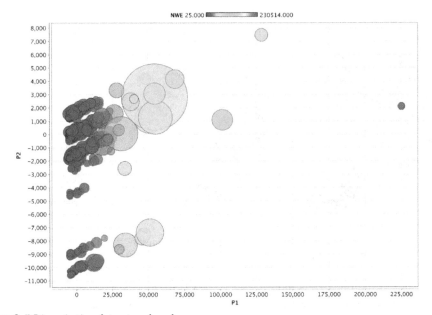

Figure 6. PCA projection dataset analyzed

The three projects that are outside normal behavior groups have been removed from the dataset, since these are projects that may be actually developed under these conditions, but they are not representative for this dataset.

PIT variable has been taken out of the dataset due to the large amount of missing values presented, which would greatly reduce the dataset. After cleaning missing values, filtering outliers and creating dummy variables, the dataset for effort model contains 409 projects and 16 attributes.

The same filters as for the above variables shall be applied on the dataset for defect models. In the case of the efforts for each phase, it shows a lot of missing values, but the total project effort has been collected.

The effort profile that a project may present over its life cycle, depends on the type of tasks it contains. This distribution of effort throughout tasks could be grouped into one of the following profiles: uniform, increasing, decreasing, bell, initial peak, final peak, and two peaks among others. Since the projects stored in the database are very different from each other, a clustering is made to identify groups using a SOM network and using the k-means clustering technique (Kanungo *et al.*, 2002).

The minimum number of clusters that produces less error in classification is three, as seen on the left side of the figure. Clusters labeled as Cluster1 and Cluster3 are a very small group of projects, for the Cluster1 the effort of the design phase is very high, while in the Cluster3 the effort of design phase is almost nonexistent. The cluster labeled as Cluster2 contains 94% of the projects studied, so that its distribution throughout the project life cycle is representative.

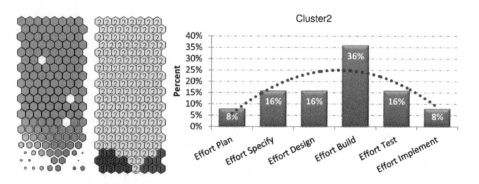

Figure 7. Identification of the load distribution of effort in the majority cluster

On the right side of the figure it can be seen the average performance of the projects that are labeled Cluster2. As it is shown, it follows a bell distribution, focusing efforts on building phase, which is standard in software projects. This distribution will be used to generate the missing values of attributes EP, ES, ED, EB, ET and IE.

Deleting cases with missing values has serious effects on the target variables defects, which are chosen to define different data sets to ensure that the target variables are representative. Thus, datasets were generated for MiD model with 413 projects, MaD model with 333 projects and ExD model with 466 projects.

5.3. Modeling effort and predicting quality through forecasted defects

Several models are built to identify factors that affect the effort and software quality, measured as defects. Afterwards, the influence of the attributes in the target variables is analyzed.

It has been decided to use Adaptive Regression Splines Multivariate MARS (Friedman, 1991) as a technique for modeling, since it is adapted to the problem using its unique characteristics and it is a promising technique in modeling complex nonlinear problems.

The characteristics that have been decisive to select MARS algorithm are, among others: robustness against collinearity of the input variables, their ability to select relevant variables and to identify the interactions between them.

Another reason for the selection of MARS algorithm was its achieving good results with dataset that do not have an abundant number of cases, provided that these are representative of the target. This dataset has been reduced, since the phases of cleaning and data filtering have reduced 10% of the initial dataset.

MARS has been used for the selection of input variables and to perform an analysis of relevant factors to be taken into consideration for estimating the effort and risk in software projects.

The process followed for training is a set of steps that begin by defining two dataset. The cases for each dataset have been selected at random. One will have 85% of the initial dataset and will be used to the model training and the remaining cases are allocated to the test dataset, whose purpose is to test the generalization of training performed. This is done to verify the model results obtained with a set of projects that have not been used for training.

In the training phase of the MARS algorithm models, it has been taken different options in algorithm configuration parameters. Different parameter settings have been tested for basic functions parameter (Friedman's nk), i.e., maximum number of model terms before pruning, as well as other parameters such as the degree of interaction (Friedman's me).

It aims to achieve a model with minimum prediction error and the least number of input attributes. In order to reduce the dimension (the number of attributes involved in the model) attributes are removed from the dataset that do not add value or have a void relative importance.

Also different combinations of variables were tested, which in theory could provide the same information to the model. An example of this combination of attributes is the case of using Functional Size (FS) next to Value Adjustment Factor (VAF) and Adjusted Function Points (AFP) in another model, since the latter is the product of two factors above, something similar is the case of PDR, NWE and FS.

In order to compare the quality of the models, it has been used Root Mean Square (RMS), which is the square root of Mean Squared Error (MSE), defined as the average difference between predicted and actual values squared.

In the case of NWE model, dimensions have been reduced to seven parameters, which are those that have obtained significant importance.

The table shows the percentage of success rate achieved by the model in each error range, both in train and in test; it also shows the results obtained by the reference model for the same interval. The column "Relative error" is the percentage of value related to the range in which effort varies, i.e. an error of less than 300 hours is around 1% of the range in which the effort is varied.

Relative error	Absolute error	NWE Train	NWE Test	Reference
1%	300	29%	26%	16%
3%	700	54%	55%	25%
7%	1500	80%	75%	44%
15%	3000	95%	89%	60%
25%	5000	97%	90%	62%
50%	10000	99%	93%	76%
75%	15000	100%	95%	80%

Table 3. Success of reference model and NWE model in training and test

To test the model results, a reference indicator on effort has been searched. Other authors have defined models for the effort but have used the variable transformations, and models were optimized for another dataset release that contains different attributes (Angelis *et al.,* 2001). Since values for the project elapsed time (measured on months) and the average team size are known in the dataset, effort is the product of time by team. It has been assumed an average of 160 hours monthly work to calculate the expected effort for the project regardless of the functional size and other factors. This way it can be checked if the model is able to extract information from the rest of attributes to provide better results in prediction. This is the reference indicator that is taken in the table.

The prediction model of effort (NWE) has an RMS of 1509 in test and the reference model has an RMS of 7212.

The figure shows the attributes that are part of the model and the relative importance of the variables for the model. The most important attribute for prediction of the effort is Average Team Size (AVT). Also, Adjusted Function Points (AFP), Project Elapsed Time (PET) and Development Type (DT) provide significant information; DT attribute describes whether the development was a new development, enhancement or re-development. Also it was involved the value "Yes" in the use of CASE tools (CTU_Y), the value "Yes" in using Methodology (UM_Y) and whether the type of project is a custom package (PC_Y).

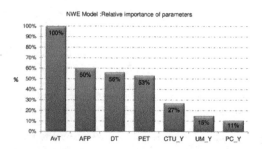

Figure 8. Relative importance of parameters in the model of NWE

For the prediction of potential software defects and therefore the prediction of the product quality that will generate, three models have been developed to perform predictions on:

Minor Defects (MiD), Major Defects (MaD) and Extreme Defects (ExD). The same methodology as for the previous model has been used.

The table shows the results of the three models for both train and test. Since there is no reference model on the prediction of possible defects in the software product, it was decided to take as reference what an organization involved in project management will do. Next, information on historical data available are collected and compiled in the dataset, and then it was taken as reference an average of defects reported in previous projects.

MiD				MaD				ExD			
Error	Train	Test	Ref.	Error	Train	Test	Ref.	Error	Train	Test	Ref.
0	46%	40%	0%	0	20%	17%	0%	0	94%	94%	0%
1	60%	57%	78%	1	44%	43%	2%	1	99%	98%	98%
2	73%	62%	82%	2	61%	59%	3%	2	99%	98%	98%
3	85%	71%	85%	3	72%	72%	8%	3	100%	100%	100%
4	91%	81%	88%	4	79%	79%	13%	4	100%	100%	100%
5	93%	83%	91%	5	82%	80%	19%	5	100%	100%	100%
10	98%	90%	95%	10	92%	87%	94%				
15	99%	95%	97%	15	97%	96%	95%				
20	99%	99%	98%	20	99%	99%	96%				

Table 4. Success of reference model and Defects models in training and test

The number of defects has been distributed with an increase in one unit until case of 5 defects and, from this point onwards, the increase has grown, because the more number of defects, the more uncertainty it presents.

The model predicting the number of minor defects has a RMS of 3.4 in test and the reference model has a RMS of 10.1. The model which presents a major number of defects has a RMS of 8.4 in test and the reference model has a RMS of 28.4. The prediction of extreme defects has a RMS of 0.3 in test and the reference model has a RMS of 0.5.

The figure shows the attributes that are part of each of the models as well as the relative importance of the variables for each model. The dimension of each problem has been diminished, in the case of MiD there are eleven attributes that define the model, eight are needed to MaD and ExD is defined by five variables.

Each model selects the attributes that best define your target attribute, but there are some attributes common to all but with different relevance.

The functional size, whether expressed as FS and VAF or AFP, appears in all models. In the case of the breakdown of the effort phases of the project life cycle, it has retained all the attributes so that the graphics are more comparable, although some do not provide information to some models.

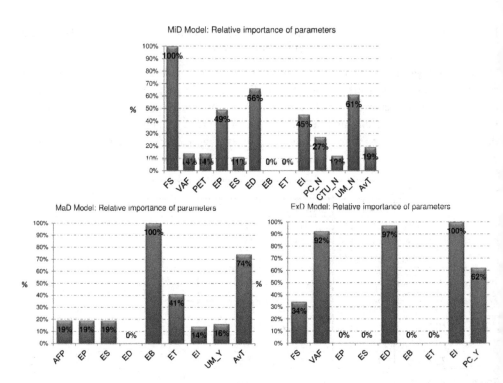

Figure 9. Relative importance of parameters in the models of defects

Other attributes as PC, CTU and UM varies depending on the model, for example, the attribute UM in the MiD model, affects the negation of the use of methodology, while MaD model affects the affirmation. Another variable that affects two models is AVT.

6. Discussion

During the data analysis, several problems associated with the great amount of nominal variables have been found (having too many levels), as well as a major presence of missing values in both nominal and numeric fields. This problem forced the rejection of many variables that could provide information to the analysis, but if missing values are filtered, it will greatly reduce the final dataset, leaving a non-representative dataset.

Next, we will proceed to analyze the results and the behavior of the most significant variables in the model to define the behavior of the effort.

The model error is less than the reference model, as the RMS of the model is much lower than the reference. Besides, the results of model tests are higher than the reference model used, therefore we can deduce that the model has been able to extract information from other attributes in addition to the team size and project time. When comparing the linear regression between model estimation and the real value of the effort we achieve a r-squared of 0.884, which is very similar to the linear adjustment obtained by other studies performing regressions (Angelis *et al.*, 2001). Considering this, it can be assumed that the model is valid to analyze and identify behaviors of the variables which give meaning to the effort. If we consider that in the dataset, the average project elapsed time is around 150 days and the average team size is about 7 resources, this implies that 300 hours of effort is equivalent to a week of work in the project. This amounts to a good estimate for an initial phase of the project, when it is important to learn about an effort in order to perform a budget as tight as possible.

We performed a sensitivity analysis to know the behavior of the model as regards the variation of one of the inputs. This is analyzed as it affects the increase or decrease of one variable with respect to the output, which is the effort.

We proceed to discuss the most significant changes that have been found in the variables that form the model of effort.

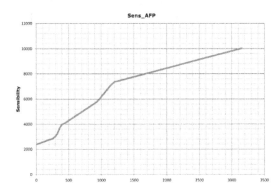

Figure 10. Sensibility of AFP in the NWE model

In some variables such as the affirmation of use of methodologies (UM_Y) it is implied that the effort is greater than in those where it is not used. However, this must not be understood as if the use of methodologies increases the effort, but that projects that often use a methodology are larger and, therefore, require more effort. Something similar occurs with the classification by the Development Type (DT); the effort increases, with the lowest type "Enhancement" followed by "New Development" and higher "Re-development". For the variable (AVT) there was an increase of the effort for average team sizes above 12.

In the case of Adjusted Function Points (AFP), the trend of the effort grows directly with AFP, but not linearly, since the slope is smooth in projects with a value of AFP higher than 1200. With elapsed time, the effort has a more stable growth for projects lasting less than one year and a half, while it increases for longer projects. This may be caused by a decrease in the number of large projects and an increase of long term uncertainty.

Predictive models of defects have a lower RMS than the reference models. Reference models are characterized by their inability to detect the absence of defects. This aspect is important since it allows us to identify the conditions that define a better quality project.

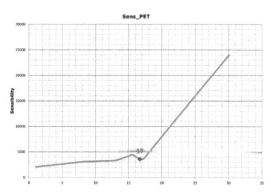

Figure 11. Sensibility of PET in the NWE model

The MiD model is able to separate in test 40% with a zero error range, and succeed 90% for a margin of 10 defects error in a range that varies 150. This model with a threshold of 2 defects achieves 90% of true positive, i.e., projects with zero minor defects are identified as such by the model.

In the case of the MaD model, it apparently reduces the scope for identification of projects without major defects and a range of 15 defects is needed in order to ensure a success of 96%, but although it seems worse than the previous model, it must be commented that the variation range is 285 defects, which implies that a margin of 15 defects is much less than that of MiD model. If we analyze only the projects that have zero major defects, this model guarantees 90% of success with a threshold of 5 defects.

After filtering, the dataset of ExD model has the variation range of 5 extreme defects. The model succeeds in nearly all cases and achieves 98% of true positives. Although this seems the best of the three when compared to the reference model, it does not improve much with the exception that it is able to guarantee 98% of true positives i.e., the model ensures zero defects in projects that really had zero extreme defects.

Analyzing the attributes that add value to the model, we observe that the functional size is always part of all models.

What makes variables PC, CTU and UM remarkable is that, for some models, it is significant the presence of dummy variable "Yes", and for other models, it is significant the presence of dummy variable "No". In the case of MiD model, the attributes PC_N, CTU_N and UM_N affect the increasing in the number of errors, so it follows that projects that do not use a methodology or do not use CASE tools, have a greater number of minor defects. For the model MaD, UM_Y, it has an indirect influence, i.e. their presence does reduce the number of major defects. For ExD model, if it is a customization package project, the number of extreme defects is reduced.

As efforts broken down in the project life cycle tend to have a direct tendency to the number of defects, with the exception of Design Effort (ED) and Implement Effort (EI).

The minor defects are related to efforts to design and implement (architecture and implementation phases) tending to reduce the defects, the major defects are directly related to efforts to build and test (code development phases), and extreme defect are directly related to efforts to design and implement (architecture and implementation phases).

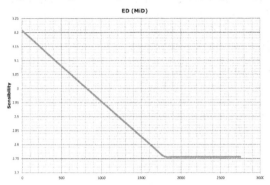

Figure 12. Sensibility of Effort Design (ED) in the MiD model

The final phase of a data mining project is the deployment of a model in an organization for which a solution is proposed. This model will be an ensemble model based on historical data from closure projects, which are provided for NWE model. Its output goes back to the repository, however at the same time it will also be an input to an NWE effort transformer into effort by phases (EP, ES, ED, EB, ET and IE; according to historical information or by type of project). Output transformation of NWE model will be the input for the three defects models, along with the information needed by each model. In this way, the four models will be linked to predict the effort and quality of the software product.

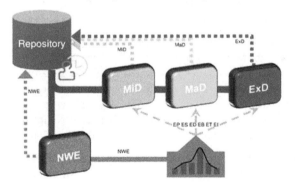

Figure 13. Ensemble model to estimate effort and defects

7. Conclusion

Software projects are involved in a changing environment, both in human and technological aspects, and do not allow generalization of models. On the contrary, data mining techniques are compatible with all project management methodologies, which aim to collect information and indicators from the project closure for its later post-mortem analysis with the aim of continuous improvement.

The general aim of this study consists in developing a method or system which facilitate the process of time and cost estimation, as well as estimate the quality of the final product by the potential risk of software defects. With the defined models, it has been achieved a process which allows us to analyze its behavior and develop perform effort estimations and estimations of risk of not meeting the quality requirements.

Given the amount of nominal variables, it is necessary to transform them so that they can provide information to the models. Most of the performed transformations have positively contributed to the improvement of several models, as in the case of the Development Type (DT) or the dummy variables of Used Methodology (UM_N, UN_Y) or CASE Tool Used (CTU_N, CTU_Y).

The key phases to model this problem have been: the selection of dataset, the stage of filtering, cleaning of outliers, as well as the use of projection techniques, whether with space dimension reduction or using self-organizing nets.

Bearing in mind that the other problem of dataset are the missing values, it can be highlighted the advantage of using clustering techniques which permit finding projects with similar characteristics, and substitute the cluster prototype where it belongs for the missing value.

The defined models allow us to make estimations since the initial phases of the project (with high level of uncertainty), with higher number of success that those of the reference models. The effort model extracts information of adjusted functional size to the technological environment where it is performed, the type of development, the use of CASE tools and the use of methodologies, among others. Defect models do not behave the same, since for instance, in the case of minor defects FS is de highest influence, for major defects the highest influence is EB and for extreme defect, it is EI and ED.

The use of databases as ISBSG, allows the contrast of process and models performed on similar datasets, although the different versions provide new fields and new projects that may make non-comparative results. These models developed from this type of database, may not be directly extrapolated to the situation of an specific organization, since the projects stored in the database have been developed under a much different work environment from the organization's. However, the applied methodology is indeed completely extrapolated, since the steps followed can be repeated on the specific data of another organization.

Finally, what has been exposed is an application process of data mining techniques to project management, and thus it may be also applied to a wider sector, it is not restricted just to the software projects.

Author details

Joaquin Villanueva Balsera, Vicente Rodriguez Montequin,
Francisco Ortega Fernandez and Carlos Alba González-Fanjul
Project Engineering Area, University of Oviedo, Spain

8. References

Acock, A. C. (2005). Working With Missing Values. *Journal of Marriage and Family, 67*(4), 1012–1028. doi: 10.1111/j.1741-3737.2005.00191.x.

Albrecht, A. J. & Gaffney, J. E. (1983). Software Function, Source Lines of Code, and Development Effort Prediction: A Software Science Validation. *IEEE Transactions on Software Engineering, SE-9*(6), 639– 648. doi: 10.1109/TSE.1983.235271.

Andreou, A. S. & Papatheocharous, E. (2008). Software cost estimation using fuzzy decision trees. *ASE 2008 - 23rd IEEE/ACM International Conference on Automated Software Engineering, Proceedings* (pp. 371–374).

Angelis, L., Stamelos, I. & Morisio, M. (2001). Building a software cost estimation model based on categorical data. *Software Metrics Symposium, 2001. METRICS 2001. Proceedings. Seventh International* (pp. 4 –15). doi: 10.1109/METRIC.2001.915511.

Boehm, B., Abts, C. & Chulani, S. (2000). *Software development cost estimation approaches – A survey*. Annals of Software Engineering.

Boehm, B., Clark, B., Horowitz, E., Westland, C., Madachy, R. & Selby, R. (1995). *Cost Models for Future Software Life Cycle Processes: COCOMO 2.0*.

Boehm, B. W. (1981). *Software engineering economics*. Prentice-Hall.

Briand, L. C., Basili, V. R. & Thomas, W. M. (1992). A pattern recognition approach for software engineering data analysis. *Software Engineering, IEEE Transactions on, 18*(11), 931 –942. doi: 10.1109/32.177363.

Chapman, P., Clinton, J., Kerber, R., Khabaza, T., Reinartz, T., Shearer, C., *et al.* (2000). *CRISP-DM 1.0 Step-by-step data mining guide*. Retrieved March 27, 2012, from http://www.crisp-dm.org/CRISPWP-0800.pdf.

Chemuturi, M. (2009). *Software estimation best practices, tools & techniques: a complete guide for software project estimators*. J. Ross Publishing.

Cuadrado-Gallego, J. J., Buglione, L., Domínguez-Alda, M. J., Sevilla, M. F. d., Antonio Gutierrez de Mesa, J. & Demirors, O. (2010). An experimental study on the conversion between IFPUG and COSMIC functional size measurement units. *Information and Software Technology, 52*(3), 347–357.

Dolado, J. . (2001). On the problem of the software cost function. *Information and Software Technology, 43*(1), 61–72. doi: 10.1016/S0950-5849(00)00137-3.

Friedman, J. H. (1991). Multivariate Adaptive Regression Splines. *The Annals of Statistics, 19*(1), 1–67. Retrieved April 2, 2012, .

Huang, S.-J., Lin, C.-Y. & Chiu, N.-H. (n.d.). Fuzzy decision tree approach for embedding risk assessment information into software cost estimation model. *Journal of information science and engineering, 22*(2), 297–313. Retrieved April 10, 2012, .

ISBSG. (2012). Estimation Techniques, Software Benchmarking, Software Estimation, Software Standards. *The International Software Benchmarking Standards Group Limited*. Retrieved from http://www.isbsg.org/.

ISO/IEC 19761. (2003). *Software Engineering COSMIC - Functional Size Measurement Method*. Genève: ISO, International Organization for Standardization.

ISO/IEC 20926. (2003). *Software Engineering IFPUG 4.1 Unadjusted Functional Size Measurement Method. Counting Practices Manual*. Genève: ISO, International Organization for Standardization.

ISO/IEC 20968. (2002). *Software Engineering Mk II Function Point Analysis. Counting Practices Manual.* Genève: ISO, International Organization for Standardization.

ISO/IEC 24750. (2005). *Software Engineering NESMA Functional Size Measurement Method, Version 2.1, Definitions and counting guidelines for the application of Function Point Analysis.* Genève: ISO, International Organization for Standardization.

ISO/IEC 29881. (2008). *Software Engineering, FiSMA Functional Size Measurement Method, Version 1.1.* Genève: ISO, International Organization for Standardization.

Kanungo, T., Mount, D. M., Netanyahu, N. S., Piatko, C. D., Silverman, R. & Wu, A. Y. (2002). An efficient k-means clustering algorithm: analysis and implementation. *Pattern Analysis and Machine Intelligence, IEEE Transactions on,* 24(7), 881 –892. doi: 10.1109/TPAMI.2002.1017616.

Lock, D. (2007). *Project Management.* Gower Publishing, Ltd.

MacDonell, S. G. (2005). Visualization and analysis of software engineering data using self-organizing maps. *2005 International Symposium on Empirical Software Engineering, 2005.* IEEE. doi: 10.1109/ISESE.2005.1541820.

Montequín, V. R., Balsera, J. V., González, C. A. & Huerta, G. M. (2005). Software project cost estimation using AI techniques. *Proceedings of the 5th WSEAS/IASME International Conference on Systems Theory and Scientific Computation,* ISTASC'05 (pp. 289–293). Stevens Point, Wisconsin, USA: World Scientific and Engineering Academy and Society (WSEAS). Retrieved April 22, 2012, from http://dl.acm.org/citation.cfm?id=1373616.1373665.

Parkinson, C. N. (1955). Parkinson's Law. *The Economist.*

Pearson, K. (1901). On lines and planes of closest fit to systems of points in space. *Philosophical Magazine,* 2(6), 559–572.

PMI. (2009). *A Guide to the Project Management Body of Knowledge (PMBOK® Guide).* PMI, Project Management Institute.

Putnam, L. H. (1978). A General Empirical Solution to the Macro Software Sizing and Estimating Problem. *Software Engineering, IEEE Transactions on,* SE-4(4), 345 – 361. doi: 10.1109/TSE.1978.231521.

Putnam LH & Ann Fitzsimmons. (1979). Estimating software cost. *Datamation.*

Spector, A. & Gifford, D. (1986). A computer science perspective of bridge design. *Commun. ACM,* 29(4), 267–283. doi: 10.1145/5684.6327.

Standish Group. (1995). The CHAOS Report (1994). *Group,* 11–13.

Standish Group. (2010). *CHAOS Report 2009.* Standish Group.

Tadayon, N. (2005). Neural network approach for software cost estimation. *Information Technology: Coding and Computing, 2005. ITCC 2005. International Conference on* (Vol. 2, pp. 815 – 818 Vol. 2). doi: 10.1109/ITCC.2005.210.

Xu, Z. & Khoshgoftaar, T. M. (2004). Identification of fuzzy models of software cost estimation. *Fuzzy Sets and Systems,* 145(1), 141–163. doi: 10.1016/j.fss.2003.10.008.

Chapter 3

Explaining Diverse Application Domains Analyzed from Data Mining Perspective

Alberto Ochoa, Lourdes Margain, Rubén Jaramillo,
Javier González, Daniel Azpeitia, Claudia Gómez,
Jöns Sánchez, Julio Ponce, Sayuri Quezada,
Francisco Ornelas, Arturo Elías, Edgar Conde, Víctor Cruz,
Petra Salazar, Emmanuel García and Miguel Maldonado

Additional information is available at the end of the chapter

1. Introduction

This chapter proposal explains the importance of adequate diverses application domains in different aspects in a wide variety of activities of our daily life. We focus our analysis to different activities that use social richness data, analyzing societies to improve diverse situational activities based on a decision support systems under uncertaainty. To this end, we performed surveys to gathering information about salient aspects of modernization and combined them using social data mining techniques to profile a number of behavioural patterns and choices that describe social networking behaviours in these societies.

We will define the terms "Data Mining" and "Decision Support System" as well as their contrast and roles in modern societies. Then we will describe innovative models that captures salient variables of modernization, and how these variables give raise to intervening aspects that end up shaping behavioural patterns in social aspects. We will describe the data mining methodologies we used to extract these variables in each one of these diverse application domains including the analysis of diverse surveys conducted in diverse societies, and provide a comparative analysis of the results in light of the proposed innovative social model.

On the rest proposed chapter, we will describe how our model can be extended to provide a means for identifying potential social public politics. More particularly, we make allusion to behavioural pattern recognition mechanisms that would identify the importance of use techniques from Data Mining. We will close with concluding remarks and extended discussions of our approach and will provide general guidelines for future work in the area of application of Data Mining in diverse application domains, including further analysis on how those public politics organize and operate in social rings, and how they use technology to that end. While our main focus will be on pure social networks such as Facebook. Our literature review will include cases of implementation of correct public politics, and some issues, challenges, opportunities, and trends about this diverses social problems.

The proposal of this chapter is to explain the importance of use Social Data Mining in a wide variety of activities in our daily life, many of these activities, which are online and involve many social networkings using in many ways using Media Richness. Social Data Mining techniques will be useful for answering diverse queries after gathering general information about this given topic. This kind of behaviors will be characterized by take a real implementation of a correct solution, each one of these taking diverse models or multi agents systems for adequate this behavior to obtain information to take decisions that try to improve aspects very important of their lifes organized in different application and fields of knowledge.

First, in section 1 of this Social Data Mining techniques will be useful for answering diverse questions after gathering general information about the given topic. This type of behaviors will be characterized by a real application of a correct solution, each one of these taking diverse models or multi agents systems. This is for adequate this behavior to have information and make decisions that try to improve aspects very important of their lifes organized in different application and fields of knowledge.

First, in section 1 of this chapter explain the concept of Social Data Mining and as this behavior affect in different way to people in differnet aspects in societies' people –Viral Marketing to determine boughts on inmobilarie sector–. In other sections we explain the way to generate a correct analysis In correspondent sections we explain the way to make a correct analysis of diferent activities of daily life as in Electrical Industry (section 2), Classification of Images and its analysis which explain the effects in their analysis including Medical advances (section 3), a comparative analysis using people profile according to describe a possible social benefits in diverse applications domains (section 4). In section 5 we explain the results obtained in e-commerce data mining and emergent kind of techniques which resolve and propose specific kind of marketing according at life style of consumers, and in the section 6 are try to describe the use of Data Mining to Mobile Ad Hoc Networks Security which will be used to determine the possible changes on our modern society. In section 7 we described another specfic applications domains as: organizational models, organizational climate, zoo applications to classify more vulnerable species or identify the adequate kind of avatars on a roll multigame players and finally our conclusions about the future of Data Mining in diverses uses to different activities of our daily life.

2. Data mining and their use on viral marketing

The use of traditional media like radio, television and newspaper, has been replaced by new digital media like social networks Facebook and Twitter. According to (Salaverría, 2009) the increase of broadband users, both on mobile devices, home and workplace, has raised the replacement of traditional media by digital media. Likewise, mentions that these new tools allow the user to interact with the issuer, thanks to several factors that facilitate interaction such as, frequency of updates, including multimedia such as videos and photographs, among others.

On the other hand, (Orihuela, 2002) mentions that existing Internet interactivity has been subverting the paradigms within communication processes in mass media. As (Salaverría, 2009), mentions the ability of interactivity, customization and upgrade, as central in replacing traditional media to digital (Figure 1).

Figure 1. Interaction between users of social networks.

In their study, (Orihuela, 2002), concludes that the public announcement raised in the new digital media is sufficient justification to redefine the requirements in the media, the procedures and content of information, all within trends changing as a result of network usage.

Due to the above, the social networks like Facebook, are an important tool in the marketing strategy of companies. Its low cost (sometimes zero) helps not only in communicating the customer value, but also improves the customer-consumer relationships. According to (Orihuela, 2002), social networks like Facebook sometimes take characteristics of traditional media, however, incorporate a higher level of interaction.

2.1. Corporate use of social networks

After analyzing the above, we can say that the use of social networks helps greatly reducing advertising costs and implementation of new marketing strategies. But even if there are different tools to monitor and observe the behavior of users, there is little research evidence that reveals different patterns of consumption, transmission of messages or lack of them, and observes the behavior of these consumers on trademarks and their experiences with them within the social networks like Facebook.

According to (Salaverría, 2009) the online advertising industry grew by 800 percent from 2004 to 2009 demonstrating a steady development in which social networks and contextual advertising play an important role in the marketing or advertising on social networks, without But there is no scientific evidence on the behavior of users in such networks and the dissemination of messages received and sent within these networks and what encourages you to do or not.

(Sandoval et al., 2010) mentions that social networks have changed the human relations approach and have potentiating its most important feature: Easy to find and develop relationships with other members with similar interests. Similarly mention that social networking services have proliferated targeting people in specific regions or some similar interests as, ethnic, religious, sexual and political (Figure 5). Thus, the fact of having a community segment showing a potential interest in a particular company or product, is useful when performing a specific marketing strategy. In addition to marketing strategies, companies can use such networks in the recruitment, internal communication and interaction with consumers.

Figure 2. Nested groups of similar interests.

2.2. Research objectives

Having analyzed the use of social networks in business, the importance of the restaurant industry in Mexico and specifically the problem of insecurity in Juarez, perform the following research questions:

- What specific objectives seek restaurant sector companies to use social networks?
- What digital social network use most frequently?
- What percentage of these companies has replaced the traditional media advertising advertising on social networks?
- What marketing strategies used in online social networks?
- What correlation is there between; use of social networks and increased sales?
- When beginning their presence within social networks?
- How many users is made up your network?
- How often publish information within social networks?
- What correlation exists between the periodicity of the publications and the time spent in the network, with the number of users in the network?

2.3. Methodology

The conclusive results of this research were obtained through an exploratory study of the use of social networks in companies in the restaurant industry in Juarez and factorial designs were performed to find some correlations between different variables.

First we made a query of the restaurant industry to recognize his presence in Mexico and in the locality. This was done through the National Chamber of the Restaurant Industry and Seasoned Foods (CANIRAC) and National Chamber of Commerce (CANACO) found in the locality.

From the list of registered companies in the industry by these cameras restaurateur, was searched to select those that were present within the digital social networks, regardless of upgrade or number of users connected to their groups. Were interviewed and application of survey of 20 companies with the largest number of users within your network, to meet their business openly in online social networks, specifically Facebook. Took place through a careful study of social networks to find that participation in that network have to know the frequency and topics of their publications, as well as general information of relevance to publish within their Facebook page. He knew the date they started their activities in the network.

Once the information was held after his capture to be analyzed in statistical software to find relevant values.

3. Competitive learning for self organizing maps used in classification of partial discharge

Competitive learning is an efficient tool for Self Organizing Maps, widely applied in variety of signal processing problems such as classification, data compression, in anothers. With the huge volumes of data being generated from the different systems everyday, what makes a system intelligent is its ability to analyze the data for efficient decision-making based on known or new cluster discovery. **The partial discharge (PD) is a common phenomenon which occurs in insulation of high voltage, this definition is given in [1]. In general, the partial discharges are in consequence of local stress in the insulation or on the surface of the insulation.** We evaluate the performance of algorithms in which competitive learning is applied of partial discharge dataset, quantization error, topological error and time in seconds per training epoch. The result from classification of PD shows that *Winner-takes-all* **(WTA)** has better performance than *Frequency Sensitive Competitive Learning* **(FSCL)** and *Rival Penalized Competitive Learning* **(RPCL)**. The first approach in a diagnosis is selecting the different features to classify measured PD activities into underlying insulation defects or source that generate PD's (Figure 3).

The phase resolved analysis investigates the PD pattern in relation to the variable frequency AC cycle (Cheng et al., 2008). The voltage phase angle is divided into small equal windows. The analysis aims to calculate the integrated parameters for each phase window and to plot them against the phase position (ϕ).

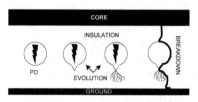

Figure 3. Example of damage in polymeric power cable from the PD in a cavity to breakdown.

- $(q_m - \phi)$: the peak discharge magnitude for each phase window plotted against ϕ, where q_m is peak discharge magnitude.

3.1. Self organizing map

The Self Organizing Map developed by Kohonen, is the most popular neural network models (Kohonen, T., 2006 & Rubio-Sánchez, M., 2004). The SOM is a neural network model that implements a characteristics non-linear mapping from the high-dimensional space of input signal onto a typically 2-dimensional grid of neurons. The SOM is a two-layer neural network that consists of an input layer in a line and an output layer constructed of neurons in a two-dimensional grid.

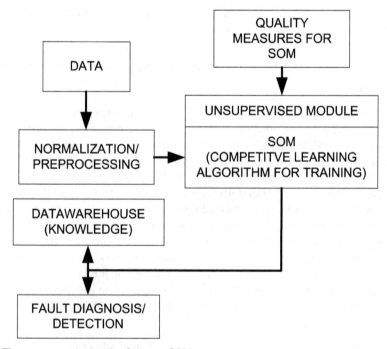

Figure 4. The component interaction between SOM.

PD measurements for power cables are generated and recorded through laboratory tests. Corona was produced with a point to hemisphere configuration: needle at high voltage and hemispherical cup at ground. Surface discharge XLPE cable with no stress relief termination applied to the two ends. High voltage was applied to the cable inner conductor and the cable sheath was grounded, this produces discharges along the outer insulation surface at the cable ends. Internal discharge was used a power cable with a fault due to electrical treeing. Were considered the pattern characteristic of univariate phase-resolved distributions as inputs, the magnitude of PD is the most important input as it shows the level of danger, for this reason the input in the SOM the raw data is the peak discharge magnitude for each phase window plotted against (qm −φ). **Figure 2** shows the conceptual diagram training. In the cases analyzed, the original dataset is 1 million of items, was used a neurons array of 10×10 cells to extract features. As it is well known, in fact, a too small number of neurons per class could be not sufficient to represent the variability of the samples to be classified, while a too large number in general makes the net too much specialized on the samples belonging to the training set and consequently reduces its generalization capability. Moreover a too large number of neuron per class implies a long training time and a possible underutilization of some of the neural units. PD patterns recognition and classification require an understanding of the traits commonly associated with the different source and relationship between observed PD activity and responsible defect sources. This paper shows the performance of SOM using different competitive learning algorithms to classify measured PD activities into underlying insulation defects or source that generate PD's, its showed that WTA is the better algorithm with less error and training time, but its overall performance are not always satisfactory, being alternative in accord at the performance FSCL or RPCL algorithms.

4. Classification of images using Naive Bayes and J48

This research work's approach is related to artificial vision due to extraction from information contained in images (human faces) by using methods to obtain RGB coloration and statistic values. Extraction takes place by performing several tests of image splitting into different sizes, later classifying sets of instances with data mining techniques, and analyzing classification results to determine which of the algorithms is the best for this particular case.

Knowledge database contains 100 images built from 20 people and 5 pictures each. Mean and standard deviation were employed as statistic values, which are also used as attributes of the instances classified by Naïve Bayes and WEKA J48. It is important to mention that no pixel is disregarded to obtain instances, both of the pixel groups the ones inside face and outside of it are considered. Impact of splitting images into parts.

Table 1 shows that splitting images into both 16 and 64 obtain the same amount of correctly classified instances except with NaiveBayes classifier under cross validation where splitting into 16 obtains 3% better of correctly classified instances, partial conclusion from this table is splitting images into both 16 and 64 is better than splitting them into 4 and no splitting them.

Table 2 shows both Naïve Bayes and J48 under use training test option obtain 100 % of correctly classified instances from splitting images into 4 parts which reveals splitting images helps for classification process.

Classifier	Test options	Parts			
		1	4	16	64
NaiveBayes	use training set	94%	100%	100%	100%
J48	use training set	97%	100%	100%	100%
NaiveBayes	cross validation folds 10	85%	90%	97%	94%
J48	cross validation folds 10	71%	86%	85%	85%
NaiveBayes	percentage split 66%	76.4706%	70.5882%	88.2353%	88.2353%
J48	percentage split 66%	64.7059%	55.8824%	64.7059%	64.7059%

Table 1. Results of splitting images into parts including all attributes.

Classifier	Test options	Parts			
		1	4	16	64
NaiveBayes	use training set	90%	100%	100%	100%
J48	use training set	92%	100%	100%	100%
NaiveBayes	cross validation folds 10	72%	93%	97%	96%
J48	cross validation folds 10	69%	83%	84%	89%
NaiveBayes	percentage split 66%	58.8235%	88.2353%	94.1176%	94.1176%
J48	percentage split 66%	61.7647%	70.5882%	73.5294%	76.4706%

Table 2. Results of splitting images into parts including best 30% attributes.

4.1. Impact of attribute selection

Table 3 shows that for any test option, both classifiers obtain greater amount of correctly classified instances considering all of the attributes which are 6.

Table 4 shows that both classifiers obtain 100% of correctly classified instances under use training set test option. Under cross validation Naïve Bayes classifies 3% better selecting 8 attributes and J48 classifies 3% considering all of the attributes. Finally under percentage split both classifiers perform better selecting 8 attributes.

Classifier	Test options	6 attributes	2 attributes
NaiveBayes	use training set	94%	90%
J48	use training set	97%	92%
NaiveBayes	cross validation folds 10	85%	72%
J48	cross validation folds 10	71%	69%
NaiveBayes	percentage split 66%	76.4706%	58.8235%
J48	percentage split 66%	64.7059%	61.7647%

Table 3. Results of attribute selection without splitting images.

Classifier	Test options	24 attributes	8 attributes
NaiveBayes	use training set	100%	100%
J48	use training set	100%	100%
NaiveBayes	cross validation folds 10	90%	93%
J48	cross validation folds 10	86%	83%
NaiveBayes	percentage split 66%	70.5882%	88.2353%
J48	percentage split 66%	55.8824%	70.5882%

Table 4. Results of attribute selection splitting images into 4 parts.

Table 5 also shows a 100% of correctly classified instances for both classifiers under use training set test option. Under cross validation , Naïve Bayes classifies equal amount of correctly classified instances selecting 29 attributes as selecting all of them, similar situation occurred with J48 with 1% greater for selecting all of the attributes. Finally, under percentage split both of the classifiers perform better selecting 29 attributes.

Classifier	Test options	96 attributes	29 attributes
NaiveBayes	use training set	100%	100%
J48	use training set	100%	100%
NaiveBayes	cross validation folds 10	97%	97%
J48	cross validation folds 10	85%	84%
NaiveBayes	percentage split 66%	88.2353%	94.1176%
J48	percentage split 66%	64.7059%	73.5294%

Table 5. Results of attribute selection splitting images into 16 parts.

Table 6 shows once again a 100 % of correctly classified instances under use training set test option for both cases of attribute selection. Under cross validation and percentage split both of the classifiers perform better selecting 116 attributes.

Classifier	Test options	384 attributes	116 attributes
NaiveBayes	use training set	100%	100%
J48	use training set	100%	100%
NaiveBayes	cross validation folds 10	94%	96%
J48	cross validation folds 10	85%	89%
NaiveBayes	percentage split 66%	88.2353%	94.1176%
J48	percentage split 66%	64.7059%	76.4706%

Table 6. Results of attribute selection splitting images into 64 parts.

4.2. Analysis of classifiers effectiveness based on test options

Table 7 shows that J48 performs better than Naïve Bayes without splitting images but not in a significant way. Considering any other splitting image scheme or attribute selection show a 100 % of correctly classified instances.

		Classifiers	
Attributes	Parts	NaiveBayes	J48
All of them	1	94%	97%
30%	1	90%	92%
All of them	4	100%	100%
30%	4	100%	100%
All of them	16	100%	100%
30%	16	100%	100%
All of them	64	100%	100%
30%	64	100%	100%

Table 7. Results of classifiers effectiveness under use training set.

Table 8 shows Naive Bayes performs better than J48 for any splitting image scheme and attribute selection.

		Classifiers	
Attributes	Parts	NaiveBayes	J48
All of them	1	85%	71%
30%	1	72%	69%
All of them	4	90%	86%
30%	4	93%	83%
All of them	16	97%	85%
30%	16	97%	84%
All of them	64	94%	85%
30%	64	96%	89%

Table 8. Results of classifiers effectiveness under cross validation.

Table 9 shows Naïve Bayes performs better than J48 except for selecting best 30% attributes without splitting images. Experiments of splitting images into parts allow concluding that splitting images into 16 parts is enough for satisfactory classification. Statement from previous paragraph can be asserted due to results in Table 1 show splitting images into 64 parts obtains equal amount of correctly classified instances as performing such split into 16 parts, Table 1 even shows a reduction of 3% in correctly classified instances for NaiveBayes classifier under cross validation. Next stage of experiment consisted on selecting best 30%

attributes, which reveals Naïve Bayes generates greater amount of correctly classified instances from splitting images into 16 parts, J48 obtains 5% better in 64 parts under cross validation and 2.9412% in 64 parts under percentage split. Due to improvement for 64 parts is not significant, it is concluded splitting into 16 parts is enough. Experiments of attribute selection allow concluding that selecting best 30% is enough. This can be validated from both table 1 and table 2 which show that splitting images into 64, 16, and 4 parts selecting best 30% obtains greater amount of correctly classified instances than considering all attributes. J48 throws 1% better for splitting into 16 parts and 3% better into 64 parts with all attributes, but this is disregarded due to it is not significant. Experiments analyzing effectiveness of classifiers allow to conclude Naïve Bayes performs better due to it obtains greater amount of correctly classified instances under most splitting images case and test option except for use training set test option and no splitting images.

Attributes	Parts	Classifiers	
		NaiveBayes	J48
All of them	1	76.4706%	64.7059%
30%	1	58.8235%	61.6747%
All of them	4	70.8552%	55.8824%
30%	4	88.2353%	70.5882%
All of them	16	88.2353%	64.7059%
30%	16	94.1176%	73.5294%
All of them	64	88.2353%	64.7059%
30%	64	94.1176%	76.4706%

Table 9. Results of classifiers effectiveness under percentage split.

4.3. Medical visualization in data mining

A field that is becoming a rich area for the application of data mining is that of medical imaging. The tremendous advance in imaging technologies such as X-rays, computed tomography, magnetic resonance, ultrasound and positron emission tomography has led to the generation of vast amounts of data (Figure 5). Scientists are interested, of course, in learning from this data, and data mining techniques are increasingly being applied in these analyses.

There are interesting techniques for finding and describing structural patterns in data as a tool for helping to explain that data and make predictions from it. The data will take the form of a set of examples from the patients. The output takes the form of predictions about new examples. Many learning techniques look for structural descriptions of what is learned, descriptions that can become fairly complex and are typically expressed as sets of rules. Because they can be understood by people, these descriptions serve to explain what has been learned and explain the basis for new predictions. People frequently use data mining to gain knowledge, not just predictions. Databases are rich with hidden information that can be used for intelligent decision making. Classification and predictions are two of data analysis that can be used to extract models describing important data classes or to predict future data trends. Such analysis can help provide us with a better understanding of the data at large.

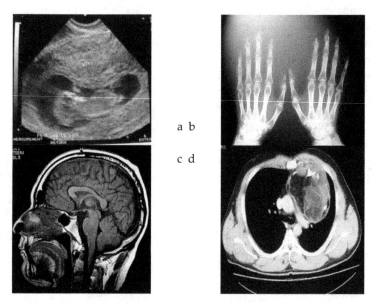

a b

c d

Figure 5. Examples of medical imaging. (a) Ultrasound. (b) A-rays. (c) Magnetic resonance. (d) Computed tomography.

4.3.1. Classification and prediction

A medical research wants to analyze breast cancer data in order to predict which one of three specific treatments a patient should receive. In the example, the data analysis task is classification, where a model o classifier is constructed to predict categorical labels, such as treatment A, treatment B, or treatment C for the medical data. These categories can be represented by discrete values, for example, the values 1, 2, and 3 may be used to represent treatment A, B, and C.

The implementation methods discussed are particularly oriented toward show different tools for analyzes medical data.

4.3.2. Classification by decision tree induction

Decision tree induction is the learning of decision trees from class-labeled training tuples. A decision tree is a flow-chart-like tree structure, where each internal node (nonleaf node) denotes a test on an attribute, each brand represents an outcome of the test, and each leaf node (or terminal node) holds a class label. The topmost node in a tree is the root node. The learning of decision trees from class-labeled training tuples is named decision tree induction. A decision tree can be viewed as a flow-chart-like tree structure, where each internal node (nonleaf node) represents a test on an attribute, each brand represents an outcome of the test, and each leaf node (or terminal node) holds a class label. The root node is the principal node (highest node) in a tree.A typical decision tree is shown below (Figure 6).

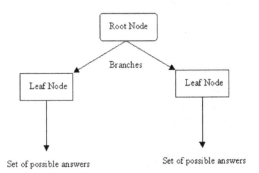

Figure 6. Decision Tree Induction

ID3 is an algorithm which generates a decision tree based on input data by looking at the amount of information contents contained in the various input attributes. At each step in the decision tree, it chooses the attribute which provides the biggest information gain and uses that attribute to classify data further. Its pseudo code is summarized as follows:

Input: Set S of positive and negative examples, Set F of features
ID3(F, S)
1. if S contains only positive examples, return "yes"
2. if S contains only negative examples, return "no"
3. else
*   choose best feature f in F which maximizes the information gain*
*   for each value v of f do*
*   add arc to tree with label v, along with the sub tree for that new branch*

Like an example, the input and output variables and their domains are specified in the list below:

1. Input variables (from clinical observations):
    a. Extent (Size of Spreading): {E1, E2, E3, E4}
    b. Hypoxia: {H1, H2}
    c. Surface (surface marker): {S1, S2, S3}
    d. LOH: {M1, M2, M3}
2. Final result/outcome:

    Outcome: {P (progressed to cancer), NP (didn't progress to cancer)}

The ID3 algorithm as implemented and the following decision tree are generated (Figure 7):

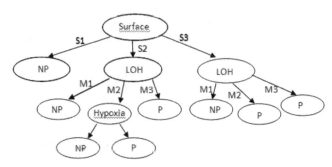

Figure 7. Decision Tree Induction for the medical data.

The decision tree method produces a reasonably good estimate on the outcome based on the inputs. This estimate is about 92% accurate, which is above the acceptable level of accuracy as proposed by the clinical researchers.

4.3.3. Classification by Back-propagation

An artificial neural network (ANN) is a computational model that is inspired by the structure and functional aspects of biological neural networks. They are usually used to model complex relationships between inputs and outputs and find patterns in data. In other words, we wish to infer the mapping implied by the data. The cost function is related to the mismatch between our mapping and the desired outcome. One very commonly used approach to train neural network from input examples is the back-propagation algorithm. Back-propagation algorithm is a common supervised-learning method that teaches an artificial neural network on how to perform a given task. The neural network is modeled as a set of neurons which take inputs, apply certain weights to each input and propagate the result forward into the next layer of units. Each unit in a particular layer is essentially a linear function of the input units from its previous layer. Eventually, the data gets propagated into the output layer where the results are presented.

Another important aspect is this algorithm is able to learn by propagating the errors in the output layer backwards into the inner layers by adjusting the weights between the input and hidden layer and between hidden and output layer in order to reduce the error on the output. The algorithm continues to do this until either the maximum number of epochs is reached or the errors at the output are within an acceptable range. This technique is also referred to as "back-propagation", as denoted in its name. A very typical neural network consists of 3 layers – input, hidden, and output layer. In practice, it is possible to have more than one hidden layers. The back-propagation algorithm used for this project is based on such a 3-layer neural network as illustrated in the figure 8.

The pseudo code for the back-propagation algorithm is as follows:

Initialize the weights in the network (randomly between -0.5 and 0.5)
Do
For each example e in the training set

O = neural-network-output(network, e) ; forward pass
T = desired output for e
Calculate error (T - O) at the output units
Compute delta_wh for all weights from hidden layer to output layer
Compute delta_wi for all weights from input layer to hidden layer
Update the weights in the network to reduce error
Until all examples classified correctly or stopping criterion satisfied
Return the network

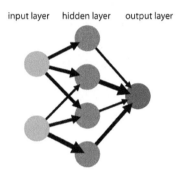

Figure 8. A simple neural network.

The output from the neural network is a simple binary value {0, 1} representing whether or not the patient's tumor progresses into malignant cancer. the classification boundary value to be the half-way point 0.5, so if the neural network's output value turns out to be above 0.5, it is categorized as 1; and values below 0.5 gets categorized as 0. The next important step is to determine the appropriate number of hidden variables in the neural network to avoid both under-fitting and over-fitting. The number of hidden variables should be strictly less than the number of inputs to the neural network, which is 4 in this case.

4.3.4. Classification by Bayesian networks

The naïve Bayesian classifier makes the assumption of class conditional independence, that is, given the class label of tuple, the value of the attributes are assumed to be conditionally independent of one other. This simplifies computation. When the assumption holds true, then the naïve Bayesian classifier is the most accurate in comparison with all other classifiers. However, dependencies can exist between variables. Bayesian networks specify joint conditional probability distributions. They allow class conditional independencies to be defined between subsets of variables. They provide a graphical model of causal relationships, on which learning can be performed. The learning can be perfomed in the graphical model of causal relationships, that they provide. Trained Bayesian belief networks can be used for classification.

A belief networks is defined by two components –a directed acyclic graph and a set of conditional probability tables (e.g., Figure 9). Each node in the directed acyclic graph represents a random variable. The variables may b discrete o continuous-valued. They may correspond to actual attributes given in the data to form a relationship (e.g., in the case of medical data, a hidden variable may indicate a syndrome, representing a number of symptoms that, together, characterize a specific disease). Each arc represents a probabilistic dependence. If an arc is drawn from a node Y to a node Z, then Y is a parent or immediate predecessor of Z, Z is a descendant of Y. Each variable is conditionally independent of its no descendants in the graph, given its parents, as is possible see in Figure 9.

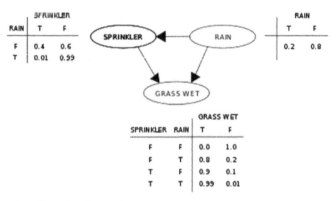

Figure 9. A example of Bayesian Network.

The Figure 10 is a simple Bayesian network for six Boolean variables. The arcs in figure 10 (a) allow the representation of causal knowledge. For example, having lung cancer is influenced by a person's family history of lung cancer, as well as whether or not the person is a smoker. The arcs also show that the variable *LungCancer* is conditionally independent of *Emphysema*, given its parents, *FamilyHistory* and *Smoker*.

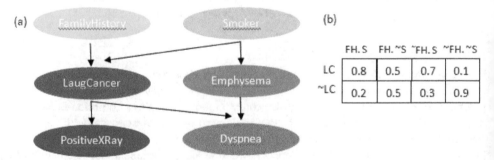

Figure 10. A simple Bayesian network: (a) A proposed casual model, represented by a acyclic graph. (b) The conditional probability table for the value of the variable LungCancer (LC) showing each possible combination of the values of its parents nodes, *FamilyHistory* (FH) and *Smoker* (S).

A belief network has one conditional probability table (CPT) for each variable. The CPT for a variable Y specifies the conditional distribution $P(Y|Parents(Y))$, where *parents(Y)* are the parents of Y. Figure 6 (b) shows a CPT for the variable *LungCancer*. The conditional probability for each knows value of *LungCancer* is given for each possible combination of values of its parents. For instance, form the upper leftmost and bottom rightmost entries, respectively, we see that

P(LungCancer = yes | FamilyHistory = yes, Smoker = yes) = 0.8

P(LungCancer = no | FamilyHistory = no, Smoker = no) = 0.9

A node within the network can be selected as an "output" node, representing a class label attribute. There may be more than one output node. Various algorithms for learning can be applied to the network. Rather than returning a single class label, the classification process can return a probability distribution that gives the probability for each class.

4.3.5. Visual data mining

Visual data mining discovers implicit and useful knowledge from large data Visual data mining have the capacity to find implicit and useful knowledge from great amount of data sets using data and/or knowledge visualization techniques. The human visual system is controlled by the eyes and brain, the latter of which can be thought of as a powerful highly parallel processing and reasoning engine containing a large knowledge base (Figure 11). Visual data mining essentially combines the power of these components, making it a highly attractive and effective tool for the comprehension of data distribution, patterns, clusters, and outliers in data. the eyes and brain, the latter of which can be thought of as a great highly parallel processing and reasoning engine that contain a large knowledge base (Figure 11). Visual data mining combines the power of these components, making it a highly attractive and effective tool for the comprehension of data patterns, clusters, distribution and outliers in data.

Figure 11. Human interact and processing large knowledge base.

Visual data mining can be viewed as an integration of two disciplines: data visualization and data mining. It is also closely related to computers graphics, multimedia systems, human computer interaction, pattern recognition, and high-performance computing. In general, data visualization and data mining can be integrated in the following ways:

Visual data mining can be viewed as an integration of two disciplines: data visualization and data mining. It is also closely related some disciplines: human computer interaction, pattern recognition, high-performance computing, computers graphics and multimedia systems. Data mining and data visualization can be integrated in the next ways:

- Data visualization: Data in a database or data warehouse can be view at different levels of granularity of abstraction, or as different combination of attributes or dimensions. Data can be presented in various visuals forms, such a boxplot, 3-D cubes, data distribution charts, curves, surfaces, link graphs, and so on. An example represented below:

  Data visualization: Data in a database or data warehouse can be view at different levels of granularity of abstraction, or as different combination of attributes or dimensions. Data can be presented in various visuals forms, such a data distribution charts, boxplot, curves, 3-D cubes, link graphs, surfaces, and so on. An example represented below:

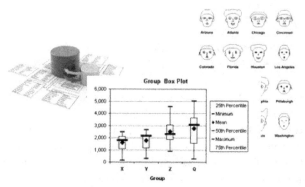

Figure 12. Boxplots showing multiple variable combinations in datasets.

- Data mining result visualization: Visualization of data mining results is the presentation of results or knowledge obtained from data mining in visual forms. Such forms may include scatter plots and boxplots, as well as decision tree, clusters, outliers, generalized rules and so on (Figure 9).

  Data mining result visualization: It means use techniques with which is possible the visual representation of results or knowledge that is obtained from data mining process. Such vicual forms may include scatter plots and boxplots, decision tree, clusters, outliers, generalized rules and so on (Figure 13).

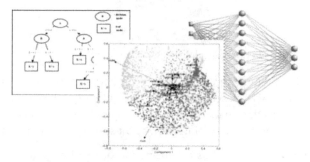

Figure 13. Visualization on data mining results.

- Interactive visual data mining: In visual data mining, visualization tools can be used in the data mining process to help users make smart data mining decisions. For example, the data distribution in a set of attributes can be displayed using colored sectors (where the whole space is representing by a circle). This display helps users determine which sector should first be selected for classification and where a good split point for this sector may be.

The data mining process can be supported by visualization tools to help users to make smart data mining decisions. For example, in a circle that represents a whole space, the data distribution in a set of attributes can be displayed using colored sectors. With this visual representation the users can determine which sector should first be selected for classification and where a good split point for this sector may be.

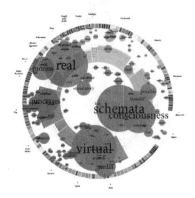

Figure 14. Example for circular data representation.

5. Analyzing people profile

The concept also is used to describe to the set of the characteristics that characterize to somebody or something. In the case of the human beings, the profile is associate to the personality. On the other hand, the word profile also is used very many to designate those particular characteristics that characterize a person and by all means they serve to him to be different itself from others. Your profile is built on other people's impressions and opinions, from the first time they hear your group's name or come into contact with one of its members. To some extent, you can control what people think and feel about your group, building a strong profile that will help you achieve action success. See Figure 15.

Orkut is a system of social networks used in Brazil by 13 million users, many of them, create more of a profile, and generate different relationships from their different profiles, this takes to think that they develop Bipolar Syndrome, to be able to establish communications with people of different life styles, and when they doing to believe other users that they are different people (Zolezzi-Hatsukimi, 2007).

The false profiles are created for: to make a joke, to harass other users, or to see who visualizes its profile. As the profile is false, the friends of this profile are also generally false, making difficult the tracking of the original author (Ochoa et. al., 2011). Using the tool of Data Mining denominated WEKA, it was come to develop a denominated "Ahankara" Model which perits reaize prediction of profiles in users of Orkut, which al-lows to understand the motivations of this type of profile and to determine if it has generated Syndrome Bipolar, to see figure 3 (Ponce et al., 2009). The model obtained Ahankara once used WEKA to look for the relations that us could be of utility to process the data. see Figure 16.

Figure 15. The profile show characteristics of a person or a group of people

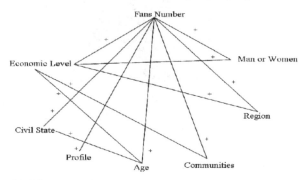

Figure 16. Ahankara Model

Waste. It is something that we produce as part of everyday living, but we do not normally think too much about our waste. Actually many cities generates a waste stream of great complexity, toxicity, and volume (see figure 17). In the management of solid waste have the problem relates to the household waste is the individual decision-making over waste generation and disposal. When the people decide how much to consume and what to consume, they do not take into account how much waste they produce (Ochoa et al., 2011).

E-commerce is the term use to describe the consumers that use the Internet for making purchases, usually refers typically to business to business type activities rather than consumer activity. It maybe more appropriate to refer to consumer activity in relation to purchasing goods and services on the Internet as on-line shopping (see figure 18). E-commerce is the term use to describe the consumers that use the Internet for making purchases, generally refers activities thath involve some business between two or more entities, rather than only consumer activity. This is more related to purchasign goods and services on the Internet rather than on-line shopping (see figure 18).

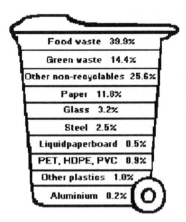

Figure 17. Example of composition by weight of household garbage

One of the important factors in the world of E-commerce is that it is much more than just a change in the way payments are made; E-commerce may not involve money at all. It gives customers the choice of making a wide range of transactions electronically rather than over the telephone, by post or in person. The E-commerce is not only a different way that the people use to pay for any thing, because, it is not simply money; this implies transactions that could be done by telephone, by post or in person, which the costumer can done electronically.

Figure 18. The people can buy services or things online

The major benefits of E-commerce are that it can help organizations to:

- improve working processes and service delivery;
- understand their customers better; and
- reduce costs through elimination of paperwork and bureaucracy.

Some of the most important benefits of E-commerce for the organizations are:

- The service delivery and the working process are improved.
- The organizations can understand their customers.

- They can reduce the costs caused by paperwork and bureaucracy.

In the e-commerce we has two different profile, the buyers and salesman profile, in this case we work with the buyers profile, In (Cocktail Analysis and Google, 2011) is sow a research about the buyers of fashionable clothes, in this work we can see that 42% of the people they have bought some article of clothes by Internet. They describe five different profiles only for the buyers of clothes, also it shows the relation of the purchases online with those of the physical stores. Data mining process can be used to determine the buyers profile, the enterprise can use this information to realize market studies in order to offer to the people specific products to them on the basis of its profile of purchases. Also the analysis ot profiles is very important like dominion application of the data mining, can help to determine landlords us of conducts, habits, or of a single person or of a group, these data allow us to make predictions and can be used of diverse ways.

6. Data mining for E-comerce

The e-commerce is one of the profound changes that internet has induced in the people's lifestyle and in the way of doing business and transactions. The way that the consumers buy has been modified, appearing trends, patterns and preferences in specific groups. Some characteristics that can affect the consumerism by internet are: gender, age, social status, economic status, financial status, studies, culture, technology, knowledge of technology, geographic location, politics and others. In the early years of e-commerce, buying online was an erudite activity strictly dominated by "techies" and semi-technology literate individuals. These individuals were mostly made up of 20 to 35 year old males. This demographic were more comfortable and in tune with Internet's capabilities. But in recent years, the numbers of females making the technology leap to shop online is surging. Females are starting to harness Internet to make their lives easier and efficient (Christopher, 2004) . In the early years of e-commerce, buying online was an erudite activity. The individuals were mostly made up of 20 to 35 year old males. In recent years, the numbers of females making the technology leap to shop online is surging. (Christopher, 2004) . Data Mining (DM) has been applied successfully to find the patterns that the consumers create in the navigation trough the different web sites giving the opportunity to the enterprises to offer a better service.

6.1. Trends in E-commerce

In the e-commerce, the behavior of the consumers creates trends that change in the time for different variables. (Audette, 2010), mention three important trends in 2010 that should be considered by the people involved in the e-commerce (brands, retailers, and others).

6.1.1. Consumer focus is on price

The consumer always is looking for the lowest prices, it means, the best product for the best price or sometimes only the best price.

The consumer also looks for special offers that can balance that price was not the lowest. The offers can be the free shipping.

6.1.2. Riding the next wave: Video and visual search

It's very important now a day, the visual experience in the e-commerce because it is more attractive for the consumer and can be a reason to decide to buy something. The people spend a lot of time watching videos. A case is Mexico where the viewers watched 5 hours of video in YouTube in September 2011, and the audience has grown 17% to reach 20.5 million viewers, representing 85% of the total online population, according to a study by comScore. The next graphic shows video properties that prefer the viewers in Mexico.

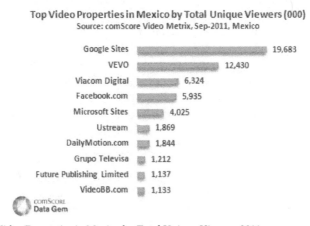

Figure 19. Top Video Properties in Mexico by Total Unique Viewers 2011

The video experience can improve the process information in a 30%, according Bing, and this can be explained because 65% are visual learners.

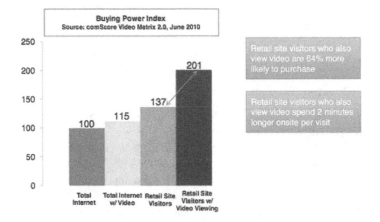

Figure 20. Buying Power Index 2010

6.1.3. Trend in technical SEO

SEO (Search Engine Optimization) is a technique which helps search engines find and rank your site higher than the others millions in response to a search query. This is based primarily in text. Google Instant had a little noticeable effect in the ecommerce clients.

6.2. Data mining and E-commerce

Data Mining (DM) have been applied to study the behavior of the users of different services (entertainment, mail, e-commerce, social network, among others) that internet provides. Many enterprises like Amazon and eBay have invested many resources to understand the consumers. Authors like (Sankar et al., 2002) explain why Web Mining, concept used for the first time by (Etzioni, 1996), is considered like sub-field of Data Mining. They say that Web Mining can be defined as "the discovery and analysis of useful information from the World Wide Web". The source of data can be the server, client, proxy server, or data bases of some enterprise. The web mining is divided in: Web content mining, Web structure mining, Web usage mining (Sankar et al., 2002). The principal tasks/phases of Web mining are: Information retrieval (resource discovery), information extraction (selection/preprocessing), Generalization (pattern recognition/machine learning), Analysis (validation/interpretation).

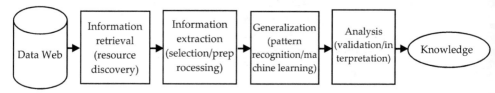

Figure 21. Tasks of Web Mining

The Data Mining, or in this case Web mining, which is known, needs some problems with certain characteristics to obtain the major benefits. Those characteristics are (Ansari, Suhail, 2000):

- Large amount of data
- Rich data with many attributes
- Clean data collection
- Actionable domain
- Measurable return-on-investment

The e-commerce has every characteristics being a "Killer Domain" of Data Mining (Ansari, Suhail, 2000). The attributes more important in the e-commerce are RFM (Recency, Frequency and Monetary). Examples of these attributes are date, time, duration session, quantity, purchase (Ansari, Suhail, 2000). Other attributes are IP address, URL, error code, among others; however these are common in logs that are not created for analysis (De Gyves Camacho, 2009). The attributes (columns) related with time and date are used to find important hidden patterns. One of the applications of Web mining is the learning of Navigation patterns (Web usage Mining).

6.3. Artificial immune system applied to web mining

The Artificial Immune System (AIS) is a bio-heuristic based in the Natural Immune System (NIS). One of the characteristics that make interesting the NIS are: highly distributed, highly adaptive, self-organising, maintain a memory of past encounters, and learn of new encounters. Some algorithms that have been proposed to use in data mining, are based in theories like negative selection, clonal selection and immune network. However new algorithms have been created inspired in other characteristic or theories. In order to approximate a solution of the learning of navigation patterns an immune-inspired algorithm is proposed which is based in the immune network and was developed by (Timmis et al., 2000). The AIS has some characteristics that can be improved but is good for a first approximation. This algorithm is proposed to clustering the similarities of the users' behavior and according of the pattern, in a next step, suggest the best structure of the web site to the consumers to improve their experience. In this way, the companies con offer a better service, adapted to the consumers' necessities and finally increase sales.

7. Data mining to mobile ad hoc networks security

Mobile radio technologies, for both voice and data communication, has experienced a rapid growth and diverse concepts have been introduced in networking. However the concept of ad hoc network is not new, the paradigm started from the beginning of late 90's and gradually became popular with the wide range of deployments of IEEE 802.11x based WLAN, despite regularly ad hoc networks are based on single-hop peer-to-peer networking between several wireless devices, in different specialized scenarios such as control applications, logistics and automation, surveillance and security, transportation management, battlefields, environmental monitoring, unexplored and hazardous conditions, home networking, etc. multi-hop wireless networks are used. Multi-hop wireless ad hoc network consists of a number of self-configurable nodes (e.g. IEEE 802.11-based WLAN, 802.16-based WiMAX, ZigBee, Bluetooth, etc.) to establish an on-demand network using multiple hops paths if required where no network infrastructures pre-exist. The basic block of multi-hop ad hoc networking can be divided into four major specialized categories – Mobile Ad hoc Networks (MANET), Wireless Mesh and Hybrid Networks (WMN), Vehicular Ad hoc Networks (VANET) and Wireless Sensor Networks (WSN) (Kamal, 2010). MANET is the most theoretically researched arena of ad hoc networking which is a collection of autonomous and mobile network objects of any kind with truly dynamic and uncertain mobility that communicate with each other by forming a multi-hop radio network and maintaining connectivity in a decentralized manner. Nowadays, MANET has become a practical platform for pervasive services, i.e., the services that are requested and provided anywhere and anytime in an instant way. This kind of service is very valuable for mobile users, especially when fixed networks (e.g. Internet) or mobile networks are temporarily unavailable or costly to access. A generic concept of the general-purpose pure MANET is shown in Figure 22.

In Figure 22, let's suppose that node A wants to send data to node C but node C is not in the range of node A. Then in this case, node A may use the services of node B to transfer data since node B's range overlaps with both the node A and node B. In MANET, no fixed infrastructure, like base station or, mobile switching center is required. Instead, every possible wireless mobile host within the perimeter of radio link acts as an intermediate switch and participates in setting up the network topology in a self organized way.

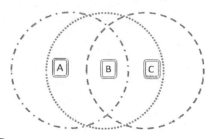

Figure 22. A Simple MANET

7.1. Data mining to deal with vulnerabilities of MANET

Despite the advantages, accord to Nakkeeran, the nature of mobility creates new vulnerabilities due to the open medium, dynamically changing network topology, cooperative algorithms, lack of centralized monitoring and management points and yet many of the proven security measures turn out to be ineffective (Nakkeeran et al. , 2010). Despite the advantages, accord to Nakkeeran, the nature of mobility creates new vulnerabilities due to the open medium, dynamically changing network topology, cooperative algorithms, lack of centralized monitoring and management points and yet many of the proven security measures turn out to be ineffective (Nakkeeran et al. , 2010). All these mean that a wireless ad-hoc network will not have a clear line of defense, and every node must be prepared for encounters with an adversary directly or indirectly. In order to avoid such circumstances requires the development of novel architectures and mechanisms that protect wireless networks and computer applications. Hence diverse research scopes do exist. Unfortunately, investigations are principally targeted towards routing, scheduling, address assignment, developing protocol stack etc. These are mainly functional properties. However, as nomadic and ubiquitous computing reaches its full potential, semantics and security will play the leading role, because the flexibility in space and time induces new challenges towards the security infrastructure. Due to in the case of the securtiy infraestructure, the flexibility in space and time will generate new challenges. Therefore, the traditional way of protecting wired/wireless networks with firewalls and encryption software is no longer sufficient. A very recurrent solution are Intrusion Detection Systems (IDS) (Mishra, 2004). Generally IDS can be defined as the detection of intrusions or intrusions attempts either manually or via software, through the use of schemes that collects the information and analyzing it for uncommon or unexpected events. Intrusion Detection (ID) is the process of monitoring and analyzing the events which occurred in a digital network in order to detect signs of security problems (Shirbhate, 2011). Then the ID is data analysis process, for this reason, as well as the growth of volume of existing data and insufficiency of data storage capacity leads us to the dynamic processing data and extracting knowledge. So the nature solution is utilizing data mining techniques, for example, anomaly detection techniques could be used to detect unusual patterns and behaviors, link analysis may be used to trace the viruses to the perpetrators, classification may be used to group various cyber attacks and then use the profiles to detect an attack when it occurs, prediction may be used to determine potential future attacks depending in a way on information learnt about terrorists through email and phone conversations (Khalilian, 2011). Data mining can improve variant detection rate, control false alarm rate and reduce false dismissals (Jianliang, 2009).

7.2. Intrusion detection methodologies

If we want to categorize intrusion detection methods, we will recognize two main aspects for grouping approaches, which one group refers to type of attack according to the kind of input information the analyze includes host based, network based, wireless and Network Behavior Analysis (NBA). Another group of approaches refers to solutions techniques which are misuse detection, anomaly detection methods and hybrid methods (Khalilian, 2011).

a. Host based methods.
   This methods are based on data source category; consequently, its data comes from the records of various activities of hosts, including system logs, audit operation system information, etc. the main architecture for this kind of methods is similar to network based.

b. Network based methods.
   These systems analyze network packets that are captured on a network. Network packet is the data source for network intrusion detection system.

c. Wireless methods.
   Wireless intrusion detection system monitors wireless network traffic and analyzes its wireless networking protocols to identify suspicious activity involving the protocols themselves. It cannot identify suspicious activity in the application or higher-layer network protocols such as TCP, UDP that the wireless network traffic is transferring. So each node is responsible for detecting signs of intrusion locally and independently, but neighboring nodes can collaboratively investigate in a broader range.

d. Network Behavior Analysis.
   NBA which examines network traffic to identify threats that generate unusual traffic flows, such as distributed denial of service (DDoS) attacks, certain forms of malware such as worms, backdoors, and policy violations. NBA systems are also deployed to monitor flows on an organization's internal Networks, and are also sometimes deployed where they can monitor flows between an organization's Networks and external networks such as the Internet.

Figure 23 shows the basic architecture for NIDS in data mining, which is very similar to the other detection methods

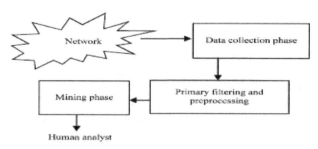

Figure 23. Basic NIDS architecture

e.   Misuse based methods.
     Misuse detection which the main study is the classification algorithms relics on the use
     of specifically known patterns of unauthorized behavior. In misuse detection related
     problems, standard data mining techniques are not applicable due to several specific
     details that include dealing with skewed class distribution, learning from data streams
     and labeling network connections. The problem of skewed class distribution in the
     network intrusion detection is very apparent since intrusion as a class of interest is
     much smaller i.e. rarer than the class representing normal network behavior. In such
     scenarios when the normal behavior may typically represent 98-99% of the entire
     population a trivial classifier that labels everything with the majority class can achieve
     98-99% accuracy (Dokas, 2002). It is apparent that in this case classification accuracy is
     not sufficient as a standard performance measure. ROC analysis and metrics such as
     precision, recall and F-value have been used to understand the performance of the
     learning algorithm on the minority class. A confusion matrix as shown in Table 1 is
     typically used to evaluate performance of a machine learning algorithm.

Confusion matrix (Standard metrics)		Predicted connection label	
		Normal	Intrusions (Attacks)
Actual connection label	Normal	True Negative (TN)	False Alarm (False Positive)
	Intrusions (Attacks)	False Negative (FN)	Correctly Detected Attacks (True Positive)

Table 10. Standards metrics for evaluations of intrusions (attacks)

     In addition, intrusions very often represent sequence of events and therefore are more
     suitable to be addressed by some temporal data mining algorithms. Finally, misuse
     detection algorithms require all data to be labeled, but labeling network connections as
     normal or intrusive re-quires enormous amount of time for many human experts. All
     these issues cause building misuse detection models very complex.

f.   Anomaly based methods.
     Misuse detection system unable to detect new or previously unknown intrusions
     occurred in computer system or digital network. Novel intrusions can be found by

anomaly detection which the main study is the pattern comparison and the cluster algorithms ((Khalilian, 2011). The basic idea of clustering analysis originates in the difference between intrusion and normal pattern; consequently, we can put data sets into different categories and detect intrusion by distinguish normal and abnormal behaviors. Clustering intrusion detection is detection for anomaly with no supervision, and it detects intrusion by training the unmarked data.

Most anomaly detection algorithms require a set of purely normal data to train the model, and they implicitly assume that anomalies can be treated as patterns not observed before. Since an outlier may be defined as a data point which is very different from the rest of the data, based on some measure. In statistics-based outlier detection techniques the data points are modeled using a stochastic distribution and points are determined to be outliers depending upon their relationship with this model. However, with increasing dimensionality, it becomes increasingly difficult and inaccurate to estimate the multidimensional distributions of the data points. However, recent outlier detection algorithms are based on computing the full dimensional distances of the points from one another as well as on computing the densities of local neighborhoods. Nearest Neighbor (NN), Mahalanobis-distance Based Outlier Detection and Density Based Local Outliers (LOF) are approaches for recent outlier detection algorithms.

g.   Hybrid methods.

Through analyzing the advantages and disadvantages between anomaly detection and misuse detection, a mixed intrusion detection system (IDS) model is designed. First, data is examined by the misuse detection module, and then abnormal data detection is examined by anomaly detection module. The intrusion detection system (IDS) is designed based in the advantages and disadvantages of the models of intrusion detection that are: anomaly detection and misuse detection. The first step is examine the data with de misuse detection module and in the second step, the anomaly detection module analyze the atypical data detected.

7.3. New trends in safety MANET

The ultimate goal of the security solutions for wireless networks is to provide security services, such as authentication, confidentiality, integrity, anonymity, and availability, to mobile users. The final goal of the security solutions for wireless networks is to offer security services to mobile users. This services are authentication, integrity, confidentiality, anonymity, and availability. This kind of schemes depend on cooperation amongst the nodes in a MANET for identifying nodes that are exhibiting malicious behaviors such as packet dropping, packet modification, and packet misrouting, so most of this methods assume that this problem can be viewed as an instance of detecting nodes whose behavior is an outlier when compared to others. Some novel solutions incorporate mobile agents (Nakkeeran et al., 2010) to provide solution against security issues in MANET networks. With the help of home agent and mobile agents, it gathers information from its own system and neighboring system to identify any attack and through data mining techniques to find out the attacks has been made in that networks. With the help of home agent and mobile agents, it is possible to extract information from both, own system and neighbor system, to identify any attack and with data mining techniques try to find the attacks that has been perpetrated in such networks. Home agent is present in each system and it gathers information about its system from application layer to routing layer.

Each system have a home agent, which should obtain iformation about the system from application layer to routing layer.

Mobile agents are a special type of agents defined as "processes capable of roaming through large networks such as the ad hoc wireless network, interacting with machines, collecting information and returning after executing the tasks adjusted by the user". Mobile agents are a special type of agents defined as "processes capable of roaming through large networks such as the ad hoc wireless network, interacting with machines, which return the colected information when finishing the execution of the tasks of the user". Often such proposals provide the three different techniques to provide suffice security solution to current node, Neighboring Node and Global networks.

Frequently, the proposals afford the three differents techniques that are used to offer security solution to current node, Neighboring and Global networks.

The trust together cooperation are another kind of novelty solution (Li, 2009); the idea of them consists in an algorithm to can help us identify the outliers, which are generally the nodes that have exhibited some kind of abnormal behaviors. Given the fact that benign nodes rarely behave abnormally, it is highly likely that the outliers are malicious nodes. Moreover, a multi-dimensional trust management scheme is proposed to evaluate the trustworthiness of the nodes from multiple perspectives. There are many techniques that have been discussed to prevent attacks in wireless ad hoc networks but most of them have in common that are based on cooperation and on methods based on the principle of anomalies.

8. Conclusions and another specific application domains improved with data mining

Diverse applications based on Data Mining have the objective to learn the patterns of the users' interaction with the Web or Data Repository. The data includes user profiles, registration profiles, user queries, and any data generated by the users' interaction with the web. This is useful, for example, to restructure the web page according the preferences of the users. This means that the web site is going to provides information, special offers, and others, that can be interesting for the consumers according their patterns of interaction or according the hour of the day. Also, this can be used to design offline strategies. One process to make projects of web usage mining is described in (DAEDALUS, 2002). To find the patterns in Web usage mining, the techniques used are: Clustering and Classification, Association rule detection, Path analysis, Sequential patterns detection. The use of any technique mention above to analyze automatically the data implies difficulties by the complexity of the problem (heterogeneous data, and others) and the limitations of the existing methodologies. To overcome that difficulties and limitations is necessary to use other techniques and methodologies like soft computing. Some algorithms developed to address Data Mining using techniques of Soft Computing are revised by (Mishra el al., 2004). Other application of Data Mining using evolutionary algorithms were proposed by (Ochoa et al., 2011) obtaining good results. In addition, we described another specfic applications domains such as: Deterining Euskadi ancesters based on family names and compare the anthropmetry of the individuals to found patterns of their ancesters; Organizational Models to supporting little and medium business related with Regional Development; Organizational Climate to identify cases of Burnout Syndrome characterized by high expectatives of productivty and Organizational Culture (Hernández et al, 2011); Identification of the use of new languages related with the songs from Eurovision for exameple Udmurt language in the entry from Russia to Eurovision Song Contest'2012; Analysis of Pygmalion Effect on people from Pondichérry in India whom be considering more closely culturally of Francophonie because the French influence in their past lifes; Zoo applications to classify more vulnerable species in an interactive map (see figure 24) or identify the adequate kind of avatars on a roll multigame players associated with cultural aspects in this case Brazilian people and their selections of features related with spcific skills (see figure 25).

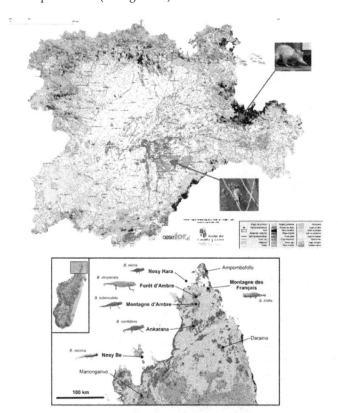

Figure 24. Interactive map based on data mining, locating the habitats of species of reptils, birds and mammals specifying the ubiquity of their behavior –changes provoked by the human- during the time.

Figure 25. Cultural Avatars related with traditional aspects and antropometry from Brazlian people used in Multi player games according of specific skills used on the online game.

In addition Tatebanko traditional Japanese Dyoram is using new ideas based with a Hybrid Algorithm conformed by the use of Data Mining and a Bioinspired Algorithm to built 3D scenario (Ochoa et al., 2012) including issues of specific time and location by each one.

Author details

Alberto Ochoa, Daniel Azpeitia, Petra Salazar, Emmanuel García and Miguel Maldonado
Juarez City University, México

Rubén Jaramillo and Jöns Sánchez
LAPEM, México

Javier González and Claudia Gómez
ITCM, México

Julio Ponce, Sayuri Quezada, Francisco Ornelas and Arturo Elías
UAA, México

Edgar Conde and Víctor Cruz
Veracruzana University, México

Lourdes Margain
Universidad Politécnica de Aguascalientes, México

9. References

Ansari, Suhail; Kohavi, Ron; Mason, Llew and Zheng, Zijian. Integrating E-Commerce and Data Mining: Architecture and Challenges. WEBKDD'2000 workshop: Web Mining for E-Commerce -- Challenges and Opportunities, 2000.

Audette Adam. Founder and Presidente of AudetteMedia., Nov 29, 2010 http://searchengineland.com/3-important-trends-to-watch-in-ecommerce-56890

Cocktail Analysis and Google (2011). El comportamiento del Comprador de Moda OnLine. http://tcanalysis.com/

Cheng, Ri; Kai, L.; Chun, B.; Shao-Yu, D.; Gou-Zheng, X. Study on Partial Discharge Localization by Ultrasonic Measuring in Power Transformer Based on Particle Swarm Optimization. *International Conference on High Voltage Engineering and Application.* (2008). 600-603.

Christopher, James. E-Commerce: Comparison of On-line Shopping Trends, Patterns and Preferences against a Selected Survey of Women. Kingston University. MSC Business Information Technology Program. November 2004.

DAEDALUS – Data, Decisions and Language, S.A.: Minería Web: Documentos básico DAEDALUS. White Paper, C-26-AB-6002-010, Noviembre 2002. http://www.daedalus.es

De Gyves Camacho, Francisco Manuel. Web Mining: Fundamentos Básicos Doctorado en informática y automática Universidad de Salamanca. Informe Técnico, DPTOIA-IT-2006-003. Mayo 2009.

Dokas, P., et al. *Data mining for network intrusion detection.* in *In Proceedings of the NSF Workshop on Next Generation Data Mining.* 2002. Baltimore, MA.

Etzioni, O. The world-wide web: Quagmire or goldmine?, Communications of the ACM, vol. 39, pp. 65-68, 1996.

Hernández, Alberto et al. Aplicación de la minería de datos para la toma de decisiones: El Caso de la cultura organizacional en una tienda del IMSS, XVI Congreso Internacional de Contaduría, Administración e Informática, 2011.

Jianliang, M., S. Haikun, and B. Ling. *The Application on Intrusion Detection Based on K-means Cluster Algorithm.* in *Information Technology and Applications, 2009. IFITA '09. International Forum on* 2009. Chengdu IEEE, Press.

Kamal, J.M.M., *A Comprehensive Study on Multi-Hop Ad hoc Networking and Applications: MANET and VANET,* in *Faculty of Computing, Engineering and Technology.* 2010, Staffordshire University: Stafford. p. 155.

Khalilian, M., et al., *Intrusion Detection System with Data Mining Approach: A Review.* Global Journal of Computer Science and Technology (GJCST), 2011. 11(5): p. 29-34.

Kohonen T. Engineering Applications of Self Organizing Map. *Proceedings of the IEEE.* (1996).

Li, W., J. Parker, and A. Joshi, *Security through Collaboration in MANETs Collaborative Computing: Networking, Applications and Worksharing,* E. Bertino and J.B.D. Joshi, Editors. 2009, Springer Berlin Heidelberg. p. 696-714.

Mishra, A., K. Nadkarni, and A. Patcha, *Intrusion detection in wireless ad hoc networks* Wireless Communications, IEEE 2004. 11(1): p. 48-60.

Nakkeeran, R., T. Aruldoss Albert , and R. Ezumalai, *Agent Based Efficient Anomaly Intrusion Detection System in Adhoc networks.* IACSIT International Journal of Engineering and Technology, 2010. 2(1): p. 52-56.

Ochoa, Alberto; Castillo, Nemesio; Yeongene, Tasha & Bustillos, Sandra. Logistics using a new Paradigm: Cultural Algorithms. Programación Matemática y Software, Vol. 1. No 1. Dirección de Reservas de Derecho: 04-2009-011611475800-102. 2011.

Ochoa, Alberto et al. New Implementations of Data Mining in a Plethora of Human Activities. In Knowledge-Oriented Applications in Data Mining, ISBN 978-953-307-154-1, 2011.

Ochoa, Alberto et al. Developing a Traditional Tatebanko Dyoram using Cultural Algorithms V Workshop Hybrid Intelligent Systems at MICAI'2012 to publish.

Orihuela, José Luis. Nuevos Paradigmas de la Comunicación. Retrieved March. Vol. 12, España (2002).

Ponce, Julio; Hernández, Alberto; Ochoa, Alerto et al. Data Mining in Web Applications. In Data Mining and Knowledge Discovery in Real Life Applications, ISBN 978-3-902613-53-0, 2009.

Rubio-Sánchez, M. *Nuevos Métodos para Análisis Visual de Mapas Auto-organizativos*. PhD Thesis. Madrid Politechnic University. (2004).

Salaveria, Ramón (2009). El Impacto de Internet en los Medios de Comunicación en España. Comunicación Social Ediciones y Publicaciones. Pp. 11-15, 2009.

Sandoval, Rodrigo, Saucedo Nancy Karina. Grupos de Interés en las Redes Sociales: El caso de Hi 5 y Facebook en México. Tecnociencia Chihuahua. Vol. IV, No. 3, 2010.

Sankar K. Pak, Varun Talwar, Pabitra Mitra. Web Mining in Soft Computing FrameWork: Relevance, State of the Art and Future Directions. IEEE Transactions on Neural Networks Vol. 13, No. 5 pp 1163-1177, September 2002.

Shirbhate, S.V., V.M. Thakare, and S.S. Sherekar, *Data Mining Approaches For Network Intrusion Detection System*. International Journal of Computer Technology and Electronics Engineering (IJCTEE), 2011. 2(2): p. 41-44.

Timmis, J, Neal, M and Hunt, J. An Artificial Immune System for Data Analysis.*Biosystems*. *55(1/3)*, pp. 143-150. 2000.

Zolezzi-Hatsukimi, Z. Implement social nets using Orkut, Proceedings of CHI'07, Nagoya, Japan, 2007.

Chapter 4

Research on Spatial Data Mining in E-Government Information System

Bin Li, Lihong Shi, Jiping Liu and Liang Wang

Additional information is available at the end of the chapter

1. Introduction

E-Government Information System is the idiographic application of GIS in the field of government departments in the world[1]. There are large amounts of data stored in the database of E-Government Information System. 80 percent of the data is concerned with spatial location. In fact, there are little applications of these data. A great deal of the data is idle, which has caused a huge waste of data due to rarely effectively utilization in practice. Actually, Spatial Data Mining, i.e.SDM, is a kind of important and useful tool in the practical application of E-Government Information System database, and is very useful to find and describe a hidden mode in the particular multi-dimensional data aggregation. It is very necessary to deal with the task of spatial data mining based on E-Government Information System database with different data resources, data types, data formats, data scales. "Mass spatial data and poor knowledge" has become a gap for the development of geo-spatial information science, which requires necessary data mining. SDM can mine automatically or semi-automatically unknown, creditable, effective, integrative or schematic knowledge which can be understood from the increasingly complex spatial database and enhance the ability of interpreting data to generate useful knowledge. And with time goes on, from its beginning, SDM has attracted more and more attention, and achieved some academic and applied results in the field of artificial intelligence, environmental protection, spatial decision-making support, computer-aided design, knowledge-driven image interpretation, intelligent geographic information systems (GIS), and so on.

Although SDM is a kind of important tool in the practical application, it is very difficult to find information manually because the data in the data set grows rapidly. The algorithms on data mining allow automatic mode search and interactive analysis.

This chapter consists of six components. The first section is the introduction. Section 2 provides the data characteristics analysis of E-Government Information System. The third section describes the course of spatial data mining. And section 4 presents the examples of spatial data mining. The next section gives the conclusions. And the last one is the acknowledgement. Especially, in this chapter, a useful application example on land utilization and land classification in a certain county of Guizhou Province, China, is presented to describe the course of SDM. Thereinto, a derived star-type model was used to organize the raster data to form multi dimension data set. Under these conditions, clustering method was utilized to carry out data mining aiming at the raster data. Based on corresponding analyses mentioned in this chapter, users could find out which types of vegetation were suitable for being cultivated in this region by using related knowledge in a macroscopic view. Therefore, feasible service information could be provided to promote economic development in the region.

2. Data characteristics analysis of E-Government Information System

The construction of E-Government Information System is complex with the character of being Systemic, which involves different fields. And the data used in the system is also complex with many types. In a whole, the data character can be described as follows.

1. Diversity of data with multi sources
    The data used in the E-Government Information System mainly comes from different departments at different level. And it includes various kinds of basic geographical data and monographic data with different scales. According to the spatial partition of data type, it includes DLG, DRG, DEM and remote sensing image with multi spectrum, scale, time, etc. And non-spatial data has the different types of statistical information, multimedia text, image, video, and sound, etc. The multi types or forms of data format, data represent, database structure and data store have been produced owe to the diversion of data source.

2. Great amount of data content
    There are large amount of different kinds of data stored in the database of E-Government Information System. Thereinto, the majority part of data capacity is spatial data, especially the image, DEM data. Besides, the video content belonging to non-spatial data is also very large. With the development of new information revolution, E-Government will face new demands. And more and more new data will be produced to meet the need or require of E-Government Information System. Meanwhile, those old data must also be restored in the database as the history data in case of recovering.

3. Temporal character of data change
    With the development of E-Government Information System, the data used in the system is constantly extended with more and more amount, content and type. Therefore, the relational data is often changed and update with temporal character. Temporal sequence is also the main character of spatial data, which is often used to make the comparison to show the development of the task.

4. Spatiality character
    Spatiality is the main character of spatial data compared to non-spatial data, which includes mainly geographical location and form of spatial object. The former often

includes geographical coordinate, postal code, administrator code, toponym, address, etc.

3. Process of spatial data mining

The detailed process of SDM can be divided into five phases described as follows: demand investigation, data selection, data pre-processing, data conversion, data mining, knowledge representation and evaluation. In figure 1, the flow of SDM can be described.

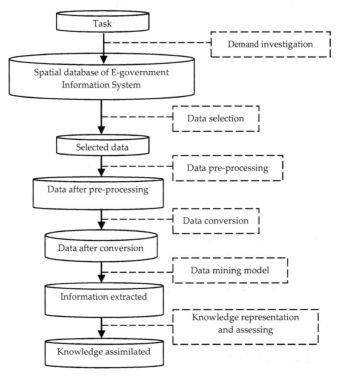

Figure 1. Process of SDM

3.1. Demand investigation

It is necessary to understand the existing data and business information before data mining. Understand fully the problems to be solved and give a clear definition on the goal of data mining. Therefore, demand investigation is the necessary and first step of SDM according to the task oriented to actual application.

3.2. Data selection

Data selection is carried out after finishing demand investigation and knowing unambiguous demand. Data selection is the course of ascertaining data source to be used in data mining and collecting data records stored in the database in accordance with the standards of being established. Some rules or methods of data selection must be made or adopted to select the needed data during the process.

3.3. Data processing and conversion

After the completion of data selection, it is necessary to make data pretreatment. The Main work in this step is to carry out data cleaning aiming at the data stored in the database of E-Government Information System and delete unnecessary information[9], and transform the required data into a unified data format. Besides, data conversion will be made through the process of data merger and integration to convert them into data with identification after data pretreatment.

3.4. Data mining model construction

It is the important step to construct the data mining model. Corresponding data mining models are to be constructed aiming at different demands, such as decision tree, clustering, etc. It is decisive for data pretreatment to select a certain type of model. Data mining can be made aiming at the data stored in the database of E-Government Information System and pattern extraction can also be done after determining the data mining model.

3.5. Knowledge representation and assessing

The results should be interpreted when data mining is completed. During the course, some of the process may be returned to the front processing steps in order to obtain more efficient knowledge. And knowledge extraction can be made repeatedly so as to gain more effective information to be interpreted as the knowledge for decision-making in the future. Finally, performance of the applied model needs assessing and constantly improving the algorithm to meet the needs of different actual application[13].

4. Realization of spatial data mining

There are lots of microcosmic data existing in the E-Government Information System coming from different sectors and different periods of time, which mainly includes vector data, raster data, attribute data and a lot of statistical data, etc[2]. It is necessary for the above-mentioned data to be stored in the multi dimension data set in accordance with multi topics to achieve the course of fixed and random dynamic data query processing, comprehensive analysis. Users can access the multi dimension data set in the end of client and extract correlative data from the data set in the background according to different rights, and selected theme demands and finally generate a variety of visual results, such as various statistical graphics (histograms, pie charts, pyramid diagram, etc.) and statistical analysis of statements, and so on. Meanwhile, some corresponding multi-dimensional analysis aiming at disposal results, such as cluster analysis, can also be made. In the next section, the raster data mining will be made as an example to prescribe the whole process[10,11].

4.1. Raster data processing and importing

Raster data roots in 1:250,000 DEM data cropped in a certain region of Guizhou Province, China. Grid processing is completed by using grids (each grid represents 100 meters x 100 meters) in the region. A pivot can be got in each grid and imported into the relational database to be a record. The picked data includes grid number, terrain slope, terrain aspect, grid coordinates, land use type and land cover type, etc. There are more than 280 records generated in the region.

Slope and aspect, which are correlative each other, are parameters commonly used to describe the terrain. Slope reflects the inclination degree of slope and the latter represents the direction which the slope faces. In terms of land use and land cover, the slope and aspect have many uses. For example, the slope exceeding 35 degrees should not be developed in general in the agricultural land development. Slope is the function of points, which is the angle between the normal direction N and vertical direction Z aiming at a certain point in the surface and can be represented using α. In practice, it is no use in computing the slope of each point[2]. Average slope of a basic grid unit is often used to represent corresponding signification. Aspect is the angle between the projection of normal direction and the due direction, that is, the direction of azimuth between the projection vectors. B is often to be described to represent the aspect. See fig.2.

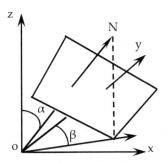

Figure 2. Terrain slope and aspect

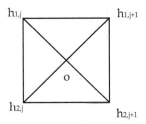

Figure 3. Elevation representation

$$\alpha = arctg\left(u^2 + v^2\right)^{1/2}, u = \left(h_2 - h_3\right)/\left(2^{1/2} * d\right), v = \left(h_1 - h_4\right)/\left(2^{1/2} * d\right)$$

Thereinto: *h1, h2, h3, h4* is respectively the elevation of four corner points in the grid, *d* is the grid length of each side.

$$\beta = tan^{-1}\left(dx * a_j / dy * b_j\right), a_j = h_{1,j+1} + h_{2,j+1} - h_{1,j} - h_{2,j}, bj = h_{2,j} + h_{2,j+1} - h_{1,j} - h_{1,j+1}$$

Similarly, *dx, dy* represents respectively grid length of horizontal or vertical side, $h_{1,j+1}$, $h_{2,j+1}$, $h_{1,j}$, $h_{2,j}$ denotes respectively the elevation of four corner points in the grid. See fig.3.

The created content of data during the course of being cropped can be described as follows, which takes slope for example. See fig.4.

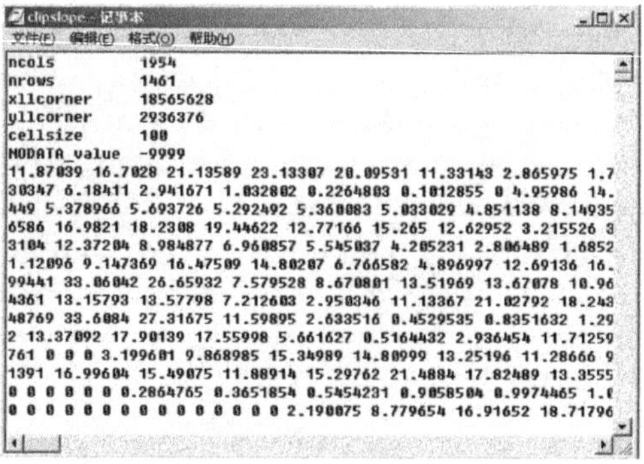

```
clipslope - 记事本
文件(F) 编辑(E) 格式(O) 帮助(H)
ncols         1954
nrows         1461
xllcorner     18565628
yllcorner     2936376
cellsize      100
NODATA_value  -9999
11.87039 16.7028 21.13589 23.13307 20.09531 11.33143 2.865975 1.7
30347 6.18411 2.941671 1.032802 0.2264803 0.1012855 0 4.95986 14.
449 5.378966 5.693726 5.292492 5.360083 5.033029 4.851138 8.14935
6586 16.9821 18.2308 19.44622 12.77166 15.265 12.62952 3.215526 3
3104 12.37204 8.984877 6.960857 5.545037 4.205231 2.806489 1.6852
1.12096 9.147369 16.47509 14.80207 6.766582 4.896997 12.69136 16.
99441 33.06042 26.65932 7.579528 8.670801 13.51969 13.67078 10.96
4361 13.15793 13.57798 7.212603 2.950346 11.13367 21.02792 18.243
48769 33.6084 27.31675 11.59895 2.633516 0.4529535 0.8351632 1.29
2 13.37092 17.90139 17.55998 5.661627 0.5164432 2.936454 11.71259
761 0 0 0 3.199601 9.868985 15.34989 14.80999 13.25196 11.28666 9
1391 16.99604 15.49075 11.88914 15.29762 21.4884 17.82489 13.3555
0 0 0 0 0 0 0.2864765 0.3651854 0.5454231 0.9058504 0.9974465 1.0
0 0 0 0 0 0 0 0 0 0 0 0 0 0 0 2.190075 8.779654 16.91652 18.71796
```

Figure 4. Slope data in a certain region

In Fig.4, *ncols* represents the lists of the raster and *nrows* shows the rows. And *x11corner, y11corner* represent respectively the coordinates of left underside corner in the whole raster range. Besides, *cellsize* denotes the grid size, which can be expressed in the manner of meter. Corresponding values can be got by using procedures to import the above-mentioned data into the relational databases of SQL Server2000. These values may be arranged in the sequence of known row or list number. For example, corresponding value is *(i, j), (i, j +1)* respectively when *id* equals 1, 2. Similar conclusions can also be made. The arrangement method of raster data can be described in table 1 and figure 5.

i,j	i,j+1	i,j+2	i,j+3	i,j+4	……	i, ncols
i+1,j	i+1, j+1	i+1, j+2	i+1, j+3	i+1, j+4	……	i+1, ncols
i+2,j	i+2, j+1	i+2, j+2	i+2, j+3	i+2, j+4	……	i+2, ncols
i+3,j	i+3, j+1	i+3, j+2	i+3, j+3	i+3, j+4	……	i+3, ncols
……	……	……	……	……	……	……
nrows, j	nrows, j+1	nrows, j+2	nrows, j+3	nrows, j+4	……	nrows, ncols

Table 1. Arrangement method of raster data

clipslope: 表

id	坡度值
1	16.7028
2	21.13589
3	23.13307
4	20.09531
5	11.33143
6	2.865975
7	1.718358
8	8.608027
9	16.05001
10	18.1099
11	18.13732
12	19.48674
13	23.64088
14	26.06059
15	22.87004
16	17.85436
17	12.38021
18	6.901349
19	2.849875
20	.8102307
21	.1012855
22	3.097377
23	11.25166
24	17.76293

记录: 1

Figure 5. Arrangement method of slope

4.2. Construction of derived star-type model based on raster data

Each star-type model includes a fact table and some corresponding dimension tables. All the fact tables and dimension tables are stored in the SQL Server2000 database. The key of constructing a star-type model is to design right fact table and dimension table as well as establish mutual connections between them[14]. These tables can reflect the complex relationship among different data. Furthermore, too much redundant data can be produced if using one dimension table to describe due to corresponding complexity of relationship and data in the dimension in practice. Here, the dimension can be divided once again. Some branches will appear from the angle of "star", thus, a derived star-type model, which is also called snowflake-type model, would come into being [2]. The derived star-type model established in this section has a specific theme on land use and land cover. Here is an example happened in a certain region of Guizhou Province.

4.2.1. Construction of fact table

In the fact table, i.e. Combine Table, it mainly stores the main code, which is represented with gridid, and the values of slope and aspect in each grid. The latter can be extracted automatically from DEM by making use of relevant designing program. Designed fact table can be described as follows in figure 6.

Figure 6. Designed fact table

4.2.2. Construction of dimension table

Dimensional tables mainly include three tables, thereinto, dimensional table of grid can store each grid's main code used to link fact table, row number, list number, coordinates and the codes of land use and land cover. The dimensional table of land cover can store corresponding attributed value, such as land cover denomination, region name. The dimensional of land utilization, similar to land cover table, stores the attributed value corresponding with grid table, such as land utilization denomination, region name, etc.

Dimensional tables of *land cover, land utilization, grid* can be described respectively as follows in fig.7, fig.8 and fig.9.

Figure 7. Dimension of land cover

Figure 8. Dimension of land utilization

4.3. Construction of multi dimension data set based on raster data

Compared with traditional approach, the main difference of constructing multi dimensions data set based on raster data in this section is the dissimilarity of forming star-type model.

Necessary data grouping processing can be adopted in order to improve the system function because the raster data amount is quite larger. In this section, all the raster data can be divided into more than 700 groups. Data of each group may arrange in the sequence of keyword.

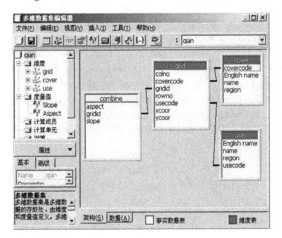

Figure 9. Dimension of grid

New multi dimensions data set can be constructed after adopting snowflake-type framework. As shown in figure 10, dimensions of *land cover* and *land utilization* act as the branches of dimension of *grid*.

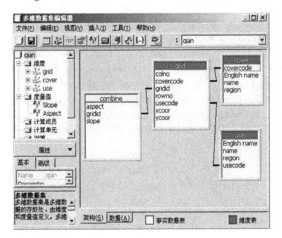

Figure 10. Multi dimension data set

4.4. Data mining based on raster data

Process of data mining based on raster, similar to the one of data mining based on vector, has also included model creation, example dimension choice and forecasting the entities and data to be trained as well as the model processing, and so on.

4.4.1. Outline of spatial data mining algorithm

At present, there are many spatial data mining algorithms, such as statistical analysis, neural networks, clustering, decision trees, genetic algorithm, classification, etc. In this section, clustering algorithm is mainly used to deal with the raster data stored in E-Government Information System. In the processing course of clustering algorithm, diverse data can be divided into different categories in order to make the difference between categories as big as possible and inner differences in the category as small as possible[4]. Clustering algorithm, which is also called aggregation algorithm, is an indirect data mining algorithms and does not use independent variables to get designated output. Different from classification model, clustering algorithm does not know beforehand that there are several categories to be divided and what these categories are. And it does not know how to define these categories according to some data items. Although it cannot predict unknown data value, while classification algorithm can, it provides a way to find similar records. These records can be considered the components of given clusters according to self-determined algorithm itself[3]. The following section has described the course of data mining by using constructing clustering.

In this section, data mining is made based on the algorithm of EM. The algorithm is one of spatial clustering algorithms, which adopts the probability method of distribute each data to the determined classification instead of calculating directly the distance.

Set up a closed curve in each dimension as the clustering criteria, and calculate the mean and standard variance. If the point falls within the closed curve, then they have a certain probability of belonging to the given classification. Since the different curve of corresponding classification is not only, so the data point may also fall in multiple classification curves and is given a different probability[6,7]. During the course of implementation, the initial classification model is repeatedly made to finish the step of optimization by the algorithm to fit the data, and determine the probability of data point existing in a classification. When the probability model fits the data, the algorithm terminates the process[19]. The function to determine the suitability is the logarithmic likelihood data fitting the model. In this process, if an empty classification is generated or the membership of one or more categories is less than a given threshold, new data point will be reseed in the classification with low fill rate, and the algorithm will re-run.

As the results of the EM cluster analysis algorithm is probabilistic, which means that each data point belongs to all categories[20], and calculates a probability for each combination of data point and the classification, but the data point is allocated to the classification of each with a different probability.

This method allows the classification overlap, so the total number of items in the all categories may exceed the total number of items in the training set[8,12]. Aiming at the mining model results, the instructions to support the scores can be adjusted accordingly in order to illustrate this situation.

4.4.2. Merit of the algorithm

Compared to the traditional clustering algorithms, the algorithm has several merits.

1. The algorithm is better than the sampling algorithm with foretype.
2. The algorithm has better efficiency in working, which scans the database only once.
3. There is little influence in executing the algorithm.

4.4.3. Implementation of the algorithm

In brief, the algorithm includes two steps as follows.

Step 1. Estimation.
Step 2. Maximization.

Suppose existing n sample ($n>0$), which come from K Gaussian Mixture Distribution. Each distribution is mutually independent[21].

The parameter of Gaussian Mixture Distribution can be estimated to determine the Mean Value, Variance, prior probability of each distribution.

The probability density function can be described as follows.

$$n_j(\vec{x}, \vec{\mu}_j, \Sigma_j) = \frac{1}{\sqrt{(2\pi)^m |\Sigma_j|}} \exp[-\frac{1}{2}(\vec{x} - \vec{\mu})^T \Sigma_j^{-1}(\vec{x} - \vec{\mu})]$$

Thereinto, $\vec{x}$ is observed data vector, $\vec{\mu}$ is the corresponding data mean. And i, j is the different data object, m is the variance.

The priori probability meets:

$$\sum_j \pi_j = 1$$

The maximum likelihood estimation is expressed as follows.

$$P(\vec{x_i}) = \sum_{j=1}^{k} \pi_j n(\vec{x_i}; \vec{\mu}_j, \Sigma_j)$$

Suppose $\theta_j = (\vec{u}_j, \Sigma_j, \pi_j)$ is the parameter of the jth Gaussian Mixture Distribution, and the parameter space to be estimated can be described as follows.

$$S = (\theta_1, \cdots, \theta_k)^T$$

The probability formula of sample X is

$$l(X \mid S) = \log \prod_{i=1}^{n} \sum_{j=1}^{k} \pi_j n_j(\vec{x_i}, \vec{\mu}_j, \Sigma_j)$$
$$= \sum_{i=1}^{n} \log \sum_{j=1}^{k} \pi_j n_j(\vec{x_i}; \vec{\mu}_j, \Sigma_j)$$

Continuously make the steps of iterative estimation and maximization, and compute repeatedly the above-mentioned three parameters until $l(X|S)$ meets the condition of no significant increase again[22].

4.5. Example of spatial data mining

An idiographic example on land utilization and land cover, which happened in a certain region of Guizhou Province, can be used to describe how to create a mining model. Land utilization and land cover are the most prominent landscape signs in the earth surface system. Land utilization is a process of making natural state of the land into the one of artificial ecosystems. And the latter represents objective existence of the earth's surface with specific spatial and temporal attributes. Generally, land types can be identified indirectly according to combination of land cover and structure. The created data mining model can be described as follows in figure 11.

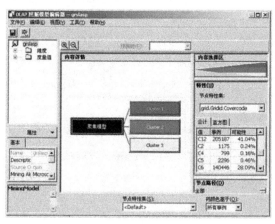

Figure 11. Data mining based on clustering

As shown in figure 11, the original data set is divided into three categories. Thereinto, C6, C8, C12 represent respectively land cover type of lush shrubbery, flourish grassland and cropland. The three land cover types account for the vast majority of the total number of all types. The amount is about 96.15%. Simultaneously, other land cover types had little proportion and can be almost negligible.

In-depth analysis to *Cluster 1* node can be made. As shown in figure 12, in this category, most of land cover types are *C6* and *C8*. The proportion is about 95.51%. That is, the type of land cover in this region is basically shrubbery and grassland. It is more suitable for the development of animal husbandry in a view of economic factor.

Click the node feature set *usecode*, the data in the table can be changed accordingly. As shown in figure 13, all the land utilization type appeared in the *Cluster 1* node is *U10*, which represents the forest. By adopting similar steps, corresponding results can be shown in the whole region included by *Cluster 1* node. For example, the average slope and aspect are respectively 12.51, 184.22 degree. Based on these analyses, users can find out which types of vegetation are suitable for being cultivated in this region by using related knowledge in a macroscopic view[16,17]. Besides, light conditions may also be considered to improve the development of vegetation. Therefore, feasible service information can be provided to promote economic development in the region.

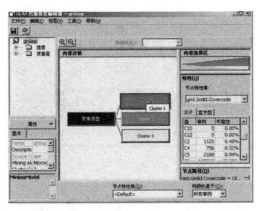

Figure 12. The dominant type of land utilization

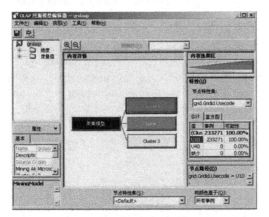

Figure 13. The single type of land utilization

Similarly, analysis to node *Cluster 2* or *Cluster 3* is analogous to the node *Cluster 1*.

In another view, distribution information in the whole categories can be found in accordance with node feature set characteristics on the contrary. Likewise, the distribution of other node feature sets characteristics is similar to the above-mentioned instance. As shown in figure 14, it represents the type of land cover of *C6*.

In figure 14, the most part of land cover type *C6* belongs to the code *Cluster 1*. And if the land cover type is switched from *C6* to *C12*, the most part of land cover type *C12* will belong to the code *Cluster 2*, the proportion of which is about 97.7%.

The distribution character of other node feature set is similar to the above-mentioned part.

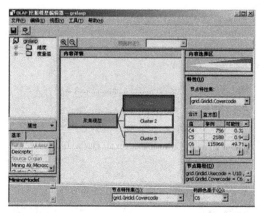

Figure 14. The type of land cover of *C6*

5. Conclusions

In this chapter, spatial data and corresponding attribute data of E-Government Information System were mined deeply by applying the technology of data mining such as Cluster. And some useful information and knowledge were extracted. For example, the correlative relationship of land utilization and land classification could be found. It was convenient for the departments of different level to make aided decision-making. Although the different applications of SDM have been increasingly extended than ever, there are still some limitations on applicability and efficiency existing in the actual application system[5,15]. At the same time, SDM is also a new study field with more attraction and challenges[18]. With the enhancement of information and the development of soft, hardware and other technology, SDM can possess mighty knowledge discovery function, and can still effectively bring into play known or potential value especially in E-Government Information System.

Author details

Bin Li, Lihong Shi, Jiping Liu and Liang Wang
Chinese Academy of Surveying and Mapping, Beijing, China

Acknowledgement

The work presented in this chapter has been funded by Fundamental Scientific Research Foundation (No.7771204, No.G71012, No.77738). And all the data used in this chapter comes from the database of Government GIS. Thank all my colleagues for their enthusiastic supports and helps.

6. References

[1] Qingpu Zhang, Foxiao Chen(1999) Basic conception and construction mode of Government GIS. Remote Sensing Information, supplement,

[2] Bin Li(2002) Research on construction of Governmental GIS Spatial Data Warehouse. The master's paper of Bin Li's published by Chinese Academy of Surveying and Mapping.

[3] Bin Li(2002) Study of Construction and Application of Data Warehouse for Government GIS. Bulletin of Surveying and Mapping, 2002(2): 4-6

[4] Bin Li, Lihong Shi, Jiping Liu(2009) A method of raster data mining based on multi dimension data set. The 6th International Conference on Fuzzy Systems and Knowledge Discovery, FSKD

[5] ChinaKDD(2008) Schedule of clustering arithmetics on data mining, http://www.dmresearch.net

[6] Li Deren, Shuliang Wang, Wenzhong Shi, Jizhou Wang(2001) On Spatial Data Mining and Knowledge Discovery. Wuhan University Transaction, Vol 26(2):491-498

[7] Genlin Gi, Zhihui Sun(2001) Jou rnal of Image and Graphics. Vo l. 6 (A) , No. 8: 715-721

[8] Xingli Li, Peiun Du,etc(2006)SCIFNCE & TECHN0LOGY lnformation, Vol (6) : 158-160

[9] Miller H J, Han J(2001) Geographic Data Mining and Knowledge Discovery. London and New York:Taylor and Francis

[10] Wang S L,Wang X Z,Shi W Z(2003)Spatial Data Cleaning. In:Zhang S C,Yang Q,Zhang C Q, Terrsa M. Proceedings of the First International Workshop on Data cleaning and Preprocessing. Maebashi City, Japan:88-98

[11] Deren Li(2002) Spatial Data Mining and Knowledge Discovery Theory and Methods. Journal of Wuhan Univsrsity-Information Science, Vol(27) : 221-233

[12] Tongming Liu9(2001) Technology and application of data mining. Beijing: National Defence Industry Press

[13] Shengwu Hu(2006) Quality assessment and reliability analysis. Beijing: Surveying and Mapping Press

[14] Hernandez M A, Stolfo S J(1998)Real-world data is dirty: data cleaning and the merge/purge problem. Data Mining and Knowledge Discovery,2: 1-31

[15] Aspinall R.J,Miller D R., Richman A R(1993)Data quality and error analysis in GIS: measurement and use of metadata describing uncertainty in spatial data. In Proceedings of XIIIth Annual ESRI User.Palm Springs: 279-290

[16] Pawlak Z (1997)Rough Sets.In:Lin Y,cercone N.Rough Sets and Data Mining Analysis for Imprecise Data. London: Kluwer Academic Publishers: 3-7

[17] Kaichang Di(2000) Spatial data mining and knowledge discovery. Wuhan: Wuhan University Press

[18] Kelleller A, Abbaspour K, Schulin R(2000) Uncertainty Assessment in Modelling Cadmium and Zinc accumulation in Agricultural Soils. In:Heuvelink G B M, Lemmens M J P M. Accuracy 200:Proceedings of the 4th International Symposium on Spatial Accuracy Assessment in Natural Resource and Environmental Science. Amsterdam,The Netherlands:Univcrsity of Amsterdam: 347-354

[19] Sheikholeslami G, Chatterjee S, Zhang A(1998) Wave-Cluster: A multi-resolution clustering approach for very large spatiall databases. In: Proceedings of the 24th International Conference on Very Large Databases. New York, 428-439

[20] Caiping Hu(2007) Spatial data mining research review. Computer Science, vol (5): 14-17

[21] Clementin E,et al (2000) Mining Multiple Level Spatial Association Rules for Objects with a Broad Boundary. Data and Knowledge Engineering, vol(34): 251-270

[22] Kacar E,et al(2002)Discovery Fuzzy Spatial Association Rules,Data Mining and Knowledge Discovery: Theory Tools and Technology IV. In: Dasarathy B V, ed. Proceedings of SPIE, Vol(4730): 94-102

Chapter 5

Using Neural Networks in Preparing and Analysis of Basketball Scouting

Branko Markoski, Zdravko Ivankovic and Miodrag Ivkovic

Additional information is available at the end of the chapter

1. Introduction

"I don't believe in keeping statistics. Only statistics that is important is the final result."

This used to be true, mostly because opponents also did not keep or use statistics. However, the times have changed. Final result is still the most important thing, but a way in which such result is obtained is also of great importance.

Basketball is the one of most popular sports, in Serbia and in the world. It is a team sport. Actors of a basketball game are the players from two opposing teams, their team officials with coaches, assistant coaches, doctors and officials (commissioner, referees, table officials, statisticians). Every team, depending on a league or competition, may have no more than 12 or 10 players per game, and of those 5 are actively engaged in the game [1]. Basketball game would not start without 5 players from each game on the court. In Europe, regular basketball game is divided into 4 quarters of 10 minutes each, while in NBA every quarter is 2 minutes longer. If a result is draw, after regular time additional time of 5 minutes is played, as many times as necessary to decide a winner of a game.

There is no limitations regarding a number of substitutions of players during a game, but there is a limitation regarding personal fouls. If a player gets fifth personal foul, he must leave the court and may not play any more.

A basket scored gets 2 or 3 points, depending on a distance from which the ball has been thrown. A line discerning two cases is drawn on the court.

In the times past, basketball statistics used to be a luxury, available only to big professional teams [2]. First beginnings of a basketball statistics started in 1969, when it was first introduced at the NBA game. Statisticians were keeping only one- or two- point scores for every player. During next two years, statistics has been developing and had sixteen events that statisticians had to keep track. Slowly but steadily, it gradually took a central position in analysis and preparation of a game, for individual players and for the team as a whole. Every team in the NBA had four statisticians, keeping track how a team is doing in offence and in defense. In those times, basketball was more oriented to offensive activities than defensive ones. There was even a name for such type of basketball: "Run and gun". For the average coach, statistics was a nightmare: it required a great deal of time and effort, first at collecting statistical data, then in manual computing various joint statistical parameters [3]. For most coaches, statistics was simply not worth the effort.

Having in mind characteristics of information quality, manual keeping of statistics, using a pencil and paper, has several flaws. The most important one is incompleteness, since due to restricted paper area evidence is kept only to most basic statistics parameters, sixteen in this case. Presently, 38 standard statistical parameters are being kept. This demands exceptional knowledge of basketball game. Moreover, it takes time to write a data on statistics sheet, and to compute data afterwards [4]. There is a considerable possibility to calculate data incorrectly, not to mention long time needed to calculate data or to write it on a paper. Since there were special forms for statistics, statisticians had to write data in a precisely defined spots, and therefore probability to omit one or more actions happening on the court was considerable. In addition, if one or more actions were omitted, there is no real information or real data. There is a thin line between win and loss [5] and every bit of information is invaluable preparations for the game, for every player and for team as a whole. Because of this, it is essential that statisticians know basketball very well, and their training is of utmost importance in order to achieve certain speed and to "catch" all actions on the basketball court. Considering the statistical sheet used for keeping statistics manually, it is evident that noted data are (un)intelligible, especially in comparison to those processed on computer and printed, with abundance of computed summary and other parameters [6]. Time and effort that must be invested in manual computing of different summary statistical parameters are enormous. Therefore, summary data may not be available at the moment when they are needed most. Moreover, possibility of human error in this kind of calculation is considerable, so even the accuracy is compromised. Coaches often could not obtain quick and precise information that was necessary in order to react in a right moment to help the team.

It should be noted that, after "manually extracting parameters", statistics had been sent to the Basketball Federation, where all sheets from all courts were again manually processed in order to try to find some regularities. Another manual statistics was kept for needs of referee commission [7]. In other words, there were other types of statistics in need. Regarding manually kept statistics, we must emphasize that this is a very difficult task; for instance, one cannot obtain total shots of a player, or a number of turnovers because time is needed to "count and add" all the data. In addition, there was a possibility to omit something and therefore to obtain incorrect data [8].

Information technologies development and their integration in all areas of social and business life have not bypassed the sports. Increasing professionalism and competition cause clubs to approach all their activities in more and more systematic way. Considerable progress is being noted in training system and in analysis of opponent teams and players, so-called scouting. Introduction of computers was helpful, releasing assistant coaches from responsibility for keeping statistics, and at the same time providing a number of information that they could only dream of twenty years a go. Moreover, computers and software are now widespread and relatively inexpensive, so information is accessible to everyone.

At the beginning of a season, coaches are mostly interested in using different statistical reports for analyzing and evaluation of individual players. Once they have insight into advantages and flaws of their players, their interest is moving towards the team as a whole. They want to know how good the team is. The team statistics therefore becomes most important. After all, a basketball is still a team sport. Finally, having in mind that different statistic reports may be used also for analyzing opponent's play, coaches' interest is moved during a season towards their opponents. More often than not, well-analyzed opponents' play means a difference between winning and losing.

Statistics is not used solely by coaches. On the contrary, whole population of sport lovers and fans is able, due to mass usage of technology and media such as television and internet, to follow efficiency of individuals and teams. Numerous professions, for instance journalists and commentators, have use of statistics in doing their job, while for some, as sports managers, it is of vital importance for their profession. In last decades, sport became more than a game: it is a large business with considerable amounts of money invested.

The final result is not the only thing important any more...

Computers are used in NBA for a some time now. Question is how the statistics is kept. Until 2000, a very popular program has been used, where actions were entered using the mouse and the keyboard. At every game there had to be five people: two keeping statistics for one team, two for another, and one person was a supervisor, controlling every step. There had to be yet another person at every game, as a substitute. Two statisticians in charge for one team were organized in such a way that one of them follows attack ant other a defense. These two could never switch, for instance taking turns for every game. Therefore, they were offense and defense specialists. Since 2001, statistics is kept using voice. This is a modern technology that slowly comes even to Serbia. In this case, one must "train" the computer to his or her voice, and to be careful to use only those words that are present in a database, or else such action would not be noted in a database. Another aggravating issue for this kind of keeping statistics is noise. Statisticians became skilled and hold microphone very close, in order to minimize noise. This manner of keeping statistics, using voice, considerably facilitates a process because the statistician may observe much more details when he is not busy with a mouse or keyboard. There is another way of keeping statistics, using PDA devices, where actions are entered using a pen. [9]

We will describe only some of differences in keeping statistics. Let us start from assists, which is probably most controversial one, besides rebounds and turnovers. In Europe, assist is noted only if a player passes the ball to another player on a good shooting position. This other player must score, for two or three points. Until recently, assists were noted only if a player is alone in the paint, but presently they are valid wherever the player is in a position to shoot and score two or three points [10]. In USA, this is quite different, whether in NBA, NSA or WNBA. There the assist is noted if a ball was passed to other player when he/she is alone on a shooting position, even if he/she was fouled after that. Assist is noted since the first player has done everything right. We had quite a discussion with Mr. Aleksandar Đikić regarding this, because we think this is quite logical because it is not assisting player guilt that receiving player did not score. Then again, basketball is a team sport. We have often witnessed situations when assisting player does everything right, and shooting player misses and assist is not noted.

This problem demands deeper analysis in order to find the best solution. In USA it is also noted where assist occurred, whether in the paint, outside the paint or at perimeter. We have a type of report saying which player assists which player the most. This is a good detail to estimate the teams' play.

Another category differing between Europe and USA is difference between steal and defensive rebound. This caused a lot of controversy in our country too. In USA, after every shot, a defensive rebound ensues and there is no problem whatsoever. However, what if after shot ball drops to the ground, or if after a free-throw shot ball bounces to the player's hands? Is this still a rebound or maybe a steal? We have spoken to a number of coaches and our only conclusion is that there is no rule. Opinions differ. In Serbia, when a ball bounces to hands after a free throw it is noted as a steal. In USA, steals are kept differently, every good defense is noted as a steal; for instance, when a good defense forces a player to step out. In such case this ball is stolen. There are several instances when after jump ball, the ball is won and noted as a rebound, and not a steal. Another interesting issue is a turnover. There are nineteen types of turnover in present basketball. Most turnovers during a game are due to bad pass. For statistician it is often hard to determine whether it was bad pass or bad catch [11], especially since statisticians are mostly seated at relatively unfavorable positions, below or around the basket. It would be much better to be placed close to scorers table, where they would have good view and could easily process disputable cases. In addition, coordination with scorers table would be easier if they note that something is not right. One of turnovers is when a player stays in paint for five seconds (three seconds in Europe). This rule was literally introduced for Shaquille O'Neal; as a dominant centre, he often entered "down the paint" and easily scored. Until recently there was another type of turnover: illegal defense. It was up to referees to recognize this. In our country, in younger categories zone defense is illegal; referees, if note this, are to warn the coach. Until two years a go, first time was the warning, and every next time was technical foul for the coach. In USA, first one was the warning, and every next time there was a free throw. There is also another type of scouting close to statistics – a way and type of defense. They must recognize a type of defense and therefore to determine a shot by a player: successful for two or three points in zone or on man [12]. Therefore, in order to keep statistics successfully, a person must know rules very fell. A number of sports organizations have their own information system regarding membership, spectators, caterers, competitors, employees, resources etc. Building an effective information system is important in order to enable easier accomplishing goals and mission defined in strategic analysis of the sport organization. It is important to collect enough information, but not too much in order to avoid information overload. In such situations, decision makers who should benefit from information gathered are unable to reach right decision due to too much information. Developing a good information system is a dynamic process. First, it should be determined which information is to be collected and how to do it. When data are collected, they must be processed and analyzed. Finally, information must be stored in a way that provides easy use and adaptation of different analysis to fit new situations [13]. System storing information regarding a sports organization is called database. Use of computers and appropriate software (database) provides quick access, analyze and report regarding huge number of important aspects in work and development of the sports organization.

2. Scouting and data mining techniques

The main reason for scouting is to know the opponent in all stages of basketball. Scouting is done at team and individual level. Team level reviews opponents systems of playing the game in offense, defense and transition; how the team acts in all kinds of defense, how it attacks after outs and how it transits from defense to offence. Every stage may be statistically shown as number of tries, lines of offense and percentage. In addition, good and bad sides of team's and individual game may be shown. Individual scouting reviews performance of every individual player in all game stages, his statistical performance, his good and bad sides. For example, from which action he attacks most frequently and most successfully or in which actions he has lower performance, as well as in how he (or she) performs in different kinds of defense (what he defends worst?)

All in all, scouting shows how to attack the opponent in most efficient way and how to handle defense. Therefore, statistics and scouting are important part of every analysis required in order to prepare for future games. A good scouting often requires to follow several games of the opponent team, mostly last four (two at home and two away). This requires exceptional knowledge about basketball and computers as well. Scouts often need several days to prepare players and coach for the next opponent. With present rhythm, playing games twice a week (Wednesday – Sunday), scouts often don't have enough time to cover all opponents, so some teams have two or even more scouts in order to analyze every next opponent. Naturally, there is a question of a mean to shorten the time for the scout, but in such a way that he still obtains good quality information that will provide advantage over the opponent. There is a powerful and good-quality tool today: "data mining in sport" techniques. Data mining techniques in sports, especially in basketball, are in rise recently. Those tools and techniques are developed with the aim to measure performances of individual players and of the team as a whole. Since the sport is one of most profitable industries, these methods, as well as performances of players and teams, attracts much attention of sport clubs and managing companies. Before data mining and its advantages, analysis of opponents, as well as preparation of tactics for the game, was a task of professional scouts. Since the number of games constantly increased, and scouts could not manage large number of games and corresponding amount of information, new methods were sought in order to extract knowledge from raw data. Every team could choose between two ways. One was to engage professional statisticians who had deep knowledge about concrete sport, in his case basketball, and who would enable the team to reach right decisions. Other way was to find methods that will shorten the time, and still provide precious knowledge; in other words, to start data mining techniques. When appropriately used, data mining techniques may result in better preparation of the game, and better performances of the team and players. This means that players may be prepared for certain events that may occur at the game, using all downsides and flaws of the opponent team.

In order to analyze the opponent, we need information. Knowing individual qualities of players and their habits, in both offence and defense, we may easily predict where advantages or problems will occur in individual situations at offence and defense. Having this in mind, we will pay more or less attention to certain segments of opponent's game, thus reducing the number of information and allowing all players of the team the clear and identical idea how to play that game. When number of misunderstandings decrease, power of team play rises. Therefore for appliance of data mining quality and precise data are necessary. One of definitions in FIBA manual [14] is: Basketball is a complex game between two opposing teams with the aim to score most points and win. During the game, a vast number of events occur, and it is very hard or even impossible to note them all. Besides basic events as shots, assists, turnovers and steals, offensive and defensive rebounds, there are a number of relevant events such as movements of player across the court with and without the ball, a type of defense played by a team, and which player is the weakest point in which defense. We must emphasize that there are measurable and non-measurable part in statistic [15]. Measurable part is the one that may be presented in statistics, but there is also a part that is not noted anywhere, for instance the last good defense, last wrong foul, last turnover or steal...

We must emphasize that during a game every team has its statistical unit that processes data and gives their coaches printed materials with information so that they react during a game and reach the right decision, and to prepare information relevant for next game or the next opponent. Due to amount and complexity of data, basketball is extremely quick and dynamic game and therefore suitable for application of data mining techniques, especially neural networks that enable extraction of conclusions from raw data. Having this in mind, we will pay more or less attention to certain segments of opponent's game, lowering number of information and allowing all players to have a clear and identical idea how to play that particular game. We do not want players to choose one or two information according to their will. We want players to choose and implement two identical information, even if those have only secondary influence on opponent's game. Therefore, it is not a bad idea to test your team during a preparation period and determine how they accept information. By using neural networks, as one of integral and indispensable technologies in data mining used most frequently in basketball data mining, patterns were discerned pointing to influence of different parameters of basketball game. In order to check correctness of results obtained, input data were analyzed using C5.0 decision tree. It is important to say that a basketball court is divided into zones, and basic division is to six fields [16].

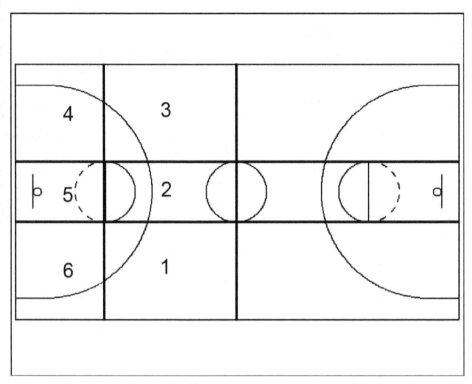

Figure 1. Division of a basketball court

This is of utmost importance since we may know how players, or a team, shoot for two or three points. By using data mining techniques, we consider influence of shot from certain positions in a field and in general. Influence of all gathered parameters is considered (shots for one, two and three points, offensive and defensive rebounds, turnovers, steals, assists, blocks). By using these technologies, models are created in order to predict the result of the game.

According to [17], "Data mining is a process of discovering new sensible correlations, patterns and guidelines by observing a large amount of information stored, and by using pattern recognition technologies and statistical and mathematical techniques". There are also other definitions:

- "Data mining is the analysis of (mostly large) observed data set in order to find certain connections and to sum up data in new ways, being intelligible and useful to the data owner" [18].
- "Data mining is an interdisciplinary bough merging techniques from machine learning, pattern recognition, statistics, databases and visualization, in order to solve the question of obtaining information from large data bases" [19]

Some companies are trying to use data mining in their own way, depending on level of inertia in certain departments. Inter-industrial standard was obviously necessary, being independent on industry branch, independent on tools and independent on application. For this purpose, special international industrial standard has been developed, independent on industry type, tool and application. Analysts from DaimlerChrysler, SPSS and NCR have developed the Cross-Industry Standard Process for Data Mining (CRISP-DM) in 1996. The CRISP is a non-profit standard freeware, intended for fitting of data mining to general problem-solving strategies for business and research purposes. Most often tasks given to data mining are: Description, Estimation, Prediction, Classification, Clustering and Association. We will touch every one with few lines. Regarding description, we must say that researchers and analysts are trying to find ways to describe patterns and tendencies present in given data. Data mining models must be as transparent as possible. This means that results of data mining model must explain clear patterns responsible for intuitive interpretation and explanation. Regarding estimation, it is similar to classification except variables sought are numerical and not categorical. Models are built using "complete" records, providing values for target variables, and predictors (defining variables). For new observation, estimated values of target variables are given regarding values of predictor. Prediction is similar to classification and estimation, except that result of prediction is located in the future. Examples of prediction in business and science areas may be predicting a winner of this year's championship in football, basketball or any other sport, based on comparing statistics of given teams. Any method or technique used for classification and estimation may also be used for prediction, under certain conditions. We also must emphasize that traditional statistical methods must be included, such as point estimation and estimation of confidence intervals, linear regression, correlation an multiple regression, as well as data mining methods and methods of retrieving knowledge such as neural networks, decision trees and methods of k-closed neighbor. Regarding classification, we must point that there is a target variable belonging to some category. Data mining model investigates a large set of records, where every record contains information about target variable and a set of predictor variables. Clustering goes for grouping records, and for observing and sampling classes of similar objects. Cluster is a collection of records similar to each other, and different from records in other clusters. Clustering is differing from classification since there is no target variable for clustering. Task of clustering is not to classify, estimate or predict value of target variable. Cluster algorithms tend to divide a data set to relatively homogenous subgroups (clusters), with maximum similarity between records, while similarities between records in different clusters are minimal. Aim of associations in data mining is to find out which attributes "belong together". This is prevailing technology in a business world, where it is called affinity analysis or market analysis. Its task is to find rules to describe connections between several attributes. Rules of association are in "*if hypothesis then consequence*" form, together with measurements of support and confidence associated to a rule.

3. Neural network

The modern discipline of neural networks was created as a combination of several quite different ways of research: signal processing, neurobiology and physics [20] and therefore is a typical interdisciplinary branch of science [21]. It is basically an effort to comprehend intricacies of a human brain, as well as to apply new insightsto processing complex information [22]. There is a number of progressive, non-algorithmic systems, as learning algorithms, genetic algorithms, adaptive memory, associative memory, fuzzy logic. General opinion is that neural networks are presently the most mature and most applicable technology [23].

Conventional computers' work is based on logic: deterministic, sequential or with a very low level of parallelism. Software written for such computers must be literally perfect in order to work properly. This requires a long and therefore expensive process of perpetual design and testing.

Neural networks belong to the category of parallel asynchronous distributed processing. The network is damage-resilient or only a relatively low number of neurons falls out of function. It is also tolerant to noise in input signal. Every memory element is delocalized - situated in network as a whole - and it is impossible to identify in which part it is stored. Classic addressing is nonexistent, since memory is approached using contents, and not the address [24].

Basic component of neural network is a neuron, as shown in figure 4:

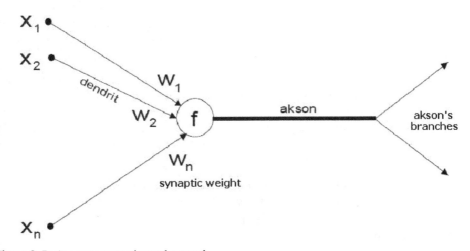

Figure 2. Basic components of neural network

3.1. Backward propagation

Neural network is a controlled learning method, demanding a large training set of complete records, including target variable. Since every observation from training set is conducted through the network, output value is obtained at the output node. This value is compared to the real value of target variable for given observation in training set, and the difference between the real and the predicted value is calculated. This prediction error is corresponding to prediction error in regression model. In order to measure how much the output prediction is consistent to real target value, most neural networks uses sum of error squares (SSE):

$$SSE = \sum_{records} \sum_{output\ nodes} (actual - output)^2 \tag{1}$$

where prediction error square is summed over all output nodes and all records in a training set.

The main problem is therefore to create set of difficulty models, which would minimize the SSE. In this way, difficulties correspond to parameters of the regression model. "Real" values of difficulty that would minimize SSE are unknown, so it is our task to assume ones for the input data set. Due to non-linear nature of the sigmoid function extending through the network, there is no ready-made solution for minimizing SSE.

3.2. Sensitivity analysis

One of downsides of neural networks is their vagueness. The same exquisite flexibility that enables a neural network to model a wide range of nonlinear behaviors, at the same time limits our ability to interpret results using easily formulated rules. Unlike decision trees, there is no clear procedure for translating complexities of neural network to a compact set of decision rules.

There is still a procedure that may be used – sensitivity analysis, enabling us to measure relative effect of every attribute on output result. By using testing data, this analysis works as follows:

1. Generates a new observation x_{mean}, where every attribute value in x_{mean} is equal to mean value of different attributes for all records in a testing data set.
2. Finds network output for x_{mean} input. We will call it *output mean*.
3. One attribute at a time, changes x_{mean} in order to represent attribute minimum and maximum. Then it finds network output for every variation and compares it to *output mean*

Sensitivity analysis will determine that change of certain attributes to minimum value has more effect on resulting output of a network than some other attributes.

3.3. C4.5 algorithm

C4.5 algorithm is a Quinlan extrapolation of its own ID3 algorithm for creating a decision tree [25]. It recursively visits every decision node, choosing optimal division while divisions are possible. The basic properties of the C4.5 algorithm are:

*   C4.5 algorithm is not limited to binary divisions; it creates trees with triple, or multiple branching.
*   For categorical attributes, C4.5 by default creates separate branch for every value of a categorical attribute. This may bring to excessive complexity, since some values may have very low frequency or be connected to other values.

C4.5 algorithm uses concept of information gain of entropy reduction in order to choose optimal division. Let us suppose that we have variable X with k possible values with probability $p_1, p_2, ..., p_k$. Which is the minimal number of bits needed, in average per symbol, to conduct a sequence of symbols representing values for X observed? Answer is called entropy for X and it is defined as:

$$H(X) = -\sum_j p_j \log_2(p_j)$$

Where this entropy formula comes from? For event with value p, average amount of information in bits needed to conduct result is $-log_2(p)$. For instance, result of coin toss-ups, with probability 0.5, can be conducted using $-log_2(0.5) = 1$ bit, i.e. zero or one, depending on toss-up result. For variables with several possible outcomes, we use difficulty sum for $log_2(p_j)$, with difficulties equal to probabilities of outcomes as seen in formula

$$H(X) = -\sum_j p_j \log_2(p_j)$$

C4.5 uses entropy concept in a following way. Let us suppose that we have potential division S, which divides training data set T to several subsets, $T_1, T_2, ..., T_k$. Mean information demands may be calculated as a difficulty sum of entropy for all individual subset:

$$H_s(T) = -\sum_{i=1} P_j H_s(T_j)$$

where P_i is a data proportion in subset i. Then we may define our information gain as $gain(S) = H(T) - H_s(T)$, or as increase of information brought by division of training set T by potential division S. At every decision node, C4.5 chooses optimal division with highest information gain, $gain(S)$.

4. Data mining in sport

Huge amounts of data are present in all areas of sport. These data may show particular traits of any player, or events that happened during a game, and/or how a team is performing as a unit. It is important to determine which data to store and to comprise a way for their best usage [26]. By finding the best method to obtain new facts from these information and to transform it to a particular data, sports organizations provide themselves a leverage in comparison to other teams [27]. Such approach to knowledge seeking may be applied to a whole organization – from players who may improve their performance using techniques of video analysis, to scouts who use statistic analysis and projection techniques in order to identify which talented youth would develop the most and become a good player [28].

The first part of a problem is to determine performances metrics [29]. A lot of present sports metrics may be used in an inappropriate way (performances are not measured with the aim to score more points than opponent, which is an ultimate goal of every sport organization).

The second part is to find patterns of interest in data observed. These patterns may include tendencies and tactics of opposing players or teams, origin of player's injuries based on monitoring exercise performances, as well as predictions based on earlier data. Professional sports organizations are the multi-million companies and certain decisions are worth large amounts of money. With this kind of capital, a single wrong decision may potentially set them years back. Due to high risk and need to make correct decisions, sport industry is just the right environment to apply data mining technologies.

Different sports associations have varying approach to such data. This approach may be divided into five levels:

- There is no connection between sports data and their use
- Experts from a given field are working on predictions using their instinct and hunch
- Experts from a given field are working on predictions using data collected
- Use of statistics in decision-making process
- Use of data mining in decision-making process.

The first type of approach is when there is no connection between sports data and their use. These sport organizations often obtain certain information about players during their games and they ignore all of it. This is characteristic for amateur sports clubs, since their emphasis is on fun or on introducing the sports basics.

The next type of approach is based on an expert from a given field who is predicting based on his personal experience. It used to be widely accepted notion that these experts (coaches, managers, scouts) might efficiently use their insights and experience in order to reach correct decisions. Decisions made from this type of approach are usually based on predictions or instincts, and not on real data and information. These decisions may include playing certain types of actions or certain player changes since such decision "looks right".

The third type approach is the one when experts start using collected data. Decisions on this level include playing with certain players, for which it was proven that they cooperate well and using actions that score points more often.

The fourth type of approach includes use of statistics as a help in decision-making process. Such statistical measurements may be simple, for instance the frequency of certain events, or complex, dividing performance of a whole team and assigning merits to each player for every game or the competition. Statistics is used as a tool, thus helping experts in making right decisions.

The fifth type of connection between sports information and their use is using the data mining techniques, since they certainly might help predictions. Statistics techniques are still in the core of data mining, but statistics is being used to extract from the background noise a pattern or any other underlying system (inclinations of opponent players). Statistics or statisticians never elucidate relations between such data, since this is a task of data mining. This type of method may be used either in order to help other professionals to make appropriate decision or to make such decisions even without experts. Use of data mining techniques without human influence is often exempted from certain errors. For instance, a scout may especially appreciate certain qualities in a player, neglecting some flaws. Most of sports organizations use the third or fourth type of approach, somewhere in between data and their use, and only a small number of them use data mining techniques. Although data mining was relatively recently introduced in sport, results of teams who apply these methods are outstanding [30]. Estimations are being done using strong analysis and scientific investigations. Rising number of sports organizations embrace the digital era, and it is possible that sport will soon became a battle of better algorithms or better metrics for performances measurement, so analysts will be equally important as players.

Applying statistics in decision-making process is certainly a step forward in comparison to decisions based on hunch, but statistics may also sway decisions to wrong direction, if there is no knowledge regarding base of a problem. This may happen because of imprecise measurements of performances of due to over-enhancement of certain quality by sports community [31]. For example, certain player may have extraordinary individual statistics, bit he or she still may have only a minor influence on the team as a whole. Sports statistics suffers from imprecision, since statistical metrics may not measure completely influence of all players. For instance, defensive rebound is a measure how many times certain player in defense caught a ball after unsuccessful shot by opponent players. In order to have a defensive rebound, other player from his team must block opponent players and therefore they are equally important in this action. Having in mind the way of noting rebounds, only the player who caught the ball is noted in statistics and rewarded a defensive rebound.

Besides imprecision and incorrect use, another problem in sports statistics is how to determine a risk value. Defense player may risk by sliding in order to intercept the ball. It may result in his fall out of the game so opponent team may have an extra man and score easily. However, if the player succeeds in intercepting the ball, this is a big plus for his team since they obtain a new attack.

4.1. Effect of shot percentage on winning

Basketball is a competitive game between two teams with the aim to win. A win is accomplished by scoring more points than the other team. Sometimes, coaches like to claim that the aim is to receive less points than the opponent does, so the game is won by defense actions. In both cases, the winner is decided by the number of points scored by shots.

Shots may be scored in several ways, and therefore are bringing different points. The hardest to achieve are long-distance shots, so they bring the most points. There is a line drawn on the floor at 6.25 meters from the basket, and shots from outside this line bring three points (in some leagues this border line is drawn even further from the basket in order to be more difficult to score, and therefore make the game more interesting to the spectators). If attempted from inside of this line, every succesful shot brings two points. During a game, sometimes a player is irregularly interrupted by rival players, and this is called a foul. If the foul is done during an attempt to score, or if the team committing the foul have already surpassed the limit (four fouls committed during one period, or quarter), then fouled player gets a chance to score from the free-throw line. Every shot scored from this line brings one point. Depending on whether a foul was committed while a player was trying to score for two or three points, he or she will have opportunity to try two or three free throws, respectively. [32]

When shooting for two points, three points and when throwing free throws, a player may make the shot or miss the shot, i.e. score or miss, respectively.The ratio between shots and scores is called shooting percentage. In basketball statistics, there are separate percents for one-, two and three point shots

The aim of this paper is to measure effect on shooting percentage from different position on outcome of the game, in order to establish at which position it is most important to be precise.

4.1.1. Data understanding phase

In keeping statistics for the Serbian First "B" basketball league for men, Basketball Supervisor (BSV) software is used. This program allows noting all data relevant for a basketball game. At the end of each quarter, statistics collected by this program is printed and distributed to home and visiting players, commissioner, TV crew (if it is covered live) and journalists covering the game. After the game, all collected data are being sent to the Basketball Federation of Serbia where, they are stored for further analysis.

In this paper we analyzed statistics collected at all the games of the Serbian First "B" Basketball league for men for 2006/07, 2007/08, 2008/09, 2009/10 and 2010/11 seasons. Databases used for storing data are named yubadata_0607, yubadata_0708, yubadata_0809, yubadata_0910 and yubadata_1011.

The database is organized in such way that shooting data are entered to a table *utstat*. Appearance of this table is given at the Figure 3. It comprises of a large number of various parameters, and for us the following are of interest:

- ID_GAME – identification of the game being observed
- ID_CLUB – identification of the club
- ID_PLAYER – identification of the player for which statistics is entered
- P1OK – successfully realized one-point shots for the observed player
- P1SUM – total number of one-point shots for the observed player
- P21OK – successfully realized two-point shots from position one for the observed player
- P21SUM – total number of two-point shots from position one for the observed player
- P22OK – successfully realized two-point shots from position two for the observed player
- P22 SUM - total number of two-point shots from position two for the observed player
- P23OK - successfully realized two-point shots from position three for the observed player

- P23 SUM - total number of two-point shots from position three for the observed player
- P24OK - successfully realized two-point shots from position four for the observed player
- P24 SUM - total number of two-point shots from position four for the observed player
- P25OK - successfully realized two-point shots from position five for the observed player
- P25 SUM - total number of two-point shots from position five for the observed player
- P26OK - successfully realized two-point shots from position six for the observed player
- P26 SUM - total number of two-point shots from position six for the observed player
- P31OK - successfully realized three-point shots from position one for the observed player
- P31 SUM - total number of three-point shots from position one for the observed player
- P32OK - successfully realized three-point shots from position two for the observed player
- P32 SUM - total number of three-point shots from position two for the observed player
- P33OK - successfully realized three-point shots from position three for the observed player
- P33 SUM - total number of three-point shots from position three for the observed player
- P34OK - successfully realized three-point shots from position four for the observed player
- P34 SUM - total number of three-point shots from position four for the observed player
- P36OK - successfully realized three-point shots from position six for the observed player
- P36 SUM - total number of three-point shots from position six for the observed player

This table comprises all data regarding a shot. It does not comprise a final result of the game, i.e. who won. These data are given in table *game*. Parameters of interest in this table are:

- ID_GAME – identification of the game observed
- ID_CLUB1 – identification of the host club
- ID_CLUB2 – identification of the guest club
- SCORE_HOME – number of points scored by the host club
- SCORE_AWAY– number of points scored by the guest club

4.1.2. Data preparation phase

Data in a base are connected to particular players. Within analysis in this paper, we intend to compare the effect of shot precision for one, two and three points on win of observed team. Therefore, it is necessary to sum data regarding players, and to obtain data for a team as a whole.

Before summing up, we will merge tables *GAMESTAT* and *GAME*. This will be done using attribute *ID_GAME* so in every observed line we will have not only existing data, but also data regarding a result.

UTSTAT	
PK	**ID_STAT**
	ID_UTAKMICA
	ID_KLUB
	ID_IGRAC
	DRES
	P1OK
	P1UK
	P21OK
	P21UK
	P22OK
	P22UK
	P23OK
	P23UK
	P24OK
	P24UK
	P25OK
	P25UK
	P26OK
	P26UK
	P31OK
	P31UK
	P32OK
	P32UK
	P33OK
	P33UK
	P34OK
	P34UK
	P36OK
	P36UK
	SKOKO
	SKOKN
	ASISTENCIJA
	UKRADENA
	IZG1
	IZG2
	IZG3
	IZG4
	IZG5
	BLOK
	BLOKNA
	LG
	TG
	LGNA
	MINUTA

Figure 3. Appearance of the *utstat table*

UTAKMICA	
PK	**ID_UTAKMICA**
	NAZIV
	ID_LIGA
	ID_KLUB1
	ID_KLUB2
	ID_TRENER1
	ID_TRENER2
	ID_DELEGAT
	ID_SUDIJA1
	ID_SUDIJA2
	ID_STAT1
	ID_STAT2
	KOLO
	GRAD
	MESTO
	DATUMVREME
	BR_GLEDALACA
	REZDOM
	REZGOSTI
	STAT
	TVPRENOS
	PLAYOFF
	ID_SUDIJA3

Figure 4. Appearance of the *game* table

Since we are interested in shot percent from certain positions, after summing up data for those positions we will divide values for successful shot from the position to values for total number of shots.

Appearance of a SQL command for selecting appropriate data is as follows:

select

        sum(p1ok)/sum(p1uk) p1_procenat,

        (sum(p21ok)+sum(p22ok)+sum(p23ok)+sum(p24ok)+sum(p25ok)+sum(p26ok))/

        (sum(p21uk)+sum(p22uk)+sum(p23uk)+sum(p24uk)+sum(p25uk)+sum(p26uk))

p2_procenat,

        (sum(p31ok)+sum(p32ok)+sum(p33ok)+sum(p34ok)+sum(p36ok))/

               (sum(p31uk)+sum(p32uk)+sum(p33uk)+sum(p34uk)+sum(p36uk))

p3_procenat,

        if(id_klub1=id_klub,

```
                    if(rezdom > rezgosti, 'pobeda', 'poraz'),
                    if(rezdom < rezgosti, 'pobeda', 'poraz')) rezultat
from yubadata_0506.utakmica ut, yubadata_0506.utstat st
where ut.id_utakmica = st.id_utakmica
group by ut.id_utakmica, st.id_klub
union
select
        sum(p1ok)/sum(p1uk) p1_procenat,
        (sum(p21ok)+sum(p22ok)+sum(p23ok)+sum(p24ok)+sum(p25ok)+sum(p26ok))/

        (sum(p21uk)+sum(p22uk)+sum(p23uk)+sum(p24uk)+sum(p25uk)+sum(p26uk))
p2_procenat,
        (sum(p31ok)+sum(p32ok)+sum(p33ok)+sum(p34ok)+sum(p36ok))/
                (sum(p31uk)+sum(p32uk)+sum(p33uk)+sum(p34uk)+sum(p36uk))
p3_procenat,
        if(id_klub1=id_klub,
                if(rezdom > rezgosti, 'pobeda', 'poraz'),
                if(rezdom < rezgosti, 'pobeda', 'poraz')) rezultat
from yubadata_0607.utakmica ut, yubadata_0607.utstat st
where ut.id_utakmica = st.id_utakmica
group by ut.id_utakmica, st.id_klub
union
select
        sum(p1ok)/sum(p1uk) p1_procenat,
        (sum(p21ok)+sum(p22ok)+sum(p23ok)+sum(p24ok)+sum(p25ok)+sum(p26ok))/

        (sum(p21uk)+sum(p22uk)+sum(p23uk)+sum(p24uk)+sum(p25uk)+sum(p26uk))
p2_procenat,
        (sum(p31ok)+sum(p32ok)+sum(p33ok)+sum(p34ok)+sum(p36ok))/
                (sum(p31uk)+sum(p32uk)+sum(p33uk)+sum(p34uk)+sum(p36uk))
p3_procenat,
        if(id_klub1=id_klub,
                if(rezdom > rezgosti, 'pobeda', 'poraz'),
                if(rezdom < rezgosti, 'pobeda', 'poraz')) rezultat
from yubadata_0708.utakmica ut, yubadata_0708.utstat st
where ut.id_utakmica = st.id_utakmica
group by ut.id_utakmica, st.id_klub
union
select
        sum(p1ok)/sum(p1uk) p1_procenat,
        (sum(p21ok)+sum(p22ok)+sum(p23ok)+sum(p24ok)+sum(p25ok)+sum(p26ok))/
        (sum(p21uk)+sum(p22uk)+sum(p23uk)+sum(p24uk)+sum(p25uk)+sum(p26uk))
p2_procenat,
```

```
        (sum(p31ok)+sum(p32ok)+sum(p33ok)+sum(p34ok)+sum(p36ok))/
                (sum(p31uk)+sum(p32uk)+sum(p33uk)+sum(p34uk)+sum(p36uk))
p3_procenat,
        if(id_klub1=id_klub,
                if(rezdom > rezgosti, 'pobeda', 'poraz'),
                if(rezdom < rezgosti, 'pobeda', 'poraz')) rezultat
from yubadata_0809.utakmica ut, yubadata_0809.utstat st
where ut.id_utakmica = st.id_utakmica
group by ut.id_utakmica, st.id_klub
union
select
        sum(p1ok)/sum(p1uk) p1_procenat,
        (sum(p21ok)+sum(p22ok)+sum(p23ok)+sum(p24ok)+sum(p25ok)+sum(p26ok))/

        (sum(p21uk)+sum(p22uk)+sum(p23uk)+sum(p24uk)+sum(p25uk)+sum(p26uk))
p2_procenat,
        (sum(p31ok)+sum(p32ok)+sum(p33ok)+sum(p34ok)+sum(p36ok))/
                (sum(p31uk)+sum(p32uk)+sum(p33uk)+sum(p34uk)+sum(p36uk))
p3_procenat,
        if(id_klub1=id_klub,
                if(rezdom > rezgosti, 'pobeda', 'poraz'),
                if(rezdom < rezgosti, 'pobeda', 'poraz')) rezultat
from yubadata_0910.utakmica ut, yubadata_0910.utstat st
where ut.id_utakmica = st.id_utakmica
group by ut.id_utakmica, st.id_klub;
```

By execution of inquiry, we obtain following data: one-point shot percentage, two-point shot percentage, three-point shot percentage and information whether the team has won or lost the game, in all games in five competition seasons. A part of data obtained is shown in Table 1:

p1_percent	p2_percent	p3_percent	result
0.5652	0.5789	0.3636	'win'
0.7273	0.3556	0.4211	'loss'
0.6500	0.5517	0.2083	'win'
0.6200	0.4722	0.3333	'loss'
0.7368	0.5641	0.5333	'loss'
0.7368	0.7632	0.5882	'win'
...	...	...	...

Table 1. Example of modeling data

Total of 1920 lines is obtained. This means that during five seasons, 960 games were played (1920 / 2 = 960), since for every game table contains data for home and guest team.

Following graphs represent analysis of statistic parameters in the First "B" Basketball league of Serbia for men. In this league, 130 games are played per year, including play off and play out. At every histogram, color blue is a number of losses by teams from competition observed. Red color shows number of wins by those teams.

Graph 1. shows effect of one-point shot on final outcome of the game. It is visible that number of wins abruptly rises when one point shot percent exceeds 65% limit. Since number of wins and losses is approximately linear, regardless of the percent, it may be supposed that one-point shot is not crucial for outcome of the game. If one-point shot percent is below 65%, teams in most cases lose that game.

Statistical minimum for one-point shot percent is 25%, and statistical maximum is 96.2%. Average value for this type of shot, regarding all games in this league, is 71.4%. Standard deviation is 0.11.

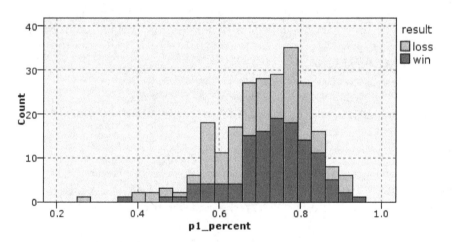

Scheme 1. Effect of one-point shot percent on final outcome of the game

Graph 2 shows effect of two-point shots on final outcome of the game. Blue color is a number of losses by teams from competition observed. Red color shows number of wins by those teams. Graph shows that number of wins rises when a two-point shot percent is above 58%. Therefore, we may conclude that a two-point shot gas significant effect on outcome of a game. If two-point shot percent is below 58 %, number of losses is higher.

Statistical minimum for two-point shot percent is 39.5%, and statistical maximum is 83%. Average value for this type of shot, regarding all games in this league, is 58.2%. Standard deviation is 0.083. Two-point shot percent has higher minimum and lower maximum than one-point shot percent, because during a game shots for two points prevail.

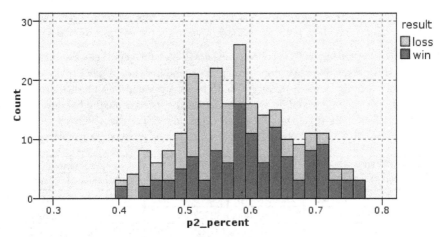

Scheme 2. Effect of two-point shot percent on final outcome of the game

Graph 3 shows effect of three-point shots on final outcome of the game. Blue color in histogram is a number of losses by teams from competition observed. Red color shows number of wins by those teams. Graph shows that number of wins rises when a three-point shot percent is above 38%. If a team has three-point shot percent close to 80%, it will win all games. If this percent is above 59%, the team rarely loses a game. Three-point shot percent between 30 and 59% has less effect on the final outcome of a game, since number of wins and losses is approximately equal. If a three-point shot is below 30%, team loses a game more often. Therefore, we may conclude that a three-point shot percent has significant effect on outcome of a game.

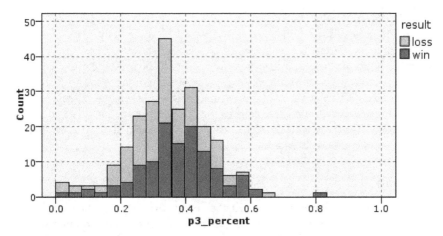

Scheme 3. Effect of three-point shot percent on final outcome of the game

Statistical minimum for three-point shot percent is 0%, when a team does not score three-point shots at all and statistical maximum is 83%. Average value for this type of shot, regarding all games in this league, is 34.9%. Standard deviation is 0.349 Three-point shot has more extreme values than two-point shot due to lower number of shots during a game.

When data about opponent team are collected, they will pass through three filters and get color and clarity during analyzing, selection, presentation and practicing game plan against this opponent. Every activity done in training should be incorporated into the overall game plan and in purpose of the game. Scouting system must also be incorporated in the demands of the game, and must be highly organized. When scouting, individual characteristics and habits of players from the database collected during the previous season must be taken into account.

1p season 2006/07				2p season 2006/07				3p season 2006/07			
Min %	Max %	MEAN	S.DEV	Min %	Max %	MEAN	S.DEV	Min %	Max %	MEAN	S.DEV
24.00	95.20	0.814	0.121	38.50	74.40	0.516	0.071	0.00	85.30	0.311	0.125
1p season 2007/08				2p season 2007/08				3p season 2007/08			
Min %	Max %	MEAN	S.DEV	Min %	Max %	MEAN	S.DEV	Min %	Max %	MEAN	S.DEV
0.00	94.10	0.561	0.127	27.10	81.2	0.581	0.101	0.00	74.00	0.290	0.156
1p season 2008/09				2p season 2008/09				3p season 2008/09			
Min %	Max %	MEAN	S.DEV	Min %	Max %	MEAN	S.DEV	Min %	Max %	MEAN	S.DEV
24.99	95.80	0.712	0.119	38.50	76.40	0.581	0.081	0.00	81.10	0.399	0.124
1p season 2009/10				2p season 2009/10				3p season 2009/10			
Min %	Max %	MEAN	S.DEV	Min %	Max %	MEAN	S.DEV	Min %	Max %	MEAN	S.DEV
23.01	91.21	0.735	0.123	39.50	73.40	0.216	0.091	0.00	82.10	0.411	0.129
1p season 20010/11				2p season 20010/11				3p season 20010/11			
Min %	Max %	MEAN	S.DEV	Min %	Max %	MEAN	S.DEV	Min %	Max %	MEAN	S.DEV
0.00	94.10	0.561	0.127	27.10	81.2	0.581	0.101	0.00	74.00	0.290	0.156

Table 2. Comparative review of one-, two- and three-point shots

Table 2. shows comparative review of one-, two- and three-point shots for First "B" Basketball league of Serbia for men in all 5 seasons observed. For the coach, these parameters are of utmost importance, especially one-point shots. At the every pause during a training, coaches ask players to practice one-point shots in order to improve this segment of the game. Table also shows that in a number of games there were no successful three-point shots, so this segment of a game calls for further improvements. It is also visible that teams were best at free throws in 2008-2009 seasons, at two-point shots in 2007-2008 season, at three-point shots in 2006-2007 season.

5. Conclusion

Basketball game is progressing rapidly. Number of quality players and teams is quickly growing. At high levels of competition, there are no teams that can count on a safe win for every game. Good preparation for the game may mean the difference between the average and best results. Scouting opponents is an important and indispensable element in these preparations. Scouting targets are not only players or team game, but also coaches, who usually have consistent approach to the game (coach philosophy). Use of data mining techniques provides knowledge about individual qualities of players and their habits, in both offence and defense, so it is easier to predict where advantages of problems will occur in individual offence or defense situations. Having this in mind, a coach may pay more or less attention to certain segment of a game, reducing the number of information and allowing all players of the team the clear and identical idea how to play that game. When number of misunderstandings decrease, power of team play rises.

As a general conclusion of all analyses, it could be said that game under the hoop is a key to winning a game. In defense, it is very important to catch a ball after opponents shot and prevent them from another attack, while in offence it is important to maintain a high level of two-point shots and not to miss "safe shots".

Data collected are applicable for Basketball league of Serbia for men, and such a model may be applied to other leagues of similar quality. It is to be expected that higher-quality leagues (NBA) or those for younger players (juniors or cadets) would create somewhat different models.

Author details

Branko Markoski, Zdravko Ivankovic and Miodrag Ivkovic
University of Novi Sad, Technical Faculty "Mihajlo Pupin", Zrenjanin, Serbia

Acknowledgement

This work was partially supported by the Serbian Ministry of Education and Sciences (Grant No: 171039).

6. References

[1] FIBA - Official Basketball Rules. (2011)
[2] Markoski, B., Radosav, D., Vasiljević, P. Milošević, Z.: Košarkaška statistika,. International Conference Dependability and Quality Management ICDQM 2009, Belgrade, Serbia, 776—781 (2009)
[3] Markoski, B., Adžić, Đ.: Razlike u vođenju statistike. Trener X, broj 42, Serbia, 24-27 (2006)
[4] Markoski, B., Adžić, Đ.: Statistika - neki problemi u praksi. Trener XI, broj 46-47, Serbia, 24-28 (2007)
[5] Oliver, D.: Basketball on paper - Rules and tools for performance analysis. Washington DC (2004)
[6] Vasiljević P., Markoski B., Ivanković Z., Ivković M., Šetrajčić J., Milošević Z. "Basket Supervisor - collecting statistical data in basketball and net casting", Technics Technologies education management, Vol.6-2011, 169-178, TTEM, ISSN 1840-1503
[7] Trninić, S.: *Analiza i učenje košarkaške igre.* (1996)
[8] B. Markoski, M. Ivković, P. Vasiljević, P. Pecev, Z. Milošević, "Collecting statistical data in basketball", Information and Communication Technologies for Small and Medium Enterprises, ICT-SME's 2011, Aranđelovac, Republic of Serbia, 2011

[9] José Manuel Sánchez Santos, Ana Belen Porto Pazos, Alejandro Pazos Sierra, "Team Performance in Professional Basketball: an Approach Based on Neural Networks and Genetic Programming", XIII IASE and III ESEA Conference of Sports, Prague, May 2011.

[10] B. Markoski, P. Pecev, L. Ratberg, M. Ivković, Z. Ivanković, "Appliance of Neural Networks in Basketball - Basketball board for Basketball Referees, CINTI 2011 - 12th IEEE International Symposium on Computational Intelligence and Informatics, Budapest, Hungary, 2011, pp 133 – 137.

[11] Bernard Loeffelholz, Earl Bednar, Kenneth W. Bauer "Predicting NBA Games Using Neural Networks", Journal of Quantitative Analysis in Sports: Vol. 5, Issue 1, Article 7, 2009.

[12] Michael E. Young, "Nonlinear Judgment Analysis: Comparing Policy Use by Those Who Draft and Those Who Coach", Psychology of Sport and Exercise, Volume 9, Number 6, November 2008.

[13] Ratgeber, L. Play from a Game: (Head Coach). Mizo Pecs 2010. 2007/2008. Mizo Pecs 2010 vs. Euroleasing Sopron.

[14] FIBA - Official Basketball Rules. (2012)

[15] Markoski B., Ivetić D., Šetrajčić J., Mirjanić D., Ivanković Z., "Košarkaški scauting", Infoteh Jahorina BIH, Volume 8, ref. E - III - 24, P. 628-630 mart 2009

[16] Markoski B., Ivanković Z., Ivković M., Ivković F., Nikolić M., Berković I. "Application of on line transmission in basketball", International symposium ZEMAK 2010, FYROM Macedonia,

[17] Bhandari, I., E. Colet, et al. 1997. Advanced Scout: Data Mining and Knowledge Discovery in NBA Data. *Data Mining and Knowledge Discovery* 1(1): 121-125

[18] David Hand, Heikki Mannila, and Padhraic Smyth, *Principles of Data Mining*, MIT Press, Cambridge, MA, 2001

[19] Peter Cabena, Pablo Hadjinian, Rolf Stadler, JaapVerhees, and Alessandro Zanasi, *Discovering Data Mining: From Concept to Implementation*, Prentice Hall, Upper Saddle River, NJ, 1998

[20] Reed, R.D., and Marks, R.J, II (1999), Neural Smithing: Supervised Learning in Feedforward Artificial Neural Networks, Cambridge, MA: The MIT Press.

[21] Quinlan, J. Ross (1992) *C4.5 Programs for Machine Learning* Morgan Kaufman Publishers Inc.

[22] Fitzgerald, R., Blackall, L., Lyons, K., & Neill, J. (2011). eResearch in .... Data. *Data Mining* and Knowledge Discovery (2005). Ausport, September, 20.

[23] O'Reilly, N. & P. Knight 2007. Knowledge Management Best Practices in National Sport Organizations. *International Journal of Sport Management and Marketing* 2(3): 264-280

[24] Markoski B., Ivanković Z., Šetrajčić J., Vasiljević P., Milićević V., "Razmena on-line podataka upotrebom Web Servisa", Zbornik radova konferencije Informacione tehologije i razvoj tehničkog informatičkog obrazovanja", Zrenjanin 2009, Serbia, 158-162

[25] Peter Cabena, Pablo Hadjinian, Rolf Stadler, JaapVerhees, and Alessandro Zanasi, *Discovering Data Mining: From Concept to Implementation*, Prentice Hall, Upper Saddle River, NJ, 1998

[26] Stefani, R. 1999. "A Taxonomy of Sports Rating Systems", *IEEE Transactions on Systems, Man, and Cybernetics - Part A* 29(1): 116-120.

[27] Branko Markoski, Predrag Pecev, Laszlo Ratgeber, Miodrag Ivković, Zdravko Ivanković, "A new approach to decision making in basketball – BBFBR program", Acta Polytechnica Hungarica Vol. 8, No. 6, 2011

A Generic Scaffold Housing the Innovative Modus Operandi for Selection of the Superlative Anonymisation Technique for Optimized Privacy Preserving Data Mining

J. Indumathi

Additional information is available at the end of the chapter

1. Introduction

The genesis of novel data mining techniques has given an impetus to the privacy risks which has kept growing leaps and bounds. This is unquestionably plausible, owing to the probability fact to strappingly coalesce and interrogate gigantic data stores accessible on the web, in the midst of fumble of prior mysterious out of sight patterns. Privacy issues also augment its convolution because of new upcoming technologies; which are linking enormous number of reciprocally strange and erratic people, to make a worldwide economy. This scenario is of serious apprehension challenging consideration. This state of situation is like a life dealing with lemons. As learned folks we have to make lemonade, from the lemons necessitating this research, where the outcome is a generic scaffold.

The principal stipulation wished-for privacy is a high-quality data fortification modus operandi known as data mystification techniques. The importance of Privacy Preserving Data Mining (PPDM) down to the core is hackneyed not only from its ostentation to heave out crucial knowledge, but also from its resistance to assault*PPDM is a discipline whose desire is to authorize delivery transmits of respondent data while preserving respondent privacy.*It introduces solutions to problems where the question is how to get hold of data mining results without violating privacy.

In the proposition of novel solutions there are two vital things to be highlighted. The first one is *Privacy* of users and personal data within strenuous environments and implicit communities. The second one is *Information Security* as it relates to privacy and the information resources provided in the same environments. This chapter aspires to contribute to the solution of a specific problem, namely, the problem of sharing sensitive data. Developing new, improvising existing algorithms and techniques for PPDM is endeavored.

1.1. Motivation

In the midst of the implausible detonation of data garnering, data dissemination, internet technologies and the manifestation of susceptible applications, security issues in knowledge discovery have reached the pinnacle. The chic data analysis and mining techniques have produced a sharp awareness of their potential, compromising privacy, and has posed challenges of controlling data access in accordance with privacy policies. The escalating exploitation done by them have reached the zenith, and have surfaced as a central and ubiquitous problem. To safeguard knowledge and wisdom, which, is pre-eminence as can be seen in figure 1, but as humble users of the most modern technologies we are pitted with possessions that may even make us paranoidconcerning usage of a computer. This chapter will bring to the surface, the modus operandi needed to shield privacy.

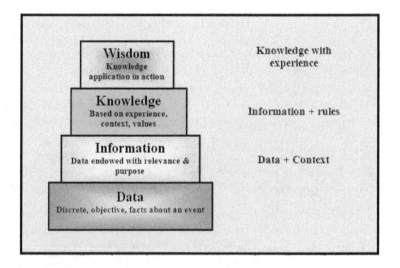

Figure 1. Data Pyramid

The objective of Privacy-Preserving Data Mining(PPDM)as can be seen in figure 2, is to release a privacy preserved dataset which will spot and protect the sensitive information in the data (with high probability),so that researchers can study the data without compromising privacy of any individual. The task of PPDM force's a central thrust on establishing a world with robust data security, where knowledge users persist to profit from data without compromising the data privacy (Indumathi, J. et al.,(2007a))

A Generic Scaffold Housing the Innovative Modus Operandi
for Selection of the Superlative Anonymisation Technique for Optimized Privacy Preserving Data Mining

135

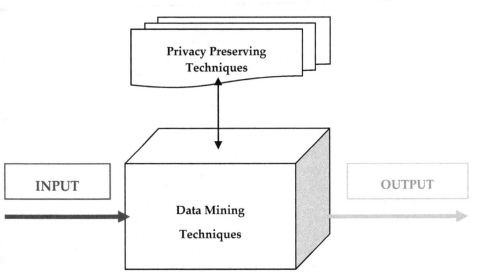

Figure 2. A Framework for Privacy Preserving Data Mining Systems: High-Level

PPDM like data mining is an interdisciplinary field, as can be seen in figure 1.3,involving the confluence of a set of disciplines, including database technology, statistics, machine learning, visualization, and information science etc., Not only that it is also divided based on the data mining approaches used, the kinds of data to be mined or on the given data mining application, the data mining system may also integrate techniques from spatial data analysis, image analysis, signal processing, computer graphics, economics, business, bioinformatics, or psychology etc.,

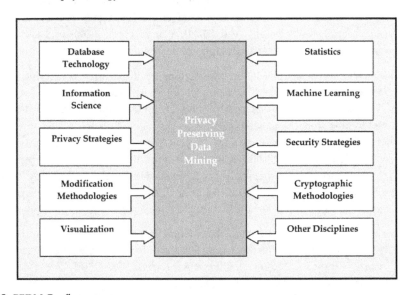

Figure 3. PPDM Confluences

2. Literature survey

This part deals with a meticulous survey bringing to limelight scores of works on the various existing privacy preserving techniques, their advantages and deficiencies. The majority techniques for privacy computation use some form of transformation on the data in order to perform the privacy preservation. Characteristically, such methods decrease the granularity of representation or limit access to resources in order to reduce the privacy. This dwindling in granularity results in some trouncing of efficacy of data mining algorithms. This is the normal trade-off between information loss and privacy. Researchers developed methods to enable data mining techniques to be applied while preserving the privacy of individuals. Though several approaches have been proposed for privacy preserving data mining, at this point we would like the reader to read Verykios et al (2004 b), Mohammad Reza Keyvanpour et al.,(2011) for a quick overview. Verykios et al (2004 b) gives a detailed survey on some of the techniques used for PPDM. Mohammad Reza Keyvanpour et al.,(2011) proposed a classification based on three common approaches of Privacy Preserving data mining, namely, Data modification approach, Data sanitization approach and Secure Multi-party Computation approach.

Atallah et al. (1999)considered the problem of limiting disclosure of sensitive rules[Statistical Disclosure Control(SDC)], aiming at selectively hiding some frequent itemsets from large databases with as little impact on other, nonsensitive frequent itemsets as possible. Specifically, the authors dealt with the problem of modifying a given database so that the support of a given set of sensitive rules, mined from the database, decreases below the minimum support value.

Most data mining techniques, i.e. association rule mining and classification, are well studied by followers of both approaches. Agarwal et al.,(2000) and Vassilios et al.,(2004) for data sanitization techniques; Kantarcioglu et al.,(2004), Vaidya et al.,(2002) and Du, W., Zhan (2002) are based on secure multi-party computation techniques.

Jian Yin et al.,(2005), proposed model-based solutions for the privacy preserving clustering problem. Data holder parties build local models of their data that is subject to privacy constraints. Then a third party builds a global model from these local models and cluster the data generated by this global model. All of these works follow the sanitization approach and therefore trade-off accuracy versus privacy. Except Jian Yin et al.(2005), none of them address privacy preserving clustering on horizontally partitioned data. Privacy preserving techniques for clustering over vertically partitioned data was proposed by Vaidya et al.(2002) . Ali Inan et al.,(2006) and Oliveira et al.,(2004) mainly concentrate on finding object based dissimilarity for privacy preservation.

Having thoroughly investigated the available diverse techniques for privacy preservation, we find that *the level of Privacy Preservation involved is* only *of* a single level. *Even the newly proposed Privacy Preservation techniques*([i.e., A comparative study on the various cryptographic methods for future work(Vasudevan.V et al. 2007); the flustering *technique*(Indumathi.J et al.2007c)] was implemented and evaluated on our own conceptual frameworks(Indumathi.J et al. 2007a,b, Gitanjali.J et al. 2007, Indumathi.J et al. 2008a,b) *to prove their efficiency. They are also of single level ones. The framework* was used to compare and contrast each and every one of the techniques in a general podium which will be the basis for ascertaining the suitable technique for a given type of application of privacy preserving shared filtering. Nonetheless, there are situations where the sharing of data can lead to general gain as in the case of privacy preserving secure accord as mentioned (Indumathi.J et al.,2007b).

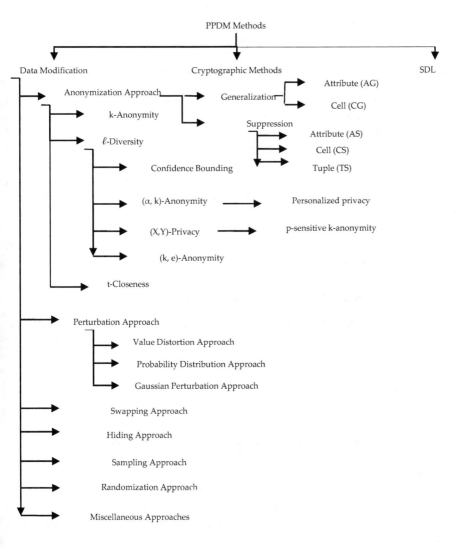

Figure 4. Proposed PPDM Taxonomy

3. Proposed taxonomy

In spite of the different categorizations available for PPDM, we propose a new taxonomy based on the procedures involved as shown in figure 4. Our earlier proposed taxonomy for PPDM (Indumathi.J et al. 2007c) is further subdivided into perturbation-based, swapping-based, hiding -based, sampling -based, randomization -based, anonymization-based techniques etc.,

PPDM Methods are broadly categorized into Data Modification based methods, cryptographic based methods; Statistical Disclosure Limitation (SDL) based methods. The data modification methods are further subdivided into perturbation-based, swapping based, hiding -based, sampling -based, randomization -based, anonymization-based techniques etc., (Indumathi.J et al. 2007c). We will pin down onto the anonymization-based techniques.

3.1. Significance of study for anonymisation based technique

Anonymity is a derived from the Greek word α 'νωνυμ'ια, *anonymia*, which means "without a name" or "namelessness". In conversational use, anonymous typically refers to a person, and often means that the personal identity, or personal identifiable information of the given person is unidentified. Anonymityis frequently observed as the *superlative way to protect individual privacy in the biomedical background*. For instance, numerous cases in biomedical law prove that anonymity can serve as a warranty for self-sacrifice. It is also seen as a protection against scientific and other biases in research. Contributing an organ donation/blood to an identified person and to receive an organ donation/blood from an identified person creates a special and complicated interpersonal relationship between the donor and the recipient. Amongst the various techniques the identities of the donor and recipient are hidden through anonymisation.

3.2. Sub-classification of anonymisation based technique

Anonymization is a process that confiscates identity information from a communication or record by making it pseudonymous, in which case the same subject will always have the same replacement identity but cannot be identified as an individual.

3.2.1. Generalization & suppression

3.2.1.1. Generalization

Generalization consists of replacing with attribute values with semantically consistent but less precise values. For example, the place of birth can be replaced by the country of birth which occurs in more records so that the identification of a specific individual is more difficult. Generalization maintains the correctness of the data at the record level but results in less specific information that may affect the accuracy of machine learning algorithms applied on the k-anonymous data set. Different systems use various methods for selecting the attributes and records for generalization as well as the generalization technique [Friedman.A,et al.,(2008)].

Generalization can be applied at the following levels:

- **Attribute (A_G):** In this sub-type, generalization is executed at the level of column; a generalization step generalizes all the values in the column.
- **Cell (C_G):** In this sub-type, generalization is executed on single cells; as a result a generalized table may contain, for a specific column, values at different generalization levels. For instance, in the date of birth column.

3.2.1.2. Suppression

Suppression refers to removing a certain attribute value and replacing occurrences of the value with a special Value?, indicating that any value can be placed instead. Suppression can drastically reduce the quality of the data if not properly used [S.V. Iyengar(2002)].

Suppression can be applied at the following levels

- **Tuple (T_S):** In this sub-type, suppression is executed at the level of row; a suppression operation removes a whole tuple.
- **Attribute (A_S):** In this sub-type, suppression is executed at the level of column; a suppression operation obscures all the values of the column.
- **Cell (C_S):** In this sub-type, suppression is executed at the level of single cells; as a result a k-anonymized table may wipe out only certain cells of a given tuple/attribute.

3.2.2. K-anonymity technique

In this technique each record within an anonymized table must be indistinguishable with at least k-1 other record within the dataset, with respect to a set of QI attributes or if one record in the table has some QID, at least k-1 other record also have the value QID. QID should have at least k minimum group size value. In particular, a table is K-anonymous if the QI attributes values of each record are identical to those of at least k-1 other records. To achieve the K-anonymity requirement, generalization or suppression could be used [P. Samarati et al.,(1998), L. Sweeney(2002)].

Advantages

- Individual record hidden in a crowd of size k

Disadvantages

- Identifying a proper QID is a hard problem.
- Finding a k-anonymity solution with suppressing fewest cells

Attacks

- Homogeneity and background knowledge attack.
- Record linkage.

3.2.3. ℓ-diversity

An equivalence class is said to have ℓ-diversity if there are at least one "well-represented" values for the sensitive attribute. i.e., ℓ-diversity requires every QID group to contain at least one "well represented" sensitive values.ℓ-Diversity provides privacy preserving even when the data publisher does not know what kind of knowledge is possessed by the adversary.

The main idea of ℓ-diversity is the requirement that the values of the sensitive attributes are well-represented in each group. The k-anonymity algorithms can be adapted to compute ℓ-diverse tables [A.Machanavajjhala et al,(2006)]. ℓ-Diversity resolved the shortcoming of k-anonymity model.

Advantages

• It prevents homogeneity and background knowledge attack.

Disadvantages

• ℓ-diversity may be difficult and unnecessary to achieve.
• ℓ-diversity is insufficient to prevent attribute disclosure (i.e., it tends to skewness and similarity attack).
• Distinct ℓ-diversity does not prevent probabilistic attack.

3.2.3.1. Confidence bounding

Wang et al. [2005, 2007] considered bounding the confidence of inferring a sensitive value from a QID group by specifying one or more *privacy templates* of the form, $QID \rightarrow s$, h_; s is a sensitive value, QID is a quasi-identifier, and h is a threshold.

Advantages

• It allows the flexibility for the data publisher to specify a different threshold h for each combination of QID and s according to the perceived sensitivity of inferring s from a group on QID

Disadvantages

• It does not prevent attribute linkage attack.

3.2.3.2. (α, k)-Anonymity

Wong et al. [2006] proposed a similar integrated privacy model, called (α, k)-*anonymity*, requiring every QID in a Table T to be shared by at least k records and $conf\,(QID \rightarrow s) \leq \alpha$ for any sensitive value s, where k and α are data publisher-specified thresholds. Nonetheless, both (X,Y)-Privacy and (α, k)-anonymity may result in high distortion if the sensitive values are skewed.

3.2.3.3. (X,Y)-Privacy

(X,Y)-anonymity states that each group on X has at least k distinct values on Y (e.g., diseases). However, if some Y values occur more frequently than others, the probability of inferring a particular Y value can be higher than $1/k$. To address this issue, Wang and Fung [2006] proposed a general privacy model, called (X,Y)-Privacy, which combines both (X,Y)-

anonymity and confidence bounding. The general idea is to require each group x on X to contain at least k records and $conf (x \rightarrow y) \leq h$ for any $y \in Y$, where Y is a set of selected sensitive values and h is a maximum confidence threshold.

3.2.3.4. (k, e)-Anonymity

Most work on k-anonymity and its extensions assumes categorical sensitive attributes. Zhang et al. [2007] proposed the notion of (k, e)-anonymity to address numerical sensitive attributes such as salary. The general idea is to partition the records into groups so that each group contains at least k different sensitive values with a range of at least e. However, (k, e)-anonymity ignores the distribution of sensitive values within the range λ.

3.2.4. t-Closeness

An equivalence class is said to have t-closeness if the distance between the distribution of a sensitive attribute in this class and the distribution of the attribute in the whole table is no more than a threshold t. ℓ-diversity principle represents an important step beyond k-anonymity in protecting against attribute disclosure. However, it has several shortcomings, such as ℓ-diversity may be difficult and unnecessary to achieve and it is insufficient to prevent attribute disclosure. N. Li et al.,(2007) proposes a new privacy measure is called t-Closeness, which requires that the distribution of a sensitive attribute in any equivalence class is close to the distribution of the attribute in the overall table.

Advantages

- It prevents skewness attack.
- It provides efficient closeness by using earth mover distance.

Disadvantages

- It lacks in flexibility specifying different protect levels for different sensitive value.
- EMD function is not suitable for preventing attribute linkage on numerical sensitive attribute
- It greatly degrades the data utility because it requires the distribution of sensitive attributes to be the same in all QID groups.

Diving down into the contemporary literature with the intention of hauling pearl, one finds that only a handful faction have navigated the area but no one has ever projected anapt explication or endeavored their implementation in the real world..Having discussed all the existing literature on the Optimality Criteria, definitions of safety (privacy), validity (utility) we can now try to illustrate how they are used for the comparison of alternative data releases and how we can customize our Modus Operandi for selection of the best PPDM Technique for any real–time Application. Moreover, we have already implemented and evaluated the true efficiency of the PPDM techniques [(Indumathi.J et al.,2007b,2008d,2009)] on our own conceptual frameworks [Indumathi.J et al.,2007,2008a].In this paper we have attempted to structure and suggest the Modus Operandi for Selection of The Best Anonymity based PPDM Technique for any real time application.

4. Problem statement

Prescribe a new generic scaffold which will obscure data sets (while still preserving certain statistical characteristics of the data) by choosing the best **anonymisation** technique with the intention of trying to improve the level of privacy protection and to maintain a perfect balance between privacy and utility.

4.1. Problem description

We have determined (Indumathi.J et al., (2009)to put forward a new generic scaffold solution for Data-Garnering and PPDM System as shown in figure 5.and incorporate five aims, in five steps namely:

a. An improved preference mechanism to determine the best optional privacy-preserving method as shown in figure 5 not only for data mining but also in shielding the information resources;
b. Develop notation for assessment and evaluation of alternative concealed data PPDM;
c. Guard data in database structures and erstwhile forms of information possessions;
d. Apply the guideline, database principle to enforceable security policies and procedures; and Implement the solution and validate it in real world situation.

It is already (Indumathi.J et al., (2009)stated that the state of being free from unsanctioned intrusion is known privacy. It limits the risk of disclosure of confidential information. Utility of concealed data is to measure how closethe concealed data are to their unconcealed version. There is no general accord that assessment and evaluation of alternative concealed data ought to be done on the foundation of the privacyand utilitythat these produce; these tend to be ambiguous concepts.

5. Architecture of the proposed system

A privacy-enhancing three tier architecture that enables to preserve the privacy of data by combining three best methods for Privacy Preservation, namely access control limitation technique, randomization and Privacy Preserving Clustering (PPC) shows an increase in the performance by modifying the algorithm so that the dissimilarity matrix is found only once by the third party instead of it being found by each local party (Indumathi.J et al.,2007c).].

In this paper we have improvised on the access control mechanism by surrogating it with the Purpose Based Access Control (PBAC) which confers us with three benefits viz., First, PBAC models include features to establish role hierarchies; second, RBAC policies change very little over time; third, it naturally supports delegation of access permissions.

As depicted in Figure 5, our framework encompasses a transactional database (modelled into a text database), a set of algorithms used for flustering data from the database, a transaction retrieval engine for fast retrieval. We amend (Indumathi.J et al., (2009) and bring out a diagrammatic representation of the architecture as shown in figure 5 and 6 involved in the proposed architecture.

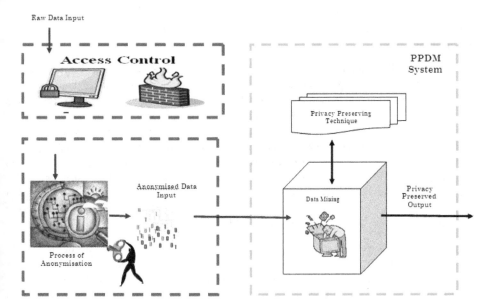

Figure 5. The PPDM Framework: High-Level

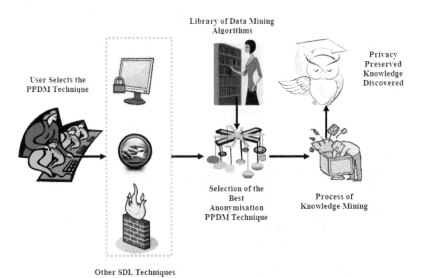

Figure 6. Modus Operandi for selecting the Best Anonymisation PPDM Technique for an Application-High Level Diagram.

Data concealingis used to limit the revelation of data by applying a mystification process to the originally collected data and publishing it the public (Indumathi.J et al., (2009). We refer synonymously the Mystification process of the original data as data befuddling; the terms concealed data set represents the output of such mystification; the concealed data set refers both to the published data and the information provided to the users about the mystification.

Data collectors collect data from data providers. These heterogeneous data can be protected by limiting the data access using password, firewalls etc., Owing to the versatility of thedata mining tasks, any one best suitable technique can be selected from a family of privacy-preserving data mining (PPDM) methods using the technique selector. This technique is used for protecting privacy before data are shared. The technique selector can either use the PPDM Ontology to select the desired technique. The algorithms are used for modifying the unique facts by some means, with the intention that the private data and private knowledge linger private even subsequent to the mining process. Metrics is used to find the measure of these techniques. The input to this block is unpreserved data whereas its output is privacy preserved and befuddled data. This is given as an input and is subject to any of the data mining techniques.The figure 7 shows the Modus Operandi for selecting the Best PPDM Technique for an Application.

From a privacy-preserving data mining (PPDM) methods pool we select(Indumathi.J et al., (2009) any one best suitable anonymisation technique can be selected using the technique selector. This technique is used for protecting privacy before data are shared. The technique selector can either use the PPDM Ontology (Indumathi.J et al., (2009) to select the desired technique. The algorithms are used for modifying the unique facts by some means, with the intention that the private data and private knowledge linger private even subsequent to the mining process. Metrics is used to find the measure of these techniques. The input to this block is unpreserved data whereas its output is privacy preserved and befuddled data. This is given as an input and is subject to any of the data mining techniques.The figure 4.3 shows the Modus Operandi for selecting the Best anonymisation PPDM Technique for an Application.

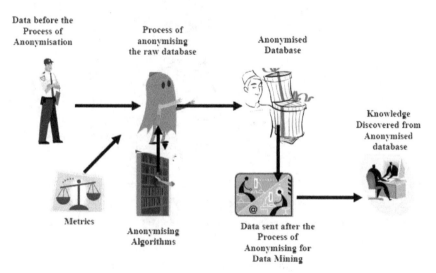

Figure 7. Modus Operandi for Selecting the Best Anonymisation PPDM Technique for an Application-Middle Level Diagram.

6. System architecture design

Problem Formulation: Specification of an appraisal framework in order to compare and contrast each and every one of the techniques in a general podium which will be the basis for ascertaining the suitable technique for a given type of application.

6.1. Subsystem architecture of the purpose based access control framework for PPDM systems

One main motive of the project work is to discuss how to address privacy issues, that is, how a business providing organization can ensure that the privacy of its consumers is protected. The project implements an approach based on intended purpose and access purpose. Intended purpose implies the intended usage of data. The purpose for which a data element is accessed is implied by access purpose. The purpose compliance check introduces some overhead. Two different granularity levels are used for purpose compliance and the overhead incurred in each scheme is noted. In addition, the approach is implemented on data that is reliable and of good quality in order to make important decisions based on that data. The concept of obtaining quality data using confidence policies is implemented in the project.

First, the emphasis is laid on the importance of privacy protection with respect to any business providing organization. While enforcing good privacy practice helps attract customers, there is a possibility of potential lawsuits by customers if the privacy of their data is violated. This prompts organizations to ensure and focus on privacy protection. One model that aims at protecting the privacy is purpose based access control for relational databases. In this model, purpose information is associated with a given data element. Such a privacy protecting access control model is desired since privacy protection cannot be easily achieved by traditional access control models .The concept of purpose is thus introduced in access control models. The proposed approach introduces access purpose and intended purpose. Intended purpose specifies the intended usage of data, and access purposes specifies the purposes for which a given data element is accessed. If privacy officers desire that data should not be allowed for certain purposes, this model can be used since it supports prohibitions. The granularity of data labeling, i.e., the units of data with which purposes can be associated is introduced using two schemes. In one scheme, purpose is associated with every data element in a relation and in the other; it is associated with each attribute in a relation. The role based access control (RBAC) is chosen as the underlying model to implement the purpose concept. RBAC, by itself, is a way of enforcing access to system resources for authorized users. Such a mechanism will be helpful in designing applications which aim at preserving data privacy.

6.1.1. High level design of purpose based access control framework for PPDM systems

The features of the proposed Purpose Based Access Control are as follows:

1. An access control model for privacy protection based on the notion of purpose was implemented.

2. The overhead incurred by using the purpose compliance checks was calculated for two labeling schemes using synthetic datasets.
    - The element based scheme (finest granularity) had significant overhead   compared to the attribute based labeling.
    - Thus, the response time increased as granularity of labeling became finer.
3. Providing high quality data to decision makers using confidence values associated with data was implemented. A greedy algorithm was implemented which dynamically incremented data confidence values in order to return query results that satisfied the stated confidence policies.

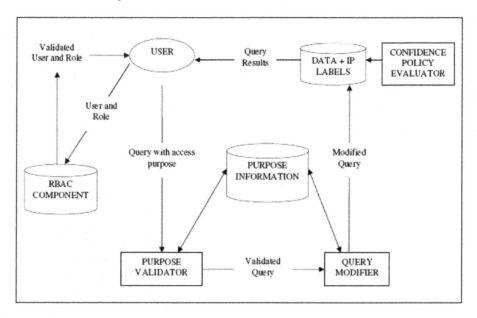

Figure 8. Block Diagram of the proposed Purpose Based Access Control Privacy Protection System

The details of the architecture are discussed. In figure 8, the overall picture of the privacy protection system is shown. The system's architecture consists of the six main components: The RBAC component, Purpose Management component, Query Modification mechanism, Confidence Policy Evaluation, Data which includes the intended purpose labels.

The RBAC component includes role and user creation, role assignment to users and role activation.

The Purpose Management component includes purpose storage and validation. In the purpose creation, we identify a purpose tree based on the organizational needs and create a purpose table to store the hexadecimal encodings of each purpose node. In purpose validation, we first find the conditional role of a user giving the role as an input. We also verify the access purpose of the user. The allowed intended purpose (AIP) and prohibited intended purpose (PIP) of a data element is also found. Finally, we check the compliance between the access purpose given by the user and the intended purpose (AIP and PIP) of the data element as decided by the privacy policy.

The query modification component returns the results of the query after the purpose compliance check. If the access purpose is non-compliant with the intended purpose of the data element, the corresponding result of the data element should not be displayed.

The confidence policy evaluation ensures that the data is of good quality and reliable in order to make important decisions. It includes confidence assignment, whereby each data item in the concerned relations is assigned a confidence value of around 0.1, confidence evaluation of the query results, policy evaluation which returns only those results with confidence value higher than the threshold specified in the confidence policy to the user (one who is managing the data). Finally, strategy finding and data quality improvement can be used to dynamically increment the confidence level of data to return query results that satisfy the stated confidence policy.

The flow is as follows. The Confidence Policy Evaluation first improves the quality of the data which will later be used for the privacy protection process. Before the user can issue a query, he should be assigned user name and a role in the database. The query is then passed onto the purpose validator component.

6.2. Subsystem architecture of the framework for PPDM systems

The architecture of the proposed system has two major subsystems called Privacy Preserving Framework, Data Mining Subsystems.Our already implementedAgent Based PPDMT Selector Module of PPDM Methods (Indumathi.J et al., (2009) intelligently decides the best suited technique as it is the routine that waits in the background and performs an action when a specified event occurs.

The PPDM Framework sub system is designed as a generalized approach to support privacy-preserving data doling. Most work in this field has been extremely specialized by edifying a new all-purpose framework, we anticipate facilitating the application of privacy-preserving mechanisms and data doling to a broader variety of fields. Furthermore, this approach has been purposeful en route for the development of a practical combined infringement discovery structure. The methods in this thesis have been distinctively spear-headed for real-world solutions that establish privacy requirements.

6.2.1. Privacy preserving framework subsystem

The Privacy Preserving Framework subsystem [Indumathi.J et al.,(2007)]has components, namely, metrics module, Library of algorithms module, technique selector module. The Privacy Preserving Framework categorically decides the Privacy preservation mode of selection (manual or automatic or interactive) of technique from the technique selector module, with the help of Library of algorithms module. The metrics module is used to quantify the work.

Library of algorithms - presents the taxonomy of the anonymisation based PPDM algorithms.

Metrics Module - Evaluator sub system has four components, namely, the performance measurer, data utility measurer, level of uncertainty measurer, resistance measurer. A introductory list of appraisal parameters to be used for assessing the worth of privacy preserving data mining algorithms, is given below:

i.   Performance of the proposed algorithms

The performance of the proposed algorithms in stipulations of time requirements, that is the time essential by each algorithm to conceal a particular set of susceptible information; assess the time needs in terms of the standard number of operations, essential to decrease the incidence of facade of explicit sensitive information below a specified threshold.

The *communication cost* incurred through the barter of information among a number of collaborating sites, should be painstaking. It is crucial that this cost must be reserved to a minimum for a distributed privacy preserving data mining algorithm.

ii.   Data utility

The data utility after the submission of the privacy preserving technique, which is equal with the minimization of the information loss or else the loss in the functionality of the data; the measure used to evaluate the information loss depends on the specific data mining technique with respect to which a privacy algorithm is performed. Information loss in the background of association rule mining, classification, will be calculated either in terms of the amount of rules that were both residual and lost in the database after sanitization, or even in terms on the reduction/increase in the support and confidence of all the rules. For clustering, the variance of the distances among the clustered items in the original database and the befuddled database, can be the basis for evaluating information loss in this case.

iii. Uncertainty level

The *level of uncertainty is defined as* with which the sensitive information that have been hidden can still be predicted; these privacy preservation strategies, demote the information to facilitate protection below certain thresholds.

iv.   Fortitude of confrontation to diverse Data Mining techniques

The fortitude of confrontationisaccomplished by the privacy algorithms; to different data mining techniques. The aim of algorithms is the fortification of susceptible information against illegal disclosure. The intruders and data terrorists will try to conciliate information by using various data mining algorithms.

6.3. Subsystem architecture of the framework for data mining systems

The Data Mining subsystem as shown in figure 9. have five components, namely, Database Server Module, Data Warehouse Server Module, Visualization Module, Data Mining

A Generic Scaffold Housing the Innovative Modus Operandi
for Selection of the Superlative Anonymisation Technique for Optimized Privacy Preserving Data Mining

149

Module and Data Preprocessing Module. Data Mining Module has been confined only to three components, namely, association, classification, clustering.

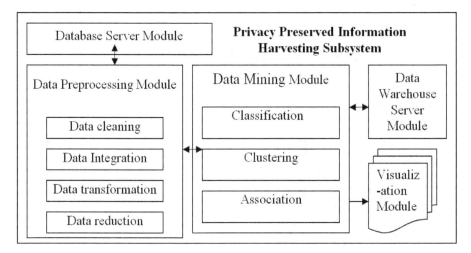

Figure 9. Privacy Preserving Data Mining Framework Subsystem.

7. Evaluation and experimental results

7.1. Data structure design and datasets used

The framework is tested and implemented for patient data collection in health care systems. The collected patient details are mined for finding the relationship between the eating habits and the diseases that are caused due to it.We have used the geneId dataset, and datasets collected from health care centres around Vellore and transmitted to Vellore City hospitals where the specialists advice the patients based on the outcomes.

User characteristics-The target user is expected to have knowledge about the data used in the system. The user should have experience in working with the standard windows environment.

Operating Environment-The operating environment of the software is in the Data Mining area at Health Care domain.

7.2. Metrics

Data Utility is the percentage of similarity between the data mined results from original data and randomized data.

Data Privacy: For quantifying privacy provided by a method, we use a measure based on how closely the original values of a modified attribute can be estimated. If it can be estimated with c % confidence that a value x lies in the interval [x1; x2], then the interval width (x2 - x1) defines the amount of privacy at c % confidence level. Based on the above factor we are going to analyze the various anonymity approaches that have been implemented.

Varied QI size for *k = 5, l = 5*

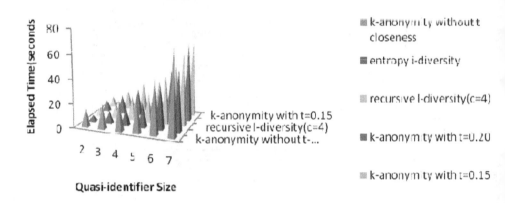

Figure 10. Elapsed time Vs. quasi-identifier size for diverse anonymity techniques

Figure 10. shows that as the data size /dimensions are increasing there is an decrease in the data utility.

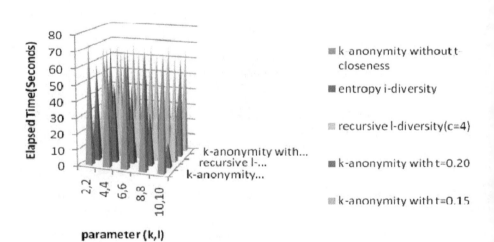

Figure 11. Elapsed time Vs. parameter for diverse anonymity techniques

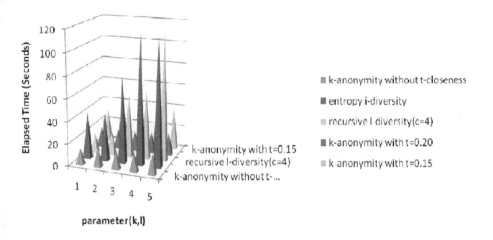

Figure 12. Elapsed time Vs. parameter for diverse anonymity techniques

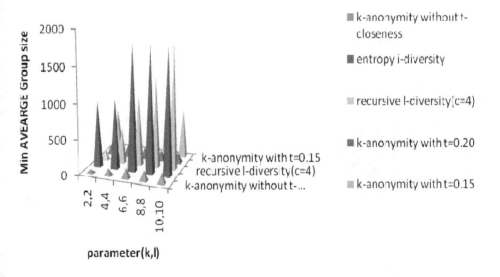

Figure 13. Elapsed time Vs. parameter for diverse anonymity techniques

Figure 11, 12, 13. shows Elapsed time Versus parameter for diverse anonymity techniques.

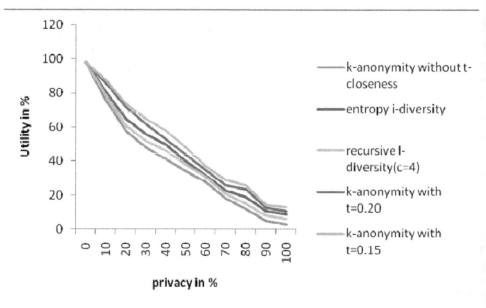

Figure 14. Data Utility Versus Privacy for diverse anonymity techniques

Figure 14. shows that as the **Privacy** increases there is an decrease in the data utility.

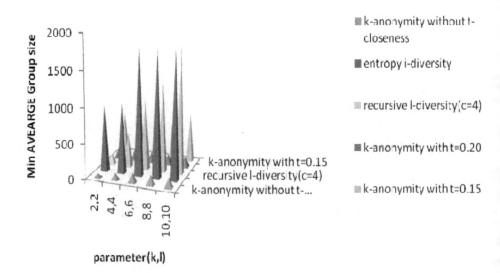

Figure 15. Minimum Average group size Versus Parameter for diverse anonymity techniques

Figure 15. shows Minimum Average group size Versus Parameter for diverse anonymity techniques.

Summarizing the main points we understand that if data utility is of primary concern in a domain, then our rating will be in the order of k-anonymity without t-closeness followed by k-anonymity with t=0.20 followed by k-anonymity with t=0.15 followed by recursive l-diversity(c=4) followed by entropy i-diversity.From the perspective of projection it will be Orthogonal projection followed by sparse projection and at last the Random projection.

Incase of Privacy, is our Spartan we select Random projection as the first choice followed by Orthogonal projection and finally sparse projection. Amongst the different classification algorithms KNN provides better balance between data utility and data privacy than the SVM Classification methods.

The system also caters to the non-functional requirements viz., Reliability, Availability, Maintainability, Portability, Security.

8. Conclusion and future work

In this chapter we propose the new appraised generic scaffold housing the innovative modus operandi for selection of the superlative Anonymity based Privacy Preserving Data Mining (PPDM) Modus Operandi for optimized privacy preserving data mining. We pin our attention on the quandary of rating discretionary concealed data sets on the basis of the values of data privacy and data utility that the Anonymisation produces. Moreover, we have proposed a generic scaffold housing the innovative modus operandi for selection of the superlative anonymisation technique for optimized PPDM; and we have contradistinguished the diverse anonymity techniques and argue solutions to tackle the problems of security threats and attacks in the PPDM in systems.

We (Indumathi, J. et al., (2009)will be able to understand the potential impact of the various Anonymisation based PPDM Techniques only when we model in full-scale applications. We do deem, nonetheless that our argument should make others vigilant to the perils intrinsic to heuristic approaches to Anonymisation based PPDM Limitations. Heuristic methods are based on assumptions which are tacit and not implicit. If for a given data Anonymisation based PPDM limitation problem, the execution of model-based solutions emerges to be too complicated or too costly to carry out, heuristic approaches need to be incorporated with a meticulous analysis aimed at probing the extent to which the approach formalizes rational group inclination structures and/or data user behaviors.

We (Indumathi, J. et al., (2009) have a wealthy plan for future research. We require considering more complicated models of user performance to take into account pragmatic circumstances where numerous users act concurrently and alliances are possible. This will escort logically to such issues as the incorporation of priors and utilities which need special attention.

Author details

J. Indumathi

Department of Information Science and Technology, College of Engineering, Anna University, Chennai, Tamilnadu, India

9. References

A.Machanavajjhala, J Gehrke, and D.Kifer, et al,(2007) "ℓ-diversity: Privacy beyond k-anonymity", ACM Transactions on Knowledge Discovery from Data (TKDD) Volume 1 Issue 1, March 2007 Article No. 3.

Aggarwal, C. and Yu, P (2004),'A Condensation Approach to Privacy Preserving Data Mining', In Advances in Database Technology - EDBT, pp. 183-199.

Ali Inan, Yucel Saygin, Erkay Savas, Ayca Azgin Hintoglu and Albert Levi (2006), 'Privacy preserving clustering on horizontally partitioned data', Proceedings of the22nd International Conference on Data Engineering Workshops, IEEE.

Atallah, M.J., Bertino, E., Elmagarmid, A.K., Ibrahim, M. And Verykois, V.S. (1999), 'Disclosure limitation of sensitive rules', Proceedings of the IEEE Knowledge and Data Engineering Workshop , IEEE Computer Society Press, Chicago, IL, USA, pp.45–52.

Du, W. and Zhan, Z. (2002), 'Building decision tree classifier on private data', Proceedings of the IEEE ICDM Workshop on Privacy, Security and Data Mining, p.1–8.

Friedman.A, R. Wolff, and A. Schuster, 'Providing k-Anonymity in Data Mining, Int'l J. Very Large Data Bases', vol. 17, no. 4, pp. 789-804, 2008.

Gitanjali, J., Shaik Nusrath Banu, Geetha Mary,A., Indumathi, J. and Uma, G.V. (2007), 'An agent based burgeoning framework for privacy preserving information harvesting systems', Computer Science and Network Security, Vol. 7, No. 11, pp.268–276.

Indumathi J., Uma G.V.(2008), 'A Novel Framework for Optimized Privacy Preserving Data Mining Using the innovative Desultory Technique', International Journal of Computer Applications in Technology ; Special Issue on: "Computer Applications in Knowledge-Based Systems". Vol.35 Nos.2/3/4, pp.194 – 203.

Indumathi, J. and Uma, G.V. (2007 c), 'A new flustering approach for privacy preserving data fishing in tele-health care systems', International Journal on Healthcare Technology and Management (IJHTM) (Special Issue on Tele-Healthcare System Implementation, Challenges and Issues). Vol. 1, Nos. 1/2/3, pp.43–52.

Indumathi, J. and Uma, G.V. (2007a), 'Customized privacy preservation using unknowns to stymie unearthing of association rules', Journal of Computer Science, Vol. 3, No. 12, pp.874–881.

Indumathi, J. and Uma, G.V. (2007b), 'Using privacy preserving techniques to accomplish a secure accord', Computer Scienceand Network Security, Vol. 7, No. 8, pp.258–266.

Indumathi, J. and Uma, G.V. (2008a), 'An aggrandized framework for genetic privacy preserving pattern analysis using cryptography and contravening-conscious knowledge management systems', Molecular Medicine and Advance Sciences, Vol. 4, No. 1, pp.33–40.

Indumathi.J, Dr.G.V.Uma.(2008 c), 'A Panglossian Solitary-Skim Sanitization for Privacy Preserving Data Archaeology',International Journal of Electrical and Power Engineering . Volume 2 Number 3, pp-154 -165, January 2008.

Indumathi.J, K. Murugesan, J.Gitanjali, D. Manjula(2009), "Sprouting Modus Operandi for Selection of the Best PPDM using Agent Based PPDMT in the Health Care Domain," International Journal of Recent Trends in Engineering, Vol. 1, No. 1, pp.627-629May 2009

Jian Yin, Zhi-Fang Tan, Jiang-Tao Ren and Yi-Qun Chen (2005)'An efficient clustering algorithm for mixed type attributes in large dataset', Proceedings of the 4th InternationalConference on Machine Learning and Cybernetics,Guangzhou, Vol. 18–21, pp.1611–1614.

Kantarcioglu, M. and Clifton, C. (2004), 'Privacy-preserving distributed mining of association rules on horizontally partitioned data', IEEE Transactions on Knowledge and Data Engineering, Vol. 16, No. 9, pp.1026–1037.

L. Sweeney, "k-anonymity: a model for protecting privacy", International Journal on Uncertainty, Fuzziness and Knowledge based Systems, 2002, pp. 557-570.

MohammadReza Keyvanpour et al.,(2011),'Classification and Evaluation the Privacy Preserving Data Mining Techniques by using a Data Modification–based Framework,' International Journal on Computer Science and Engineering (IJCSE), Vol. 3, No. 2, pp. 862–870.

N. Li, T. Li, and S. Venkatasubramanian, (2007)"t-Closeness: Privacy Beyond k-anonymity and l-Diversity", In Proc. of ICDE, 2007, pp. 106-115.

Oliveira, S.R.M. and Zaïane, O.R. (2004), 'Privacy preserving clustering by object similarity-based representation and dimensionality reduction transformation', Proceedings of the 2004 ICDM Workshop on Privacy and Security Aspects of Data Mining, pp.40–46.

P. Samarati and L. Sweeney(1998), "Protecting privacy when disclosing information: k-anonymity and its enforcement through generalization and suppression", In Technical Report SRI-CSL-98-04, SRI Computer Science Laboratory, pp.1-191998.

S.V. Iyengar(2002), 'Transforming Data to Satisfy Privacy Constraints', Proc. Eighth ACM SIGKDD, pp. 279-288, 2002.

Vaidya, J. and Clifton, C. (2002), 'Privacy preserving association rule mining in vertically partitioned data', Proceedings of the 8th ACM SIGKDD International Conference on Knowledge Discovery and Data Mining, pp.639–644.

Vassilios, S.V., Elmagarmid, A., Bertino, E., Saygin, Y. And Dasseni, E. (2004), 'Association rule hiding', IEEE Transactions on Knowledge and Data Engineering, Vol. 16, No. 4, pp. 434–447.

Vasudevan, V., Sivaraman, N., Senthil Kumar, S., Muthuraj, R., Indumathi, J. and Uma, G.V. (2007), 'A comparative study of SPKI/SDSI and K-SPKI/SDSI SYSTEMS', Information Technology Journal, Vol. 6, No. 8, pp.1208–1216.

Verykios V. S., Bertino. E., Fovino I. N., Provenza L. P., Saygin Y.and Theodoridis. Y. (2004 b),'State-of-the-art in privacy preserving data mining',ACM SIGMOD Record, Vol.33, No.1.

Wang, K. and Fung, B. C. M. (2006),". Anonymizing sequential releases,". In Proceedings of the 12th ACM SIGKDD Conference. ACM, New York.

Wang, K., Fung, B. C. M., AND YU, P. S. (2005)," Template-based privacy preservation in classification problems," In Proceedings of the 5th IEEE International Conference on Data Mining (ICDM). 466–473.

Wang, K., Fung, B. C. M., and Yu, P. S.(2007)," Handicapping attacker's confidence: An alternative to k-anonymization,".Knowl. Inform. Syst. 11, 3, 345–368.

Wong, R. C. W., Li., J., Fu, A. W. C., and Wang, K. (2006),". (a,k)-anonymity: An enhanced k-anonymity model for privacy preserving data publishing,". In Proceedings of the 12th ACM SIGKDD. ACM, New York,754–759.

Zhang, Q.,Koudas, N., Srivatsava, D., and Yu, T. (2007),". Aggregate query answering on anonymized tables,". In Proceedings of the 23rd IEEE International Conference on Data Engineering (ICDE).

Data Mining in Medical Applications

Chapter 7

Incorporating Domain Knowledge into Medical Image Mining

Haiwei Pan

Additional information is available at the end of the chapter

1. Introduction

Advances in image acquisition and storage technology have led to tremendous growth in very large and detailed image databases [2]. A vast amount of image data is generated in our daily life and each field, such as medical image (CT images, ECT images and MR images etc), satellite images and all kinds of digital photographs. These images involve a great number of useful and implicit information that is difficult for users to discover.

Image mining can automatically discover these implicit information and patterns from the high volume of images and is rapidly gaining attention in the field of data mining. Image mining is more than just an extension of data mining to image domain. It is an interdisciplinary endeavor that draws upon computer vision, image processing, image retrieval, machine learning, artificial intelligence, database and data mining, etc. While some of individual fields in themselves may be quite matured, image mining, to date, is just a growing research focus and is still at an experimental stage.

Broadly speaking, image mining deals with the extraction of implicit knowledge, image data relationship, or other patterns not explicitly stored in the images and between image and other alphanumeric data. For example, in the field of archaeology, many photographs of various archeological sites have been captured and stored as digital images. These images, once mined, may reveal interesting patterns that could shed some lights on the behavior of the people living at that period of time. Clearly, image mining is different from low-level computer vision and image processing techniques. The focus of image mining is in the extraction of patterns from a large collection of images, whereas the focus of computer vision and image processing techniques is in understanding and/or extracting specific features from a single image. While there seems to be some overlap between image mining and content-based retrieval (since both deals with large collection of images), image mining goes beyond the problem of retrieving relevant images. In image mining, the goal is the discovery of image patterns that are significant in a given collection of images and the related alphanumeric data. Perhaps the most common misconception of image mining is that image mining is yet another term for pattern recognition. While the two fields do share a large number of common functions such as feature extraction, they differ in their fundamental assumptions. In pattern recognition, the objective is to recognize some specific patterns; whereas in image mining, the aim is to generate all significant patterns without prior knowledge of what patterns may exist in the image databases. Another key difference is in the types of patterns examined by the two research fields. In pattern recognition, the patterns are mainly classification patterns. In image mining, the patterns types are more diverse. It could be classification patterns, description patterns, correlation patterns, temporal patterns, and spatial patterns. Finally, pattern recognition deals only with pattern generation and pattern analysis. In image mining, this is only one (albeit an important) aspect of image mining. Image mining deals with all aspects of large image databases which imply that the indexing scheme, the storage of images, and the retrieval of images are all of concerns in an image mining system[3]. A few interesting studies and successful applications involving image mining have been reported. For example, [4] describes the CONQUEST system that combines satellite data with geophysical data to discover patterns in global climate change. The SKICAT system [5] integrates techniques for image processing and data classification in order to identify "sky objects" captured in a very large satellite picture set. A multimedia data mining system prototype MultiMediaMiner [2, 6] uses a data cube structure for mining characteristic, association, and classification rules. However, the system does not use image content to the extent we wanted. In [7], localization of the visual features, their spatial relationships and their motion in time (for video) are presented. A discovering association rules algorithm based on image content from a simple image dataset is presented in [8]. [9]

Research in image mining can be broadly classified into two main directions [3]. The first direction involves domain-specific applications where the focus is to extract the most relevant image features into a form suitable for data mining [10, 11]. The second direction involves general applications where the focus is to generate image patterns that maybe helpful in the understanding of the interaction between high-level human perceptions of images and low level image features [2, 8, 12]. Clustering medical images belongs to the first direction.

Image clustering is unsupervised classification of images into groups. The problem in image clustering is to group a given collection of unlabeled images into meaningful clusters according to the image content without a priori knowledge [13]. The fundamental objective for carrying out image clustering in image mining is to acquire content information the users are interested in from the image group label associated with the image[3]. Image clustering is usually performed in the early stages of the mining process. Feature attributes that have received the most attention for clustering are color, texture and shape. Generally, any of the three, individually or in combination, could be used. There is a wealth of clustering techniques available: hierarchical clustering algorithms, partition-based algorithms, mixture-resolving and mode-seeking algorithms, nearest neighbor clustering, fuzzy clustering and evolutionary clustering approaches. Once the images have been clustered, a domain expert is needed to examine the images of each cluster to label the abstract concepts denoted by the cluster. Chang et al. use clustering technique in an attempt to detect unauthorized image copying on the World Wide Web [3, 14]. Yu and Zhang present an unsupervised clustering and query approach (also known as ACQ for Automatic Clustering and Query) for large-scale image databases [15]. ACQ does not require the number of clusters to be known a priori and is insensitive to noise. By intelligently applying wavelet transforms on the feature space, this clustering can effectively and efficiently detect clustering of arbitrary shape of high dimensional feature vectors. Kitamoto apply clustering methods such as k-means and the self-organizing map (SOM) for visualizing the distribution of typhoon cloud patterns on a two-dimensional space [3, 11].

Some algorithms used in the medical images [16, 17, 18] are generally for classification. [19, 20, 21] propose some new clustering methods in relational databases. They are not suitable to cluster the medical images because there are important differences between relational databases versus image databases: (1) Absolute versus relative values. In relational databases, the data values are semantically meaningful. For example, one item is milk is well understood. However, in medical image databases, the data values themselves may not be significant unless the domain of medicine supports them. For example, a grey scale value of 46 could appear darker than a grey scale value of 87 if the surrounding context pixels values are all very bright. (2) Spatial information (Independent versus dependent position) [9]. Another important difference between relational databases and medical image databases is that the implicit spatial information is critical for interpretation of image contents but there is no such requirement in relational databases. As a result, image miners try to overcome this problem by extracting position-independent features from images first before attempting to mine useful patterns from the images[3]. (3) Unique versus multiple interpretation. A third important difference deals with image characteristics of having multiple interpretations for the same visual patterns. The traditional data mining algorithm of associating a pattern to a class (interpretation) will not work well here. A new class of discovery algorithms is needed to cater to the special needs in mining useful patterns from images[3].

Association rule mining from medical images is another significant research topic in the field of image mining. Finding these valuable rules is typically done in two steps: discovering frequent itemsets and generating association rules. The second step is rather straightforward, and the first step dominates the processing time, so we explicitly focus this chapter on the first step. A number of efficient association rule mining algorithms have been proposed in the last few years. Among these, the Apriori algorithm by Agrawal, R., Imielinski, T [22][23] has been very influential. Later, many scholars have improved and optimized the Apriori algorithm and have presented new Apriori-like algorithms [24][25][26][27][28]. The Apriori-like algorithms consist of two major procedures: the join procedure and the prune procedure. These algorithms require a huge calculation and a complicated transaction process during the two procedures. Therefore, the mining efficiency of the Apriori-like algorithms is not very good when transaction database is very large.

L.Jaba Sheela proposed the FAR algorithm [29] in 2009. This algorithm transforms a transaction database into a Feature matrix stored in bits. Meanwhile it uses the Boolean vector "relational calculus" method to discover frequent itemsets. This method uses the fast and simple "and calculus" in the Feature matrix to replace the calculations and complicated transactions that deal with large number of itemsets [32]. It scans the database only once and has a good efficiency. But there is a great shortcoming in FAR algorithm. The generating of candidate itemsets relies on the combination of column of feature matrix. When the number of column of feature matrix is very large, that is to say the number of items in transaction database is very large, FAR algorithm will cost much time to do useless calculus.

In this chapter, we firstly quantify the domain knowledge about brain image (especially the brain symmetry), and then incorporate this quantified measurement into the clustering algorithm. Our algorithm contains two parts: (1) clustering regions of interest (ROI) detected from brain image; (2) clustering images based on the similarity of ROI. We apply the method to cluster brain images and present results to demonstrate its usefulness and effectiveness[1]. Secondly, we proposed the GMA (association graph and matrix pruning algorithm) algorithm to solution this problem. Yen and Chen proposed the DLG (Direct Large Itemset Generation Algorithm) algorithm [30][31] based association graph for the first time in 1996. GMA algorithm adopts both association graph and matrix pruning to reduce the generation of candidate itemsets. It also scans database only once and generates frequent itemsets by the "and calculus". Throughout the chapter we try to provide a general framework to understand these approaches. We believe many of the problems we are facing are likely to appear in other domains. As such this work tries to isolate those problems which we consider will be of most interest to the database community doing research on clustering [9] and association rule mining.

The rest of the chapter is organized as follows: section 2 is pre-processing describing an algorithm to detect objects in medical images [9]. Section 3 presents the medical image clustering algorithm. This section includes four parts: (1) Feature extraction is to extract the most relevant features from the object with the direction of domain knowledge; (2) Object clustering. We define the similarity measurement according to the above features and present OCA algorithm to cluster objects into some groups; (3) Image clustering. We firstly determine weights of objects that appear in images based on term frequency and inverse document frequency, similar to IR. Each image will then be represented by a vector, where a vector contains a set of weights that correspond to the importance of the objects that appear in the image. Finally ICA algorithm is presented to cluster medical images; (4) Experiment results. This part reports the results of our experiments and performance study. Section 4 presents the association rule mining algorithm. This section includes three parts: (1) Basic concept. We define Support, Confidence, Association Graph and Feature Matrix, etc. to describe this problem; (2) GMA algorithm. The GMA algorithm consists of four phases as follows: generating feature matrix and association graph, pruning the feature matrix, selecting and extending by the association graph and generating the set of frequent-k itemsets; (3) Experiment results give the experiment results and analysis. Section 5 introduces the future work. Section 6 concludes the study in this chapter.

2. Preprocessing

Since the images we studied were raw Computerized Tomography (CT) scans that were scanned at different illumination conditions, some of them appeared too bright and some were too dark. We should digitize them to no loss, no compression and 256 gray scale images through special medical scanner. We used CT scan images because this modality is the most used in radiotherapy planning for two main reasons. The first reason is that scanner images contain anatomical information which offers the possibility to plan the direction and the entry points of the radiotherapy rays which have to target the tumor and to avoid some risk organs. The second reason is that CT scan images are obtained using rays, which is the same physical principle as radiotherapy. This is very important because the radiotherapy rays intensity can be computed from the scanner image intensities[33].

In this section, we firstly use progressive water immersion method with guidance of domain knowledge to detect region of interest (ROI) in medical images, then we combine these ROIs with their location, size and other descriptors to form a table for mining.

Water immersion algorithm is considered to be a powerful technique for ROI detection. It works by grouping pixels with similar gradient information. Direct application of water immersion method to the digitized medical images typically produces over-segmentation of the trivial regions. Instead, we propose a progressive water immersion algorithm with guidance of domain knowledge to cope with this situation [34]. Details of the algorithm follow.

First, a N×N window is used to locate the local optimal points in the image. For each segmented patches, we place the center of the window over each pixel in the patches. If the grey level of the central pixel is optimal with respect to all the other pixels in the window, we say that the central pixel is a local optimum; otherwise, the window will move to be centered at another pixel to continue the search for all local optimal points. At the end of this phase, all the optimum is marked and they will be treated as the starting seeds for water immersion method. One advantage of using the sliding window approach is that with the appropriate window size, it is possible to eliminate a large amount of optimal points that correspond to the light and dark reflection regions thus removing false detection. This is because the grey level of the optimal points corresponding to the light and dark reflection patches are generally lower and higher than that of potential ROI. Given that the distances between the optimal points of the light and dark reflection patches and the nearest optimal points of the neighboring ROI are generally less than that between two touching ROI, it is possible to set the window size in such a way that these false optimal points are 'absorbed' by the neighboring ROI optimal points while the true optimal points are not affected.

Having identified the true optimal points, water immersion process starts from these detected points and progressively floods its neighboring pixels. The neighboring pixels are defined to be the 8-direction neighbors. These neighbors are placed in a growing queue structure sorted in descending order of the grey level of the pixels. The lowest and highest grey pixel in the growing queue will be 'immersed' first but respectively and it is marked as belonging to the same region label as the current seed. The marked pixel is then removed from the growing queue. All neighboring pixels whose grey level is lower or higher than the marked pixel are added to the growing queue. This immersion process continues until the growing queue is empty [9].

Unfortunately, simple application of the water immersion technique has the tendency of over-flooding. To overcome this problem [9], we firstly give some definitions.

1. We partition all pixels in pixel set P into m blocks. Pixels in the same block have the same grey level and pixels in the different blocks have the different grey level. Let $G(P)=\{g_1, g_2, ..., g_m\}$ be P's grey-scale (GS) set if G(P) is an ascending sort set of g_1', g_2', ..., g_m' and g_i' is grey level of pixels in the ith block, where g_i (i=1,...,m) is the ith GS, g_1' and g_m' are P's minimum and maximum GS respectively. The GS of pixel p_i is denoted as $g(p_i)$ [33].

2. We call $g_{mean}(P)$ the mean GS if

$$g_{mean}(P)= \sum_{i=1}^{|P|} g(p_i)/|P|.$$

3. For any P and distance function $DisA=|g_k - g_{mean}(P)|$, mid-value GS is a middle value in the GS set that minimizes DisA. Mid-value GS set is a set of mid-value GS [33].

4. For any P, if

a. Mid-value GS set includes one element g_{mid}, and g_s is the minimum value between g_{mean} and g_{mid};

b. Mid GS set includes two elements, g_s is the minimum value between these two values; g_s is called Benchmark GS and another one is denoted as g_s' [33].

5. For pixel set P, let

$g^{(l)}=\{g_i \mid g_1 \leq g_i \leq g_1+|g_1-g_s|/2\}$ be low bound GS;
$g^{(h)}=\{g_i \mid g_m-|g_m-g_s'|/2 \leq g_i \leq g_m\}$ be high bound GS;
$g^{(b)}= g^{(l)} \cup g^{(h)}$ be bound GS; [33]

Our progressive water immersion ignores all those pixels whose grey level doesn't belong to the bound GS. Bound GS is defined with guidance of domain knowledge that describes the degree of dark and light. So the optimality of point in a certain region is defined as follows [9]:

$$optimality=\begin{cases} \text{maximal grey level, if point belongs to high bound pixel set ;} \\ \text{minimal grey level, if point belongs to low bound pixel set ;} \end{cases}$$

The pseudo-codes for the progressive water immersion algorithm are given as follows.

Input: medical image
Output: objects in this medical image

```
   WHILE(image scan not finished)
{
    IF(the first scan)
       initialize slide window;
    ELSE
       relocate initial position of the slide window;
    WHILE (1)
    {
        compare pixel grey value in the window and find the optimal point;
            IF (the optimal point is the center of the window)
                this point is stored as seed;
                Break;
          ELSE
           move the slide window and make the optimal point as the center of window;
    }
}
Count=1;
Con_th= seed-to-pixel contrast threshold;
FOR(each seed)
{
        FOR (each 8-directional neighbor pixel of the seed)
           IF (absolute value of seed-to-neighbor pixel contrast is less than Con_th)
           {
              push this pixel into queue and mark this pixel;
              Count++;
           }
        WHILE (Count!=0)
        {
           sort pixel in queue in descent order according to the grey value;
           pop the last pixel from queue;
           Count--;
           FOR (each 8-directional neighbor pixel of the last pixel)
            IF(absolute value of seed-to- neighbor pixel contrast is less than Con_th)
            {
               push this pixel into queue and mark this pixel;
               Count++;
            }
        }
}
```

After the above process, all the ROIs are detected and we will call them objects later, see figure 1. Next, images with many different objects are represented by transactions and we use a table to describe these transactions, see table 1 [9].

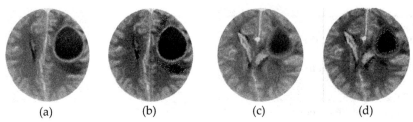

(a)   (b)   (c)   (d)

Figure 1. Figure (a) and (c) are two original abnormal brain images. Progressive water immersion algorithm is used to mark the objects with dotted line in figure (b) and (d).

In table 1, the first column is the medical image id. The second column is the objects in each image. The other columns are the features extracted from the object.

Image ID	Object ID	feature$_1$	...	feature$_n$
IM$_1$	O$_1$	feature$_1$_v	...	feature$_n$_v
IM$_1$	O$_2$	...	...	...
IM$_1$	O$_3$	...		
IM$_2$	O$_1$	...		
IM$_2$	O$_2$	...		
...	...	...		
IM$_n$	O$_n$	...	...	...

Table 1. Images are modeled by transactions

3. Medical image clustering

By applying progressive water immersion algorithm, we segment images into objects. Let IM={IM$_1$, IM$_2$, ..., IM$_N$} be a image set. After the above algorithm, Each image IM$_j$ contains k objects R$_{j1}$, R$_{j2}$, ..., R$_{jk}$. For different image, k may be not equal. Let the total of objects in IM be M, then we denote the object set as R={ R$_1$, R$_2$, ..., R$_M$}.

3.1. Feature extraction

For each extracted object R$_i$, we need to extract relevant information for features mining to take place. The domain knowledge of the brain image characteristics indicates that the normal persons have nearly the same brain structure that is evident to be bilateral symmetry. That is, the distribution of density in the left hemisphere of the brain is almost identical with the right, see figure 2 [9]. The pathological regions result in irregularly shaped grey level distribution in the CT scan images and destroy the symmetry, see figure 1. At this point, the following relevant features are able to provide sufficient discriminative power to cluster objects into different groups: (1) grey level of the object of interest; (2) area of the object of interest; (3) location of the object of interest; (4) elongation of the object of interest; (5) direction of the object of interest; and (6) symmetry of the object of interest.

Brain midline

Figure 2. Normal person's brain image

With the above method, the object extracted from brain image is either brightness or darkness. So we define grey level as GL= 0 (brightness), or 1 (darkness). The second feature we have found useful relate to the size of the region in the form of the area of the region. Area of the region of interest is defined as the total number of pixels within the region, up to and including the boundary pixels. The location of an object of interest is defined as a ratio. The coordinates of the centroid of the object [9] are computed with the formula (1).

$$\bar{x} = \frac{1}{k}\sum_{j=1}^{k} x_j \qquad \bar{y} = \frac{1}{k}\sum_{j=1}^{k} y_j \tag{1}$$

k is the number of the pixels of the object and the location is ($\bar{x}$ /|x|, $\bar{y}$ /|y|).

The fourth feature is the elongation of an object which is defined as the ratio of the width of the minor axis to the length of the major axis. This ratio is computed as the minor axis width distance divided by the major axis length distance, giving a value between 0 and 1. If the ratio is equal to 1, the object is roughly a square or is circular in shaped. As the ratio decreases from 1, the object becomes more elongated. Major axis is the longest line that can be drawn through the object. The two end points of the major axis are found by selecting the pairs of boundary pixels with the maximum distance between them. This maximum distance is also known as the major axis length. Similarly, the minor axis is defined as the line that it is perpendicular with respect to the major axis and the length between the two end points of the line intersected with the object is the longest which is called the width of the minor axis. The ratio, elongation, is a measure of the degree of elongation of an object.

$$elongation = len_{major} / len_{minor} \tag{2}$$

where len_{major} is the major axis length of the object and len_{minor} is the minor axis length of the object. We establish a common coordinate with brain midline as y and perpendicular line going through the midpoint of midline as x. With the major axis of the object, we define the next feature, direction of the object, as the inclination θ of the major axis and x positive direction and $\theta \in [0,180]$ [9].

Before introducing the final feature, we will give some definitions.

6. Pixel set of IM_p is defined as P={p_i | p_i is the pixel with coordinate (x_i, y_i) in the image IM_p}, P(L) and P(R) are pixel set of IM_p(L) and IM_p(R) respectively [33].
7. For any $p_{li} \in$ P(L), $p_{rj} \in$ P(R), they are symmetric pixel if the line between p_{li} and p_{rj} is halved vertically by brain midline. They are denoted as p_{li} and p_{ri} below [33].

8. $\Delta g(P)$ is IM_p's difference set if for any symmetrical pixel p_{li} and p_{ri}, $\Delta g(P)=\{ \Delta g_i | \Delta g_i = g(p_{li})-g(p_{ri}), i=1,2,...,|p|/2 \}$, where $g(p_{li})$ and $g(p_{ri})$ are grey level of these two pixels respectively.

Now we define the sixth feature as following.

9. An object of interest R_{pk} is symmetrical if for IM_p and R_{p1}, R_{p2}, ..., R_{pk}, $P' = P - \sum_{i=1}^{k} P(R_{pi})$, the mean grey level of $\Delta g(R_{pk})$, $mean(\Delta g(R_{pk}))$, and the mean grey level of $\Delta g(P')$, $mean(\Delta g(P'))$, satisfy the following condition:

$$|mean(\Delta g(R_{pk})) - mean(\Delta g(P'))| < \varepsilon.$$

Theorem 1: If for IM_p, an object of interest R_{pk} is symmetrical, then there must exist another object of interest R_{pt} that satisfies the following conditions: (1) R_{pk} and R_{pt} must lie in different side of the midline; (2) R_{pk} and R_{pt} are either two different objects or the same one.

Proof: According to the definition of symmetric pixel and object symmetry, condition 1 is evident. For the second condition, it is also evident for R_{pk} and R_{pt} to be two different objects. If R_{pk} bestrides two hemispheres and is symmetrical, it satisfies the definition of object symmetry. Actually, R_{pt} is the part of R_{pk} that lies in the other side of the brain midline. Both of them belong to the same object.

3.2. Object clustering

Now, we would like to determine similarity between two objects based on these features. For an object R_i, a vector $V_i(v_{i,1}, v_{i,2}, ..., v_{i,k})$ is constructed and similarity between object R_i and object R_j is as follows [9]:

$$Sim^R(R_i,R_j) = \Delta v_{ij,1} * (\sum_{h=2}^{k-1} v_{i,h} * v_{j,h}) / (\sqrt{\sum_{h=2}^{k-1} v_{i,h}^2} * \sqrt{\sum_{h=2}^{k-1} v_{j,h}^2}) \tag{3}$$

According to domain knowledge, we let $v_{ij,1}$ be GL. Two objects are not possible to be similar if one is very darkness and the other is very brightness. So we let $\Delta v_{i,1}$ be 1 if $v_{i,1} = v_{j,1}$, or 0 if $v_{i,1} \neq v_{j,1}$ in formula (3) [9]. Another similar rule is that if two objects R_i and R_j satisfy the second condition in theorem 1, they will be grouped into the same cluster. This rule is prior to the above similarity function.

It is difficult for us to know the number of the clusters in advance. So we use DBscan algorithm to group these objects. We use a non-negative threshold T_R to construct object clusters. If similarity between two objects is smaller than T_R, then the two objects can be in the same group [9].

10. For an object R_j, its ε-neighborhood, denoted by ε-$N(R_j)$, is defined by:

$$\varepsilon\text{-}N(R_j) = \{X \in R | Sim^R(R_j,X) \leq T_R \}$$

11. R_i is core object (c-object) if its $\varepsilon\text{-}N(R_i)$ involves no less than MP objects, that is, $|\varepsilon\text{-}N(R_i)| \geq MP$.
12. R_i is directly density reachable from R_j if $R_i \in \varepsilon\text{-}N(R_j)$ and $|\varepsilon\text{-}N(R_i)| \geq MP$ (R_i is c-object).
13. R_1 is density reachable from R_k if there is a chain of objects $R_1, R_2, ..., R_k$, any object R_{i+1} is directly density reachable from R_i.
14. R_i is density connected to R_j if there is an object R_k that is density reachable from not only R_i but also R_j.

Density-connectivity is a symmetric relation. For density reachable points, the relation of density-connectivity is also reflexive. The key idea is that for each object of a cluster the neighborhood of a given radius has to contain at least a minimum number of objects, i.e. the density in the neighborhood has to exceed some threshold. The shape of a neighborhood is determined by the similarity function. To find a cluster, OCA starts with an arbitrary object R and retrieves all objects density-reachable from R. If R is a core object, this procedure yields a cluster. If R is a border object, no objects are density-reachable from R and OCA visits the next object of the dataset.

If two clusters C_1 and C_2 are very close to each other, it might happen that some object R belongs to both C_1 and C_2. Then R must be a border object in both clusters because otherwise C_1 would be equal to C_2 since we use global parameters. In this case, object R will be assigned to the cluster discovered first. Except from these rare situations, the result of our algorithm is independent of the order in which the objects of the database are visited.

In the following, we present the Object Clustering Algorithm (OCA) [9].

Object Clustering Algorithm (OCA):
Input: object set R, T_R and MP
Output: p clusters
    1. Assume that the size of object set R is M and examine $\varepsilon\text{-}N(R)$;
    2. For k = 1 to M {
    3.   If (Ri is *unclassified*) Then
    4.   If ($\varepsilon\text{-}N(Ri)$ involves more than MP objects) Then {
    5.   mark Ri as the core object;
    6.   Cluster_Expanding(Ri);
    7.   else mark Ri *classified*;
    8.   }
    9. }

The function *Cluster_Expanding()* is most important for discovering arbitrary shape clusters. It is presented bellow [9].

Cluster_Expanding(Ri)

1. While(all core objects) {
2.   mark Ri *classified*;
3.   cluster all density reachable objects;
4.   record all the core objects;
5.   mark those non-core objects as *classified*;
6. }

The average run time complexity of this algorithm is $O(M\log M)$ with spatial index. Otherwise, it is $O(M^2)$.

3.3. Image clustering

The OCA algorithm clusters these M objects into p groups which we denoted as RC={C_1, C_2, ..., C_p}. Image clustering is based on image similarity. To calculate image similarity, we construct a vector $W_i(w_{1,i}, w_{2,i}, ..., w_{p,i})$ for an image IM_i. $w_{p,i}$ is the weight of object cluster C_p in image i. In this vector we keep the weight of each group. Thus, the size of vector W_i is same as the total number of object clusters (=p). It is possible that the weight of a group may be zero. This is because no object of an image may be a participant of that group during clustering. To determine an image vector, we adopt the idea from the area of information retrieval. Here, images correspond to documents, and object clusters correspond to terms (keywords) [9].

15. Let $CIM_{j,i}$ be the times of objects of cluster C_j in image IM_i, IMC_j be the number of images in which objects of cluster C_j appear. We define

$$iIMC_j = \log (N/IMC_j) \tag{4}$$

where N is the size of the image set [9].

IMC_j is used to evaluate the function of C_j to measure the similarity of two images. For $iIMC_j$, the higher its value is, the more impact C_i has to distinguish two different images.

16. For a vector $W_i(w_{1,i}, w_{2,i}, ..., w_{p,i})$, we define

$$w_{j,i} = CIM_{j,i} * iIMC_j \tag{5}$$

After computing image vectors, we get similarity between any two images using cosine similarity:

$$\text{Sim}^{IM}(IM_i, IM_j) = (\sum_{h=1}^{p} w_{h,i} * w_{h,j}) / (\sqrt{\sum_{h=1}^{p} w_{h,i}^2} * \sqrt{\sum_{h=1}^{p} w_{h,j}^2}) \tag{6}$$

The higher the value of Sim^{IM} is, the more similar the two images are [9].

When two microclusters, each of which includes more than two images, are to be grouped into a new cluster, we redefine the similar function to measure the similarity of two microclusters.

$$\text{Sim}^{MC}(MC_i, MC_j) = (\sum_{h=1}^{p} \overline{w}_{h,i} * \overline{w}_{h,j}) / (\sqrt{\sum_{h=1}^{p} \overline{w}_{h,i}^{2}} * \sqrt{\sum_{h=1}^{p} \overline{w}_{h,j}^{2}}) \tag{7}$$

where $\overline{W}_i(\overline{w}_{1,i}, \overline{w}_{2,i}, ..., \overline{w}_{p,i})$ is the centroid of all vectors within microcluster MC_i.

The algorithm will stop when the images are clustered into k group.

Image Clustering Algorithm (ICA):
Input: Image set IM and the number of clusters k;
Output: k clusters
    1. Each element of IM is regarded as an atomic cluster and compute Sim^{IM};
    2. Find the biggest Sim^{IM} and Amalgamate to form a new cluster;
    3. While (the number of clusters is not equal to k) {
    4. If all R_is in one image are symmetrical
    5. Then cluster this image to *special* cluster;
    6. Compute Sim^{MC};
    7. Cluster the sub-clusters or images; }

The average run time complexity of this algorithm for the worst case is $O(n^2)$. The clustering algorithm starts with each input image as a separate cluster, and at each successive step merges the closest pair of clusters. In order to compute the distance between a pair of clusters, for each cluster, c representative images are stored. These are determined by first choosing c well scattered image within the cluster, and then shrinking them toward the mean of the cluster by a fraction α. The distance between two clusters is then the distance between the closest pair of representative images - one belonging to each of the two clusters. Thus, only the representative images of a cluster are used to compute its distance from other clusters.

The c representative images attempt to capture the physical shape and geometry of the cluster. Furthermore, shrinking the scattered images toward the mean by a factor α gets rid of surface abnormalities and mitigates the effects of outliers. The reason for this is that outliers typically will be further away from the cluster center, and as a result, the shrinking would cause outliers to move more toward the center while the remaining representative images would experience minimal shifts. The larger movements in the outliers would thus reduce their ability to cause the wrong clusters to be merged. The parameter α can also be used to control the shapes of clusters. A smaller value of α shrinks the scattered images very little and thus favors elongated clusters. On the other hand, with larger values of α, the scattered images get located closer to the mean, and clusters tend to be more compact [9].

3.4. Experiment results

The main reason why we study on real brain CT images instead of any simulative data is to avoid insignificance and uninterestingness and the reliability of the discovered knowledge [9]. On the other hand, it is because brain tissue is human's advanced nerve center, its function is particularly important. The disease affecting the brain has received much attention in the domain of medicine. In China, about 40,000 to 60,000 persons suffer from brain tumor every year. Especially during these years, the incidence of brain disease (especially brain tumor) has increased significantly. Therefore, the early diagnosis of brain diseases is becoming more and more crucial and is directly working on patients' treatment [33]. To have access to real medical images is a very difficult undertaking due to legally privacy issues and management of hospital. But with some specialists' help and support, we got 618 precious images and their corresponding diagnosis records which, for simplicity, we generalized to normal(N) and abnormal(A) [9].

Our algorithm is written in Visual C++ and compiled by Microsoft Visual Studio 6.0. All of experiments are performed on Acer computer using a 2.8GHZ Intel PC, 512MB of RAM, and 1024MB of virtual memory. The operating system in use was the Microsoft Windows XP.

To measure the quality of a cluster, we use precision, recall, and E measure. Recall is the ratio of relevant images to total images for a given category. Precision is the ratio of relevant images to images that appear in a cluster for a given category.

$$\text{Precision(P)} = \frac{\text{number of images correctly classified into each class}}{\text{number of total images}}$$

$$\text{Recall(R)} = \frac{\text{number of images correctly classified into one certain class}}{\text{number of images in one certain class}}$$

E measure is defined as follows:

$$E(p,r) = 1 - \frac{2}{1/p + 1/r}$$

where p and r are the Precision and Recall of a cluster. Note that E (p, r) is simply one minus harmonic mean of the precision and recall; E (p, r) ranges from 0 to 1 where E (p, r) =0 corresponds to perfect precision and recall, and E (p, r) corresponds to zero precision and recall. Thus, the smaller the E measure values the better the quality of a cluster [9].

The existing image clustering methods generally include two parts: (1) extract related features from image to form feature vector; (2) use distance function as the image similarity measurement to cluster images. Therefore, we design an image feature-based method as the comparison with our ROI-based method (ICA). Firstly, two related features we extract from medical images are asymmetry and grey level mean difference. Then, k-means algorithm is used to cluster these medical images. In the experiment, we sample five patients' images each time to test two clustering algorithms. Each patient has an image sequence. All the images in the same sequence, which are similar since they belong to the same patient, should be clustered into one group. In this way, we sample five times from the medical image dataset and get the average value of precision, recall and E value for each time, see figure 3-5. It is obviously that ICA is better than the image feature-based method because the precision and recall of ICA is higher than the image feature-based method and E value is lower.

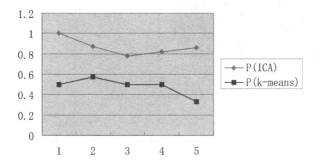

Figure 3. Precision for different number of sampling

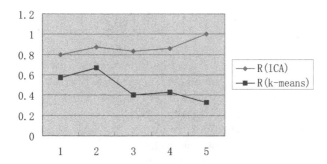

Figure 4. Recall for different number of sampling

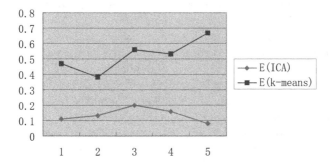

Figure 5. E measure for different number of sampling

In figure 3-5, x axis represents different sample time and the y axis represents p, r and E respectively. We have observed that precision and recall are higher for medical images.

Figure 6 shows an instance of our clustering algorithm.

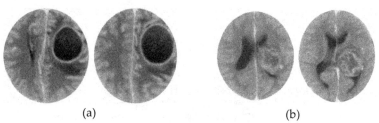

(a)   (b)

Figure 6. (a) and (b) show two images of two different clusters

In any case fairly large medical data sets exist but they are not available to us. Also, it would be interesting to apply these ideas in other domains where large complex data sets are available [9].

4. Association rule mining

In this section, we proposed the improved algorithm that generating candidate itemsets based association graph and matrix algorithm (GMA). That is, the GMA algorithm's candidate itemsets is the intersection of DLG and FAR algorithm's candidate itemsets. Experiments show that, GMA algorithm reduced the candidate itemsets generation greatly and had higher efficiency compared with other algorithms. The DLG algorithm's main idea is to construct a direct edge for every itemset of frequent-2 itemsets L_2. So L_2 can be mapped to a digraph, association graph. DLG algorithm uses the information of association graph to mine the frequent-k itemsets, where k is an integer. The FAR algorithm's main idea is to map the transaction database to a matrix with elements values of '0' and '1'. In order to mine frequent itemsets fast, it deletes some column and row to prune the matrix. Moreover, it must consider column of the matrix first, then consider the row of the matrix. The FAR algorithm also needs to generate the candidate itemsets. The candidate-k itemsets generate from k-vectors combination of columns of matrix. If the feature matrix has n columns, the number of candidate-k itemsets is C_n^k. Then it do "and calculus" for each combination of k-vectors. If the sum of element values in the "and" calculation result is not smaller than the minimum support, the k-itemsets corresponding to this combination of k-vectors are the frequent k-itemsets and are added to the set of frequent k-itemsets Lk [32]. DLG algorithm relies on the information of association graph to generate candidate itemsets, but when the transaction database is very large, the association graph is large, and the number of candidate itemsets also is very large. FAR algorithm generates the candidate-k itemsets by arbitrary k-vectors combination, that is C_n^k. The column of matrix is very large normally, so the number of candidate itemsets is also large.

4.1. Basic concept

A formal statement of the association rule is shown in Definition 1, 2 and 3.

17. Let I = {I_1, I_2, ..., I_m} be a set of m distinct attributes, also called literals. Let D be a database, where each record (tuple) T has a unique identifier, and contains a set of items

such that $T \subseteq I$. An association rule is an implication of the form $X \Rightarrow Y$, where X, $Y \subset I$, are sets of items called itemsets, and $X \cap Y = \phi$. Here, X is called antecedent, and Y consequent [3].

Two important measures for association rules, support (s) and confidence (α), can be defined as follows.

18. The support (s) of an association rule is the ratio (in percent) of the records that contain $X \cup Y$ to the total number of records in the database.
19. For a given number of records, confidence (α) is the ratio (in percent) of the number of records that contain $X \cup Y$ to the number of records that contain X.

Mining of association rules from a database consists of finding all rules that meet the user-specified threshold support s and confidence a.

20. Let D be a transaction database. L_k is the set of frequent-k itemsets, where k is an integer, for each itemset of L_k, it occurs with a frequency that is greater than or equal to the user-specified threshold support, s.
21. Association Graph.

For a directed graph $G = \{V, E\}$. $V(G)$ is the collection of vertex in G. $E(G)$ is the collection of edge in G. $<V_i, V_j>$ is a direct edge that from vertex of V_i to $V_j\{i < j\}$. Suppose that V_i, V_j mapped to item O_i, O_j in transaction database DB. Moreover, G can meet the following conditions:

$$V(G) = \{V_i \mid O_i \in L_1\},$$

$$E(G) = \{<V_i, V_j> \mid \{O_iO_j\} \in L_2, i<j\}$$

G is the association graph of the transactions database .

Property 1. Suppose the directed graph G is the association graph of image database D, the number of edge in G is equal to the number of frequent-2 itemsets $|L_2|$ in image database D.

22. Association Graph Extend and Join

Suppose $X = \{O_1O_2...O_k\}$ is a k-itemset of the database, if the association graph G of database has a direct edge $e = <V_k,V_j>$, X can be extended and joined to $X' = \{O_1O_2...O_k,O_j\}$.

Property 2. Suppose $X = \{O_1O_2...O_k\}$ is a k-itemset of the database, $X' = \{O_1O_2...O_k,O_j\}$ is a (k+1)-itemset which extended from k-itemset X by the association graph G. The number of X' is equal to the outdegree of the vertex V_k in G.

23. Feature Matrix

For a transaction database D, T is the transactions and O is the set of item in D. R is the binary relation from $T = \{T_1T_2,...,T_m\}$ to $O = \{O_1,O_2,...,O_n\}$, R: if the item O_i occur in transaction T_i, set $R(T_i,O_j) = 1$; else set $R(T_i,O_j) = 0$. FM is the feature matrix of the transaction database D. We denote the feature matrix as $FM = (r_{ij})_{m \times n}$, $(r_{ij}) = R(T_i, O_j)$.

For the sake of convenience, we denote the feature matrix $FM_{m \times n}$ and item O_j as $A_{m \times n}$ and I_j respectively.

4.2. GMA algorithm

This section proposed the GMA algorithm to mine the association rules for ROI in medical images database. In this section, we will give the algorithm details. In general, the GMA algorithm consists of four phases as follows: generating feature matrix and association graph, pruning the feature matrix, selecting and extending by the association graph, generating the set of frequent-k itemsets Lk(k>2).

4.2.1. Generating Feature Matrix and Association Graph

In the first phase, GMA algorithm has two steps. One is to transform the medical image transaction database into the feature matrix and get the set of frequent-1 itemsets L_1. The other is to get the set of frequent-2 itemsets L_2 and the association graph of medical image database.

Suppose that the mined medical image transaction database is D, with D having m images and n categories of ROI. First, GMA algorithm transforms the medical image transaction database into the feature matrix. Let $T=\{T_1,T_2,...,T_m\}$ be the set of transactions and $I=\{I_1,I_2,...,I_n\}$ be the set of items. So the D can be mapped to a matrix $A_{m \times n}$ relative to ROI which has m rows and n columns. Scanning the image transaction database D, if item I_j is in transaction T_i, where $1 \leq j \leq n, 1 \leq i \leq m$, the element value of A_{ij} is '1', otherwise the value of A_{ij} is '0' [32].

After transforming, GMA algorithm scans the ROI matrix, computes the supports of all items, and generates the set of frequent-1 itemsets L_1. The support number I_j.support of item I_j is the number of '1' in the jth column of the feature matrix $A_{m \times n}$. If I_j.support is not smaller than the minimum support, I_j.support$\geq$min_sup, I_j will be added to the set of frequent-1 itemsets L_1. Otherwise the column of the jth will be deleted from the feature matrix.

The phase of Generating feature matrix can be detailed in Algorithm 1.

Algorithm 1: Feature Matrix Construction
Input: DB, min_sup.
Output: Feature Matrix A, L_1.
Method :
for i = 1 to m
  for j = 1 to n
    set A_{ij} = 0;
Scan the DB;
for j = 1 to n
  for i = 1 to m
    if item j in the ith transaction do begin
      set A_{ij} to 1;
    end

```
end
L₁= Φ;
Scan Feature Matrix A;
for i = 1 to n do
    denote the 1's counts of the column of Aj as sum(Aj);
    if sum(Aj) ≥ min_sup
        L₁=L₁∪{Ij};
        else delete Aj from A;
end
```

The set of frequent-2 itemsets generates to construct the association graph. For each itemset I_i of L_1, a node is allocated for item I_i and I_i.link = NULL. For every combination of I_i and I_j (i<j) in L_1, the ith and jth column of feature matrix are two vectors, the "and" relational calculus $I_i \wedge I_j$ is done. If the sum of element values in the "and" calculation result is not smaller than the minimum support number min_sup, sum($I_i \wedge I_j$) ≥min_sup, a directed edge from item I_i to item I_j is constructed and add itemset $\{I_iI_j\}$ to the set of frequent-2 itemset L_2. So after generating the L_2, we can get the association graph, see Algorithm 2 [32].

```
Algorithm 2: Association Graph Construction
Input: L₁, min_sup.
Output: L₂, Association Graph.
Method:
if L₁ ≠Φ, do
    allocate a node for every item Ii of L₁, and do
    Item[Ii].link = NULL; then do
        produce every 2-vectors Ai, Aj(i < j) combination
        B=Ai∧Aj;
        if the 1 counts of vector B, sum(B) ≥ min_sup do
            allocate a node p;
            p.link = Item[Ii].link; p.Item = Item[Ij];
            Item[Ii].link = p; L₂ = L₂ ∪{Ii,Ij};
        end
    end
```

4.2.2. Pruning matrix

In order to introduce the pruning principle clearly, we give two properties and their proof in the following.

Proposition 1. Let X is a k-itemset, $|L_{k-1}(j)|$ presents the number of items 'j' in all frequent (k-1)-itemsets of the frequent set L_{k-1}. There is an item j in X. If $|L_{k-1}(j)|$ < k-1, itemset X is not a frequent itemset.

Proposition 2. For each row vector A_i in the feature matrix of the transaction database D, If the sum of '1' in a row vector A_i is smaller than k, it is not necessary for A_i attending calculus of the k- supports . [32]

Algorithm3:OptMatrix( )
Input: L_{k-1}, Feature Matrix $A_{m \times n}$.
Output: Matrix $B_{p \times q}$.
Method:
Scan the matrix A;
for j = 1 to n
    if $|L_{k-1}(A_j)| < k-1$
        Delete the column A_j of Matrix A;
    for i = 1 to m
    Compute the 1'counts of A_m;
        if sum(A_m) < k
            Delete the row A_m of Matrix;
    for i = 1 to p
    for j = 1 to q
        Output the corresponding matrix B_{ij};

Pruning the matrix means deleting some rows and columns from it. According to the proposition 1 and proposition 2, we can get the pruning principle. The pruning principle can be described as Algorithm 3. First, the column of the feature matrix is pruned. This is described in detail as: Let I' be the set of all items in the frequent set L_{k-1}, where k>2. Compute all $|L_{k-1}(j)|$ where $j \in I'$, and delete the column of correspondence item j if $|L_{k-1}(j)|$ is smaller than k-1. Second recompute the sum of the element values in each row in the feature matrix. These rows of the feature matrix whose sum of element values is smaller than k are deleted from this matrix. [32]

4.2.3. Selecting and extending by association graph

GMA algorithm generates the candidate-k itemsets depending on selecting and extending the frequent-(k-1) itemset by the association graph. For a (k-1)-itemset of L_{k-1}, if it do not contain the item j which the corresponding column of feature matrix was deleted by pruning in the (k-1)th pass. GMA extends it to a k-itemset as a candidate-k itemset.

In order to generate candidate-k itemsets, GMA need to consider all itemsets of L_{k-1}. However, this procedure performed following the feature matrix pruning procedure. That is to say, when GMA mine the frequent-k itemsets, it must do the two steps, one is the feature matrix pruning, the other is selecting and extending frequent-(k-1) itemsets to generate the candidate-k itemsets. If there is a column of matrix has been deleted by optimizing matrix, we will not consider the itemset of L_{k-1} which contains the corresponding of item. Otherwise, for each itemset $\{I_1, I_2, ..., I_{k-1}\}$ of L_{k-1}, finding edges that from vertex I_{k-1} to other vertex in association graph. If there is an edge from vertex I_{k-1} to vertex u, the itemset $\{I_1, I_2, ..., I_{k-1}, u\}$ is a candidate-k itemset. Not that all (k-1)-itemset needs to extend, this idea can be described by Algorithm 4.

Algorithm 4: SEJ( ) Select to Extend and Join
Input: L_{k-1}, Association Graph.
Output: Candidate-k itemset C_k.

    $C_k = \Phi$;
    Scan the L_{k-1};
    for i = 1 to $| L_{k-1} |$
        if $\{I_1, I_2, ..., I_{k-1}\} \in L_{k-1}$&& $\{I_1, I_2, ..., I_{k-1}\}$ not contain item I_d
        which the corresponding column of matrix was deleted
        do begin
          pointer = Item[I_{k-1}].link;
          while (pointer $\neq$ NULL) do begin
            u = pointer.Item;
            $C_k = C_k \cup \{I_1, I_2, ..., I_{k-1}, I_u\}$;
            pointer = pointer.link;
      end
    end

4.2.4. Generating Frequent-k Itemsets Lk(k>2)

The most important phase in GMA algorithm is to generate the set of frequent-k itemsets L_k (k>2). In order to find the set of frequent-k (k>2) itemset, GMA algorithm firstly optimizes the matrix. Afterwards it generates the candidate-k itemsets using the information of association graph and matrix pruning. At last it verifies whether the candidate-k itemset is a frequent-k itemset. The details of above procedures are described as follows.

Proposition 3. $|L_k|$ presents the number of k-itemsets in the frequent set L_k. If $|L_k|$ is smaller than k+1, the maximum length frequent itemsets is k.

Most of algorithm for mining frequent-k itemsets's terminal condition is that L_{k-1} is null. However, GMA algorithm terminal condition is described by Property 3. that is to say, when GMA get the L_k, it examine the number of L_k, if $|L_k|$ is smaller than k+1, GMA algorithm terminate to perform the the k+1th mining.

In order to generate the set of frequent-k itemsets L_k, GMA must obtain the candidate-k itemsets, then to verify by the "and calculus" operation. We can get the candidate-k itemsets by the Algorithm 4. GMA algorithm is an iterative to mine the frequent itemsets.

GMA algorithm does the "and" relational calculus to verify whether the candidate-k itemset is a frequent-k itemset of L_k. The "and" relational calculus is for combination of k vectors which corresponding to the candidate-k itemset $\{I_1, I_2, ..., I_{k-1}, u\}$. Then make k=k+1, do this again to find all frequent-k itemsets, see Algorithm 5.

Algorithm 5: Frequent-k (k>2)Itemset Generation
Input: L_{k-1}, min_sup.
Output: L_k.
Method:
   while ($|L_{k-1}| \geq k$) do begin
   $L_k = \Phi$;
      OptMatrix(A);
      SEJ(L_{k-1}, Association Graph);
   for i = 1 to $|\check{C}_k|$
   if $C_k = \{I_1, I_2, ..., I_{k-1},u\}$&&
   sum($A_1 \wedge A_2 \wedge ... \wedge A_{k-1} \wedge A_u) \geq$ min_sup do
      $L_k = L_k \cup \{I_1, I_2, ..., I_{k-1},I_u\}$;
   end
   k = k+1;
end

4.3. Experiment results

In order to appraise the performance of the GMA algorithm, we conducted an experiment using the DLG algorithm, the FAR algorithm and GMA algorithm. These algorithms were implemented in C and tested on Windows XP SP3 Operating system, Mobile Intel Pentium 4 1.89GHz CPU，1024MB DDR RAM，VC++6.0 compiler platform. The test database T10I4D100K was generated   synthetically by an algorithm designed by the IBM Quest project. The number of items N is set to 1000; $|D|$ is the number of transactions; $|T|$ is the averages size of transactions, and $|I|$ is the average size of the maximum frequent itemsets. Fig. 7 presents the experimental results for different values of minimum supports.

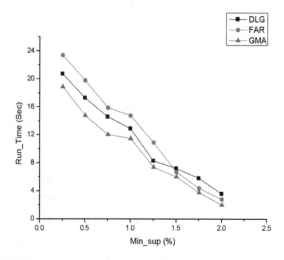

Figure 7. The performance comparisons of DLG,FAR and GMA

Experiment shows that, we can get the same set of frequent-k itemsets using three algorithms. However, the run_time of the algorithms execution is not same. DLG algorithm is better than FAR algorithm when the min_sup is small. FAR algorithm excels DLG algorithm as the value of min_sup increasing. Because when the min_sup increase, the efficiency of matrix pruning is better. In general, GMA algorithm is outperform the two algorithms whatever the value of min_sup is.

5. Further research

Based on the above work, the further research involves the following 3 parts:

i.   Semantic cluster concept generation. The above clustering method allows us to automatically obtain the information regarding the spatial layout, the area and the density of a specific cluster. Based on these information, we are able to define a few semantic cluster concepts, such as center cluster, left cluster, dense cluster, sparse cluster, big cluster, small cluster and so on.

ii.   Semantic concept image indexing and retrieval. After the generation of cluster semantic concepts, semantic concept indexing of medical images is built to support high-level image retrieval based on these semantic concepts. Examples of such image retrieval are:"retrieval all the medical images which have dense cluster in the center of the image", and "retrieval all the medical images in which the clusters located in the left and lower corners are all small ones".

iii. Trends and patterns mining. Finally, it is desirable to produce some spatial and temporal trends and patterns of the patient who have the medical images with different time. To this end, we explore the pathology cluster information to discover any spatial and temporal trends and patterns of pathology development in terms of scale, area, time duration and location. These trends and patterns are potentially useful for better understanding of the pathology behavior. [3]

6. Conclusion

In this chapter, we firstly presented a progressive water immersion algorithm with guidance of domain knowledge to preprocessing the medical image set to detect objects in medical images. Then we proposed two new algorithms with guidance of domain knowledge to cluster the medical images. We quantified the domain knowledge and use them in the clustering algorithm. Secondly, we proposed GMA algorithm for mining association rules on medical images. GMA algorithm draws on the advantages both association graph and feature matrix pruning to reduce the candidate itemsets generation. In actually, it greatly reduces the candidate itemsets and has improved the efficiency of frequent itemset mining. Experiment shows that GMA algorithm can adapt and adjust better to the change of the value of min_sup. Moreover, GMA algorithm can be used for mining association rules on medical images effectively [9]. We have described the problems with a general form to provide a common framework for other problems appeared in other domains.

Author details

Haiwei Pan
College of Computer Science and Technology,
Harbin Engineering University, Harbin, Heilongjiang, China

Acknowledgement

I would like to express my sincere gratitude to people for helping me during my study. I would especially like to thank my adviser, Jianzhong Li, for his being supportive all the time. I wish to thank Prof. Guisheng Yin, Prof. Jing Zhang, Prof. Qilong Han, Prof. for the advice and the kindness. I would also like to thank Mr. Xiaolei Tan, Ms. Chunxin Zhang, Ms. Guizhen Sun and Mr. Mingde Pan for the research and the support.

The chapter is partly supported by the National Natural Science Foundation of China under Grant No.60803036, No.60803037, Natural Science Foundation of Heilongjiang Province under Grant No.F200903, the Fundamental Research Funds for Central Universities No. HEUCFZ1010, the National High-tech R&D Program of China under Grant No. 2009AA01Z143, and Nuclear Safety & Simulation Tech. Lab Foundation under Grant No.HEUFN0802.

7. References

[1] Haiwei Pan, Jianzhong Li, Wei Zhang(2007) Incorporating domain knowledge into medical image clustering, Applied Mathematics and Computation, 15 February, V185, 844–856

[2] Osmar R. Zaiane, Jiawei Han, Ze-Nian Li, Jean Hou (1998) Mining Multimedia Data CASCON'98: Meeting of Minds, Toronto, Canada, November, 83-96.

[3] WYNNE HSU, MONG LI LEE, JI ZHANG (2002) Image Mining: Trends and Developments. Journal of Intelligent Information Systems, 2002(19-1):7–23.

[4] P. Stolorz, H. Nakamura, E. Mesrobian, R. Muntz, E. Shek, J. Santos, J. Yi, K. Ng, S. Chien, C. Mechoso, and J. Farrara (1995) Fast spatio-temporal data mining of large geophysical datasets. In Proc. Int. Conf. on KDD, 300–305.

[5] U. M. Fayyad, S. G. Djorgovski, and N. Weir (1996) Automating the analysis and cataloging of sky surveys. In U. Fayyad, G. Piatetsky-Shapiro, P. Smyth, and R. Uthurusamy, editors, Advances in Knowledge Discovery and Data Mining, AAAI/MIT Press, 471–493.

[6] O. R. Zaiane, J. Han, Z.-N. Li, J. Y. Chiang, and S. Chee (1998) MultiMediaMiner: A system prototype for multimedia data mining. In Proc. ACM-SIGMOD, Seattle, 581-583.

[7] Osmar R. Zaiane, Jiawei Han, Hua Zhu (2000) Mining Recurrent Items in Multimedia with Progressive Resolution Refinement. Int. Conf. on Data Engineering (ICDE'2000), San Diego, CA, February, 461-470.

[8] Ordonez, C. and Omiecinski, E. (1999). Discovering Association Rules Based on Image Content. In IEEE Advances in Digital Libraries Conference.

[9] Haiwei Pan, Jianzhong Li, Wei Zhang(2005) Medical Image Clustering for Intelligent Decision Support, Proceedings of the 2005 IEEE Engineering in Medicine and Biology 27th Annual Conference, Shanghai, China, September, 3308-3311

[10] Wynne Hsu, Mong Li Lee, Kheng Guan Goh (2000) Image Mining in IRIS: Integrated Retinal Information System, In Proc. 2000 ACM-SIGMOD Int. Conf. Management of Data (SIGMOD'00). 2000:176~177

[11] Kitamoto.A (2001) Data Mining for Typhoon Image Collection. In Second International Workshop on Multimedia Data Mining (MDM/KDD'2001). 2001:68~78

[12] Ashraf Elsayed, Frans Coenen, Marta García-Fiñana, Vanessa Sluming(2009) Segmentation for Medical Image Mining, A Technical Report, 24 June.

[13] Jain, A.K., Murty, M.N., and Flynn, P.J. (1999) Data Clustering: A Review. ACM Computing Survey, 1999:31~58

[14] Chang, E., Li, C., and Wang, J. (1999) Searching Near-Replicas of Image via Clustering. In SPIE Multimedia Storage and Archiving Systems VI. 1999:89~100

[15] Yu, D. and Zhang, A. (2000) ACQ: An Automatic Clustering and Querying Approach for Large Image Databases. IEEE International Conference on Data Engineering. 2000:58~69

[16] Wynne Hsu, Mong Li Lee, Kheng Guan Goh. (2000) Image Mining in IRIS: Integrated Retinal Information System. Proceedings of the ACM SIGMOD, Dellas, Texas, U.S.A., May 2000, pp. 593.

[17] Maria-Luiza Antonie, Osmar R. Zaiane, Alexandru Coman. (2001) Application of Data Mining Techniques for Medical Image Classification. Proceedings of the Second International Workshop on Multimedia Data Mining (MDM/KDD'2001).

[18] Osmar R. Zaiane, Maria-Luiza Antonie, Alexandru Coman. (2002) Mammography Classification by an Association Rule-based Classifier. Proceedings of the Third International Workshop on Multimedia Data Mining (MDM/KDD'2002).

[19] Christian Bohm, Karin Kailing, Peer Kroger, Arthur Zimek. (2004) Computing Clusters of Correlation Connected Objects. In Proc. 2004 ACM-SIGMOD Int. Conf. Management of Data (SIGMOD'04), 2004:455-466.

[20] Anthony K. H. Tung, Xin Xu, Beng Chin Ooi (2005) CURLER: Finding and Visualizing Nonlinear Correlation Clusters, Proceedings of the ACM SIGMOD International Conference on Management of Data (SIGMOD), 2005: 518~529

[21] Hans-Peter Kriegel,Martin Pfeifle (2005) Density-Based Clustering of Uncertain Data, Proceedings of the Eleventh ACM SIGKDD International Conference on Knowledge Discovery and Data Mining (KDD), 2005:672~677

[22] Rakesh Agrawal, Tomasz Imielinski and Arun N. Swami (1993) Data Mining: A Performance perspective, IEEE Transactions on Knowledge and Data Engineering, 1993, Vol.5, pp.914-925.

[23] Rakesh Agrawal and Ramakrishnan Srikant (1994) Fast Algorithms for Mining Association Rules in Large Databases, Proceedings of the Twentieth International Conference on Very Large Databases, Santiago, Chile, pp.487-499.

[24] Mika Klemettinen, Heikki Mannila, Pirjo Ronkainen, Hannu Toivonen and A. Inkeri Verkamo (1994) Finding Interesting Rules From Large Sets of Discovered Association

Rules, Proceedings of the Third International Conference on Information and Knowledge Management (CIKM'94), Gaithersburg, USA. pp.401-407.

[25] Jiawei Han, Jian Pei, Yiwen Yin (2000) Mining frequent patterns candidate generation," In proceedings of the 2000 ACM SIGMOD International Conference on Management of Data (SIGMOD'2000), Dallas, TX, 2000, pp.1-12.

[26] J.S. Park, M.S. Chen, P.S. Yu (1995) An effective hash-based algorithm for mining association rules, Proc. 1995 ACM-SIGMOD Int.Conf. Management of Data (SIGMOD'95), San Jose, CA, l995, pp.175-186.

[27] Liu, D. & Kedem, Z. (2002) An Efficient Algorithm for Discovering The Maximum Frequent Set, IEEE Transaction on Knowledge and Data Engineering, 2002, Vol.14, No.3, pp.553-566.

[28] Savasere, E.Ohniecinski, S.Navathe (1995) An efficient algorithm for mining association rules in large databases, Proc.1995 Int. Conf. Very Large Data Bases (VLDB'95), Zurich, Switzerland, l995, pp.432-443.

[29] L.Jaba Sheela , V. Shanthi , D.Jeba Singh (2009) Image Mining using Association rules derived from Feature Matrix, In proceedings of the 2009 International Conference on Advances in Computing, Communication and Control (ICAC3'09), Mumbai, Maharashtra, India, 2009, pp.440~443.

[30] YEN SJ, CHEN ALP (1996) An Efficient Approach to Discovering Knowledge from Large Database, Proceedings of the IEEE/ACM International Conference on Parallel and Distributed Information Systems, Los Angeles, USA, 1996, pp.8~18.

[31] YEN SJ, CHEN ALP (2001) A Graph-Based Approach for Discovering Various Types of Association Rules, IEEE Transactions on Knowledge and Data Engineering, 2001, Vol.13, No.5, pp.839~845.

[32] Pratima Gautam, K. R. Pardasani(2010) A Fast Algorithm for Mining Multilevel Association Rule Based on Boolean Matrix, International Journal on Computer Science and Engineering, Vol. 02, No. 03, 746-752

[33] Haiwei Pan, Xiaolei Tan, Qilong Han, Guisheng Yin(2011) Information Engineering and Electronic Business, A Domain Knowledge Based Approach for Medical Image Retrieval, March, 16-22

[34] Bin Fang, Wynne Hsu, Mong Li Lee(2002) Tumor Cell Identification using Features Rules, SIGKDD , July 23-26

Chapter 8

Electronic Documentation of Clinical Pharmacy Interventions in Hospitals

Ahmed Al-Jedai and Zubeir A. Nurgat

Additional information is available at the end of the chapter

1. Introduction

The documentation of interventions by hospital pharmacists has been on-going for over three decades through various available means; with recent national surveys suggesting that the majority of hospital pharmacists continue to document their interventions on a daily basis.[1-5] Pharmacist intervention encompasses all activities relating to safe medication utilisation and optimising therapeutic outcomes for patients in conjunction with other health care professionals which ultimately improves patient management or therapy'.[5'6]

The percentage of hospital pharmacists documenting and collecting data on a regular basis has been shown to vary from as high as 72% to 50% in various countries.[1-5] The specialty of individual pharmacist's clinical practice does not seem to significantly influence the number of documentation of interventions with 86% of intensive care pharmacists and 74% of various clinical specialties reported documenting their interventions on a daily basis.[5] However, there seems to be significant differences in the number of documented interventions between clinical pharmacists with respect to the level of managerial responsibilities.[5,7] Clinical pharmacists with managerial responsibilities have variable workloads, while those without have more time allocated to spend on rounds with the medical team, enabling them to document all of their interventions. In addition, the significant effect of education level of clinical pharmacists and the number of interventions documented has been previously published.[7] Clinical pharmacists with postgraduate qualifications seem to document significantly more interventions than those without.[7] This is not surprising that post doctorate pharmacists contribute more interventions due to their higher level of training, experience and confidence than those without a post graduate degree.

Various guidelines and suggestions, including recommendations made by the professional regulatory bodies have been published on pharmacists' interventions. The American Society of Health-System Pharmacist (ASHP) has recommended that, as integral members of the health care team, pharmacist must document the care they provide.[8] The Practice and Quality

Improvement Directorate of the Royal Pharmaceutical Society (RPS) has provided guidance on when an intervention is of sufficient significance for it to be recorded; the contents of the records made; where the record should be made; how the records could be utilised to improve efficiency and safety; and the length of time the records need to be retained for.[9]

2. Benefits and outcomes of pharmacists' interventions

Various reasons have been given for the recording of interventions by the RPS; to ensure patient safety and improve the quality and continuity of care; to provide evidence of the additional value of the pharmacist professional input; to have an accurate record available for scrutiny where decisions could be challenged; and to provide an incident or near miss monitoring process as part of the an organisation's clinical governance framework. The RPS recommends that interventions should be made as soon as possible after the event has occurred as this would enable the recording of details to be more accurate. Further recommendations include the recording of interventions into the patient's medication records either manually or electronically and they should be used to ensure consistency and continuity of standards and for reflective learning within the pharmacy team. [9]

The benefits of pharmacists' interventions in improving patient care is already well established, with no evidence of harm done to the patients.[10] The contribution made by pharmacists have not gone unnoticed and as a result was recognized as essential aspect in safe medication use. The close collaboration with the physician through participation in medical rounds has been suggested to improve medication safety and has been described as important.[10] As a result, traditional dispensing part of the hospital clinical pharmacist's job has all but disappeared and has undergone a paradigm shift by working directly with patients through the multidisciplinary teams consisting of physicians, nurses and other allied health professionals.

The outcome of pharmacists interventions have led to a reduction in mortality rates, drug costs and length of hospital stay.[11-13] In addition, it has resulted in improvements in medication appropriateness, pharmacoeconomics, health-related quality of life, and patient satisfaction.[14-17] Furthermore, these interventions have significantly reduced the number of drug interactions, medication errors, and adverse drug events. [19-23]

The benefits of pharmacists' intervention have been exploited for the expansion of the clinical pharmacists scope of practice.[14] New pharmacy positions such as technicians have been created to fill in for the technical duties of pharmacists as a result of the expanded role of clinical pharmacists.[14] The end result has been a reported lower medication error rate as the number of clinical pharmacists increased per occupied bed.[15]

There are, however, discrepancies between consensus recommendations of intervention recording and documentation of such interventions.[18] For this reason, various guidelines[7-9] and suggestions have been published on the subject as outlined above. The controversy of whether near miss or other interventions that prevent significant harm to patients by hospital pharmacist should be documented in patients' hospital health records when making recommendations will not be discussed in this chapter. Since the majority of hospitals have separate reporting systems under risk managements for near misses and adverse drug reactions this will be not be reviewed in this chapter rather pharmacy stand-alone systems for documentation purpose will be reviewed as this is the most popular way for documenting pharmacist interventions.

3. Methods of pharmacy interventions documentation - A global look

Various methods of documenting pharmacist interventions have been explored.[24-27] Earlier systems of documentation interventions used manual recording on a paper-based form and later on moved to electronic versions when they became available. Interestingly, the paper based intervention documentation system is still the preferred system of documenting of pharmacist interventions in some countries as shown by the survey of New Zealand Hospitals in 2008 where 88% collected data on paper, the majority using pre-printed forms and some using notebooks. In other countries paper based intervention documentation system has been replaced by other systems, as shown in a survey of 433 US health Care centres where only 24% documented interventions manually on a paper form.

Clinical Pharmacist Intervention Form

Pharmacist : _____   Date: _____   Serial No: _____

Drug Related Problems (DRPs)	Type of Intervention (T)	Clinical Significance (S)	Expected Outcome (O)	Acceptance (A)

1- No indication for drug therapy
2- No drug order for medical condition
3- Inappropriate drug selection
4- Inappropriate dosage regimen
  a) dose
  b) frequency
  c) route
  d) rate
5- Prescribed drug not administered
6- Experiencing ADR's or S.E.
7. Experiencing drug interactions (DI's):
  a) drug drug interactions (DDIs)
  b) drug food interactions (DFIs)
  c) drug lab test interactions (DLTIs)
8- Miscellaneous
	1- Pharmacokinetics
	
	2- Pharmacotherapeutics
	
	3- Drug Information
	
	4- Miscellaneous
		1- Potentially severe/
		   highly clinical
		   significance
		
		2- Important/serious
		   /moderately clinically
		   significance
		
		3- Minor/low clinical
		   significance
			1- Cost savings only
			
			2- Potential ADR's/
			   Toxicity prevented
			
			3- Enhanced therapeutic
			   effect
				A Accepted
				MA Modified then Accepted
				R Rejected
				
				N.B.
				if MA or R
				specify:
				a) what was the reason?
				
				b) Was it reasonable?

Pt. Account number and unit	Intervention	DRP #	T #	S #	O #	Acceptance

Pt. Account number and unit	Intervention	DRP #	T #	S #	O #	Acceptance
	Rx _____ Rec					a) b)
	Rx _____ Rec					a) b)
	Rx _____ Rec					a) b)
	Rx _____ Rec					a) b)

Figure 1. Paper based system for documenting pharmacist interventions.[18]

Nearly all of the pharmacist intervention documentations systems for recording pharmacist interventions are mostly designed in-house to meet the requirements of individual hospital's administrative data requirement. As a result, the pharmacist intervention documentation system varies from institution to institution due to different priorities of each individual institution as illustrated in tables 1 and 2 where surveys from two different countries suggest different priorities of the different institutions.[3,5]

Type of intervention	% Respondents Documenting
Change/clarify medication order	92
Therapeutic duplication	84
Drug-drug interaction	81
Adverse drug reaction	76
Formulary conversion	75
Medication selection recommendation	73
Pharmacokinetic consult	73
Therapeutic substitution	68
Medication error	67
Drug or lab level	62
Drug-food interaction	58
Drug information response	57
Potential adverse drug event	57
Patient education	45
Parenteral nutrition consult	44
Drug-disease interaction	44
Disease management recommendation	43
Drug use guidelines	40
Medication use without indication	31
Drug-herbal interaction	26
Untreated indication for medication	20
Pharmaceutical care plan	19
Admission medication history	15
Attendance at medical rounds	12
Patient medical history	11
CPR response	10
Discharge plan	9
Other	5

Table 1. Type of pharmacist Interventions Documented in US health-systems pharmacy directors survey (n=433). [5]

In a survey of US health-systems pharmacy directors,[5] the most common type of intervention documented were changing or clarifying medication order, therapeutic duplication and drug-drug interactions. Adverse drug reactions, formulary selection, medication selection and pharmacokinetic consultation were also frequently reported. Less frequently reported interventions were pharmaceutical care plans, Admission medication history and patient medication history. Whereas the survey from New Zealand,[3] free text of the intervention description was frequently reported in addition to the pharmacist identification. Less frequent documented interventions was cost savings and time spent on interventions.

Type of data	Number of hospitals collecting this data n (%)
Date of intervention	23 (96%)
Pharmacist's name/identification	21 (88%)
Place where intervention was made	21 (88%)
Classification of intervention	21 (88%)
Medication name	21 (88%)
Brief description of intervention (free text area)	21 (88%)
Patient NHI/identification	18 (75%)
Consultant name/identification	18 (75%)
Reason for making the intervention	15 (63%)
Severity/ranking of intervention	15 (63%)
Intervention accepted or declined by other health professional	13 (54%)
Time spent on intervention	12 (50%)
Effect on cost saving	8 (33%)
Drug class/therapeutic classification	6 (25%)

Table 2. Types of data collected by hospital pharmacies in the survey of New Zealand Hospitals. [3]

4. Challenges and drawbacks of current systems

The prevalence of in-house documentation systems has been the most significant drawback in terms of standardising and achieving consistency of recording of pharmacist interventions and eventually using the data as a bench mark for comparison of clinical pharmacist's contributions. This lack of standardisation of pharmacist intervention documentation has been the subject of much debate in the literature[3,5,18,28] and some have proposed to have a standard classification system like the one prevalent for Adverse Drug Reaction template imposed by the regulatory authorities.[3,5] This would make it much easier to collect meaningful statistics and comparisons be made with other centres as a bench mark for clinical pharmacy services.[28]

In a survey of US health-systems pharmacy directors, 61% of the respondents reported dissatisfaction with their current documentation systems.[5] Similar in the survey of New Zealand hospitals a large proportion of respondent believed that they had problems with their documentation systems.[3] Some have suggested that collecting data on paper was very time consuming especially if transcribing the data to an electronic storage data base and proved difficult to document all interventions. Others have reported that collecting data on pre-printed forms was cumbersome and transcribing the data was time consuming.[27] Furthermore, it was difficult to precisely audit pharmacists' workload, determine the quality of interventions and calculate cost saving, in line with what others have reported.[24-28]

With the difficulties encountered with the paper based pharmaceutical care intervention form, the challenges faced by any administrator is to implement a system that is user friendly and capture the data that is required. Another challenge is to capture all information that was previously entered on paper, increase the data-entry speed, and modify the database to address specific needs that was identified by the end users. One major advantage of an electronic system is the ease with which it facilitates monthly and annual reporting for departmental quality assurance programs. Numerous articles have been published on electronic pharmacist intervention programs in the literature and most have focused on a main frame computer terminal based in the pharmacy department. [24-28]

5. The King Faisal Specialist Hospital's experience, a personal-perspective

We had faced similar problems with our paper based documentation systems as described above, and in an attempt to improve the documentation of pharmacist's intervention we successfully developed and implemented a computerised application program to facilitate the collection and analysis of the data. Prior to this, pharmaceutical care activities and clinical interventions were either not documented or inconsistently documented (see figure 2). Later, the multi-user PC version and the subsequent enhanced version, the web based application revealed an increase in the number of interventions done by individual pharmacist with more pharmacists participating in the interventions recording regularly. We were able to show that by keeping the intervention program simple and easy to use; the contributions of individuals not only increased but were consistent. Here we describe in detail how we managed to develop our in-house documentation systems which may assist others in making similar documentation systems.

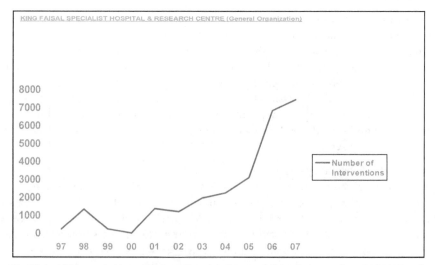

Figure 2. Clinical Pharmacist' interventions showing the trend from the paper based in 1997 to the multiuser PC (2004-2005) and finally up to the introduction of the web-based systems (2006-2007)-Unpublished Data (experience from KFSH&RC).

6. Process of documentation

6.1. The software

Traditionally two main types of electronic system of documenting of pharmacists interventions have been available to pharmacists for documentations of their interventions. One is the computer based pharmacist intervention program, multi-user PC version, restricted to a single point of entry in the pharmacy department or on the wards and the other a web based program such as based on Microsoft Visual Fox Pro® program Multi-user Application running under the Citrix® server using any terminal equipped with a Citrix® client.

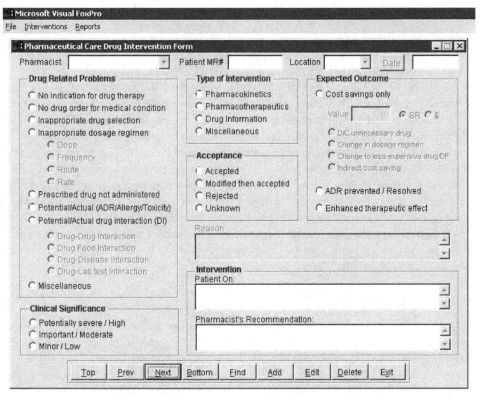

Figure 3. Main screen of the multi-user PC software intervention form. Only one outcome could be documented at a time by the clinical pharmacist. [7]

The multi-user PC version provides a platform for easy manipulation, customization, and updating the paper based program. It allows the mangers to monitor performance of individual pharmacists by evaluating the number of interventions made and the acceptance for daily interventions. In addition, it provides reports for the hospital administration on clinical pharmacists' activities and the data generated can be used to justify additional clinical pharmacists' positions. However, the system requires installation of the software in individual stand-alone personal computers (PCs). With the limited numbers of PCs that could be accessed by the pharmacists at the point of need e.g. during the physician rounds and within the pharmacy department most often the clinical pharmacists have to record the interventions manually on paper intervention form on the physician rounds and later on record their interventions on the multi-user PC version, resulting in incomplete data collection and duplication of work which was time consuming.

From our experience,[7, 18-19] the web based program of pharmacists' documentation systems facilitates ease of access and improves overall accuracy in data entry. The web based system enables the pharmacist to enter interventions from any workspace, in the clinic; on the ward; in the inpatient and outpatient dispensary. This may be achieved using any PC, laptop or even wireless personal digital assistant (PDA) connected to the hospital intranet. The ability to access the intervention program from any point is one major advantage of the web based intervention program. The web based application had one big advantage over the multi-user PC version since installation was not required in every PC and the program could be accessed from any location with intranet access. Since all in- patient areas and clinics were connected to the intranet, the easy access enabled the pharmacist to enter interventions from any workstation, in the clinics and on the ward during the physician rounds. This has been reflected in our recent study,[7] where the use of the web-based application revealed a 40% increase in the total number of documented interventions compared to multi-user PC software. In addition the time required to document an intervention using the web-based application of 66.55 ± 8.98 s (mean ± SD), is much quicker than documenting on paper base forms and as others have previously reported time of 81.8 ± 8.3 for web based program.[7,29] As the majority of dissatisfaction with the pharmacy documentations systems was reported to be a lack of time the lack of pharmacist time,[3, 5] the clinical pharmacist documentation system must be as efficient, and user-friendly as possible to be fully accepted by the end users and hence, be successfully implemented.

6.2. Intervention entry

Figure 4 depicts the "main intervention form" with the major categories e.g. Type of Intervention; Clinical Significance; Drug Related Problem; Acceptance; Expected Outcome clearly highlighted. It allows for the identification of the patient through the patient Medical Record Number (MRN), as well as the date and the location of the intervention. The pharmacist documenting the intervention is identifiable through the Drop-down pharmacists list which is password protected. The form further allows the pharmacist to document the main types of intervention inclusive of an intervention summary and the pharmacist recommendation. The web based program further enables the pharmacist to document cost saving only interventions on the main intervention form.

The cost saving interventions includes changes in dosage regimens, substitution with a less expensive drug, discontinuation of unnecessary drug and other indirect savings such as change form intravenous to oral formulation.

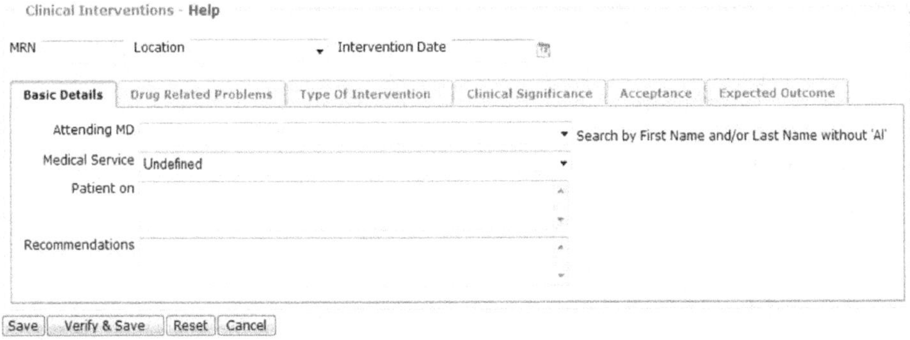

Clinical Interventions · **Help**

MRN   Location   ▾   Intervention Date

| **Basic Details** | Drug Related Problems | Type Of Intervention | Clinical Significance | Acceptance | Expected Outcome |

Attending MD   ▾ Search by First Name and/or Last Name without 'Al'

Medical Service   Undefined   ▾

Patient on

Recommendations

[Save] [Verify & Save] [Reset] [Cancel]

Figure 4. Main Data entry screen of the web based documentation application. [7] Data entry screen for the patient demographic details of the web-based application with a mixture of drop down menus and free-text entry for comments. Free text entry must be kept to a minimum, in order to keep data entry simple and to improve the retrieval of information for reporting purposes. Patient's specific data *i.e.* Medical Record Number (MRN) and the intervention details were entered by free text.

7. Database construction and use

Ideally the use of free text entry should be kept to a minimum, in order to keep data entry simple and improve retrieval of information for reporting purposes. Patient's specific data i.e. Medical Record Number (MRN) can be entered by free text. The location and the intervention date can be entered using the drop down menus and radio buttons. The radio buttons are arranged in pre-determined groups of related options on the main data entry point based on our pharmaceutical care manual intervention form i.e. basic details, drug related problems, type of intervention, clinical significance, acceptance, and expected outcomes displayed on a screen as a list. Different types of clinical interventions were available under the tab of the type of intervention i.e. pharmacokinetics, pharmacotheraputics, drug information, and miscellaneous.

8. Description of software

The construction of the database of the web based intervention program must take into consideration the feedback of the participating and non participating pharmacists, the departmental quality assurance pharmacist and the limitations of the multi-user PC version. The database must be designed to be user friendly with a multi-option of radio buttons, check boxes, and drop down menus. The free-text entry is to be kept at minimum for the descriptive nature of the interventions. The data entry must be user ID and password protected and the individual user documenting the intervention should be identifiable through their password which requires user authentication.

8.1. Data entry

The patients' number and location can be entered as free text. Using tab keys, allows the user to switch between different categories of interventions, basic details; drug related problems; type of interventions; clinical significance; acceptance; and expected outcome Activating the tab, done by a mouse click, make its associated content visible and the tab itself becomes highlighted to distinguish it from other inactive tabs. Only one tab must be activated at a time and the user cannot continue to the next step if there was missing details in the intervention form. Minimal manual data entry was required for documentations of interventions, with only the detail of the interventions done by free text.

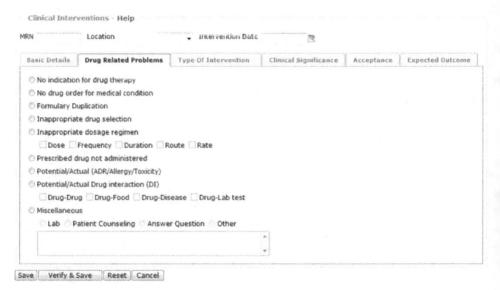

Figure 5. Data-entry screen for drug related problems of the web based documentation application.[7] The user selects the type of intervention using radio buttons and only one selection could be activated at a time. The selection of a radio button is done by clicking the mouse on the button, or the caption, or by using a keyboard shortcut. It was not possible to leave any of the radio buttons in a group unselected, as the user would not be allowed to move to the next screen.

8.2. Validation of pharmacy intervention documentation

The reliability and validity of pharmacist intervention data documented has been questioned by some and have highlighted the lack of consistency in categorising interventions.[18] The lack of reliability in the individual pharmacist coding of interventions should be of concern especially if there is a lack of the reliability of the data generated. In order to standardise the intervention data, we defined three main types of interventions, which was highlighted when the user placed the cursor on the icon; Potentially Severe / High was defined as an intervention that may have resulted in decreasing patient mortality, preventing or reducing organ damage or system failure, and resulted in cost savings; Important / Moderate intervention was defined as an intervention that may have resulted in improving the quality of patient care; and Minor / Low interventions was defined as an intervention that may have resulted in improving convenience of compliance. This allowed the user to enter the correct category as the definitions of the interventions were readily available (figure 6).

Figure 6. Data-entry screen for clinical significance of the web based documentation application. [7] The cursor highlights the definition of the intervention when it is placed on the icon, thereby ensuring consistency in the data that is collected.

8.3. Documentation of cost savings

Inaccurate cost savings projections and the difficulty in making accurate cost savings projections have been cited as one of the major shortcomings in pharmacist intervention documentation systems in the surveys of US health systems pharmacy directors and New Zealand hospital pharmacies. In these surveys only 27% of US health-systems pharmacists and 33% of New Zealand pharmacists documented cost savings interventions. Although cost saving interventions was not specifically mentioned in the recommendations posted by the professional or regulatory bodies on documenting pharmacist interventions, they easily justify their inclusion in the clinical pharmacist's documentation system. In addition to justifying the hiring of additional clinical pharmacists, cost savings information helps emphasize the critical role of pharmacy in managing hospital drug budgets. These costs have risen dramatically in the recent years and continue to climb, which has resulted in pressure from hospital administrators to contain these costs. Taken together, consideration of the cost savings that result from clinical pharmacist interventions is an important factor in modern clinical practice. With the ever increasing cost of medications and pressure from hospital administrators, the impact of clinical pharmacist on cost savings could be emphasised to the senior hospital administrators.[23]

Figure 7. Data-entry screens for cost savings of the web-based documentation application.[7] After the user selects the cost saving, specific data fields are made available that allow for the accurate reporting of cost savings using the software. The medications are pre-populated in the application. The software allows for cumulative cost savings to be calculated at the end of each financial year for each individual pharmacist.

However, the documented cost savings on drugs represent only a fraction of total cost savings as other indirect cost savings such as decreased hospital length of stay, reduction in the pharmacy and/or nursing time (e.g. switching from IV to oral medications) was not captured by our intervention program. Nevertheless, the significant sums of money involved are a justification for its inclusion in the pharmacist intervention program which was not included in the RPSGB guidance on recording of interventions. Cost savings interventions made by the pharmacists can be used to justify additional clinical pharmacist positions while emphasising the role played by the pharmacy department in managing the hospital drugs budget with the hospital administration.

9. How to use these records

The ease with which monthly or periodical reports are generated is one advantage of the web-based system. The system enables one to run monthly or periodical statistics on all interventions entered in the system. The generation of the clinical intervention reports may be utilised by the departmental managers during the annual staff appraisal and more importantly in the departmental quality assurance programs. The monthly or the periodical reports generated further ensure consistency and continuity in interventions standards. Moreover, junior pharmacists and pharmacy residents working in the department can utilise the data as a technical aid for documenting interventions. The underutilisation of the reports generated has been routinely mentioned by most hospitals and some have suggested that the reports must be shared with the medical and nursing staff through the various committees such as drug utilisation committee, quality improvement committee, senior hospital management and pharmacy and therapeutics committee.[5]

	Multiuser PC software		Web-based application	
Drug Related Problems	**Number**	**Percentage**	**Number**	**Percentage**
No Indication for drug therapy	245	4.97	523	7.65
No order for medical condition	295	5.99	642	9.39
Inappropriate drug selection	113	2.29	256	3.74
Inappropriate dosage regimen	1326	26.92	1756	25.67
Prescribed drug not administered	2	0.04	8	0.12
Potential/Actual (ADR/Allergy/Toxicity)	211	4.28	518	7.57
Potential/Actual Drug Interaction (DI)	46	0.93	517	7.56
Miscellaneous	1988	40.36	2536	37.08
Not Documented*	700	14.21	0	0
Type of Intervention	**Number**	**Percentage**	**Number**	**Percentage**
Pharmacokinetics	1273	25.84	1250	18.27
Pharmacotherapeutics	2483	50.41	5341	78.08
Drug Information	775	15.73	157	2.30
Miscellaneous	203	4.12	92	1.35
Not Documented*	192	3.90	0	0
Clinical Significance	**Number**	**Percentage**	**Number**	**Percentage**
Potentially Severe / High	337	6.84	830	12.13
Important / Moderate	3186	64.68	5495	80.34
Minor / Low	449	9.11	515	7.53
Not Documented	954	19.37	0	0
Acceptance	**Number**	**Percentage**	**Number**	**Percentage**
Accepted	4398	89.28	6288	91.93
Modified then accepted	144	2.92	178	2.60
Denied	135	2.74	150	2.19
Unknown	114	2.31	224	3.27
Not Documented*	135	2.74	0	0
Expected Outcome	**Number**	**Percentage**	**Number**	**Percentage**
Cost Saving	234	4.75	1988	29.06
- D/C unnecessary drug	344	6.98	1208	61.44
- Change dosage regimen	129	2.62	547	27.82
- Change to less expensive drug	13	0.26	109	5.54
- Indirect cost saving	23	0.47	124	6.23
Enhanced therapeutic effect	1581	32.10	3163	46.24
ADR / Toxicity prevented / resolved	2197	44.60	2628	38.42
Not Documented*	405	8.22	0	0
Interventions cost savings	132,937.99 SR ($35,347.00)		228,786.93 SR ($61,000.00)	
Total Interventions	4926		6840	

*The web-based application does not allow users to continue to the next screen unless all fields are completed thereby ensuring completeness and accuracy of the data collected.

Table 3. Clinical Interventions Report. [7] Percentages are based upon the total number of interventions.

9.1. The use of mobile devices in clinical pharmacy documentation

The utilization of informatics and information technology in health care systems in the developed country is a common practice nowadays. This has ranged from informatics systems used for direct patient care to documentation of this care to those for billing and coding requirements. Mobile Personal Digital Assistants (PDAs) and now Smart Phones (SPs) and Tablet computers (TCs) e.g iPads, have the capability, power and technology needed to run such informatics systems for health care professionals who are in constant need for instant communication. Previous studies have outlined the usefulness of these mobile devices in data collection and documentation of clinical activity by health care providers.[5,35-38] Currently used methods of documentation depend on standalone systems that are usually equipped with online access capability. Many hospitals in North America and Europe use online documentation forms hosted on their intranet that can be accessed via mobile devices equipped with wireless or cellular (3G or 4G) connectivity. The hypothesis is that this will facilitate access and eventually improve documentation.[35-38]

There are different platforms of mobile devices which employ similar applications from different manufacturers. Main platforms available in the market up until the writing of this chapter include those from Google, Inc. (Android based), Apple, Inc. (IOS based), Research in Motion (RIM), Inc. (BlackBerry based), and Microsoft, Inc. (Windows Phone based).

There has been an increased utilization of this technology for documenting pharmacists' interventions over the last few years. An earlier study in 2003 found that only 15% of surveyed hospitals used computerized tools for pharmacists' interventions documentation and only 5% of those hospitals used a mobile device technology.[5] Other reports have shown a rapid increase in adopting this technology. Another study showed up to 54% of pharmacy interventions in a single hospital were recorded via mobile devices.[38]

Advantages of using mobile devices in documenting pharmacists' interventions include more flexibility, speed and completeness. One study evaluated the completeness and speed of documentation using mobile devices compared to manual method and found out that captured fields of a single documentation was 96% vs. 86% in PDAs technology and traditional paper method; respectively.[38] More interventions were recorded in 3-10 minutes in the PDAs group compared to traditional paper method. The study concluded that the use of PDA technology was more complete and efficient that the traditional method.[38]

There are several challenges for implementation and adoption of mobile devices for documentation purposes. These include but are not limited to cost of implementation and maintenance, security of transmission, and acceptance by pharmacy practitioners. Cost of such electronic means of documentation includes hardware, software, maintenance fees and pharmacist time. In one report, the annual cost of maintaining such system was up to US 5,000 not including pharmacist time.[5]

Securing the confidentiality of transmitting patient sensitive data is of paramount importance and this has been a challenge to most hospitals. Several developed countries have legislation in existence that mandate protection of patient personal information. Both

Canada and the United States have passed the Personal Information Protection and Electronic Documents Act and the Health Insurance Portability and Accountability Act (HIPAA); respectively. Both require certain measures to ensure that only authorized users can access these devices/systems. It is recommended that data encryption and access control be implemented to protect patient information stored on these systems.[39-40]

9.1.1. Personal perspective

Our successful experience with the implementation of the web based system of monitoring pharmacist interventions has led us to move forward to adopt a more easily accessible electronic documentation method; Mobile devices. Our plan, unlike previously reported methods is to focus on utilizing an online documentation application hosted on our intranet that can be accessed via mobile devices equipped with wireless connectivity. We hypothesize that this will facilitate access and eventually improve documentation.

We also plan to develop an Android and iOS based applications that will be installed on variety of mobile devices (Android phones and tablets and iPhones and iPads). This will allow users to enter data in both passive mode (off-line) and active (on-Line) modes. Currently, all of our hospital facilities are equipped with wireless hotspots (*WiFi* 802.11n standard) that provide 100% wireless coverage. The currently used online software will be re-written with web support to suite mobile devices. We plan to have a real-time synchronization with the clinical intervention server hosted in our Information Technology (IT) department. We also plan to have the client installed on the Smart Phones and iPads to manually synchronize with the server once the devices connects to our intranet. This will allow clinicians to manually synchronize data in case of unavailability of wireless coverage.

9.2. Pharmacy data mining

Data mining in pharmacy encompasses many functions which utilize technology that gives pharmacists the ability to analyse the huge amount of data related to drugs and their clinical. By definition these functions allow pharmacists to convert the raw data into meaningful information to guide best decision making.[41] In the near past, pharmacy computer systems were standalone and closed by design. They were not integrated with other health information systems that contain important patient data e.g. laboratory, pathology, radiology, nursing and physician documentations. Over the last decade, the concept of having an integrated clinical information system has been adopted by many health care systems. This has led to an enormous increase in the amount and complexity of data that necessitated a sophisticated data warehouse or data repository. The clinical data repository collects, organizes and integrates pieces of data into what is known as data cubes or data marts. In pharmacy, these data cubes contain patient demographics, medication orders, physicians' and nurses' notes, laboratory results, and pharmacy interventions.[41]

Because of the nature and complexity of pharmacy data, clinical repositories need to be "mined" in a systematic and logical manner. To achieve the best results, these data warehouses need to be secure, easily accessible, able to capture historical and real-time data, and capable of capturing population specific data to allow identification of management and clinically oriented trends for the pharmacy department and the whole organization. Once fully integrated, the benefits of clinical repositories extend to include enhanced communication between care-givers, and improved daily patient care.

Several clinical repository tools exist in the market. These include but are not limited to MicroStrategies (http://www.microstrategy.com/), Cognos (http://www.cognos.com/), Business Objects (http://www.businessobjects.com/) and Brio Technology (http://www.brio.com/). These tools are designed to enable directors of pharmacy, clinical pharmacy coordinators and other pharmacy informatics specialists to populate and analyse the raw data to yield meaningful clinical and managerial information to guide day to day operation in addition to other strategic decisions.[41]

Over the past few years, mining pharmacy data to monitor prescribing patterns and enhance revenues of insurance companies has been widely utilized in the United States. It is estimated that one billion prescriptions per year is being mined in the US alone based on one report[2]. More than 51,000 retail pharmacies in the United States participate in data mining through 2 major data mining companies. This has resulted in significant revenues to the data miners that exceed $2 billion annually.[42] Despite the clear value of mining pharmacy data (clinically and financially), there has been some controversy over the past few years on the legality of pharmacy data mining.[42,43] Despite that data miners remove patient identifiers, several states have banned pharmacy data mining because of claims that it invades prescribers' privacy and that it violates the Health Insurance Portability and Accountability Act (HIPAA). Several lower courts have ruled that pharmacy data mining is unconstitutional, however, recently the supreme court has decided that it is in fact constitutional.[42-44]

In early 2000s, we created a data warehouse at our institution as one of the first organizations to do so in the Middle East. We currently utilize IBM Cognos Enterprise as our data warehouse and performance management tool. After the successful implementation of our Integrated Clinical System (ICIS) in 2010, we planned to design and create different pharmacy reports form this data warehouse that include work load statistics at the user level, automated score card, Medication Utilization Evaluations (MUEs), turn-around time for inpatient and outpatient prescriptions and discharge medications, prescription trends, and prescription variances.

10. Summary

The accurate and precise documentation of interventions should be seen as a barometer of pharmacist activities and it is beyond any reasonable doubt that the clinical pharmacy documentation in hospitals has made a significant impact not only amongst the hospital administrators but also amongst the medical and nursing fraternity. However, there is still room for much improvement of the documentations. Since the recording of clinical pharmacists' interventions is not mandatory in most of the institutions but it is highly recommended with little punitive action for those not recording their interventions. This non–punitive policy generally results in only a few dedicated pharmacists' documenting the interventions on a regular basis, whilst others documented infrequently and some do not participate at all. Numerous reasons have been cited for the non-participation in the recording of interventions and the repetitive nature of the program was the main reason for the non-adherence. The majority see as it as a tool for gathering statistics and time consuming. However, those institutions that have incorporated the clinical pharmacist documentation into the annual evaluations of clinical staff pharmacists have observed an increase in the number of interventions documented. This in turn gives the pharmacy administration the justification required to approve additional FTEs and/or resources for their institutions. In addition, the impact of technology on pharmacist documentation program is best described again by the increase in the documentation of clinical pharmacy services, resulting in an increase the number of clinical pharmacists. So as long as pharmacists keep documenting their interventions and the technology keeps on improving through the hand held devices or even through the use of smart phones by making the process easier and faster their role as safe custodian of medications usage should be enshrined in law.

Author details

Ahmed Al-Jedai*
Pharmacy Services Division, King Faisal Specialist Hospital and Research Centre, Riyadh, Saudi Arabia
Alfaisal University, College of Medicine, Riyadh, Saudi Arabia

Zubeir A. Nurgat
King Faisal Specialist Hospital and Research Centre, Riyadh, Saudi Arabia

11. References

[1] Pedersen CA, Schneider PJ, et al. ASHP national survey of pharmacy practice in acute care settings: Monitoring, patient education, and wellness—2000.*Am J Health Syst Pharm*.2000;57:2171–87.

[2] Pedersen CA, Schneider PJ, Santell JP.ASHP national survey of pharmacy practice in hospital settings: Prescribing and transcribing—2001. *Am J Health Syst Pharm.* 2001;58:2251–66.

[3] Miller T, Sandilya R, Tordoff J, Ferguson R. Documenting pharmacist's clinical interventions in New Zealand hospitals. Pharm World Sci. 2008;30:99–106.

[4] McLennan DN, Dooley MJ. National survey of clinical activity documentation practices. *Aust J Hosp Pharm* 2000;30:6–9.

* Corresponding Author

[5] Youngmee K, Gregory S. Pharmacist intervention documentation in US health care systems. *Hosp Pharm.* 2003;38:1141–7.

[6] Society of Hospital Pharmacists of Australia Committee of Specialty Practice in Clinical Pharmacy, Dooley et al. SHPA standards of practice for clinical pharmacy. *J Pharm Pract Res* 2005;35:122–46.

[7] Nurgat ZA, Al-Jazairi AS, Abu-Shraie N, Al-Jedai A. Documenting Clinical Pharmacist Intervention Before and After the Introduction of a Web-based Tool. *Int J Clin Pharm.* 2011 Apr; 33(2):200-7. Epub 2011 Jan 14

[8] American Society of Health –System Pharmacists. ASHP guidelines on documenting pharmaceutical care in patient medical records. Am J Health-Syst Pharm 2003;60:705-7.

[9] Royal Pharmaceutical Society of Great Britain. Guidance on recording interventions. London. RPSGB 2006: www.rpsgb.org/registrationandsupport/clinicalgovernance. Accessed 15th July 2009.

[10] Kaboli PJ, Hoth AB, McClimon BJ, Schnipper JL. Clinical Pharmacists and inpatient medical care: a systemic review. *Arch Intern Med* 2006;166:955-964.

[11] Bond CA, Raehl CL, Franke T. Interrelationships among mortality rates, drug costs, total cost of care, and length of stay in United States Hospitals: summary and recommendations for clinical pharmacy services and staffing. *Pharmacotherapy.*2001;21:129–41.

[12] Chisholm MA, Vollenweider LJ, Mulloy LL, Wynn JJ,Wade WE, DiPiro JT. Cost-benefit analysis of a clinical pharmacist- managed medication assistance program in a renal transplant clinic. *Clin Transpl.* 2000;14:304–

[13] Ghandi PJ, Smith BS, Tataronis GR, et al. Impact of a pharmacist on drug costs in a coronary care unit. *Am J Health-Syst Pharm.* 2001;58:497–503.

[14] Keely JL. American College of Physicians-American Society of Internal Medicine. Pharmacist scope of practice. Ann Intern Med 2002; 136:79-85.

[15] Bond CA, Raehl CL, Franke T. Clinical pharmacy services, hospital pharmacy staffing, and medication errors in United States hospitals. *Pharmacotherapy.* 2002;22:134–47.

[16] Scarsi KK, Fotis MA, Noskin GA. Pharmacist participation in medical rounds reduces medication errors. *Am J Health Syst Pharm.* 2002;59:2089–92.

[17] Kucukarslan SN, Peters M, Mlynarek M, NafzigerDA. Pharmacists on rounding teams reduce preventable adverse drug events in hospital generalmedicine units. *Arch Intern Med.* 2003;163:2014-2018.

[18] Al Jedai AH, Hamasni IM, Al Alhaidari KM. Documenting the value of pharmacist clinical interventions. ACCP/ESCP International congress on clinical pharmacy. *Pharmacotherapy* 1999;9:507 Poster presentation

[19] Al-Jazairi AS, Al Agil AA, Asiri YA, Al-Kholi TA, Akhras NS, Honranieh BK. The impact of clinical pharmacist in a cardiac-surgery intensive care unit. *Saudi Med J.* 2008 Feb 29(2):227-81.

[20] Cousins D, Gerrrett D, Luscombe D. Reliability and validity of hospital pharmacists clinical intervention data. *Am J Health Syst Pharm* 1997;54:1596-603.

[21] Canales PL, Dorson PG, Crismon ML. Outcomes assessment of clinical pharmacy services in a psychiatric inpatient setting. *Am J Health Syst Pharm.* 2001;58:1309-1316.

[22] Bjornson DC, Hiner WO Jr, Potyk RP, et al. Effect of pharmacists on health care outcomes in hospitalized patients. *Am J Hosp Pharm*. 1993;50:1875-1884.

[23] Haig GM, Kiser LA. Effect of pharmacist participation on a medical team on costs, charges, and length of stay. *Am J Hosp Pharm*. 1991;48:1457-1462.

[24] Boyko WL Jr, Yurkowski PJ, Ivey MF, Armitstead JA, Roberts BL. Pharmacist influence on economicand morbidity outcomes in a tertiary care teaching hospital. *Am J Health Syst Pharm*. 1997;54:1591-1595.

[25] Owens NJ, Sherburne NJ, Silliman RA, Fretwell MD. The Senior Care Study: the optimal use of medications in acutely ill older patients. *J Am Geriatr Soc*. 1990;38:1082-1087.

[26] Zimmerman CR, Smolarek RT, Stevenson JG. A computerized system to improve documentation and reporting of pharmacists' clinical interventions, cost savings, and workload activities. *Pharmacotherapy*. 1995; 15:220-7.

[27] Kanmaz TJ, Haupt BA, Peterson AM. Comparison of manual and bar-code systems for documenting pharmacists' interventions. *Am J Health-Syst Pharm*. 1997; 54:1623-6.

[28] Scott MG, McElnay JC, Burnett KM. Using bar-code technology to capture clinical intervention data in a hospital with a standalone pharmacy computer system. *Am J Health Syst Pharm*. 1996;53:651–4

[29] Schumock GT, Hutchinson RA, Bilek BA. Comparison of two system s for documenting pharmacist interventions in patient care. *Am J Hosp Pharm* 1992:49;2211-4.

[30] Mason RN, Pugh CB, Boyer SB and Stiening KK. Computerised documentation of pharmacists' interventions. *Am J Hosp Pharm* 1994;51:2131-8.

[31] Dooley MJ, McLennan DN, Galbraith KJ, Burgess NG. Multicentre pilot study of a standard approach to document clinical pharmacy activity. *Austr J Hosp Pharm* 2000;30:150–5.

[32] Fox BI, Felkey BG, Berger BA, Krueger KP, Rainer RK Jr. Use of personal digital assistants for documentation of pharmacists' interventions: a literature review. *Am J Health Syst Pharm* 2007;64(14):1516-25.

[33] Ford S, Illich S, Smith L, Franklin A. Implementing personal digital assistant documentation of pharmacist interventions in a military treatment facility. *J Am Pharm Assoc* 2006; 46(5):589-93.

[34] Lynx DH, Brockmiller HR, Connelly RT, Crawford SY. Use of a PDA-based pharmacist intervention system. *Am J Health Syst Pharm*. 2003;60(22):2341-4

[35] Prgomet M, Georgiou A, Westbrook JI. The Impact of Mobile Handheld Technology on Hospital Physicians' Work Practices and Patient Care: A Systematic Review. *J Am Med Inform Assoc*. 2009; 16(6): 792–801.

[36] Raybardhans S, Balen RM, Partovi N et al. Documenting drug related problems with personal digital assistants in a multisite health system. *Am J Health-Syst Pharm*. 2005; 62:1782-7.

[37] Silva MA, Tataronis GR, Maas B. Using personal digital assistants to document pharmacist cognitive services and estimate potential reimbursement. *Am J Health-Syst Pharm*. 2003; 60:911-5.

[38] Raybardhan S, Balen RM, Partovi N, Loewen P, Liu G, Jewesson PJ. Documenting drug-related problems with personal digital assistants in a multisite health system. *Am J Health-Syst Pharm.* 2003; 60:1772-4

[39] Liu G, Balen RM. Securing confidential data on your personal digital assistant (PDA): part 1. Using the security options built into the Palm operating system. *J Inform Pharmacother.* 2004; 15.

[40] Pancoast PE, Patrick TB, Mitchell JA. Physician PDA use and the HIPAA privacy rule. *J Am Med Inform Assoc.* 2003; 10:611-2.

[41] Felkey BJ, Liang H, Krueger KP. *US Pharm.* 2003;38:845-850.

[42] Vivian JC. Last Words: Data Mining Is Legal. *US Pharm.* 2011;36(8):68-74.

[43] Vivian JC. Mining ban unconstitutional: freedom of speech wins. *US Pharm.* 2007;32(6):67-70.

[44] Vivian JC. Pharmacists beware: data mining unconstitutional. *US Pharm.* 2009;34(6):48-49.

Chapter 9

Region Of Interest Based Image Classification: A Study in MRI Brain Scan Categorization

Ashraf Elsayed, Frans Coenen, Marta García-Fiñana and Vanessa Sluming

Additional information is available at the end of the chapter

1. Introduction

The principle challenge of MRI brain scan classification is the capture of the features of interest in such a way that relative spatial information is retained while at the same time ensuring tractability. Some popular feature representations are directed at colour, texture and/or shape. Little work has been done on techniques that maintain the relative structure of the features of interest. This chapter describes a number of mechanisms whereby this may be achieved. More specifically, the work is directed at medical image classification according to a particular feature of interest that may appears across a given image set. There are many medical studies [1, 8, 10, 12, 15, 24, 26, 32, 38, 40, 49] that demonstrate that the shape and size of specific regions of interest plays an important role in medical image classification. One example (and the application focus of the work described) is that the shape and size of the corpus callosum, a prominent feature located in brain MRI scans, is influenced by neurological diseases such as epilepsy and autism, and by special abilities (such as mathematical or musical ability) [35, 43, 47].

Given the above, the work described in this chapter is motivated by a need for techniques that can classify images according to the shape and relative size of features of interest that occur across some medical image sets. The main issue to be addressed is how best to process image collections so an efficient and effective representation can be generated suited to the classification of such images, according to some Region of Interest (ROI) contained across the image set. Given that the proposed techniques assume that some appropriate ROI exists across the image set, the techniques will not be applicable to all image classification problems, but the techniques will be applicable to the subset of problems where classification according to a ROI makes sense. The resolution of the ROI classification problem, as formulated above, requires that the following issues be addressed:

1. Any derived solution should serve to maximise classification accuracy while at the same time allowing for efficient processing (although in the medical context efficient processing can be viewed as a secondary requirement to accuracy).

2. So as to achieve the desired classification accuracy any proposed feature extraction (representation) method needs to capture the salient elements of the ROI without knowing in advance what those salient elements might be. In other words any proposed feature extraction method, whatever form this might take, must retain as much relevant information as possible.

3. Not withstanding point 2 it is also desirable to conduct the classification in reasonable time, although there tends to be a trade off between accuracy and efficiency that must also be addressed.

4. Not all potential representations are compatible with all available classification paradigms, thus different representations may require the application of different classification techniques.

The rest of this chapter is organised as follows. Section 2 provides an overview of the application domain. An essential precursor to the techniques described, although not the focus f this paper, is the registration and segmentation of the region of interest; a note on the registration and segmentation process adopted is therefore given in Section 3. The four proposed techniques for classifying MRI brain scan data according to a single object that occurs across the data, are founded on weighted graph mining, time series analysis, the Hough transform and Zernike Moments respectively. Each is described in the following four sections; Sections 4, 5, 6 and 7. Section 8 then reports on the comparative evaluation of the proposed techniques. Some conclusions are then presented in Section 9.

2. Application domain

Magnetic Resonance Imaging (MRI) came into prominence in the 1970s. MRI is similar to Computerized Topography (CT) in that cross-sectional images are produced of some object. A special kind of MRI, called Magnetic Resonance Angiography (MRA) can be used to examine blood vessels. MRI is also used for brain diagnosis, for example to detect abnormal changes in different parts of the brain. A MRI scan of the brain produces a very detailed picture. An example brain scan image is given in Figure 1. MRI brain scans underpin the diagnosis and management of patients suffering from various neurological and psychiatric conditions. Analysis of MRI data relies on the expertise of specialists (radiologists) and is therefore subjective. Automated classification of MRI image data can this provide useful support for the categorisation process and potentially free up resources.

As noted in the introduction to this chapter the focus of the work described is the classification of MRI brain scan data according to a feature called the corpus callosum. Figure 2 gives an example midsagittal slice of a MRI scan[1], the corpus callosum is located in the centre of the brain (highlighted in the lefthand image, an associated structure, the fornix, is also shown). The size and shape of the corpus callosum has been shown to be correlated to sex, age, neurodegenerative diseases (e.g. epilepsy, multiple sclerosis and schizophrenia) and various lateralised behaviour in people (such as handedness). It is also conjectured that the size and shape of the corpus callosum reflects certain human characteristics (such as a mathematical or musical ability). Within neuro-imaging research considerable effort has been directed at quantifying parameters such as length, surface area and volume of structures in living adult brains, and investigating differences in these parameters between sample groups. As noted

---

[1] The midsagittal slice is the middle slice of a sequence of MRI slices.

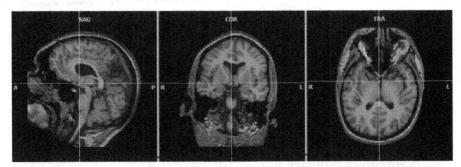

Figure 1. An example brain scan image. The three images show (from left to right) sagittal, coronal and axial planes. A common point is marked in each image.

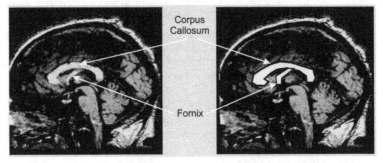

Figure 2. Midsagital MRI brain scan slice showing the corpus callosum (high-lighted in the right-hand image), the Fornix is a related feature [18].

in [33] a number of reported studies have demonstrated that the size and shape of the human corpus callosum, in humans, is related to gender[1, 12, 40], age [40, 49], handedness [10], brain development and degeneration [24, 32], conditions such as epilepsy [8, 38, 47] and brain disfunction [15, 26]. It is worth noting that although the work described in this thesis is directed at MRI brain scan classification, there are other features in MRI brain scans to which the techniques could be applied, such as the ventricles.

3. Image preproessing and registration

Although the primary concern of this chapter is the representation of images to permit classification according to some feature that appears across these images, more specifically the classification of MRI brain scans according to the nature of the corpus callosum, for this to happen images must first be segmented and registered. In our case the images were registered by trained physicians using the Brain Voyager QX software package [21] that supports registration using the Talairach transformation. Segmentation was conducted using a variation of of the Normalized Cuts (NCuts) segmentation technique. NCuts formulates segmentation as a graph-partitioning problem. The basic NCut algorithm was proposed by Shi and Malik [44]. However, the authors found that the basic NCuts algorithm did not operate well when applied to large images such as MRI brain scan images. An established enhancement to the basic NCuts algorithm, the multiscale normalized cuts algorithm proposed by Cour et al. [11], was also considered. In the context of the corpus callosum application it was found that the multiscale normalized cuts algorithm could be improved upon so as to reduce the computational resource required to achieve the segmentation. A variation of the multiscale normalized cuts algorithm, developed by the authors, was thus adopted. Details of the algorithm can be found in [17]. Alternative registration and segmentation techniques can clearly be adopted. What is important to note, with respect to the contents of this chapter, is that the start point for each of the techniques described is a segmented corpus callosum.

4. Method 1: Region of interest image classification using a hough transform signature representation

The Hough transform was originally proposed by Paul Hough in 1962 [25]. Subsequently it was refined, in various manners, with respect to a number of proposed image analysis techniques directed at a great variety of application domains. In the context of image analysis the Hough transform is principally used for the purpose of detecting parametric shapes (boxes, cylinders, cones, etc.) in image data. The Hough transform was initially used for the purpose of detecting straight lines in image data, then extended with respect to simple parametric forms, and eventually generalised to detect any parametric shape [2]. The fundamental idea behind the Hough transform is that image patterns can be "transformed" (translated) into some alternative parameter space so that the desired shape detection problem becomes one of simply identifying peaks in the new defined space. The principle disadvantages of the Hough transform are: (i) its substantial storage requirement and (ii) the associated computational overhead. The effect of these two disadvantages can be partially reduced by utilising additional information from the image data to limit the range of parameters that are required to be calculated with respect to each point in a given image. For example, Ballard [2] used gradient information to support circle detection.

The proposed image classification method, based on the Hough transform, is directed at the extraction of shape signatures which can be used as feature vectors in a classification process. It is assumed that the input image is a binary representation of a region of interest (i.e. the corpus callosum with respect to the focus of the work described in this chapter), that has been appropriately segmented from "source" MRI brain scans of the form described above. The proposed shape signature extraction method is founded on an idea first presented in Vlachos et al. [45], which gave good results when classifying simple line drawn symbol images according to their shapes. However, direct application of the Vlachos approach was found to perform consistently badly with respect to the classification of brain MRI scans according to the nature of the corpus callosum. Therefore the proposed method commences by simplifying the shape of the region of interest using a polygonal approximation method. Then the signature extraction process, using the Vlachos approach, was applied.

The proposed image classification technique based on the Hough transform comprises three majors steps. We start with a data set of pre-labelled images from which the ROI (the corpus callosum in our case) has been extracted. Then (Step 1), for each image, the ROI is processed using a Canny edge detector [6] to determine its boundary. Secondly (Step 2), a polygonal approximation technique is applied to reduce the complexity of the boundaries by approximating the boundaries with a minimum number of line segments. Thirdly (Step 3), signature extraction using the Vlachos approach is applied to extract the desired feature vectors which are then placed in a Case Base (CB). The CB ultimately comprises feature vectors extracted from all the images in the given training set and their corresponding class labels. This CB can then used, in the context of a Case Based Reasoning (CBR) framework, to classify unseen MRI brain scans according to the nature of the corpus callosum. Each of these steps is considered in further detail in the following three sub-sections.

4.1. Preprocessing (Edge detection)

As already noted the extraction of the desired shape signatures (one per region of interest within each image) commences by applying the Canny edge detector technique [6]. The Canny operator detects the edge pixels of an object using a multi-stage process. First of all, the region boundary is smoothed by applying a Gaussian filter. Then the edge strength is calculated by applying a simple 2D first derivative operator. The region is then scanned along the region gradient direction, and if pixels are not part of the local maxima they are set to zero, a process known as non-maximal suppression. Finally, a threshold is applied to select the correct edge pixels. When the edge detection technique is applied to the corpus callosum each region will be represented by its boundaries.

4.2. Polygonal approximation

The aim of the region boundary simplification step is to obtain a smooth curve over a minimum number of line segments describing the region's boundary. This process is referred to as the polygonal approximation of a polygonal curve which consists of a set of vertices. The approximation of polygonal curves is aimed at finding a subset of the original vertices so that a given objective function is minimised. The problem can be defined in a number of ways, the definition used here is referred to as the *min-# problem*. Given a N-vertex polygonal curve C, approximate it by another polygonal curve C_a with a given number of straight line segments M so that the approximation error is minimised.

One of the most widely used solutions to the min-# problem is a heuristic method called the Douglas-Peucker (DP) algorithm [14]. With respect to the work described in thus chapter the Douglas-Peucker (DP) algorithm was used to simplify the boundaries of the regions of interest before the application of the Hough transform to extract signatures. The DP algorithm uses the closeness of a vertex to an edge segment. This algorithm works in a top down manner starting with a crude initial guess at a simplified polygonal curve, namely the single edge joining the first and last vertices of the polygonal curve. Then the remaining vertices are tested for closeness to that edge. If there are vertices further than a specified tolerance, $\epsilon > 0$, away from the edge, then the vertex furthest from it is added to the simplification. This creates a new guess for the simplified polygonal curve. Using recursion, this process continues for each edge of the current guess until all vertices of the original polygonal curve are within tolerance of the simplification.

In the case of the approximation of the corpus callosum boundary as a closed curve, we have to find an optimal allocation of all approximation vertices including the starting point. A straightforward solution is to try all vertices as the starting points, and choose the one with minimal error. The complexity of this straightforward algorithm for a N-vertex curve is N times that of the algorithm for an open curve. There exist a number of heuristic approaches for selecting the starting point. In this work we adopted a heuristic approach founded on that presented in Sato [42]. In this approach, the farthest point from the centroid of the region of interest is chosen as the starting point.

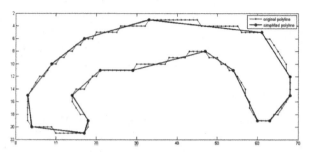

Figure 3. Polygonal approximation of corpus callosum corresponding to $\epsilon = 0.9$ ($M = 17$).

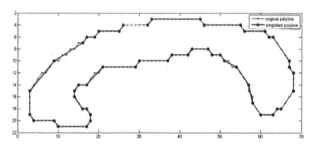

Figure 4. Polygonal approximation of corpus callosum corresponding to $\epsilon = 0.4$ ($M = 52$).

The value of the tolerance ϵ affects the approximation of the original polygonal curves. For smaller values of tolerance, the polygonal curve is approximated by a large number of line segments M which means that the approximation is very similar to the original curve. While the larger values give a much coarser approximation of the original curve with a smaller number of line segments M. Figure 3 shows an example of a simplification of the boundary of a corpus callosum using $\epsilon = 0.9$ resulting in 17 line segments. Figure 4 shows another example using $\epsilon = 0.4$ resulting in 52 line segments.

4.3. Shape signature extraction

The generation of the shape signature based on the Straight Line Hough Trans- form (SLHT) relies on creating an $M \times N$ accumulator matrix A, where (using the polar coordinate scheme) each row corresponds to one value of ρ (length), and each column to one value of θ (orientation). As already noted the he procedure for generating the feature vector from the accumulator matrix is founded on that presented in Vlachos et al. [45] and is as follows:

1. Determine the set of boundary pixels corresponding to the region of interest.
2. Transform each pixel in the set into a parametric curve in the parameter space.
3. Increment the cells in the accumulator matrix A as directed by the parametric curve.
4. Calculate a preliminary feature vector.
5. Calculate the vector mean.
6. Normalise the feature vector.

By transforming every point (x, y) in the image into the parameter space, the line parameters can be found in the intersections of the parametrized curves in the accumulator matrix as show in Figure 4.1. In step 4, the accumulator matrix is projected to a one-dimensional θ vector by summing up the ρ values in each column. Finally the feature vector is normalised according to its mean in steps 5 and 6. The extracted feature vector describing the ROI within each image can then be used as an image signature.

4.4. Classification

The signatures from a labelled training set can thus be collected together and stored in a Case Base (CB) within a Case Based Reasoning (CBR) framework. Euclidean distance may then be used as a similarity measure in the context of a CBR framework. Let us assume that we have the feature vector T for a pre-labelled image and the feature vector Q for the test image (both of size N). Their distance apart is calculated as:

$$dist(T, Q) = \sum_{j=1}^{N} (T_j - Q_j)^2 \qquad (1)$$

Here $dist = 0$ indicates a perfect match, and $dist = distmax$ indicates two images with maximum dissimilarity.

To categorise "unseen" MRI brain scans, according to the nature of the corpus callosum, signatures describing the unseen cases were compared with the signatures of labelled cases held in the CB. The well established K-Nearest Neighbour (KNN) technique was used to identify the most similar signature in the CB from which a class label was then extracted.

5. Method 2: Region of interest image classification using a weighted frequent subgraph representation

As already noted, the application of techniques to classify image data according to some common object that features across an image set requires the representation of the image objects in question using some appropriate format. The previous section considered representing image objects using a signature generation process founded on the Hough transform. In this section an image decomposition method is considered whereby the ROIs are represented using a quad-tree representation. More specifically the Minimum Bounding Rectangles (MBRss) surrounding the ROIs are represented using a quad-tree representation. The conjectured advantage offered is that a quad-tree representation will maintain the structural information (shape and size) of the ROI contained in the MBR. By applying a weighted frequent subgraph mining algorithm, gSpan-ATW [28], to this representation, frequent subgraphs that occur across the tree represented set of MBR can be identified. The identified frequent subgraphs each describing, in terms of size and shape, some part of the MBR; can then be used to form the fundamental elements of a feature space. Consequently, this feature space can be used to describe a set of feature vectors, one per image, to which standard classification processes can be applied (e.g. decision tree classifiers, SVM or rule based classifiers).

The graph based approach for image classification, as in the case of all the other methods described in this chapter, commences with segmentation and registration to isolate the Region Of Interest (ROI). Secondly, image decomposition takes place to represent the details of the identified ROI in terms of a quad-tree data structure. Feature extraction using a weighted frequent subgraph mining approach (the gSpan-ATW algorithm with respect to the evaluation described later in this chapter) is then applied to the tree represented image set (one tree per image) to identify frequent subgraphs. The identified subtrees (subgraphs) then form the fundamental elements of a feature space (a set of attributes with which to describe the image set). Finally, due to a substantial number of features (frequent sub- graphs) being generated, feature selection takes place to select the most relevant and discriminatory features. Standard classifier generation techniques can then be applied to build a classifier that can be applied to unseen data. Each of the steps involved in the process is discussed in further detail in the following subsections.

5.1. Image decomposition

Image decomposition methods are commonly used in image analysis, compression, and segmentation. Different types of image decomposition mat be adopted, with respect to the work described in this chapter a quad-tree representation is proposed. A quad-tree is a tree data structure which can be used to represent a 2D area (such as images) which has been recursively subdivided into "quadrants" [31]. In the context of the representation of ROIs in terms of quad-trees, the pixels representing the MBR surrounding each ROI are tessellated into homogeneous sub-regions [16, 17]. The tessellation can be conducted according to a variety of image features such as colour or intensity. With respect to the corpus callosum a binary encoding was used, the "tiles" included in the corpus callosum were allocated a "1" (black) and the tiles not included a "0" (white). A tile was deemed to be sufficiently homogeneous if it was 95% black or white. The tessellation continues until either sufficiently homogeneous tiles are identified or some user specified level of granularity is reached. The result is then stored in a quad-tree data structure such that each leaf node represents a tile. Leaf nodes nearer the root of the tree represent larger tiles than nodes further away. Thus the tree is "unbalanced" in that some leaf nodes will cover larger areas of the ROI than others. It is argued that tiles covering small regions are of greater interests than does covering large regions because they indicate a greater level of detail (they are typically located on the boundary of the ROI). The advantage of the representation is thus that it maintains information about the relative lo-cation and size of groups of pixels (i.e. the shape of the corpus callosum). The decomposition process is illustrated in Figures 5 and 6. Figure 5 illustrates the decomposition (in this case down to a level of 3), and Figure 6 illustrates the resulting quad-tree.

5.2. Feature extraction using gSpan-ATW algorithm

From the literature two separate problem formulations for Frequent Subgraph Mining (FSM) can be identified: (i) transaction graph based, and (ii) single graph based. In transaction graph based mining, the input data comprises a collection of relatively small graphs, whereas in single graph based mining the input data comprises a very large single graph. The graph mining based approach adopted with respect to the work described in this chapter focuses on transaction graph based mining. In the context of transaction graph based mining, FSM aims

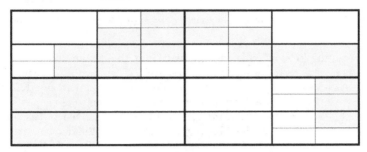

Figure 5. Hierarchical decomposition (tessellation) of the corpus callosum [18].

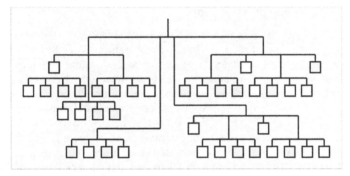

Figure 6. Tree representation of the hierarchical decomposition given in Figure 5 [18].

to discover all the subgraphs whose occurrences in a graph database are over a user defined threshold σ. Many FSM algorithms have been proposed of which the most well known is arguably gSpan [46].

Frequent subgraph mining is computationally expensive because of the candidate generation and support computation processes that are required. The first process is concerned with the generation of candidate subgraphs in a non-redundant manner such that the same graph is not generated more than once. Thus graph isomorphism checking is required to remove duplicate graphs. The second process is to compute the support of a graph in the graph database. This also requires subgraph isomorphism checking in order to determine the set of graphs where a given candidate occurs. Although algorithms such as gSpan can achieve competitive performance compared with other FSM algorithms, its performance degrades considerably when the graph size is relatively large or the graph features few node and/or edge labels. The mechanism for addressing this issue adopted here was to use weighted frequent subgraph mining.

Given the quad-tree representation a weighted frequent subgraph mining algorithm (gSpan-ATW) was applied to identify frequently occurring subgraphs (subtrees) within the tree representation. The Average Total Weighting (ATW) scheme weights nodes according to their occurrence count. The nodes in the tree (see for example Figure 6) are labelled as being either: "black", "white" or "nothing". The black and white labels are used for the leaf nodes and represent the shape of the corpus callosum. These should therefore be weighted more highly than the "nothing" nodes. It can also be argued that these should be weighted more highly because they are further away (on average) from the root than the "nothing" nodes, and therefore the leaf nodes can be said to provide more detail. The ATW scheme achieves this.

The ATW weighting scheme was incorporated into the gSpan algorithm to produce gSpan-ATW. As a result of the application of gSpan-ATW the identified frequent subgraphs (i.e. subtrees) each describing, in terms of size and shape, some part of a ROI that occurs regularly across the data set, are then used to form the fundamental elements of a feature space. Using this feature space each image (ROI) can be described in terms of a feature vector of length N, with each element having a value equal to the frequency of that feature (sub-graph).

5.3. Feature selection and classification

As noted above the graph mining process typically identifies a great many frequent subgraphs; more than required for the desired classification. Therefore a feature selection strategy was applied to the feature space so that only those subgraphs that serve as good discriminators between cases are retained. A straightforward wrapper method was adopted whereby a decision tree generator was applied to the feature space. Features included as "choice points" in the decision tree were then selected, whilst all remaining features were discarded. For the work described here, the well established C4.5 decision tree algorithm [37] was adopted, although any other decision tree generator would have sufficed. On completion of the feature selection process each image was described in terms of a reduced feature vector indicating the selected features (subgraphs) that appear in the image. Once the image set had been represented in this manner any appropriate classifier generator could be applied. With respect to the work described in this chapter the C4.5 algorithm was again adopted (both appliations of C4.5 used the WEKA implementations [23]).

6. Method 3: Region of interest image classification using a Zernike moment signature representation

This section describes the third proposed approach to image classification according to some feature that appears across the image set. The proposed approach is founded on the concept of Zernik Moments. Moments are scalar quantities used to characterize a function and to capture its significant features. They have been widely used for many years in statistics for the description of the shape of probability density functions and in classic "rigid-body" mechanics to measure the mass distribution of a body. From the mathematical point of view, moments are "projections" of a function onto a polynomial basis.

Zernike moments are a class of orthogonal moments (moments produced using orthogonal basis sets) that can be used as an effective image descriptor. Unfortunately, direct computation of Zernike moments is computationally expensive. This makes it impractical for many applications. This limitation has prompted considerable study of algorithms for the fast evaluation of Zernike moments [3, 29, 36]. Several algorithms have been proposed to speed up the computation. Belkasim et al. [3] introduced a fast algorithm based on the series expansion of radial polynomials. Parta et al. [36] and Kintner [29] have proposed recurrence relations for fast computation of radial polynomials of Zernike moments. Chong et al. [7] modified Kintners method so that it would be applicable for all cases. Unfortunately, all of these methods approximated Zernike moment polynomials and consequently, produced inaccurate sets of Zernike moments. Wee et al. [48], proposed a new algorithm that computed exact Zernike moments through a set of exact geometric moments; their method was accurate but still entailed a significant computational overhead.

The authors have thus developed an efficient method for exact Zernike Moment computation based on the observation that exact Zernike moments can be expressed as a function of geometric moments. The proposed algorithm is based on a quad-tree representation of images (similar to that described in Section 5) whereby a given pixel represented region is decomposed into a number of non-overlapping tiles. Since the geometric moment computation for each tile is easier than that for the whole region this reduces the computational complexity significantly. The algorithm proposed by Wu et al. [50] for the fast computation of geometric moments was adopted to calculate the required geometric moments. The resulting Zernike moments were then used to define a feature vector (one per image) which can be input to a standard classification mechanism.

6.1. Fast calculation of Zernike moments

As noted above a new method for Zernike Moment computation, based on the observation that exact Zernike Moments can be expressed as a function of Geometric Moments (GMs), is proposed here. The method eases the computational complexity associated with Zernike Moment calculation. Given a pixel represented object, this is first decomposed into a number of non-overlapping squares, for which GMs can be calculated.

The complex 2D Zernike moments of order p and repetition q are defined as:

$$Z_{pq} = \frac{p+1}{\pi} \int_0^{2\pi} \int_0^1 \left[V_{pq}(r,\theta) \right]^* f(r,\theta) r dr d\theta \tag{2}$$

where $p = 0, 1, 2, ..., \infty$ and q is a positive or negative integer according to the condition $p - |q| = even$, $|q| \leq p$. * Is the complex conjugate. The Zernike polynomial:

$$V_{pq}(r,\theta) = R_{pq}(r)e^{iq\theta} \tag{3}$$

describes a complete set of complex-valued orthogonal functions defined on the unit disk, $x^2 + y^2 \leq 1$, with $i = \sqrt{-1}$. The real-valued radial polynomial $R_{pq}(r)$ is defined as:

$$R_{pq}(r) = \sum_{\substack{k=q \\ p-k=even}}^{p} B_{p|q|k} r^k \tag{4}$$

where the polynomial coefficient, $B_{p|q|k}$, is defined as:

$$B_{p|q|k} = \frac{(-1)^{\left(\frac{p-k}{2}\right)} \left(\frac{p+k}{2}\right)!}{\left(\frac{p-k}{2}\right)! \left(\frac{k+q}{2}\right)! \left(\frac{k-q}{2}\right)!} \tag{5}$$

Zernike polynomials are thus defined in terms of polar coordinates (ρ, θ) over a unit disk, while the object intensity function is always defined in terms of Cartesian coordinates (x, y), therefore the computation of ZM requires an image transformation. There are two traditional mapping approaches [7]. In the first approach, the square image plan is mapped onto a unit disk, where the centre of the image is assumed to be the origin of the coordinate system. In this approach, all pixels outside the unit disk are ignored, which result in a loss of some image information. In the second approach, the whole square image plan is mapped inside the unit disk where the centre of the image is assumed to be the coordinate origin. In this paper, the second approach is used to avoid loss of information. Zernike moments can be expressed in terms of GMs as follows:

$$Z_{pq} = \frac{p+1}{\pi} \sum_{\substack{k=|q| \\ p-k=even}}^{p} \Phi \tag{6}$$

where Φ is defined as:

$$\Phi = \sum_{j=0}^{s} \sum_{m=0}^{|q|} w^m \binom{s}{j} \binom{|q|}{m} B_{p|q|k} G_{k-2j-m,2j+m} \tag{7}$$

$s = 0.5(k - |q|), i = \sqrt{-1}, G$ (a geometric moment), and:

$$w = \begin{cases} -i & \text{if } q > 0 \\ i & \text{if } q \leq 0 \end{cases}$$

To speed up the calculation of Zernike moments in terms of GMs, as noted above, a quad-tree decomposition was adopted as used in the graph based approach described in Section 5 and in [50]. The GMs for each object can then be easily calculated by summing the GMs for all the squares in the decomposition that are part of the object (the computation of GMs of squares is easier than that for the whole object).

6.2. Feature extraction based on Zernike moments

In the context of the proposed ROI based image classification approach, the calculated exact Zernike moment magnitudes were used to define a feature space representing the image set. Each image, or more specifically the object of interest within each image, can then be represented in terms of a feature vector. The feature vector $\{AFV\}_N$ will then consist of the accumulated Zernike moment magnitudes from order $p = 0$ to order $p = N$ with all possible repetitions of q. For example, where N = 4, the feature vector $\{AFV\}_4$ will consist of the set of all Zernike moments corresponding to the orders $p = 0, 1, 2, 3, 4$ coupled with all possible repetitions of $q : \{|Z_{00}|, |Z_{11}|, |Z_{20}|, |Z_{22}|, |Z_{31}|, |Z_{33}|, |Z_{40}|, |Z_{42}|, |Z_{44}|\}$. Consequently a set of images that contain a common ROI (such as the corpus callosum in the case of the brain MRI scan data of interest with respect to this chapter) can be represented as a set of feature vectors which can be input to standard classification techniques.

7. Method 4: Region of interest image classification using a time series representation

In this section the fourth proposed approach to ROIBIC, founded on a time series representation coupled with a Case Based Reasoning (CBR) mechanism, is described. In this approach the features of interest are represented as time series, one per image. There are a number of mechanisms whereby the desired time series can be generated, the method proposed in this chapter is founded on a ROI intersection mechanism. The generated time series are then stored in a Case Base (CB) which can be used to categorise unseen data using a Case Based Reasoning (CBR) approach. The unseen data is compared with the categorisations contained in the CB using a Dynamic Time Warping (DTW) similarity checking mechanism. The class associated with the most similar time series (case) in the CB is then adopted as the class for the unseen data. It should be noted that the phrase "time series" is used with respect to the adopted representation because the proposed image classification technique is founded on work on time series analysis, not because the representation includes some temporal dimension.

7.1. ROI Intersection Time Series Generation

Using the ROI intersection mechanism the desired image signature ("pseudo" time series) is generated using an ordered sequence of M "spokes" radiating out from a single reference point. The desired time series is then expressed as a series of values (one for each spoke) describing the size (length) of the intersection of the vector with the ROI. The representation thus maintains the structural information (shape and size) of the ROI. It should also be noted that the value of M may vary due to the differences of the shape and size of the individual ROI within the image data set.

Formally speaking it is assumed that there are M spokes and each spoke i, radiating out from some reference point, intersects the ROI boundary at two points $(x_1(i), y_1(i))$ and $(x_2(i), y_2(i))$; then the proposed image signature is given by:

$$D(i) = \sqrt{(x_1(i) - x_2(i))^2 + (y_1(i) - y_2(i))^2}, \qquad i = 1, 2, \ldots, M \qquad (8)$$

With respect to the corpus callosum application the time series generation procedure is illustrated in Figure 7. The midpoint of the lower edge of the object's Minimum Bounding Rectangle (MBR) was selected as the reference point. This was chosen as this would ensure that there was only two boundary intersections per spoke. The vectors were derived by rotating an arc about the reference point pixel. The interval between spokes was one pixel measured along the edge of the MBR. For each spoke the intersection distance D_i (where i is the spoke identification number) over which the spoke intersected with a sequence of corpus callosum pixels was measured and recorded. The result was a time series with the spoke number i representing time and the value D_i, for each spoke, the magnitude (intersection length). By plotting D_i against i a pseudo time series can be derived as shown in Figure 7.

7.2. Similarity measuring using dynamic time warping

The objective of most similarity measures is to identify the distance between two feature vectors. There are a number of methods where this may be achieved. In the case of time series analysis a common similarity measuring technique is Dynamic Time Warping (DTW). The DTW algorithm is a well-known algorithm in many areas. It was first introduced in 1960s [4] and extensively explored in 1970s for application within speech recognition systems. DTW operates as follows. In order to align two time series (sequences) A and B with lengths N and M, an $N \times M$ matrix (D) is constructed, where each element (i, j) of the matrix contains the distance between the points A_i and B_j. The goal is to find a path through this matrix, which

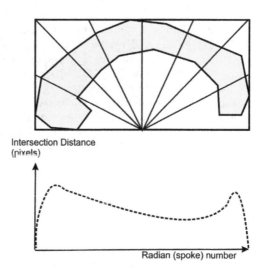

Figure 7. Conversion of corpus callosum into time series using the ROI Int. method [18].

minimises the sum of the local distances of the points. The path from $(1,1)$ to (N, M) in the matrix D is called warping path W:

$$W = \{w_1, w_2, ..., w_k\} \tag{9}$$

which is subject to the following constraints:

- **Boundary condition**: This requires the warping path to start at $w_1 = (1,1)$ and finish at $w_k = (N, M)$.
- **Continuity**: Given two consequetive points along the warping path, $w_{k-1} = (c, d)$ and $w_k = (a, b)$:

$$a - c \leq 1, \tag{10}$$

$$b - d \leq 1$$

  thus restricting the allowable steps in the warping path.
- **Monotonicity**: Given $w_{k-1} = (c, d)$ and $w_k = (a, b)$, then:

$$a - c \geq 0, \tag{11}$$

$$b - d \geq 0$$

The above inequalities forces the points in W to be monotonically spaced in time. The warping path on the D matrix is found using some dynamic programming algorithm, which accumulates the partial distances between the sequences. If $D(i, j)$ is the global distance up to (i,j) and the local distance at (i,j) is given by $d(i,j)$, then the DTW algorithm uses the following recurrence relation:

$$D(i,j) = d(A_i, B_j) + \min \begin{cases} D(i-1, j-1) \\ D(i-1, j) \\ D(i, j-1) \end{cases} \qquad (12)$$

Given $D(1,1) = d(A_1, B_1)$ as the initial condition, we have the basis for an efficient recursive algorithm for computing $D(i,j)$. The algorithm starts from $D(1,1)$ and iterates through the matrix by summing the partial distances until $D(N,M)$, which is the overall matching score of the times series (sequences) A and B.

The computational cost of the application of DTW is $O(NM)$. In order to improve the computational cost global constraints may be introduced where by we ignore matrix locations away from the main diagonal. Two well known global constraints are the "Sakoe-Chiba band" [39] and "Itakura parallelogram" [27]. The Sakoe-Chiba band runs along the main diagonal and has a fixed width R such that $j - R \leq i \leq j + R$ for the indices of the warping path $w_k(i,j)$. While the Itakura parallelogram describes a region that serves to constrain the warping path options. There are several reasons for using global constraints, one of which is that they slightly speed up the DTW distance calculation. However, the most important reason is to prevent pathological warpings, where a relatively small section of one time series maps onto a relatively large section of another. In the work described here, the Sakoe-Chiba band was adopted.

7.3. Image classification based on time series representation

The time series based image classification method commences, as in the case of the previous methods, with the segmentation and registration of the input images as described in Chapter 3. Once the ROI have been segmented and identified the next step is to derive the time series according to the boundary line circumscribing the ROI. In each case the ROI is represented using the proposed time series generation techniques described above. Each ROI signature is then conceptualised as a prototype or case contained in a Case Base (CB), to which a Case Based Reasoning (CBR) mechanism can be applied (as in the case of method 1).

As noted previously CBR can be used for classification purposes where, given an unseen record (case), the record can be classified according to the "best match" discovered in the CB. With respect to proposed technique, and in the case of the corpus callosum application, the CB comprises a set of pre-labelled ROI time series "signatures", each describing a record. The DTW time series matching strategy was then adopted to identify a best match with a new ("unseen") ROI signature. To do this each pre-labelled signature of size N is compared to the given "unseen" signature of size M using the DTW technique and a sequence of similarity measures obtained. The well established k-nearest neighbour technique (KNN) was used to identify the most similar signature in the CB from which a class label was then extracted.

8. Comparison of the proposed approaches

The four advocated approaches to ROI based image classification were evaluated in the context of the classification of brain MRI scans according to the nature of the corpus callosum, a particular ROI that appears across such datasets. This section reports on the evaluation the proposed approaches. The comparison was undertaken in terms of classification performance and run time complexity. The statistical analysis of the significance of the reported results was conducted using the best performing parameters with respect to each technique (so as to consider each technique to its best advantage). In addition the proposed approaches were compared with two notable alternative ROI representation techniques: the Curvature Scale Space (CSS) [34] and the Angular Radial Transform (ART) [5]. These two techniques were selected because in the MPEG-7 standard, CSS has been adopted as the contour-based shape descriptor and ART as the region-based shape descriptor.

8.1. Datasets

To evaluate the techniques described in this thesis to classify medical images according to the nature of the corpus callosum a number of data sets were used. As already noted the data sets were generated by extracting the *midsagittal slice* from MRI brain scan data volumes (bundles), one image per volume. Each data set comprised a number of brain MRI scans each measuring 256×256 pixels, with 256 grayscale levels and each describing a midsagittal slice. To support the evaluation the data sets were grouped as follows: (i) Musicians, (ii) Epilepsy and (iii) Handedness. Each group is described in some further detail as follows:

Musicians datasets For the musicians study the data set comprised 106 MRI scans, 53 representing musicians and 53 non-musicians (i.e. two equal classes). The study was of interest because of the conjecture that the size and shape of the corpus callosum reflects human characteristics such as a musical ability.

Epilepsy datasets For the epilepsy study a data set comprising the 106 MRI brain scans used for the musicians study complemented with 106 MRI brain scans from epilepsy patients, to give a data set totalling 212 MRI brain scans, was used. The objective was to seek support for the conjecture that the shape and size of the corpus callosum is influence by conditions such as epilepsy. It should be noted that, as far as the authors are aware, the musicians study did not include any epilepsy patents.

Handedness datasets For the handedness study a data set comprising 82 MRI brain scans was used, 42 representing right handed individuals and 40 left handed individuals. The study was of interest because of the conjecture that the size and shape of the corpus callosum reflects certain human characteristics (such as handedness).

All three brain MRI datasets were preprocessed, using the variation of the mult-iscale mormalised cuts algorithm introduced in Subsection 3, so as to extract the corpus callosum ROI. On completion of data cleaning (noise removal) a "local" registration process was undertaken by fitting each identified corpus callosum into a Minimum Bounding Rectangle (MBR) so that each identified corpus callosum was founded upon the same origin.

8.2. Experimental evaluation

Table 1 shows the TCV results obtained using the musician data set. The HT, GB, ZM, TS rows indicate the results using the Hough transform, frequent sub-graph, Zernike moments, and time series based approaches respectively. The CSS and ART rows indicate the MPEG-7 descriptors (Curvature Scale Space and the Angular Radial Transform) respectively. The

	Acc	Sens	Spec
HT	91.51	92.45	90.57
GB	95.28	96.23	94.34
ZM	96.23	98.11	94.34
TS	**98.11**	**100.00**	**96.23**
CSS	86.79	88.68	84.91
ART	89.62	90.57	88.68

Table 1. TCV Classification Results for Musicians Study

	Acc	Sens	Spec
HT	90.24	92.50	88.1
GB	93.90	95.00	92.86
ZM	93.90	95.00	92.86
TS	**96.34**	**97.50**	**95.24**
CSS	85.37	85.00	85.71
ART	87.80	90.00	85.71

Table 2. TCV Classification Results for Handedness Study

"Acc", "Sens", and "Spec" columns indicate accuracy, sensitivity and specificity respectively. The best results are indicated in bold font. Inspection of Table 1 demonstrates that the overall classification accuracies obtained using the four advocated approaches were over 90%, while the overall classification accuracy obtained using the time series based approach significantly improved over that obtained using the other three approaches. The best sensitivity and specificity were also obtained using the time series based approach (100% in the case of sensitivity). The four advocated approaches all outperformed the CSS and ART techniques. These are excellent results.

Table 2 shows the TCV results obtained using the handedness data set. The column and row headers are defined as in Table 1. Inspection of Table 2 indicates that the four advocated approaches also performed well with respect to handedness study. The best overall classification results were again obtained using the time series based approach, which showed significant improvement over the other three approaches. The best sensitivity and specificity were also obtained using the time series based approach. The four advocated approaches also outperform the CSS and ART techniques. Again, these are excellent results.

Table 3 shows the TCV results obtained using the epilepsy data set. The column and row headers were defined as in Table 1. From Table 3 it can be observed that a different result was produced than that recorded with respect to the musicians and handedness studies. The graph based and Zernike moments based approaches that consider all the pixels of each ROI in the feature extraction process outperformed the Hough transform and time series based approaches (recall that these approaches consider only the pixels of the boundary of the ROI). Again all four of the advocated approaches also outperform the CSS and ART techniques. The results for the epilepsy data set seem to be at odds with those obtained using the musicians and handedness studies reported above. Subsequent discussion with medical domain experts did not give an indication as to why this might be the case. However, the suspicion is that the results reflect the fact that although the nature of the corpus callosum may play a part in the identification of epilepsy there are also other factors involved.

	Acc	Sens	Spec
HT	76.42	81.13	71.70
GB	**86.32**	**87.74**	**84.91**
ZM	85.38	87.74	83.02
TS	77.36	82.08	72.64
CSS	68.40	72.64	64.15
ART	70.28	73.58	66.98

Table 3. TCV Classification Results for Epilepsy Study

With respect to classification accuracy in general all four ROI based image classification approaches performed remarkably well, although the time series based approach produced the best results for the musicians and handedness studies while the graph based approach produced the best results for the epilepsy study. There is no obvious reason why this might be the case, visual inspection of the MRI scans does not indicate any obvious distinguishing attributes with respect to the size and shape of the corpus callosum. Tracing the cause of a particular classification back to a particular part of the corpus callosum is thus seen as a desirable "avenue" for future research. It is also interesting to note that the Hough transform based approach performed consistently badly with respect to all of the above evaluation studies suggesting that generating shape signatures using the Hough transform is not a technique to be recommended in the context of feature based classification, although the use of the Hough transform is popular in other branches of image analysis.

In the literature there are a few reported studies on classifying medical images according to the nature of the corpus callosum. For example, Sampat et al. [41] used the cross sectional area of the corpus callosum and the inferior subolivary Medulla Oblongata Volume (MOV) to distinguish patients with Relapsing-Remitting Multiple Sclerosis (RRMS), Secondary-Progressive Multiple Sclerosis (SPMS), and Primary-Progressive Multiple sclerosis (PPMS). Their study produced a classification accuracy of 80%. Fahmi et al. [19] proposed a classification approach in order to distinguishing between healthy controls and autistic patients according to the nature of the corpus callosum. They analysed the displacement fields generated from the non-rigid registration of different corpus callosum segments onto a chosen reference within each group. Their reported result indicated that the classification accuracy was 86%. Golland et al. [22] adopted a version of "Skeletons" for feature extraction, coupled with the Fisher linear discriminant and the linear support vector machines, for the classification of corpus callosum data for schizophrenia patients. The best classification accuracy achieved using their support vector machine classification method was less than 80%. These studies indicate how comparatively effective the classification results obtained, using the four proposed approaches, are. The results obtained using the proposed methods significantly improved on the results produced in these earlier studies.

The run time complexity of the four ROIBIC approaches using the musician, handedness, and epilepsy datasets, are presented in Figures 8, 9 and 10 respectively. The classification time is the overall run time, i.e. it incorporates the feature extraction, training and testing phases. All the experiments were performed with 1.86 GHz Intel(R) Core(TM)2 PC with 2GB RAM. The graph based approach was computationally the most expensive, while the time series based approach was computationally the least expensive. However, it is worth remarking that, especially in the medical context, it is the classification accuracy, not speed, which is the most important feature of the proposed processes.

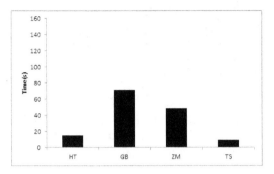

Figure 8. Run time complexity for the classification of the musician dataset.

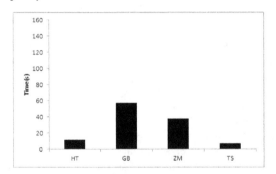

Figure 9. Run time complexity for the classification of the handedness dataset.

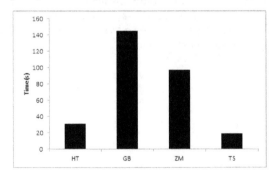

Figure 10. Run time complexity for the classification of the epilepsy dataset.

In summary we can note that there is no constant "winner" among the four proposed ROI based image classification approaches. However, excellent classification results were produced.

8.3. Statistical comparison of the proposed image classification approaches

The AUC values for the best results obtained for all five dataset are given in Table 4. It should be noted that the AUC values support the results reported in Sub-section 8.2. The Friedman's

| | Friedman test statistic = 10.68 ($p < 0.005$) | | | |
	Musician	Handedness	Eplepsy	AR
HT	92.6 (4)	91.3 (4)	78.6 (4)	4
GB	97.1 (2)	96.2 (2)	**88.3** (1)	1.4
ZM	96.4 (3)	94.7 (3)	87.2 (2)	2.4
TS	**99.1** (1)	**96.8** (1)	79.3 (3)	2.2

Table 4. Area Under the receiver operating characteristic Curve (AUC) results.

test [13, 20] was used to compare the AUCs of the different classifiers. The Friedman test statistic is based on the Average Ranked (AR) performances of the classification techniques on each data set, and is calculated as follows:

$$\chi_F^2 - \frac{12N}{K(K+1)}\left[\sum_{j=1}^{K} AR_j^2 \frac{K(K+1)^2}{4}\right] \tag{13}$$

where $AR_j = 1/N\sum_{i=1}^{N} r_i^j$, N denotes the number of data sets used in the study, K is the total number of classifiers and r_i^j is the rank of classifier j on data set i. χ_F^2 is distributed according to the Chi-square distribution with $K-1$ degrees of freedom. If the value of χ_F^2 is large enough, then the null hypothesis that there is no difference between the techniques can be rejected. The Friedman statistic is well suited for this type of data analysis as it is less susceptible to outliers than other comparison techniques. In Table 4 the numbers in the parentheses indicate the average rank of each technique. The Friedman test statistic and corresponding p-value is also shown. From the table it can be seen that these were all significant ($p < 0.005$), the null hypothesis that there is no difference between the techniques can therefore be rejected. From Table 4 the technique achieving the highest AUC on each data set and the overall highest ranked technique is indicated in bold font. From the table it can be seen that the graph based approach (GB) has the best Friedman score (average rank (AR)). The AR associated with the Hough transform approach is statistically worse than the AR associated with all the other approaches, supporting the results obtained earlier.

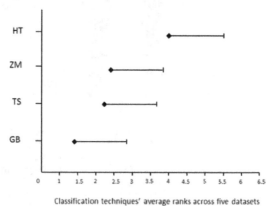

Classification techniques' average ranks across five datasets

Figure 11. Demšar significance diagram for the proposed image classification approaches.

To determine the operational difference between the individual classifiers a post hoc Nemenyi test was applied [13]. The Nemenyi test states that the performances of two or more classifiers are significantly different if their average ranks differ according to a Critical Difference (CD) value, given by:

$$CD = q_{\alpha,\infty,K} \sqrt{\frac{K(K+1)}{12N}} \tag{14}$$

where the value value for $q_{\alpha,\infty,K}$ is based on the Studentised range statistic [13]. A post hoc Nemenyi test was therefore applied to each class distribution and the results displayed using a modified version of a Demšar significance diagram [30]. A Demšar diagram displays the ranked performances of the classification techniques, along with the critical difference, to highlight any techniques which are significantly different to the best performing classifiers. Figure 11 displays the Demšar diagram for the proposed classification approaches. The diagram shows the AUC performance rank for each approach, along with the Nemenyi CD tail. The CD value for the diagram shown in Figure 11 is equal to 1.48. The diagram shows the classification techniques listed in ascending order of ranked performance on the y-axis; and the image classification techniques' average rank, across all data sets, along the x-axis. From the figure it can be seen that the graph based approach is the best performing classification technique with the time series approach coming in second. The diagram clearly again shows that, despite its popularity, the Hough transform performs significantly worse (with a value of 4) than the best performing classifiers in the context of the corpus callosum classification problem.

9. Discussion and conclusion

Referring back to Section 8 all four algorithms performed well, although the time series approach produced the best results for the musicians and handedness studies, while the graph based approach produced the best results with respect to the epilepsy study. Using the Friedman statistic and the post hoc Nemenyi test incited that the graph based technique provided the best overall performance (with the time series approach coming in second). It is interesting to note that, for all the data sets, visual inspection of the MRI scans does not indicate any obvious distinguishing attributes with respect to the size and shape of the corpus callosum. It is also interesting to note that the HT, although popular in the literature, performed consistently badly with respect to all of the above evaluation studies suggesting that generating shape signatures using the HT is not a technique to be recommended in the context of object based image classification.

Thus, in summary, four techniques for single object based image classification have been described. Although the work described focused on the classification of MRI brain scan data according to a particular object (the corpus callosum) that features within this data, the approach clearly has more general applicability. The main findings were that the graph based approach produced the best performance followed by the time series based approach. The HT based approach produced the worst performance in all cases. With respect to future work the research team are interested in developing techniques to trace the cause of a particular classification back its origin (back to a particular part of the corpus callosum).

Author details

Ashraf Elsayed
Department of Mathematics and Computer Science, The University of Alexandria, Egypt

Frans Coenen
Department of Computer Science, The University of Liverpool, UK

Marta García-Fiñana
Department of Health Sciences, The University of Liverpool, UK

Vanessa Sluming
Institute of Translational Medicine, The University of Liverpool, UK

10. References

[1] Allen, A., Richey, M., Chain, Y. and Gorski R. (1991). Sex Differences in The Corpus Callosum of The Living Human Being. Journal of Neuroscience, 11(4), pp933-942.

[2] Ballard, D. (1981). Generalizing the hough transform to detect arbitrary shapes. Pattern Recognition, 13(2), pp111-122.

[3] Belkasim, S., Shridhar, M. and Ahmadi, M. (1991). Pattern Recognition with Moment Invariants: A Comparative Study and New Results. Pattern Recognition, 24(12), pp1117-1138.

[4] Bellman R. and Kalaba, R. (1959). On Adaptive Control Processes. IRE Transactions on Automatic Control, 4(2), pp1-9.

[5] Bober, M. (2001). Mpeg-7 Visual Shape Descriptors. IEEE Transactions on Circuits and Systems for Video Technology, 11(6), pp716-719.

[6] Canny, J. (1986). A Computational Approach to Edge Detection. IEEE Transactions on Pattern Analysis and Machine Intelligence, 8, pp679-698.

[7] Chong, C., Raveendran, P. and Mukundan, R. (2003). A Comparative Analysis of Algorithms for Fast Computation of Zernike Moments. Pattern Recognition, 36, pp731-742.

[8] Conlon P. and Trimble M. (1988). A Study of The Corpus Callosum in Epilepsy Using Magnetic Resonance Imaging. Epilepsy Research, 2(2), pp122-126.

[9] Cortes C. and Vapnik. V. (1995) Support-vector networks. Machine Learning, 20, pp273-297.

[10] Cowell, P., Kertesz, A. and Denenberg, V. (1993). Multiple Dimensions of Handedness and The Human Corpus Callosum. Neurology, 43(11), pp2353-2357.

[11] Cour, T., Benezit, F. and Shi, J. (2005). Spectral Segmentation With Multiscale Graph Decomposition. Proc. IEEE Computer Vision and Pattern Recognition (CVPR'05), 2, pp1124-1131.

[12] Davatzikos, C., Vaillant, M., Resnick, S., Prince, J., Letovsky, S. and Bryan, R. (1996). A Computerized Approach for Morphological Analysis of The Corpus Callosum. Computer Assisted Tomography, 20(1), pp88-97.

[13] Demšar, J. (2006). Statistical comparisons of classifiers over multiple data sets. Journal of Machine Learning Research, 7, pp1-30.

[14] Douglas D. and Peucker, T. (1973). Algorithm for The Reduction of The Number of Points Required to Represent a Line or its Caricature. The Canadian Cartographer, 10, pp112-122.

[15] Duara, R., Kushch, A., Gross-Glenn, K., Barker, W., Jallad, B., Pascal, S., Loewenstein, D., Sheldon, J., Rabin, M., Levin, B. and Lubs, H. (1991). Neuroanatomic Differences Between Dyslexic and Normal Readers on Magnetic Resonance Imaging Scans. Archives of Neurology, 48(4), pp410-416.

[16] Elsayed, A., Coenen, F., Jiang, C., García-Fiñana, M. ana Sluming, V. (2010). Region of Interest Based Image Categorization. Proc. 12th International Conference on Data Warehousing and Knowledge Discovery (DaWaK'10), pp239-250.

[17] Elsayed, A., Coenen, F., Jiang, C., García-Fiñana, M. ana Sluming, V. (2010). Corpus Callosum MR Image Classification. Knowledge Based Systems, 23(4), pp330-336.

[18] Elsayed, A., Coenen, F., Jiang, C., García-Fiñana, M. ana Sluming, V. (2012). Classification of MRI Brain Scan Data Using Shape Criteria. Annals of the British Machine Vision Association (BMVA), Vol. 2011, No. 6, pp1-14 (2011)

[19] Fahmi, R., El-Baz, A., Abd El Munim, H., Farag, A. and Casanova, M. (2007). Classification Techniques for Autistic vs. Typically Developing Brain using MRI Data. Proc. 4th IEEE International Symposium on Biomedical Imaging: From Nano to Macro, pp1348-1351.

[20] Friedman, M. (1940). A Comparison of Alternative Tests of Significance for The Problem of m Rankings. Annals of Mathematical Statistics, 11, pp86-92.

[21] Goebel, R., Esposito, F. and Formisano, E. (2006). Analysis of Functional Image Analysis Contest (FIAC) Data with Brainvoyager QX: From Single-Subject to Cortically Aligned Group General Linear Model Analysis and Self-organizing Group Independent Component Analysis. Human Brain Mapping, 27(5), pp392-401.

[22] Golland, P., Grimson, W. and Kikinis, R. (1999). Statistical Shape Analysis Using Fixed Topology Skeletons: Corpus Callosum Study. Proc. 16th International Conference on Information Processing and Medical Imaging (IPMI'99), 16, pp382-387.

[23] Hall, M., Frank, E., Holmes, G., Pfahringer, B., Reutemann, P. and Witten, I. (2009). The Weka Data Mining Software: An Update. SIGKDD Explorations Newsletter, 11, pp10-18.

[24] Hampel, H., Teipel, S., Alexander, G., Horwitz, B., Teichberg, D., Schapiro, M., and Rapoport, S. (1998). Corpus Callosum Atrophy is a Possible Indicator of Region and Cell Type-specific Neuronal Degeneration in Alzheimer Disease. Archives of Neurology, 55(2), pp193-198.

[25] Hough, P. (1962). Method and means for recognizing complex patterns. United States Patent 3069654.

[26] Hynd, G., Hall, J., Novey, E., Eliopulos, D., Black, K., Gonzalez, J., Ed- monds, J., Riccio, C. and Cohen, M. (1995). Dyslexia and Corpus Callosum Morphology. Archives of Neurology, 52(1), pp32-38.

[27] Itakura, F.(1975). Minimum Prediction Residual Principle Applied to Speech Recognition. IEEE Transactions on Acoustics, Speech and Signal Processing, 23(1), pp67-72.

[28] Jiang C. and Coenen, F. (2008). Graph-Based Image Classification by Weighting Scheme. Proc. SGAI International Conference on Artificial Intelligence (AI'08), pp63-76.

[29] Kintner, E. (1976). On The Mathematical Properties of Zernike Polynomials. Journal of Modern Optics, 23(8), pp679-680.

[30] Lessmann, S., Baesens, B., Mues, C. and Pietsch, S. (2008). Benchmarking Classification Models for Software Defect Prediction: A Proposed Framework and Novel Findings. IEEE Transactions on Software Engineering, 34, pp485-496.

[31] Lindeberg, T. (1994). Scale-Space Theory: A Basic Tool for Analysing Structures at Different Scales. Journal of Applied Statistics, 21, pp224-270.

[32] Lyoo, I., Satlin, A., Lee, C. and Renshaw, P. (1997). Regional Atrophy of the Corpus Callosum in Subjects with Alzheimer's Disease and Multi-infarct Dementia. Psychiatry Research, 74(2), pp63-72.

[33] Lundervold, A., Duta, N., Taxt, T. and Jain, A.K. (1999). Model-guided segmentation of corpus callosum in MR images. Proc. IEEE Computer Society Conference on Computer Vision and Pattern Recognition, pp231-237.

[34] Mokhtarian F. and Mackworth, A. (1986). Scale-based Description and Recognition of Planar Curves and Two-dimensional Objects. IEEE Transactions on Pattern Analysis and Machine Intelligence, 8, pp34-43.

[35] Ozturk, A., Tascioglu, B., Aktekin, M., Kurtoglu, Z. and Erden, I. (2002). Morphometric Comparison of The Human Corpus Callosum in Professional Musicians and Non-musicians by Using in Vivo Magnetic Resonance Imaging. Journal of Neuroradiology, 29(1), pp29-34.

[36] Prata A. and Rusch W. (1989). Algorithm for Computation of Zernike Polynomials Expansion Coefficients. Applied Optics, 28, pp749-754.

[37] Quinlan. J. (1993). C4.5: Programs for Machine Learning. Morgan Kaufmann Publishers Inc.

[38] Riley, J., Franklin, D., Choi, V., Kim, R., Binder, D., Cramer, S. and Lin, J. (2010). Altered White Matter Integrity in Temporal Lobe Epilepsy: Association with Cognitive and Clinical Profiles. Epilepsia, 51(4), pp536-545.

[39] Sakoe H. and Chiba, S. (1978). Dynamic Programming Algorithm Optimization for Spoken Word Recognition. IEEE Transactions on Acoustics, Speech and Signal Processing, 26(1), pp43-49.

[40] Salat, D., Ward, A., Kaye, J. and Janowsky, J. (1997). Sex Differences in The Corpus Callosum with Aging. Neurobiology of Aging, 18(2), pp191-197.

[41] Sampat, M., Berger, A., Healy, B., Hildenbrand, P., Vass, J., Meier, D., Chitnis, T., Weiner, H., Bakshi, R. and Guttmann, C. (2009). Regional White Matter Atrophybased Classification of Multiple Sclerosis in Cross-Sectional and Longitudinal Data. American Journal of Neuroradiology, 30(9), pp1731-1739.

[42] Sato, Y. (1992). Piecewise Linear Approximation of Plane Curves by Perimeter Optimization. Pattern Recognition, 25(12), pp1535-1543.

[43] Schlaug, G., Jancke, L., Huang, Y., Staiger, J. and Steinmetz, H. (1995). Increased Corpus Callosum Size in Musicians. Neuropsychologia, 33(8), pp1047-1055.

[44] Shi, J. and Malik, J. (2000). Normalized Cuts and Image Segmentation. IEEE Transactions on Pattern Analysis and Machine Intelligence, 22, pp888-905.

[45] Vlachos, M., Vagena, Z., Yu, P. and Athitsos, V. (2005). Rotation Invariant Indexing of Shapes and Line Drawings. Proc. 14th ACM international conference on Information and knowledge management (CIKM'05), pp131-138.

[46] Yan, X. and Han, J. (2002). gSpan: Graph-Based Substructure Pattern Mining. Proc. IEEE 2002 International Conference on Data Mining (ICDM'02), pp721-724.

[47] Weber, B., Luders, E., Faber, J., Richter, S., Quesada, C., Urbach, H., Thompson, P., Toga, A., Elger, C. and Helmstaedter, C. (2007). Distinct regional atrophy in the corpus callosum of patients with temporal lobe epilepsy. Brain, 130(12), pp3149-3154.

[48] Wee C. and Paramesran, R. (2007). On The Computational Aspects of Zernike Moments. Image and Vision Computing, 25, pp967-980.

[49] Weis, S., Kimbacher, M., Wenger, E. and Neuhold, A.(1993). Morphometric Analysis of the Corpus Callosum Using MRI: Correlation of Measurements with Aging in Healthy Individuals. American Journal of Neuroradiology, 14(3), pp637-645.

[50] Wu, C., Horng, S., and Lee, P. (2001). A New Computation of Shape Moments Via Quadtree Decomposition. Pattern Recognition, 34, pp1319-1330.

Chapter 10

Discovering Fragrance Biosynthesis Genes from *Vanda* Mimi Palmer Using the Expressed Sequence Tag (EST) Approach

Seow-Ling Teh, Janna Ong Abdullah, Parameswari Namasivayam and Rusea Go

Additional information is available at the end of the chapter

1. Introduction

1.1. Orchidaceae

Orchidaceae is the largest family of angiosperms with an estimation of 17000 to 35000 species in 880 genera (Chai & Yu, 2007). In Malaysia, more than 230 orchid genera and 4000 species had been discovered (Go *et al.*, 2012). In Penisular Malaysia, a total of 898 species in 143 genera are currently recognised (Go *et al.*, 2010). The amazing vast diversity of types and forms enable the Orchidaceae to be successfully distributed and colonised almost every habitats worldwide (Arditti, 1992). As a result of selective forces from evolution, orchids are found to be evolved from its ancestral forms and adapted well to their present habitats (Aceto & Gaudio, 2011). Associated with their diverse floral morphology and physiology properties, they have drawn the attention of botanists and scientists for centuries. There are orchids which resemble moths (*Phalaenopsis*), butterflies (*Oncidium papillo*), the slippers of Aphrodite or moccasins (*Paphiopedilum* or *Cypripedium*), dancing ladies (*Oncidium*), spiders (*Brassia*), scorpions (*Arachnis*) and bees (*Ophrys*) (Teoh, 1980).

Similar to other angiosperms, two whorls of perianth segment can also be found in orchids. The outer and inner whorls of the orchid flowers consist of three petals and three sepals. The labellum or lip (one of the petals), is distinctly evolved from the other two morphologically and physically (Arditti, 1992). The lifespan of opened-orchid flowers can range from as short as one day to as long as 270 days (Micheneau *et al.*, 2008).

Most orchids are epiphytic that obtain their support from trees but not for nutrition while the rest are terrestrial plants (Rada & Jaimez, 1992). Orchids' cultivation was famous since 5000 years ago in China where *Cymbidium* was grown as potted plants, and *Vanda* and

Aerides were suspended from baskets (Teoh, 1980). Orchid hybrids can be divided into three groups which are hybrid species (produced by selfing a species or by crossing two plants belonging to the same species), inter-specific hybrid (produced from the crossing between two different species belonging to the same genus or by second crossing with other inter-specific hybrids) and inter-generic hybrid (produced from the crossings of orchids belonging to different genera).

Orchid hybrids cultivation started since 1856 by John Dominy (http://www/ionopsis.com/hybridization htm). *Calanthe dominii* was created from the crossing between *Calanthe masuca* and *Calanthe furcated*. Orchid hybrids made up majority of the commercial orchids in Malaysia and Singapore. There are lots of reasons that led to the wide area coverage of orchid hybrids cultivation, such as the ease of cultivation, free blooming habit, and compactness and fantastic arrays of shapes, colours and flowers (Kishor *et al.*, 2006).

The export of orchids from Malaysia, Thailand and Singapore contributed RM200 million annually in the world floral (Ooi, 2005). According to the Japan Florists' Telegraph Delivery Association, cut flower in Japan constituted around 13.3% of the imported market in the year 2010 with Malaysia having the largest market share of imports, which accounted for 23.4% (7,648 million yen), followed by Columbia at 19.2% and China at 10.4%. Malaysian orchids consisted of 8.1% of the imported cut flower orchid to Japan.

1.2. Vandaceous orchids

Tropical Asia is the native home for approximately 50 vandaceous orchids species. They are distributed in Sri Lanka and southern India to New Guinea, northern Australia and Solomon Islands, and north to China, Taiwan and the Philippines. Thailand was found to be predominated with 11 vanda species. In Thailand, vanda is a vital commercial orchid. Most of them exhibit monopodial growth where their leaves are varies according to habitat. Vandas have many different colours, and majority are yellowish-brown with dark brown spots.

The vanda has been designated as the 'Queen Orchid of the East' due to its robust and large rounded flowers (Teo, 1981). Most of the vandaceous orchids prefer sunlight but some are well adapted to shady areas. Like any other tropical orchids, they require warm temperature with good aeration. The vandaceous orchids take around three and half to 10 years to become mature flowering plants (Kishor *et al.*, 2008). Once matured, this orchid genus blooms every two to three months with the flowers lasting two to three weeks. As a result of land development, 28 orchid species have been listed as endangered species on Appendix II of the Convention on International Trade in Endangered Species (CITES) and prohibited from worldwide export. Among those orchids, two belong to vandas (*Vanda coerulea* and *Vanda sanderiana*).

It is impossible to differentiate or identify an orchid species based on the vegetative parts of the plant alone. Hence, a convenient and flower-independent method to allow quick assessment of a given orchid vegetative specimen for species confirmation can be achieved with the help of molecular markers. To date, approximately 50 species are registered under vandas in the Royal Horticultural Society (RHS) database due to their commercial importance.

1.3. *Vanda* Mimi Palmer

Vanda Mimi Palmer (VMP) (Figure 1) is one of those hybrids known to be highly sought after mainly for its fragrance rather than its flower shape or colour. It is a hybrid of *Vanda* Tan Chay Yan and *Vanda tessellate* (Roxb.) Hk.*f.* ex G. Don, and was registered on 1st December 1963 by the Gem Nursery, Singapore. It inherited its sweet fragrance and tri-colour flower from *V. tessellate*, while its terete-shaped is inherited from *V.* Tan Chay Yan. It has purplish green, but brown-speckled, petals and sepals with a dark blue lip. This hybrid is a frequent bloomer throughout the year with maximal floral scent emission when the flower is fully bloomed (an average bloom diameter of 5.0-7.0 cm). Fragrance emission is detected only when the flower bud starts to open as none is detected from the closed bud [average size of 0.8-1.4 cm](Chan *et al.*, 2011; Janna *et al.*, 2005). It has been recognised for its extraordinary fragrance as evident with awards won from the competitions organised by the Royal Horticultural Society of Thailand in 1993 and the 17th World Orchid Conference in 2002.

Figure 1. *Vanda* Mimi Palmer, a hybrid crossing between *Vanda* Tan Chay Yan and *Vanda tessellate* (Roxb.) Hk.*f.* ex G. Don.

Orchids cultivation entails hard work as the orchids can be easily infected by orchid-infecting viruses. More than 50 orchid-infecting viruses have been detected worldwide, with cymbidium mosaic virus (CymMV) and odontoglossum ringspot tobamovirus (ORSV) infections being the most prevalent (Sherpa *et al.*, 2007). Infected orchid cultivars usually exhibit blossoms with brown necrotic streaks and other necrosis symptoms. Infected flowers are smaller in size and poorer in quality. This has caused severe economic damages in the cut flower and potted plant industry (Ajjikuttira *et al.*, 2002; Sherpa *et al.*, 2007; Vejaratpimol *et al.*, 1999). CymMV infection is dominant and extremely stable in Orchidaceae, and it was found to be prevalent in VMP. A screen of our VMP cDNA library revealed a 1.6% contamination rate with CymMV genes (Teh *et al.*, 2011). Markers might be useful in facilitating the screening of virus-infected stock plants to minimise losses incurred in the floral industry. So far, the identification of CymMV infection is done through serological, bioassay or electron microscopy. Those techniques include enzyme-linked immunosorbent assays (ELISA), dot-blot immunoassay (DBIA), rapid immunofilter paper assay (RIPA), immunosorbent electron microscope (ISEM), DIG-labelled cRNA probes, reverse transcription polymerase chain reaction (RT-PCR), quartz crystal microbalance-based DNA biosensors and TaqMan real-time quantitative RT-PCR (Eun *et al.*, 2002; Eun & Wong, 2000; Hsu *et al.*, 1992; Hu *et al.*, 1998; Khentry *et al.*, 2006; Rani *et al.*, 2010).

2 Importance of floral fragrance

Floral fragrance plays various functions in both the floral and vegetative organs. Fragrance is defined as a highly complex component of floral phenotype for its dynamic patterns of emission and chemical composition (Raguso, 2008). Due to their restriction to specific lineages and interactions in species-specific ecology, these have led to their designation as specialized or secondary metabolites (Pichersky *et al.*, 2006).

Floral fragrance has a significant impact in plant reproduction as it is a selective attractant in a variety of animal pollinators especially insects. Pollinators such as bees, butterflies and moths are able to discriminate visitation on plants based on the compositions of the floral scent. This plant-insect interaction has led to many successful pollinations and development of fruits in many crop species (Majetic *et al.*, 2009; Shuttleworth & Johnson, 2009).

Anti-microbial or anti-herbivore properties of floral volatiles could be used by plants to protect their vital floral reproductive parts from potential predators. Two types of plant defences can be characterised based on floral volatiles property, that are direct and indirect defences such as herbivore-induced volatiles signals, and visual and olfactory floral signals to attract pollinators (Schiestl, 2010). Indirect plant defences protect the plants by minimizing damage to plant tissues through attracting arthropods that prey or parasitize the herbivores. This general property has been reported in cabbage (Park *et al.*, 2005), *Lotus japonicas* (Arimura *et al.*, 2004) and cucumber (Agrawal *et al.*, 2002). On the other hand, direct defences take place when herbivore-induced volatiles repel or intoxicate the herbivores and pathogens. For example, some herbivore-induced monoterpenes and sesquiterpenes tend to react with various reactive oxygen species and thus protect the plants from internal oxidative damage (Dudareva *et al.*, 2004). Terp *et al.* (2006) reported that lipoxygenases are produced in *Brassica napus* seeds upon wounding and pathogen attack. Complexity in floral scent chemicals was found to be useful in protecting the plants' reproductive structures from herbivores and ants (Schiestl, 2010).

Through the discovery of pollinator-attracting floral scents as the source of olfactory pleasure since ancient times, humans had figured out unique values in certain types of floral scents and exploited them to cultivate and propagate specific plant species. For centuries, flowers with vibrant colours and scents have been used by people to enhance their beauty and this was seen in almost all major civilizations. Large numbers of aromatic plants have been used as flavourings, preservatives and herbal remedies (Pichersky *et al.*, 2006). Their economic importance also relies on their petals which are found to be the main site of natural fragrances and flavourings in most of the plants (Baudino *et al.*, 2007).

2.1. Fragrance biosynthesis pathways

Plants are known with the capability of synthesizing many volatile metabolites, either primary or secondary metabolites with variety of functions (Pichersky *et al.*, 2006). However, volatile esters formation is not restricted to plant kingdom but also in yeast and fungi especially in the fermentation industry (Beekwilder *et al.*, 2004). Floral scent is made up of a complex mixture of low-molecular-weight lipophilic compounds which are typically liquids with high vapour pressures (Vainstein *et al.*, 2001). With the discovery of novel techniques including gas chromatography-nuclear magnetic resonance (GC-NMR), gas chromatography-mass spectrometry (GC-MS), headspace based techniques in volatiles detection and analyses, the number of identified volatile compounds has increased tremendously (Gonzalez-Mas *et al.*, 2008; Mohd-Hairul *et al.*, 2010; Nojima *et al.*, 2011).

Most of the volatile compounds are derived from three major biosynthesis pathways: phenylpropanoids, fatty acid derivatives and terpenoids. They are thus classified into three major categories: terpenes, lipid derivatives and aromatic compounds. The terpenes are the largest class of plant volatiles, which consist of monoterpene alcohols and sesquiterpenes. There are also other terpene derivatives like ketones that are present in low quantities but have significant contributions to the floral fragrance. The second largest family of plant volatiles is the aromatic compounds. Most of them are derived from the intermediates in the benzenoid biosynthesis pathway that resulted in the synthesis of phenylalanine from the shikimate pathway, followed by a wide range of primary metabolites (eugenol, a lignin precursor, is one of them) and secondary non-volatile compounds (this was well reviewed in Bick & Lange, 2003; Pichersky & Dudareva, 2007).

The third category of plant volatiles is the lipid derivatives from the oxidative cleavage and decarboxylation of a variety of fatty acids which lead to shorter-chain volatiles with aldehyde and ketone moieties formation (reviewed in Baysal & Demirdoven, 2007). There are also other plant volatiles especially those with nitrogen or sulfur, which are produced through the cleavage of modified amino acids or their precursors (Cherri *et al.*, 2007; Pichersky *et al.*, 2006).

2.2. Discovery of fragrance-related genes

Due to the invisibility of floral scents and its dynamic nature, the study on flower scent is limited. There is no convenient plant model system that allows chemical and biochemical studies on floral scents. The well-established *Arabidopsis* as a plant model system failed to serve this purpose as the detection of volatiles production by its flower was barely detectable (Vainstein *et al.*, 2001). To date, the characterization and elucidation of enzymes and genes involved in flower scent production are still not as advanced as the biochemical study on the scent constituents. *Petunia hybrid* is one of the plant model systems that has been used to study the biological importance of floral scent (Spitcer *et al.*, 2007). However, limited information is available for the floral fragrance synthesized in petunia flowers as well as its cell specificity in fragrance production (van Moerkercke *et al.*, 2012).

'Scent' enzymes can be identified through *in vitro* characterization of their enzymatic activities with substrates predicted to be the precursors of known products in the tissues from which they are derived (Dudareva *et al.*, 2004). Besides, they can also be determined by identifying the homologue sequences in genomic or EST databases, expressing the protein in heterologous system like bacterial system followed by biochemical testing of the enzymatic activities with various substrates (Adelene *et al.*, 2012; Bradbury, 2007).

For more than 400 orchids (including both species and hybrids) that were discovered to emit fragrance (Frowine, 2005), in-depth scientific studies on orchid fragrance barely covered 2 percents of the fragrant orchids. Sadly, fragrance study in orchid is not as well established as in other flowers such as rose (Guterman *et al.*, 2002), petunia (Verdonk *et al.*, 2003) and *Clarkia breweri* (Dudareva *et al.*, 1996; Dudareva *et al.*, 1998). The advent of GC-MS technique enabled the evaluation of floral scent components quantitatively and qualitatively (Vainstein *et al.*, 2001). Mohd-Hairul *et al.* (2010) showed that the scent of VMP was predominated by terpenoid, benzenoid and phenylpropanoid compounds through GC-MS analysis (Table 1). It was interesting to note that a comparison of the volatiles captured from VMP with both of its parents revealed that the scent was dissimilar to its fragrance parent, *V. tessellate*. Such biochemical data is useful for subsequent work in the identification of fragrance-related genes in VMP.

3. Expressed sequence tags (ESTs)

Expressed Sequence Tags (ESTs) are partial sequences generated from single-pass sequencing (5'- or 3'- end) from a reverse transcription of mRNA representing tissue of interest or a particular developmental stage of an organism (Adam *et al.*, 1991). In plant, EST approach was first used in the model plant *A. thaliana* for genome and *in vivo* analysis of their gene products (Hofte *et al.*, 1994). Generally, the generated ESTs are highly informative at the middle DNA sequences but its redundancy rate at both ends can reach up to 3% (Nagaraj *et al.*, 2006; Rudd, 2003). Thus, pre-processing of ESTs is required prior to further analyses.

EST libraries for many plant species such as *P. equestris* (Schauer) Rchb.f. (Tsai *et al.*, 2006; Tsai *et al.*, 2011), cycads (Brenner *et al.*, 2003), mints (Lindqvist *et al.*, 2006), apple (Newcomb *et al.*, 2006), *Jatropha curcas* (Chen *et al.*, 2011) and *Prunus mume* (Li *et al.*, 2010) have been developed and deposited into the GenBank database. One of the databases for the submission and deposition of ESTs sequences is the database of expressed sequence tags (dbEST). dbEST is a collection of cDNA sequences and ESTs information from different variety of organisms. From the dbEST released on April 1, 2012 (http://www.ncbi.nlm.nih.gov/dbEST/dbEST_summary.html), the publicly available ESTs data were 72,316,247.

3.1. Importance of ESTs

EST is a fast, efficient and valuable tool for gene expression, genome annotation and evolutionary studies. Analysis of ESTs provides a platform for functional genomics study as well as uncovering the potentially novel genes, and poses an avenue for genome sequencing projects (Ayeh, 2008; Kisiel & Podkowinski, 2005; Li *et al.*, 2010; Lindqvist *et al.*, 2006). Early EST projects were focused mostly on economically important plants and crop plants. In subsequent years, more EST projects on plants yet-to-achieve high economical impact started to materialise. The development of ESTs for some of the plants species from the early years until now is summarised in Table 2.

EST also proves to be a beneficial resource for comparative genomic studies in plant. Hsiao *et al.* (2006) deduced monoterpene biosynthesis pathway and identified a few fragrance-related genes in *Phalaenopsis bellina* by making a comparison with the floral EST library of *P. equestris* (scentless species). EST is also useful in the development and mining of microsatellite markers such as simple sequence repeats (SSRs) (Alba *et al.*, 2004). Lindqvist *et al.* (2006) reported the development of mint's EST for the identification of genetic markers for Hawaiian endemic mints. Moreover, EST provides the basis for the understanding of metabolic regulation mechanisms (Chen *et al.*, 2011; Li *et al.*, 2010).

Peak	Relative retention time (min)	Main spectrum fragments (m/z)	Compound name
Monoterpene			
1	8.636	36,41,53,67,79,93,105,121	Ocimene
2	9.147	41,43,59,81,93,112	Linalool oxide
3	9.592	41,43,69,71,93,107,121,136	Linalool
Sesquiterpene			
10	16.492	41,43,69,71,93,107,123,136, 162	Nerolidol
Benzenoid			
4	9.702	51,77,105,136	Methylbenzo-ate
5	10.030	39,51,65,78,91,105,122	Benzyl acetate
Phenylpropanoid			
6			
8	10.783	39,43,65,79,91,108,150	Phenylethanol
	11.926	39,43,65,78,91,104	Phenylethyl acetate
Indole			
9	13.084	39,50,63,74,90,117	Indole
Formanilide			
7	12.260	39,52,65,76,93,161	Formanilide

Table 1. Volatile compounds emitted by fully open flower of *Vanda* Mimi Palmer with **their relative retention times and spectral fragments.** This table is adapted from Mohd-Hairul *et al.* (2010).

Organism	ESTs
Zea mays (maize)	2,019,114
Arabidopsis thaliana (thale cress)	1,529,700
Glycine max (soybean)	1,461,624
Oryza sativa (rice)	1,252,989
Triticum aestivum (wheat)	1,073,877
Panicum virgatum (switchgrass)	720,590
Brassica napus (oilseed rape)	643,874
Hordeum vulgare + subsp. *vulgare* (barley)	501,838
Vitis vinifera (wine grape)	446,639
Nicotiana tabacum (tobacco)	334,384
Pinus taeda (loblolly pine)	328,662
Malus x *domestica* (apple tree)	324,742
Piceaglauca (white spruce)	313,110
Gossypium hirsutum (upland cotton)	297,239
Solanum lycopersicum (tomato)	297,142
Medicago truncatula (barrel medic)	269,238
Solanum tuberosum (potato)	249,761
Lotus japonicas	242,432
Mimulus guttatus	231,095
Raphanus sativus (radish)	110,006
Petunia x hybrid	50,705
Zingiber sp.	38,190
Elaeis guineensis	40,737
Petunia axillaris subsp. *axillaris*	11,078
Phalaenopsis equestris	5,604
Rosa hybrid cultivar	5,565
Phalaenopsis violacea	2,359
Dendrobium officinale	800
Oncidium hybrid cultivar	280
Phalaenopsis amabilis	103

Table 2. Summary of some of the plants species available in dbEST from the early years until 1 April 2012.

3.2. Discovery of fragrance-related genes from VMPESTs

Expressed sequence tags (ESTs) have been developed from many monocot plant species including *P. equestris* (Tsai *et al.*, 2006), ginger (Chandasekar *et al.*, 2009), oil palm (Low *et al.*, 2008), wheat (Zhang *et al.*, 2004) and maize (Fernandes *et al.*, 2002). To date, more than 1700 floral fragrance compounds have been identified through biochemical analysis with the majority identified from higher plants whilst others are from animals, insects, marine organisms, algae and bacteria. Unfortunately, the developments of the biochemical aspects of fragrance compounds are not in par with the molecular information on fragrance-related genes. More so, reported molecular information from the vandaceous orchids is still extremely scarce. Thus far, the only available fragrance-related molecular works on orchid are from the genera *Phalaenopsis* and *Vanda* (from our research group).

A VMP floral cDNA library was previously constructed from opened flowers at different developmental stages and time-points (Chan *et al.*, 2009). All the cDNA clones with the inserts sizes of 0.5 kb to 1.6 kb were mass excised and single-pass 5'-sequenced. From our attempt, a total of 2,132 ESTs was generated. This VMP dbEST (designated as VMPEST) was clustered, annotated and further classified with Gene Ontology (GO) identifier into three categories: Molecular Functions (51.2%), Cellular Components (16.4%) and Biological Processes (24.6%). Around 3.1% of the VMPEST had hits with other orchid species such as dendrobium, phalaenopsis, oncidium, *Aerides japiona*, and *Aranda* Deborah. A number of fragrance-related transcripts were identified (Table 3; Teh, 2011) by comparing Kyoto Encyclopedia of Genes and Genomes (KEGG) pathways with the three major volatiles biosynthesis pathways (terpenoid, benzenoid and phenylpropanoid) of well-studied scented flowers such as *Antirrhinum majus, Clarkia breweri, Petunia* hybrid and *Rosa* hybrid (Boatright *et al.*, 2004; Lavid *et al.*, 2002).

From the VMPEST, several fragrance-related transcripts were selected for full-length isolation and expression analysis using real-time quantitative RT-PCR. They were *Vanda* Mimi Palmer *acetyl-CoA acetyltransferase* (designated as *VMPACA*, in press), *Vanda* Mimi Palmer *3-hydroxy-3-methylglutaryl-coenzyme A reductase* (*VMPHMGR*), *Vanda* Mimi Palmer *1-deoxy-D-xylulose 5-phosphate synthase* (*VMPDXPS*), *Vanda* Mimi Palmer *linalool synthase* (*VMPLis*) and *Vanda* Mimi Palmer *lipoxygenase* (*VMPLox*) (Teh, 2011). Gene specific primers were designed and synthesised for 5'-RACE targeting at the incomplete 5'-ends of each of the aforementioned gene transcript. The full length cDNA sequences of those transcripts were deduced, amplified, followed by sequencing and sequence analysis. Real-time quantitative RT-PCR were performed using cDNA templates extracted from different types of VMP tissues (sepals, petals, lips, stems, stalks, columns, roots and leaves), from full-bloom flowers taken at different time points (2-hour intervals within 24-hour duration) and from different flower developmental stages (buds, blooming and full-bloom flower). Overall, the expression profiles revealed that the transcripts exhibited a developmentally regulated pattern in the different flower developmental stages. Majority of the transcripts were highly expressed in the full-bloom stage, with the sepals and petals having the highest expression levels.

GenBank Accession	dbEST id	Putative identity	E-value	Score (bits)
GW392501	68671343	3-hydroxy-3-methylglutaryl-coenzyme A reductase 2 [Gossypium hirsutum]	2.00E-108	358
GW392566	68671408	LOX1 (Lipoxygenase 1); lipoxygenase [Arabidopsis thaliana]	1.00E-50	203
GW392695	68671537	linalool synthase 2 [Clarkia breweri]	9.00E-19	97.8
CW392657	68671499	trans-caffeoyl-CoA 3-O-methyltransferase [Populus trichocarpa]	2.00E-52	209
GW392731	68671573	lipoxygenase 1 [Brassica napus]	2.00E-15	85.9
GW392740	68671582	acyltransferase [Vanda hybrid cultivar]	3.00E-70	268
GW392813	68671655	cinnamyl alcohol dehydrogenase [Populus trichocarpa]	2.00E-73	279
GW393688	68672530	carboxyl methyltransferase [Crocus sativus]	5.00E-58	228
GW392895	68671737	cinnamoyl-CoA reductase [Saccharum officinarum]	2.00E-46	189
GW392922	68671764	putative 1-deoxy-D-xylulose 5-phosphate synthase [Hevea brasiliensis]	6.00E-62	241
GW393960	68672802	putative acetyl-CoA C-acyltransferase [Oryza sativa Japonica Group]	4.00E-103	378
GW393331	68672173	lipoxygenase 1 [Brassica napus]	4.00E-27	125
GW393619	68672461	resveratrol O-methyltransferase [Vitis vinifera]	8.00E-56	221
GW393628	68672470	s-adenosylmethionine synthetase, putative [Ricinus communis]	2.00E-59	233
GW394168	68673010	linalool synthase-like protein [Oenothera arizonica]	6.00E-41	171
GW393499	68672341	acetyl-CoA acetyltransferase, cytosolic 1 [Zea mays]	1.00E-136	488

Table 3. Selected putative fragrance-related ESTs generated from *Vanda* Mimi Palmer. This table is adapted from Teh *et al.* (2011).

Among all the transcripts analysed, *VMPHMGR* was selected for functional analysis. HMGR is a very well-studied enzyme in cholesterol synthesis especially in animal system. A functional enzymatic assay performed showed *VMPHMGR* was functionally active in *Escherichia coli*, catalysing the conversion of HMG-CoA to mevalonate derivatives, which are commonly used in the metabolic biosynthesis of steroids, terpenoids and carotenoids (Teh, 2011). This VMPHMGR shows high sequence identity to the HMGR found in other plant species, with 76% sequence similarity with *Oryza sativa* Indica group. Although its N-terminal end differs distinctly in length and amino acids compositions, its C-terminal catalytic domain shows high sequence similarity with other plant species (unpublished data). This highlights the importance of information and evolution of gene of similar function in different organisms.

4. Simple sequence repeat and its importance

Simple Sequence Repeat (SSR) or microsatellite is a short tandem repeats of a unique DNA sequence with one to six nucleotides motif (Jacob et al., 1991). SSR is a famous molecular marker because of its hyper variability, relative abundance, highly reproducible, multiallelic diversity, co-dominantly inherited and extensive coverage of the genome (Mohan et al., 1997).

Owing to its desirable genetic attributes, SSRs have been utilized in genetic and genomic analyses including genetic mapping, marker assisted plant breeding, development of linkage map, and ecology studies (Kalia et al., 2011; Sonah et al., 2011; Yue et al., 2006). Yue et al. (2006) reported the usage of SSRs in the protection of new Dendrobium varieties.

To date, the used of SSRs markers have been reported in several monocot and dicot species including raspberry and blackberry (Stafne et al., 2005), rice (Chakravarthi & Naravaneni, 2006), common bean (Yu et al., 2000), Brachypodium (Sonah et al., 2011) and Dendrobium (Yue et al., 2006). However, the effort to develop SSR markers for orchids is limited to several species: Chinese orchid [Cymbidium spp.] (Huang et al., 2010), Phalaenopsis (Bory et al., 2008; Hsu et al., 2011), Brazilian orchid (Epidendrum fulgens) (Pinheiro et al., 2008), Dendrobium (Yue et al., 2006) and Vanda (Phuekvilai et al., 2009).

So far, the reported SSRs generated from vandaceous orchids were used as selective marker only. Phuekvilai et al. (2009) generated SSRs from 33 vandas species for the sole purpose of identifying and evaluating the purity of cultivar in commercial samples. However, the identification and development of SSRs for VMP will be channelled towards facilitating the screening of any potential fragrance-related transcripts from closely related species. Besides, it will be used to determine the extent of inter-species transferability of genes, which had been reported in many plant species (Chapman et al., 2009; Stafne et al., 2005; Wang et al., 2004).

4.1. Data mining of VMPEST-SSR

In recent years, genic microsatellite or EST-SSRs which is less time consuming and relatively easy to develop has replaced the genomics SSRs (Sharma et al., 2007). The publicly available ESTs sequences facilitate the development of SSRs by using the SSR identification tools. These search tools include MISA (MIcroSATellite), SSRIT (SSR Identification Tool), SciRoKo, TRF (Tandem Repeat Finder), Sputnik, SSRfinder, SAT (SSR Analysis Tool), Poly and SSR Primer. It is deemed important to choose a search tool which is user-friendly and has unlimited access to a non-redundant database (this was well reviewed by Kalia et al., 2011). The first attempt to develop such EST-SSR marker was in rice by Miyao et al. (1996).

SSRIT which is accessible at URL (http://www.gramene.org) was used to identify the SSR motifs in our VMPEST. The script assessed the sequences uploaded in FASTA-formatted files and detected the SSR motifs, the number of repeats as well as identified the sequence corresponded to the SSRs. A total of 98 (9.4%) unigenes containing 112 SSRs with motifs length ranging from two to six nucleotides were detected from VMPEST.

The VMPEST-SSRs were classified into 2 groups with 88.4% belonging to Class I ($n \geq 20$ nucleotides) and 11.6% belonging to Class II ($12 \leq n \leq 20$ nucleotides) according to their lengths and genetic marker potential (Teh et al., 2011). Such groupings had been reported in rice by Temnykh et al. (2001). In their study, they revealed that higher rates of polymorphism occurred in transcripts with longer SSR sequences. Likewise, Song et al. (2010) reported that SSR which covered longer portion of sequence (repeat number less than 35) were deemed better for development of genetic markers because they associated with expressed portion of the genome, thus facilitate better understanding of associated protein(s). From our study, majority of the EST-SSR sequences were categorised as 'ideal' repeat ($n \geq 20$ nucleotides), which correlated well to the SSRs mined from tea [Camellia sinensis L.] (Sharma et al., 2009).

Sharma et al. (2009) stressed that the length of repeats and the tools used in the EST-SSRs mining play a significant role in EST-SSR occurrences. The di-nucleotide motif (AT/TA) was present with the most abundance (33.9%) in our VMPEST-SSR. Such observation of A- and T-rich signatures being the most common repeat motifs in the VMPEST-SSRs is also reflected in the early findings of Chagne et al. (2004), Lagercrantz et al. (1993), and Morgante & Olivieri (1993). Interestingly, Blair et al. (2009) found that this motif occurred mainly in the 3'-end of the common bean cDNA clones.

Nevertheless, whatever mined results we obtained from our study, each SSR needs to be validated with further analyses such as selection of SSR primers and screening for utility in vandaceous orchids.

Besides EST-SSR, there are other alternative data mining techniques such as expressed sequence tag-single nucleotide polymorphism (EST-SNP) in maize (Batley et al., 2003), barley (Varshney et al., 2007), melon (Deleu et al., 2009), citrus (Jiang et al., 2010), and cocoa (Allegre et al., 2011), expressed sequence tag-rapid amplified polymorphic DNA (EST-RAPD) in oil palm (Balakrishnan & Vadivel, 2012), and expressed sequence tag-sequence tagged site (EST-STS) in wheat (Leonard et al., 2008; Naji et al., 2008). All the aforementioned techniques are useful for functional genetic diversity estimation of GenBank collections and valuable for use in marker-assisted programmes. However, each technique has its good and down sides that might affect its eventual development.

5. Conclusion

The VMPEST dataset is a potential asset in facilitating the molecular biology and cloning of more genes involved in the fragrance biosynthesis pathway(s). Several fragrance-related transcripts were identified from our VMPEST including VMPACA, VMPHMGR, VMPDXPS, VMPLox and VMPLis. The functional enzymatic assay that was performed on the selected transcript (VMPHMGR) proved to be functionally active in its catalysis reaction in a heterologous system. The detected SSRs loci and microsatellite motifs that had hits with fragrance-related genes in the GenBank are believed to be a valuable resource especially to researchers involved in studying diversity to access the functional diversity of fragrant vandaceous orchids and their linkages to other orchids.

Author details

Seow-Ling Teh and Janna Ong Abdullah
Department of Microbiology, Faculty of Biotechnology and Biomolecular Sciences, Malaysia

Parameswari Namasivayam
Department of Cell and Molecular Biology,
Faculty of Biotechnology and Biomolecular Sciences, Malaysia

Rusea Go
Biology Department, Faculty of Science, Universiti Putra Malaysia, Malaysia

Acknowledgement

Authors would like to thank the Ministry of Higher Education Malaysia and Universiti Putra Malaysia for financial support through the Fundamental Research Grant Scheme (02-12-10-1002FR) and Research University Grant Scheme (05-04-08-0551RU), respectively.

6. References

Aceto, S. & Gaudio, L. (2011). The MADS and the beauty: genes involved in the development of orchid flowers. *Current Genomics*, 12, 342-356.

Adam, M. D., Kelley, J. M., Gocayne, J. D., Dubnick, M.,Polymeropoulos, M. H., Xiao, H., Merril, C. R., Wu, A., Olde, B., Moreno, R. F., Kerlavage, A. R., McCombie, W. R. & Venter, J. C. (1991). Complementary DNA sequencing: expressed sequence tags and human genome project. *Science*, 252, 1651-1656.

Adelene, S. A. L., Janna, O. A., Mohd, P., Norazizah, S., Raha, A.R. & Puad, A. (2012).Functional expression of an orchid fragrance gene in *Lactococcus lactis*. *International Journal of Molecular Sciences*, 13, 1582-1597.

Agrawal, A., Janssen, A., Bruin, J., Posthumus, M. & Sabelis, M. (2002). An ecological cost of plant defence: attractiveness of bitter cucumber plants to natural enemies of herbivores. *Ecological Letters*, 5, 377-385.

Ajjikuttira, P. A., Woon, M. H., Ryu, K. H., Chang, C. A., Loh, C. S., Wong, S. M. & Ridge, K. (2002). Genetic variability in the coat protein genes of two orchid viruses: cymbidium mosaic virus and odontoglossum ringspot virus. *Archives of Virology*, 147, 1943-1954.

Alba, R., Fei, Z. J., Liu, Y., Moore, S., Debbie, P., Cohn, J., Ascenzo, M., Gordon, J., Rose, J., Martin, G., Tanksley, S., Bouzayen, M., Jahn, M. & Giovannoni, J. (2004). ESTs, cDNA microarrays and gene expression profiling: tools for dissecting plant physiology and development. *The Plant Journal*, 39, 697-714.

Allegre, M., Argout, X., Boccara, M., Fouet, O., Roguet, Y., Berard, A., Thevenin, J. M., Chauveau, A., Rivallan, R., Clement, D., Courtois, B., Gramacho, K., Boland-Auge, A., Tahi, M., Umaharan, P., Brunel, D. & Lanaud C. (2011). Discovery and mapping of a new expressed sequence tag-single nucleotide polymorphism and simple sequence repeat panel for large-scale genetic studies and breeding of *Theobroma cacao* L. *DNA Research*, doi: 10.1093/dnares/dsr039

Arditti, J. (1992). *Fundamentals of orchid biology*, John Wiley & Sons Inc., New York, USA.

Arimura, G., Ozawa, R., Kugimiya, S., Takabayashi, J. & Bohlmann, J. (2004). Herbivore-induced defense response in a model legume: two-spotted spider mites, *Tetranychusurticae*, induce emission of (*E*)-β-ocimene and transcript accumulation of (*E*)-β-ocimene synthase in *Lotus japonicas*. *Plant Physiology*, 135, 1976-1983.

Ayeh, K. O. (2008). Expressed sequence tags (ESTs) and single nucleotide polymorphisms (SNPs): emerging molecular marker tools for improving agronomic traits in plant biotechnology. *African Journal of Biotechnology*, 7, 331-341.

Balakrishnan, V. P. & Vadivel, A. (2012). In silico RAPD priming sites in expressed sequences and iSCAR markers for oil palm. *Comparative and Functional Genomics*, doi: 10.1155/2012/913709

Batley, J., Barker, G., O'Sullivan, H., Edwards, K. J. & Edwards, D. (2003). Mining for single nucleotide polymorphisms and insertions/deletions in maize expressed sequence tag data. *Plant Physiology*, 132, 84-91.

Baudino, S., Caissard, J-C, Bergougnoux, V., Jullien, F., Magnard, J-L, Scalliet, G., Cock, J. M. & Hugueney, P. (2007). Production and emission of volatile compounds by petal cells. *Plant Signal Behaviour*, 2, 525-526,

Baysal, T. & Demirdoven, A. (2007). Lipoxygenase in fruits and vegetables: A review. *Enzyme and Microbial Technology*, 40, 491-496.

Beekwilder, J., Alvarez-Huerta, M, Neef, E., Verstappen, F., Bouwmeester, H.& Aharoni, A. (2004). Functional characterization of enzymes forming volatile esters from strawberry and banana. *Plant Physiology*, 135, 1865-1878.

Bick, J. A. & Lange, M. (2003). Metabolic cross talk between cytosolic and plastidial pathways of isoprenoids biosynthesis: unidirectional transport of intermediates across the chloroplast envelope membrane. *Archives of Biochemistry and Biophysics*, 415, 146-154.

Blair, M. W., Torres, M. M., Giraldo, M. C. & Pedraza, F. (2009). Development and diversity of Andean-derived, gene-based microsatellites for common bean (*Phaseolus vulgaris* L.). *BMC Plant Biology*, 9, 100-113.

Boatright, J., Negre, F., Chen, X., Kish, C., Wood, B., Peel, G., Orlova, I., Gang, D., Rhodes, D. & Dudareva, N. (2004). Understanding *in vivo* benzenoid metabolism in petunia petal tissue. *Plant Physiology*, 135, 1993-2011.

Bory, S., Silva, D., Risterucci, A., Grisoni, M., Besse, P. & Duval, M. (2008). Development of microsatellite markers in cultivated vanilla: Polymorphism and transferability to other vanilla species. *Scientia Horticulturae*, 115, 420-425.

Bradbury, L. (2007). *Identification of the gene responsible for fragrance in rice and characterization of the enzyme transcribed from this gene and its homologs*. Doctor of Philosophy dissertation, Southern Cross University, Australia.

Brenner, E. D., Stevenson, D. W., McCombie, R. W., Katari, M. S., Rudd, S. A., Mayer, K. F., Palenchar, P. M., Runko, S. J., Twigg, R. W., Dai, G., Martienssen, R. A., Benfey, P. N. & Coruzzi, G. M. (2003). Expressed sequence tag analysis in Cycas, the most primitive living seed plant. *Genome Biology*, 4, 78-88.

Chagne, D., Chaumeil, P., Ramboer, A., Collada, C., Guevara, A., Cervera, M. T., Vendramin, G. G., Garcia, V., Frigerio, J-M, Echt, C., Richardson, T. & Plomion, C. (2004). Cross-species transferability and mapping of genomic and cDNA SSRs in pines. *Theoretical and Applied Genetics*, 109, 1204-1214.

Chai, D. & Yu, H. (2007). Recent advances in transgenic orchid production. *Orchid Science and Biotechnology*, 1, 34-39.

Chakravarthi, B. K. & Naravaneni, R. (2006). SSR marker based DNA fingerprinting and diversity study in rice (*Oryza sativa* L.). *African Journal of Biotechnology*, 5, 684-688.

Chan, W. S., Janna, O. A., Parameswari, N. & Maziah, M. (2009). Molecular characterization of a new 1-deoxy-D-xylulose 5-phosphate reductoisomerase (DXR) transcript from *Vanda* Mimi Palmer. *Scientia Horticulturae*, 121, 378-382.

Chan, W. S., Janna, O. A. & Parameswari, N. (2011). Isolation, cloning and characterization of fragrance-related transcripts from *Vanda* Mimi Palmer. *Scientia Horticulturae*, 127, 388-397.

Chandasekar, A., Riju, A., Sithara, K., Anoop, S. & Eapen, S. J. (2009). Identification of single nucleotide polymorphism in ginger using expressed sequence tags. *Bioinformation*, 4, 119-122.

Chapman, M. A., Hvala, J., Strever, J., Matvienko, M., Kozik, A., Michelmore, R. W., Tang, S., Knapp, S. J. & Burke, J. M. (2009). Development, polymorphism and cross-taxon utility of EST-SSR markers from safflower (*Carthamus tinctorius* L.). *Theoretical and Applied Genetics*, 120, 85-91.

Chen, M. S., Wang, G. J., Wang, R. L., Wang, J., Song, S. Q. & Xu, Z. F. (2011). Analysis of expressed sequence tags from biodiesel plant *Jatropha curcas* embryos at different developmental stages. *Plant Science*, doi:10.1016/j.plantsci.2011.08.003

Cherri, M., Jullien, F., Heizmann, P. & Baudino, S. (2007). Fragrance heritability in hybrid tea roses. *Scientia Horticulture*, 113, 177-181.

Deleu, W., Esteras, C., Roig, C., Gonzalez-To, M., Fernandez-Silva, I., Gonzalez-Ibeas, D., Blanca, J., Aranda, M. A., Arus, P., Nuez, F., Monforte, A. J., Pico, M. B. & Garcia-Mas, J. (2009). A set of EST-SNPs for map saturation and cultivar identification in melon. *BMC Plant Biology*, 9, 90, doi:10.1186/1471-2229-9-90

Dudareva, N., Cseke, L., Blanc, V. & Pichersky, E. (1996). Evolution of floral scent in *Clarkia*: novel patterns of S-linalool synthase gene expression in the *C. breweri* flower. *Plant Cell*, 8, 1137-1148.

Dudareva, N., D'Auria, J., Nam, K. H., Raguso, R. & Pichersky, E. (1998). Acetyl-CoA:benzylalcohol acetyltransferase - an enzyme involved in floral scent production in *Clarkia breweri*. *The Plant Journal*, 14, 297-304.

Dudareva, N., Pichersky, E. & Gershenzon, J. (2004). Biochemistry of plant volatiles. *Plant Physiology*, 135, 1839-1902.

Eun, A. J. & Wong, S. (2000). Molecular beacons: a new approach to plant virus detection. *Phytopathology*, 90, 269-275.

Eun, A. J., Huang, L., Chew, F., Li, S. F. & Wong, S. (2002). Detection of two orchid viruses using Quartz crytal microbalance-based DNA biosensors. *Phytopathology*, 92, 654-658.

Fernandes, J., Brendel, V., Gai, X., Lal, S., Chandler, V. L., Elumalai, R. P., Galbraith, D. W., Pierson, E. A. & Walbot, V. (2002). Comparison of RNA expression profiles based on maize expressed sequence tag frequency analysis and micro-array hybridization. *Plant Physiology*, 128, 896-910.

Frowine, S. A. (2005). *Fragrant orchids*, Timber Press Inc., Oregon, USA.

Go, R., Yong, W. S. Y., Unggang, J. & Salleh, R. (2010). *Orchids of Perlis, Jewels in the Forests,* Revised Edition. Perlis Forestry Department and Universiti Putra Malaysia Press, Kuala Lumpur, Malaysia, p152.

Go., R., Khor, H. E., Tan, M. C., Janna, O. A., Farah Alia, N., Ng. Y. J., Muskhazli, M., Mohd Nazre, S. & Rosimah, N. (2012). Current knowledge on orchid diversity in Peninsular Malaysia including new records and discovery. *(Manuscript submitted and under review)*

Gonzalez-Mas, M. C., Garcia-Riano, L. M., Alfaro, C., Rambla, J. L., Padilla, A. I. & Gutierrez, A. (2008).Headspace-based techniques to identify the principal volatile compounds in red grape cultivars. *International Journal of Food Science & Technology,* 44, 510-518.

Guterman, I., Shalit, M., Menda, N., Piestun, D., Dafny, Y., Shalev, G., Bar, E., Davydov,O., Ovadis, M., Emanuel, M., Wang, J., Adam, Z., Pichersky,E., Lewinsohn, E., Zamir, D., Vainstein, A. & Weiss, D. (2002). Rose scent: genomics approach to discovering novel floral fragrance-related genes. *The Plant Cell,* 14, 2325-2338.

Hofte, H., Desprez, T., Amselem, J., Chiapello, H., Rouze, P., Caboche, M., Moisan, A., Jourjon, M. F., Charpenteau, J. L., Berthomieu, P., Guerrier, D., Giraudat, J., Quigley, F., Thomas, F., Yu, D. Y., Raynal, M., Cooke, R., Grellet, F., Marcillac, P., Gigot, C., Fleck, J., Phillips, G., Axelos, M., Bardet, C., Tremousaygue, D. & Lescure, B. (1994). An inventory of 1152 expressed sequence tags obtained by partial sequencing of cDNAs from *Arabidopsis thaliana. Plant Journal,* 4, 1051-1061.

Hsiao, Y., Tsai, W., Kuoh, C., Huang, T., Wang, H., Wu, T., Leu, Y., Chen, W. & Chen, H. (2006). Comparison of transcripts in *Phalaenopsis bellina* and *Phalaenopsis equestris* (Orchidaceae) flowers to deduce monoterpene biosynthesis pathway. *BMC Plant Biology,* 6, 14-27.

Hsiao, Y. Y., Pan, Z. J., Hsu, C. C., Yang, Y. P., Hsu, Y. C., Chuang, Y. C., Shih, H. H., Chen, W. H., Tsai, W. C. & Chen, H. H. (2011). Research on Orchid Biology and Biotechnology. *Plant and Cell Physiology,* 52(9), 1467-1486.

Hsu, C. C., Chung, Y. L., Chen, T. C., Lee, Y. L., Kuo, Y. T., Tsai, W. C., Hsiao, Y. Y., Chen, Y. W., Wu, W. L. & Chen, H. H. (2011). An overview of the *Phalaenopsis* orchid genome through BAC end sequence analysis. *BMC Plant Biology,* 11, 3-13.

Hsu, H. T., Vongsasitorn, D. & Lawson, R. H. (1992). An improved method for serological detection of *cymbidium* mosaic potexvirus infection in orchids. *Phytopathology,* 82, 491-495.

Hu, W. W. & Wong, S. M. (1998). The use o DIG-labelled cRNA probes for the detection of cymbidium mosaic potexvirus (CymMV) and odontoglossum ringspot tobamovirus (ORSV) in orchids. *Journal of Virological Methods,* 70, 193-199.

Huang, Y., Li, F. & Chen, K. (2010). Analysis of diversity and relationships among Chinese orchid cultivars using EST-SSR markers. *Biochemical Systematics and Ecology,* 38, 93-102.

Jacob, H. J., Lindpaintner, K., Lincoln, S. E., Kusumi, K., Bunker, R. K., Mao, Y. P., Ganten, D., Dzau, V. J. & Lander, E. S. (1991). Genetic mapping of a gene causing hypertensive rat. *Cell,* 67, 213-224.

Janna, O. A., Tan, L., Aziz, A., Maziah, M., Puad, A. & Azlan, J. (2005). Dull to behold, good to smell... *Vanda* Mimi Palmer. *BioTech Communications,* Faculty of Biotechnology & Biomolecular Science Research Bulletin, Universiti Putra Malaysia, Malaysia, volume 1, pp21-25, ISSN 1823-3279.

Jiang, D., YE, Q. L., Wang, F. S. & Cao, L. (2010). The mining of citrus EST-SNP and its application in cultivar discrimination. *Agricultural Sciences in China*, 9, 179-190.

Kalia, R. K., Rai, M. K., Kalia, S., Singh, R. & Dhawan, A. K. (2011). Microsatellite markers: an overview of the recent progress in plants. *Euphytica*, 177, 309-334.

Khentry, Y., Paradornuwat, A., Tantiwiwat, S., Phransiri, S. & Thaveechai, N. (2006). Incidence of cymbidium mosaic virus and odontoglossum ringpot virus in *Dendrobium* spp. in Thailand. *Crop Protection*, 25, 926-932.

Kishor, R., ShaValli Khan, P. S. & Sharma, G. J. (2006).Hybridization and *in vitro* culture of an orchid hybrid *Ascocenda 'Kangla'*. *Scientia Horticulturae*, 108, 66-73.

Kisiel, A. & Podkowinski, J. (2005). Expressed Sequence Tags and their applications for plants research. *Acta Physiologiae Plantarum*, 27, 157-161.

Kishor, R., Devi, H., Jeyaram, K. & Singh, M. (2008). Molecular characterization of reciprocal crosses of *Aerides vandarum* and *Vanda stangeana* (Orchidaceae) at the protocorm stage. *Plant Biotechnology Reports*, 2, 145-152.

Lagercrantz, U., Ellegren, H. & Anderson, L. (1993). The abundance of various polymorphic microsatellite motifs differs between plants and vertebrates. *Nucleic Acids Research*, 21, 1111-1115.

Lavid, N., Wang, J., Shalit, M., Guterman, I., Bar, E., Beuerle, T., Menda, N., Shafir, S., Zamir, D., Adam, Z., Vainstein, A., Weiss, D., Pichersky, E. & Lewinsohn, E. (2002). O-methyltransferases involved in the biosynthesis of volatile phenolic derivatives in rose petals. *Plant Physiology*, 129, 1899-1907.

Leonard, J., Watson, C., Carter, A., Hansen, J., Zemetra, R., Santra, D., Campbell, K. & Riera-Lizarazu, O. (2008). Identification of a candidate gene for the wheat endopeptidase*Ep-D1* locus and two other STS markers linked to the eyespot resistance gene *Psh1*. *Theoretical & Applied Genetics*, 116, 261-270.

Li, X., Shangguan, L., Song, C., Wang, C., Gao, Z., Yu, H. & Fang, J. (2010). Analysis of expressed sequence tags from *Prunus mume* flower and fruit and development of simple sequence repeat markers. *BMC Genetics*, 11, 66-76.

Lindqvist, C., Scheen, A., Yoo, M., Grey, P., Oppenheimer, D. G., Leebens-Mack, J. H., Soltis, D. E., Soltis, P. S. & Albert, V. A. (2006). An expressed sequence tag (EST) library from developing fruits of an Hawaiian endemic mint (*Stenogyne rugosa*, Lamiaceae): characterization and microsatellite markers. *BMC Plant Biology*, 6, 16-30.

Low, E. T., Alias, H., Boon, S. H., Shariff, E., Tan, C. Y., Ooi, L., Cheah, S. C., Raha, A. R., Wan, K. L. & Singh, R. (2008). Oil palm (*Elaeis guineensis* Jacq.) tissue culture ESTs: Identifying genes associated with callogenesis and embryogenesis. *BMC Plant Biology*, 8, 62-81.

Majetic, C., Raguso, R. & Ashman, T. (2009). The sweet smell of success: floral scent affects pollinators attraction and seed fitness in *Hesperis matronalis*. *Functional Ecology*, 23, 480-487.

Micheneau, C., Fournel, J., Gaucin-Bialecki, A. & Pailler, T. (2008).Auto-pollination in a long-spurred endemic orchid (*Jumellea stenophylla*) on Reunion Island (Mascarene Archipelago, Indian Ocean). *Plant Systematics and Evolution*, 272, 11-22.

Miyao, A., Zhong, H., Monna, L., Yano, M., Yamamoto, K., Havukkala, I. & Minobe, Y. (1996). Characterization and genetic mapping of simple sequence repeats in rice genome. *DNA Research*, 3, 233-238.

Mohan, M., Nair, S., Bhagwat, A., Krishna, T. G., Yano, M., Bhatia, C. R. & Sasaki, T. (1997). Genome mapping, molecular markers and marker-assisted selection in crop plants. *Molecular Breeding*, 3, 87-103.

Mohd-Hairul, A. R., Parameswari, N., Gwendoline Ee, C. L. & Janna O. A. (2010). Terpenoid, benzenoid and phenylpropanoid compounds in the floral scent of *Vanda* Mimi Palmer. *Journal of Plant Biology*, 53, 358-366.

Morgante, M. & Olivieri, A. M. (1993). PCR-amplified microsatellites as markers in plant genetics. *Plant Journal*, 3, 175-182.

Nagaraj, S., Gasser, R, & Ranganathan, S. (2006). A hitchhiker's guide to expressed sequence tag (EST) analysis. *Briefing in Bioinformatics*, 8, 6-21.

Naji, A. M., Moghaddam, M., Ghaffari, M. R., Irandoost, H. P., Farsad, L. K., Pirseyedi, S. M., Mohammadim S. A., Ghareyazie, B. & Mardi, M. (2008). Validation of EST-derived STS markers localized on Qfhs.ndsu-3BS for *Fusarium* head blight resistance in wheat using a 'Wangshuibai' derived population. *Journal of Genetics & Genomics*, 35, 625-628.

NewComb, R. D., Crowhurst, R. N., Gleave, A. P., Rikkerink, E., Allan, A. C., Beuning, L. L., Bowen, J. H., Gera, E., Jamieson, K. R., Janssen, B. J., Laing, W. A., McArtney, S., Nain, B., Ross, G. S., Snowden, K. C., Souleyre, E., Walton, E. F. & Yauk, Y. K. (2006). Analyses of expressed sequence tags from apple. *Plant Physiology*, 141, 147-166.

Nojima, S., Kiemle, D. J., Webster, F. X., Apperson, C. S. & Schal, C. (2011). Nanogram-scale preparation and NMR analysis for mass-limited small volatile compounds. *PLoS ONE*, 6: e18178. Doi:10.1371/journal.pone.0018178

Ooi, J. M. (2005). *Screening of a random peptide library with CymMV for potential development of diagnostic kits.* Master dissertation, Malaysia University of Science and Technology, Selangor Darul Ehsan, Malaysia.

Park, Y. S., Jeong, M. H., Lee, S. H., Moon, J. S., Cha, J. S., Kim, H. Y. & Cho, T. J. (2005). Activation of defense responses in chinese cabbage by a nonhost pathogen, *Pseudomonas syringae* pv. tomato. *Journal of Biochemistry and Molecular Biology*, 38, 748-754.

Phuekvilai, P., Pongtongkam, P. & Peyachoknagul, S. (2009). Development of microsatellite markers for *Vanda* orchid. *Natural Science*, 43, 497-506.

Pichersky, E. & Dudareva, N. (2007). Scent engineering: toward the goal of controlling how flowers smell. *TRENDS in Biotechnology*, 25, 105-110.

Pichersky, E., Noel, J. & Durareva N. (2006). Biosynthesis of plant volatiles: nature's diversity and ingenuity. *Science*, 311, 808-811.

Pinheiro, F., Santos, M. O., Barros, F., Meyer, D., Salatino, A., Souza, A. P. & Cozzolino, S. (2008). Isolation and characterization of microsatellite loci in the Brazilian orchid *Epidendrum fulgens*. *Conservation Genetics*, 9, 1661-1663.

Rada, F. & Jaimez, R. (1992). Comparative ecophysiology and anatomy of terrestrial and epiphytic *Anthurium bredemeyeri* Schott in a tropical Andean cloud forest. *Journal of Experimental Botany*, 43, 723-727.

Raguso, R. (2008). Wake up and smell the roses: The ecology and evolution of floral scent. *Annual Review of Ecology, Evolution and Systematics*, 39, 549-569.

Rani, P., Pant, R. & Jain, R. (2010). Serological detection of cymbidium mosaic and odontoglossumringspot viruses in orchids with polyclonal antibodies produced against their recombinant coat proteins. *Journal of Phytopathology*, 158, 542-545.

Rudd, S. (2003). Expressed sequence tags:alternative or complement to whole genome sequences? *TRENDS IN Plant Science*, 8, 321-328.

Schiestl, F. P. (2010). The evolution of floral scent and insect chemical communication. *Ecology Letters*, 13, 643-656.

Sharma, P., Grover, A. & Kahl, G. (2007). Mining microsatellites in eukaryotic genomes.*TRENDS in Biotechnology*, 25, 490-498.

Sharma, R., Bhardwaj, P., Negi, R., Mohapatra, T. & Ahuja, P. (2009). Identification, characterization and utilization of unigenes derived microsatellite markers in tea (*Camellia sinensis* L.). *BMC Plant Biology*, 9, 53-76.

Sherpa, A., Hallan, V., Pathak, P. & Zaidi, A. (2007). Complete nucleotide sequence analysis of cymbidium mosaic virus Indian isolate: further evidence for natural recombination among potexviruses. *Journal of Bioscience*. 32, 663-669.

Shuttleworth, A. & Johnson, S. (2009). A key role for floral scent in a wasp-pollination system in *Eucomis* (Hyacinthaceae). *Annals of Botany*, 103, 715-725.

Sonah, H., Deshmukh, R. K., Sharma, A., Singh, V. P., Gupta, D. K., Gacche, R. N., Rana, J. C., Singh, N. K. & Sharma, T. R. (2011). Genome-wide distribution and organization of microsatellite in plants: an insight into marker development in *Brachypodium*. *PLoS ONE*, 6, 1-9.

Song, Q., Jia, G., Zhu, Y., Grant, D., Nelson, R., Hwang, E-Y, Hyten, D. & Cregan, P. (2010). Abundance of SSR motifs and development of candidate polymorphic SSR markers (BARCSOYSSR_1.0) in soybean. *Crop Science*, 50, 1950-1960.

Spitcer, B., Ben Zvi, M., Ovadis, M., Marhevla, E., Barkai, O., Edelbaum, O., Marton, I., Masci, T., Alon, M., Morin, S., Rogachev, I., Aharoni, A. & Vainstein, A. (2007). Reverse genetics of floral scent: application of tobacco rattle virus-based gene silencing in petunia. *Plant Physiology*, 145, 1241-1250.

Stafne, E. T., Clark, J. R., Weber, C. A., Graham, J. & Lewers, K. S. (2005). Simple sequence repeat (SSR) markers for genetic mapping of raspberry and blackberry. *Journal of American Horticultural Science*, 130, 1-7.

Teh, S. L. (2011). *Development of a floral expressed sequence tags resource from and characterization of fragrance-related gene transcripts in Vanda Mimi Palmer*. Master dissertation, Universiti Putra Malaysia, Selangor Darul Ehsan, Malaysia.

Teh, S. L., Chan, W. S., Janna, O. A. & Parameswari, N. (2011). Development of expressed sequence tag resources for *Vanda* Mimi Palmer and data mining for EST-SSR. *Molecular Biology Reports*, 38, 3903-3909.

Temnykh, S., DeClerck, G., Lukashova, A., Lipovich, L., Cartinhour,S. & McCouch, S. (2001). Computational and experimental analysis of microsatellites in rice (*Oryza sativa* L.): frequency, length variation, transposon associations and genetic marker potential. *Genome Research*, 1441-1452.

Teo, C. K. H. (1981). *Tropical orchid hybrids*, FEP International Sdn. Bhd., Singapore.

Teoh, E. S. (1980). *Asian orchids*, Times Books International, Singapore.

Terp, N., Gobel, C., Brandt, A. & Feussner, I. (2006). Lipoxygenases during *Brassica napus* seed germination. *Phytochemistry*, 67, 2030-2040.

Tsai, W., Hsiao, Y., Lee, S., Tung, C., Wang, D., Wang, H., Chen, W. & Chen, H. (2006). Expression analysis of the ESTs derived from the flower buds of *Phalaenopsis equestris*. *Plant Science*, 170, 426-432.

van Moerkercke, A., Galvan-Ampudia, C. S., Verdonk, J. C., Haring, M. A. & Schuurink, R. C. (2012). Regulators of floral fragrance production and their target genes in petunia are not exclusively active in the epidermal cells of petals. *Journal of Experimental Botany*, doi:10.1093/jxb/ers034

vanTunen, A. J., Eikelboom, W. & Angenent, G. C. (1993). Floral organogenesis in *Tulipa*. *Flowering Newsletter*, 16, 33-37.

Vainstein, A., Lewinsohn, E., Pichersky, E. & Weiss, D. (2001). Floral fragrance.New inroads into an old commodity. *Plant Physiology*, 127, 1383-1389.

Varshney, R. K., Chabane, K., Hendre, P. S., Aggarwal, R. K. & Graner, A. (2007). Comparative assessment of EST-SSR, EST-SNP and AFLP markers for evaluation of genetic diversity and conservation of genetic resources using wild, cultivated and elite barleys. *Plant Science*, 173, 638-649.

Vejaratpimol, R., Channuntapipat, C., Pewnim, T., Ito, K., Iizuka, M. & Minamiura, N. (1999). Detection and serological relationship of cymbidium mosaic potexvirus isolates. *Journal of Bioscience and Bioengineering*, 87, 161-168.

Verdonk, J. C., Haring, M. A., van Tunen, A. J. & Schuurink, R. C. (2005). *ODORANT1* regulates fragrance biosynthesis in petunia flowers. *The Plant Cell*, 17, 1612-1624.

Wang, M. L., Gillaspie, A. G., Newman, M. L., Dean, R. E., Pittman, R. N., Morris, J. B. & Pederson, G. A. (2004). Transfer of simple sequence repeat (SSR) markers across the legume family for germplasm characterization and evaluation. *Plant Genetic Resource*, 2, 107-119.

Yu, K., Park, S. J., Poysa, V. & Gepts, P. (2000). Integration of simple sequence repeat (SSR) markers into a molecular linkage map of common bean (*Phaseolus vulgaris* L.). *The American Genetic Association*, 91, 429-434.

Yue, G. H., Lam-Chan, L. T. & Hong, Y. (2006).Development of simple sequence repeat (SSR) markers and their use in identification of *Dendrobium* varieties. *Molecular Ecology Resources*, 6, 832-834.

Zhang, D., Choi, D., Wanamaker, S., Fenton, R., Chin, A., Malatrasi, M., Turuspekov, Y., Walia, H., Akhunov, E., Kianian, P., Otto, C., Deal, K., Echenique, V., Stamova, B., Ross, K., Butler, G., Strader, L., Verhey, S., Johnson, R., Altenbach, S., Kothari, K., Tanaka, C., Shah, M., Laudencia-Chingcuanco, D., Han, P., Miller, R., Crossman, C., Chao, S., Lazo, G., Klueva, N., Gustafson, J., Kianian, S., Dubcovsky, J., Walker-Simmons, P., Gill, K., Dvorak, J., Anderson, O., Sorrells, M., McGuire, P., Qualset, C., Nguyen, H. & Close, T. (2004). Construction and evaluation of cDNA libraries for large-scale expressed sequence tag sequencing in wheat (*Triticum aestivum* L.). *Genetics*, 168, 595-608.

Chapter 11

Visual Exploration of Functional MRI Data

Jerzy Korczak

Additional information is available at the end of the chapter

1. Introduction

New brain imaging techniques, such as functional Magnetic Resonance Imagery (fMRI), allow for recording and analysis of brain activity over time. A fMRI image is a great source of information about brain behaviour; it is a considerable amount of data (approximately 300000 voxels, "three-dimensional pixels", for which between 100 and 1000 observations are collected). More information about fMRI concepts, studies, data and applications can be found on a publicly accessible repository [1].

From the view point of the data mining, the brain is the most complex object to analyze. In general, the identification of the voxels of the brain that represent real activity is very difficult because of a weak signal-to-noise ratio and of the presence of artefacts. The first tests of the current classification algorithms in this field showed that their performances and their qualities of recognition are weak [2]. Because of the difficulty caused by a very large amount of registered data, the main stream of the research projects is focused on testing a model of brain behaviour by the means of univaried statistics. This is a principle of image processing software such as Statistical Parametric Mapping (SPM) [3], AFNI [4] or BrainVoyager [5], which consists of highlighting the more active voxels under comparable conditions. The statistical methods are powerful, but cannot provide conclusions apart from those prefixed by the model. Using these methods, results must inevitably be anticipated, which is not always possible.

In this article, a new interactive data-driven approach to fMRI mining will be presented. The concept of data mining appears useful as complement or as replacement of the classical methods when it is difficult to predict what will occur during acquisition. In our system, a number of clustering methods have been implemented within an interactive tool to emphasize the active zones without having to use a model. The originality of the approach is not only due to real-time clustering, but also to the insertion of domain knowledge and interactivity, directly integrating the expert-physician into the process of the discovery of functional zones in the brain and their organization. In general, the fMRI data can be analyzed from various perspectives. The three dimensional data recorded temporally can correspond to one or several patients or to the history of the same patient, and, finally, it can be completed by medical knowledge. This article focuses on the first two aspects, where the spatial and temporal dimensions of brain activity are crucial. Important consideration is given to the high volume of data, the processing time, and the noise of image acquisition.

The article is structured in the following way. In section 2, the data mining system architecture oriented toward brain exploration is described. Section 3 describes the three implemented clustering algorithms: Kohonen's Self Organizing Map [6], Fritzke's Growing Neural Gaz [7], and Goua's Clustering using Representatives (CURE) [8]. Section 4 presents the principles of user interface and tools for brain visualization. Section 5 illustrates cases of studies carried out on synthetic and real data. The final section concludes the first experiments and indicates further research perspectives.

2. Data-guided approach

The proposed interactive exploration of fMRI images can be classified as a data-guided approach assisted directly by an expert knowledge and by gathered experience. The process of data mining is composed of five phases: the acquisition and selection of the data, pre-processing, clustering, the extraction of rules and concepts, and validation [9].

The source fMRI data comes from the scanner in a form of sequences of 3D images. The cerebral activity is registered as variations of voxels intensity over time. Typically, the patient is never completely motionless and, moreover, other factors interfere with the signals of interest. Therefore the specific pre-processing must then be adapted to each identified artefact. In the clustering phase, classes are created that are composed of voxels with similar behaviour in time. In the knowledge extraction phase, the classification rules are generated describing each cluster of voxels. Once validated, the rules are saved in the knowledge base, and if required, can be reused in following diagnosis. Figure 1 presents a simplified functional schema of the system, from the fMRI acquisition to interpretation and the validation by the expert-physician, who can interact with the system on all phases.

In many cases the interpretation of fMRI data has to be done very quickly. Frequently, the physician, after obtaining the preliminary results of image clustering, is forced to change the acquisition parameters and redefine geometrical or temporal parameters (resolution, zoom, etc). The clustering and cluster explanation (shown on the right part of fig.1) help the expert to discover and understand the generated classes, and if necessary to modify the experiment directly. These modifications are based on the assumptions about cerebral activities, knowledge of brain anatomy, or about other sources of medical information.

The work presented in this article is primarily focused on the clustering phase, emphasizing interactive and dynamic aspects of algorithms of unsupervised learning. In general, it consists of regrouping voxels that have similar characteristics and behaviours into a limited number of relatively homogeneous clusters. Many clustering algorithms have already been applied to fMRI data. The most common are statistical methods such as K-means [9, 10, 11, 12, 13, 14, 15], Principal Component Analysis [15, 16,], and Independent Component Analysis [18, 19, 20, 21, 22]. Interesting results have been also obtained using fuzzy classification [17], hierarchical classifications [17; 23, 24], Kohonen's Self-Organizing Maps [25, 26]. The advantage of these methods consists of a higher level of interpretation, but these algorithms are very costly in terms of computing time and memory space.

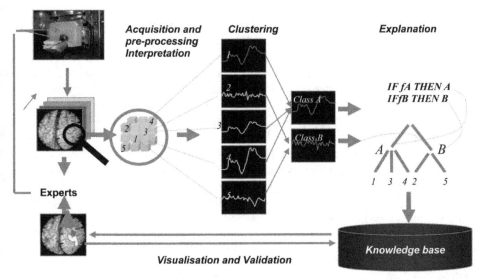

Figure 1. Schema of interactive exploration of fMRI data

In our research, we have been focused on real-time clustering algorithms able to discover as quickly as possible classes of voxels in fMRI data, allowing experts to insert their preferences, medical knowledge and spatio-temporal constraints. The interested reader may find more technical details in our previous reports and publications [27, 28, 29, 30].

3. Clustering algorithms

Clustering algorithms usually depend on a distance. A distance between voxels has to be defined. A 3D distance between voxels is irrelevant to identify voxels having the same activity. Taking the 3D distance into account would make close voxels - close from a 3D perspective - look more similar than far-away voxels having the same activity. The distance between voxels should only be defined according to their activities. It should be noted that a clustering based on the activity of the voxels without any influence of their localisation is clearly different from segmentation techniques also used to identify areas in fMRI images that relies on a comparison of neighbouring voxels.

The fMRI data are very highly noisy. The sources are many: heterogeneity of the magnetic field, thermal noises, thermal noises of examined tissues, head movements, eyes movements, breathing, internal movement related to the blood flow pulsation [27]. This list of noise disturbances is only related to the image acquisition, but not associated with the sensory or cognitive noise. Therefore a number of pre-processing operations are required to obtain the data to be analyzed. The most commonly used pre-processing refers to co-registration (correction of movements), rephasing of the brain cuts, normalisation, smoothing, spatial and temporal filtering, segmentation. More about the pre-processing methods can be found in [1, 2, 3, 4, 10].

Before clustering, the representation of each voxel has to be carefully chosen. The attributes to describe the sequence of voxel values have to be selected in such a way that the relationships and distances between voxel activities will be well established. But in clustering, the cause of difficulties may be weak a priori knowledge. The same set of data can be differently clustered depending on selected attributes and distance measure. Note that the activity of a voxel is a continuous signal. Therefore a sampling method for a signal is extremely important. One approach consists in generating different attributes describing the signal, e.g. its average, minimum and maximum values, and then using those attribute-values in a traditional attribute-value clustering system. In such an approach, the built-in distance measure of the clustering system is calculated on the intermediate attributes, e.g. the Euclidian distance between the respective average, minimum and maximum values of each voxel. Its success depends on how well the built-in distance and the generated attributes fit together. Lots of attributes can be tested. For instance, in [3] applied wavelets to transform the signal, though they made use of hidden Markov models rather than a clustering technique.

We considered an alternative approach, where the distance is directly calculated on the fMRI data. The fMRI data are transformed into a time series of voxel intensity variations relative to its average as follows:

$$I^a_{ave} = 1/n \sum I^a_i$$

where I^a_{ave} is an average intensity of voxel a of a series of n images;

$$S_a = \{\delta_1, \delta_2, \ldots, \delta_n\}, \quad \delta_i = I^a_{ave} - I^a_i$$

where S_a is fMRI signal.

The distances between two fMRI signals S_a and S_b may be computed as Euclidian distance:

$$d_E = \sqrt{(\delta^a_i - \delta^b_i)^2}$$

or Manhattan distance:

$$d_M = \sum |(\delta^a_i - \delta^b_i)|.$$

In the system different clustering algorithms can be easily developed. Currently, the five algorithms are available, notably K-means, LBG, CURE, and two neural models: Kohonen's

Self Organizing Map, and Fritzke's Growing Neural Gaz. The algorithms K-means and LGB are well known and described in many publications. Algorithms like ICA and PCM separate the fMRI signals into a set of well defined components, but have to deal with constraints of their independency and orthogonality. Therefore in the paper, the description of algorithms is only given to the three less known algorithms that enable the expert interactively to improve his or her understanding of the human brain.

Self-Organizing Maps is a topology-preserving clustering algorithm that maps high-dimensional fMRI data into low-dimensional space [24, 25]. SOM creates the map that represents the fine cluster structures and cluster relations. The specification of SOM algorithm is given below:

Algorithm Self-Organizing Map

Parameters:

t: time units

t_{max}: duration of computing

$d_{rs} = |i-k| + |j-m|$: Manhattan distance between two classes $r=a_{ij}$ and $s=a_{km}$

σ_i, σ_f, ε_i and ε_f : initial and final coefficients of adaptation

$\sigma_i = \sigma_i .(\sigma_f/\sigma_i)^{t/tmax}$: neighbouring coefficient

$\varepsilon_i = \varepsilon_i .(\varepsilon_f/\varepsilon_i)^{t/tmax}$: adaptation coefficient

$h_{rs} = exp (-d^2_{rs} / 2\sigma(t)^2)$: neighbouring function between classes r and s

$l * h$: size of the grid ; number of classes

Procedure

1. Choose parameters values: size of the grid $l * h$, the duration t_{max}, the adaptation coefficients: σ_i, σ_f, ε_i and ε_f
2. Grid initialization taking values respecting neighbouring class proximity
3. Select at random an input signal ξ.
4. Search for $a=g(\xi)$ of the winning class of ξ; the closest vector of reference
5. Adapt each class according to the formula $w_a =w_a + \varepsilon(t) . h_{a\xi}. (\xi - w_a)$
6. Increment the time $t=t+1$
7. If $t<t_{max}$, then return to step 3, else stop.

However, its fixed topological structure would not help in our application, since there is no a priori topological relationship between the classes. The problem to solve concerned the validity of discovered clusters and choosing the number of selected clusters.

Thus we have preferred the Growing Neural Gas (GNG) algorithm [7]. Its main advantage is that the number of classes is not fixed in advance, as in most clustering algorithms. The class centres can increase as well as decrease during the learning process. Moreover this algorithm easily fits in an interactive knowledge discovery application. The specification of GNG algorithm is given below:

Algorithm Growing Neural Gas

<u>Parameters</u>

$age_{(a1,a2)}$: age of connection between two classes $a1$ and $a2$
age_{max} : maximal age of connection
ε_a : error of class a
$\varepsilon_b, \varepsilon_b$: coefficient of adaptation of winning class and its neighbours

<u>Procedure</u>

1. Initialize two classes $A = \{c_1, c_2\}$, $t=0$. Initialize the connection set.
2. Select at random an input signal ξ.
3. Determine the winner s_1 and the second-nearest cluster s_2, the closest to ξ.
4. If a connection between s_1 and s_2 does not exist already, create it. Set the age of the connection to 0

$$C = C \cup \{(s_1, s_2)\}.age_{(s_1,s_2)} = 0$$

5. Add the squared distance between the input signal and the winner to a local error variable:

$$\Delta \varepsilon_{s1} = II\ \xi - w_{si}II^2.$$

6. Adapt the reference vectors of the winner and its direct topological neighbours by fractions :

$$\Delta w_{si} = \varepsilon_b*(\xi - w_{si})\ ,\ \Delta w_i = \varepsilon_n*(\xi - w_n)$$

7. Increment the age of all edges emanating from s_i
8. Remove edges with an age larger than a_{max}. If this unit has no more emanating edges, remove the unit as well.
9. If the number of input signals generated so far is an integer multiple of a parameter l, add a new unit r to the network and interpolate its reference vector from q and f, decrease the error variables of q and f.
10. If a stopping criterion (e.g., net size or some performance measure) is not yet fulfilled, continue, return to step 2.

The third algorithm, called CURE (Clustering Using REpresentatives), is an agglomerative algorithm where disjoint clusters are successively merged until the number of clusters reduces to the desired number of clusters. CURE can identify clusters that are not spherical as well as clusters with wide variances in cluster size. These features are particularly interesting while clustering medical images. The specification of CURE algorithm is given below:

Algorithm CURE

Parameters

S: n voxels in *d*-dimensional space
k: number of clusters
u,v w, and *x:* clusters
u.rep: the set of representative points in *u* cluster
u.closest: the closest cluster to *u*
kd_tree: data structure that stores the representative points for every cluster
the heap: data structure that stores the entries for various clusters u arranged in the increasing order of the distances

Procedure cluster (S,k)

```
12.   T:= build_kd_tree(S)     /*all voxels are inserted into the k-d tree */
13.   Q := build_heap(S)       /*each input voxel is considered as a separate cluster */
14.   while size(Q) > k do{
15.        u := extract_min(Q) /*extract the top element in Q */
16.        v := u.closest
17.        delete(Q,u)
18.        w := merge(u,v)     /*merge the closest pair of clusters u and v and compute new
                                  representative point for the new merged cluster w which is
                                  inserted into T */
19.        delete_rep(T,u); delete_rep(T,v); insert_rep(T,w)
20.        w.closest := x       /* x is an arbitrary cluster in Q*/
21.        for each x ∈ Q do {
22.            if dist(w,x) < dist(w, w.closest)
23.                w.closest := x
24.            if x.closest is either u or v {
25.                if dist(x,x.closest)< dist(x,w)
26.                    x.closest := closest_cluster (T,x,dist(x,w))
27.                else
28.                    x.closest :=w
29.                relocate(Q,x)
30.            }
31.            else if dist(x,x.closest) > dist(x,w) {
32.                    x.closest := w
33.                    relocate(Q,x)
34.            }
35.        }
36.        Insert(q,w)
37.   }
```

The algorithm CURE, in contrast to the previous algorithms, does not favor clusters with spherical shapes and similar volumes. The computational complexity of CURE is quadratic, so for large fMRI data it was necessary to employ random sampling of voxels, sacrificing clustering quality. More detailed discussion of CURE performance can be found in [8]

While the current approach supposes that the human expert builds up the hypothesis and the software, e.g. SPM [3], is only used to validate that hypothesis, data mining techniques can complement that approach by guiding the expert in his generation of new hypotheses, in particular by automatically showing up activated areas, and highlighting dependencies between those areas.

We have extended the SLICER system for clustering and interactive exploration of fMRI images features. In its current version, our software environment allows the physician to interact graphically with the clustering process, e.g. by modifying parameters of the algorithm, by focusing on a specific region of the brain, etc.

4. Visual data mining

The fMRI mining system integrates two functional parts: interactive clustering algorithms and visualisation package 3DSlicer developed by Harvard Medical School and AI Lab of the Massachusetts Institute of Technology (http://www.slicer.org [33]). The visualization package allows observing in 2D and 3D of the evolution of clusters discovered by data mining algorithms. The interface for interactive clustering has been also designed to engage the expert in the process of discovery. Therefore all clustering algorithms implemented in our system can be run in an interactive mode. The expert can follow the classification evolution from the beginning at regular time intervals.

Four levels of interaction can be distinguished. The lowest level corresponds to measurements provided on the state of classification and makes it possible for the user to make a decision when to interrupt the process. This interruption can be thus called upon systematically with regular intervals of times to take absolute measures on the classification and to visualize the intermediate results. This makes it possible to store or modify the current state of clustering. Thus, the expert may access the clustering algorithm and modify it at any point during its execution. Not only the parameters of the algorithm, but also the data space can be modified and refined during the clustering process. The second level concerns the definition and resizing of the data volume. The third level of interaction concerns the algorithms with the parameters that can be dynamically changed. Beyond these three levels of interaction, the management of saving and restoring the states of clustering constitutes the last level of classification interactions. Figure 2 illustrates the concepts of visual mining of fMRI data.

Three types of information are provided: statistical, temporal, and spatial. On the left part, the statistics describes the evolution of clusters; the user can examine the evolution of the errors, intra-class and inter-class inertias, the number of voxels connected to the center of each class, and the number of voxels which change class per unit time. The system provides also information that describes the dispersion of the clusters, the convergence of algorithm and the stability of clusters. Temporal information associated with each cluster represents graphically the fMRI signals over time. The signals are visualized in the form of curves on a graph. A paradigm, as in a sequence of stimuli and the model of the response, if available, can also be shown and compared online. On the right part, spatial information is simultaneously visualized in two manners: as 3D image, and as three perpendicular cuts across the brain. It is important to notice that during the clustering, the generated clusters are displayed in 2D and 3D. To facilitate interpretation, the 3D image of clusters can be superimposed, depending on the case, with a structural MRI of the subject or a standardized volume acting as an anatomical atlas.

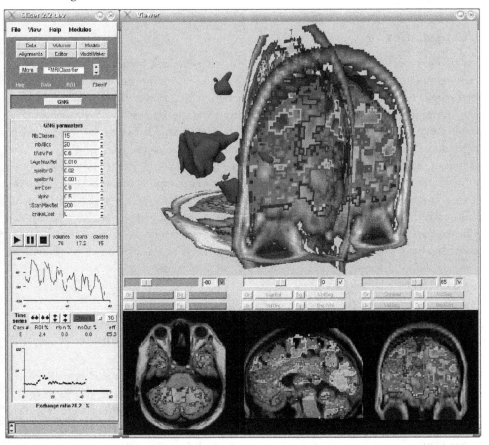

Figure 2. Interface of fMRI mining system

The user can easily optimize the clustering process by the online observation of statistical measures and their variations induced by modifications of parameters. Thus, the adjustment of the algorithm can be suitably carried out without continuously stopping and restarting the process.

To increase the speed of execution and to reduce the complexity of the results, the expert may find it beneficial to reduce the volume of the data. The space of exploration can be adjusted in several ways. The standard version of 3DSlicer assures not only the 3D visualization, but also allows the selection of volumes of interest or disinterest. The novel functionalities of the system permit the user also to restrict the space of research using anatomical structures or a subset of generated clusters. For instance, a threshold may eliminate the space that surrounds the brain. In the case of standardized images, it is possible to limit research to the grey matter. Thus, the expert can continue a classification by focusing his interest on certain regions after having eliminated voxels belonging to other non-relevant clusters.

5. Case studies

During the process of knowledge discovery, clusters generated by unsupervised classifiers must be validated by an expert, who retains only the relevant ones. Each selected cluster corresponds to a set of voxels, or zones of the brain, with a similar hemodynamic response over time. These responses can be explicitly characterized via the construction of classification rules. These rules combine observed temporal patterns with spatial information, such as the activity of voxels in neighbouring zones, or domain knowledge, such as the atlas of functional zones regions of the brain. It is important to note that the data normalisation (i.e. when the images are recalibrated to correspond to one brain type; voxels of several series of images of one person, or of several people), the voxels on the same positions correspond to the same zones of the brain. Temporal patterns can be synchronized with the paradigm, for example, to discover the interactions between areas regions of the brain used for visual memory. Temporal patterns can also be independent of any paradigm, for example, to highlight the succession of typical activations of region areas of the brain associated with hallucinations.

In the next part of the section, the performance of the clustering algorithms on the synthetic and real fMRI data will be described.

The synthetic data test

The synthetic data were composed of two parts, purely artificial simulated activations and real data. In the first experiment, the selected images corresponded to the auditive test conditions: "silence" and "talk". All the images of the "silence" condition were real data. Added to this series of 40 images were the synthetic activations formed by time series in crenel (square signal), simulating a paradigm of the block type. The localization of activations was a cubic volume of 5 voxels of each dimension. The level of average noise of these 125 voxels of the bottom was measured by taking double the variance of the intensities of the voxels over time. From this measurement, it was then possible to control the signal-to-noise ratio of the activations, by adding crenels of desired intensities to the considered voxels.

The performance evaluation was based on a confusion matrix indicating the true-positive ratios in particular. To create this matrix, it was necessary to determine the positive and negative classes. The figure 3 shows, in a simplified way, how the positive classes were defined and their coverage of a zone of activation.

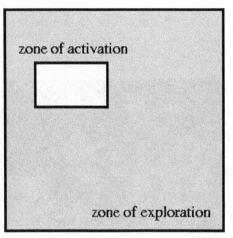 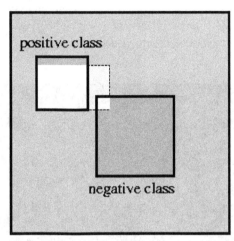

Figure 3. Simplified illustration of relation between a zone of activation and positive/negative classes

The table 1 illustrates the results of five clustering algorithms on synthetic data varying the parameter Signal-to-Noise (*S/N*). More detailed results may be found in research reports [Hommet, 2003].

S/N	GNG	SOM	LBG	K-means	CURE
1.2	55	0	0	15	52
1.4	100	0	15	35	76
1.6	100	70	55	44	72
1.8	100	100	65	50	72
2.0	100	100	69	70	72
3.0	100	100	100	82	88

Table 1. Detection frequency (%) in respect of Signal-to-Noise ratio

Amongst implemented algorithms, two of them generated relatively stable and coherent clusters. The first, the Growing Neuronal Gas algorithm [7], has been adapted to the interactive classification of fMRI images. Contrary to the majority of the other methods, the originality of the GNG lies in the fact that the number of classes is not fixed in advance. In addition, the network topology and the number of neurons can be dynamically increased or decreased during the classification, making the algorithm efficient to cluster a large volume of data. The connections between neurons have the property of aging, and disappear when they reach a preset maximum age. This property is the cause of the disappearance of neurons, which are eliminated when they are not connected any more. The creation of the new neurons is made at regular time intervals by inserting a new neuron near the neuron with the greatest error. The error of a neuron is evaluated using the sum of the distances from this neuron to the voxels that declared this neuron as a winner. Thus the network is reinforced near the neurons which traverse the longest distances or which bring together the most voxels. Our contributions pertain to two aspects of classification, in particular reducing the volume of data and setting the parameters of the algorithm with the assistance of statistical tools and visual data mining.

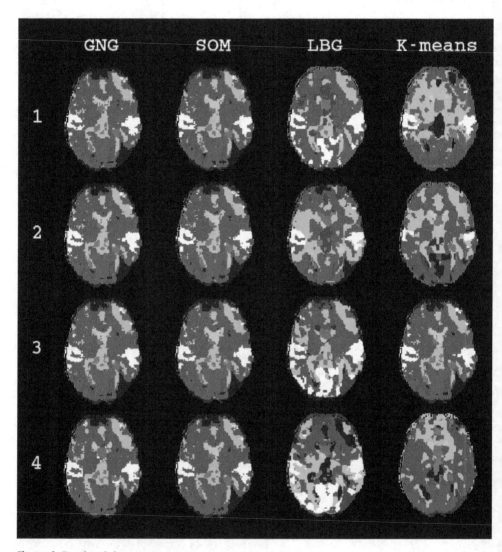

Figure 4. Results of clustering

The second algorithm, CURE [8], that has been also adapted to an interactive mode, generates clusters that have non-spherical forms with large variance, and, moreover, it allows a reduction in the processing time by aggregation and sampling fMRI data.

That the K-means had the worst level of detection is not surprising. K-means and LBG to some extent are strongly dependent on their initializations. But these two algorithms were not stripped of usefulness insofar as they did not require any parameter apart from the number of classes. This simplicity often enables them to obtain better results than GNG and SOM when the parameter setting of the latter is not optimal.

Block type data of a fMRI series of auditive tests

The real data used come from the site of the London research institute, "The Wellcome Department of Imaging neuroscience [http://www.fil.ion.ucl.ac.uk/spm/]; they form part of the test set of the program SPM99. The series was composed of 96 MRI acquisitions of the brain recorded with a repetition time of 7 s. The paradigm of the block type alternates the two following situations: a condition without stimulus and a condition of auditive stimuli consisting of repetitions of two-syllable words. With the pre-processed series, the classifications were performed by the four algorithms under the same conditions. With the rough series, one classification has been obtained using the paradigm data. The resulting classifications highlighted the most significant noises, such as the movements of the subject's head, which generated clusters along the most intense contrasts of the image. By gathering the data in agreement with the paradigm, the zone activated by the auditive test could be revealed. The paradigm of this test was of the block type, where two conditions followed one another and were repeated, forming a periodic pattern. Here, the signals tend towards two conditions during each of the 6 images and repeat 8 times. Therefore, the 8 periods have been compressed into one period made up of 12 images. Classification of this small series preferentially reveals the expected zones in the form of compact blocks of voxels. However, within a class there are also scattered voxels. The treated data was compacted by a factor 16 compared to the pre-processed series. Amongst applied algorithms, two generated relatively stable and coherent clusters: GNG and SOM. Figure 4 illustrates clustering results of 4 independent runs of four algorithms (white coloured zones on fig.4 are relevant).

This result is interesting insofar as there was no pre-processing applied and the volume of the data was extremely reduced, considerably increasing the speed of execution.

6. Conclusion

In this article, a novel approach to interactive mining of fMRI data has been presented. The engagement of a physician in the process of knowledge discovery has been discussed, as well as the specificities of fMRI clustering with weak prior knowledge. Several clustering algorithms were evaluated. The experiments have shown that the Growing Neural Gas algorithm demonstrates the highest clustering performance and acceptable robustness.

The results have also demonstrated that the proposed new approach could be applied in detecting event-related fMRI data. It is important to underline that the parameters of the exploration algorithms can be modified during the course of execution. This dynamic aspect was a determining factor in its usage in interactive data mining.

The integration of clustering algorithms with the 3D Slicer has allowed visual exploration of created clusters and has provided the physician with more comprehensible information in quasi real time. The first results on synthetic data and block type data are encouraging and allow us to extend this work towards experiments with event-driven data where the signal-to-noise ratio is particularly weak and noisy data mask the relevant information.

Author details

Jerzy Korczak
University of Economics, Wrocław, Poland

Acknowledgement

The author thanks Christian Scheiber, Nicolas Lachiche, Jean Hommet, Aurelie Bertaux from the University of Strasbourg, France, for their contributions in this research, and K. Friston and G. Rees for the data from the SPM test, as well as the students of the University of Strasbourg, H. Hager, P. Hahn, V Meyer, J. Schaeffer and O. Zitvogel, for their participation in the initial phase of the realization of this project.

7. References

[1] The fMRI Data Center, http://www.fmridc.org, accessed March 2, 2012
[2] Sommer F.T, Wichert A (2003) *Exploratory Analysis and Data Modeling in Functional Neuroimaging*, The MIT Press, Cambridge.
[3] Friston K.J, Holmes A.P, Worsley K.J, Poline J.P, Frith C.D, Frackowiak R.S (1995), *Statistical Parametric Maps in Functional Imaging: A General Linear Approach*, Human Brain Mapping, 2: pp.189-210.
[4] Cox R.W (1996) *AFNI: Software for Analysis and Visualization of Functional Magnetic Resonance Neuroimages*, Computers and Biomedical Res., 29, pp.162–173.
[5] Goebel R (1997) BrainVoyager: *Ein Programm zur Analyse und Visualisierung von Magnetresonanztomographiedaten.* In: Plesser T, Wittenburg P, Forschung und Wissenschaftliches Rechnen.
[6] Kohonen T (1982), *Self-organized formation of topologically correct feature maps*, Biological Cybernetics, 43, pp. 59-69.
[7] Fritzke B (1995) *A growing neural gas network learns topologies*, In: Tesauro G, Touretzky D.S, Leen T.K, editors, Advances in Neural Information Processing Systems 7, pp 625-632. MIT Press, Cambridge.
[8] Goua S, Rastogi R, Shim K (1998) *CURE : An Efficient Clustering Algorithm for Large Databases*, Proc. SIGMOD'98, Seattle, pp. 73-84.

[9]   Bock H.H, Diday E (2000) Analysis of Symbolic Data, Exploratory Methods for Extracting Statistical Information from Complex Data. Studies in Classification, Data Analysis and Knowledge Organization, Springer-Verlag.

[10] Clayden J.D et al. (2011) TractoR: Magnetic Resonance Imaging and Tractography with R, Journal of Statistical Software, 11, vol 44, Issue 8, pp.1-18.

[11] Lindquist M.A (2008) The Statistical Analysis of fMRI Data, Statistical Science, vol. 23 (4), pp.439-464.

[12] Dimitriadou E, Barth M, Windschberger C, Hornik K, Moser E (2002) Detecting Regions of Interest in FMRI: An Application on Exploratory-based Data Analysis, In: Proc. 2002 IEEE World Congress on Computational Intelligence (WCCI 2002), Fogel D (edidor), Honolulu, pp.1488-1492.

[13] Goutte C, Toft P, Rostrup E, Nielsen E.F, Hansen L (1999), *On clustering fMRI time series*, NeuroImage, 9(3), pp. 298-310.

[14] Moller M, et al. (2005) Real *Time fMRI: A Tool for the Routine Presurgical Localisation of the Motor Cortex.* Eur Radiol, 15, pp. 292–295.

[15] Anderson A, et al. (2011) *Large Sample Group Independent Component Analysis of Functional Magnetic Resonance Imaging using Anatomical Atlas-based Reduction and Bootstrapped Clustering.* International Journal of Imaging Systems and Technology, 21(2), pp.223–231.

[16] Viviani R, Gron G, Spitzer M (2005) *Functional Principal Component Analysis of fMRI Data, Human Brain Mapping*, 24: pp. 109-129.

[17] Baumgartner R, Windischberger C, Moser E (1998) *Quantification in Functional Magnetic Resonance Imaging: Fuzzy Clustering vs Correlation Analysis*, Magnetic Resonance Imaging, 16, pp.115-125.

[18] Beckmann C, Smith S.M, (2003) *Probabilistic Independent Component Analysis for Functional Magnetic Resonance Imaging*, IEEE Trans. on Medical Imaging, 2003.

[19] Calhoun V.D, Adali T, Hansen L.K, Larsen J, Pekar J.J (2003) *ICA of Functional MRI Data: An Overview*, Proc. 4th Internat. Symp. on Independent Component Analysis and Blind Signal Separation (ICA2003), Nara, pp.281-288.

[20] Esposito F and al. (2002) *Spatial Independent Component Analysis of functional MRI time-series: To what extent do results depend on the algorithm used?*, Human Brain Mapping, 16, pp. 146-157.

[21] Douglas P.K, Harris S, Yuille A, and Cohen M.S (2011) *Performance Comparison of Machine Learning Algorithms and Number of Independent Components used in fMRI Decoding of Belief vs. Disbelief*, Neuroimage, 56, pp.544–553.

[22] Daubechies I, et al. (2009) *Independent Component Analysis for Brain fMRI does not select for independence*, In Proc. Of the Nat. Academy of Sciences of the USA Lashkari D, et al. (2012) Search for Patterns of Functional Specificity in the Brain: A Nonparametric Hierarchical Bayesian Model for Group fMRI Data, Neuroimage 59(2), pp.1368-1368.

[23] Filzmoser P, Baumgartner R, Moser E (1999) *Interactive Clustering of Functional MR Images*. In: Magnetic Resonance Imaging, 10, pp.817-826.

[24] Liao W, Chen H, Yang Q, Lei X (2008) *Analysis of fMRI Data using Improved Self-Organizing Mapping and Spatio-temporal Metric Hierarchical Clustering*, IEEE Trans. Med. Imaging, 27(10, pp.1472-1483.

[25] Katwal S.B (2011) *Analyzing fMRI Data with Graph-based Visualizations of Self-Organizing Maps*, IEEE International Symposium on Biomedical Imaging, Chicago, pp.1577-1580.

[26] Pereira F, Mitchell T, Botvinick M (2009). *Machine Learning Classifiers and fMRI: A Tutorial Overview*, NeuroImage, 45(1 Suppl).

[27] Hommet J (2005) *Système interactif de découverte du fonctionnement du cerveau à partir d'image IRMf*, Memoire CNAM, Illkirch.

[28] Korczak J, Scheiber C, Hommet J, Lachiche N (2005) *Fouille interactive en temps réel de séquences d'images IRMf*, Numéro Spécial RNTI, Cépaduès, pp.97-124.

[29] Korczak J, Bertaux A (2006), *Extension de l'algorithme CURE aux fouilles de données volumineuses*, Revue de Nouvelles Technologies de l'Information, EGC'2006, Cépaduès, pp. 547-548.

[30] Lachiche N, Hommet J, Korczak J, Braud A (2005), *Neuronal clustering of brain fMRI images*, Proc. of Pattern Recognition and Machine Inference.

[31] Moser E, Baumgartner R, Barth M, Windischberger C (1999) *Explorative Signal Processing in Functional MR Imaging*. International Journal of Imaging Systems Technology, 10(2), pp.166-176.

[32] Ulmer S, Jansen O, editors (2010) *fMRI – Basics and Clinical Applications*, Springer.

[33] Pieper S, Halle M, Kikinis R (2004) *3D SLICER*, In: Proc. 1st IEEE International Symposium on Biomedical Imaging: From Nano to Macro, pp.632–635.

Chapter 12

Examples of the Use of Data Mining Methods in Animal Breeding

Wilhelm Grzesiak and Daniel Zaborski

Additional information is available at the end of the chapter

1. Introduction

Data mining techniques involve mainly searching for various relationships in large data sets. However, they can also be used in a much narrower range, sometimes as an alternative to classical statistics. The characteristic feature of these models is the use of a specific strategy, usually requiring the division of data into training set, sometimes also verification set, which enable the evaluation of the model quality as well as a test set for checking its prognostic or classification abilities. Among many different methods belonging to data mining, the following can be distinguished: the general models of classification and regression trees (G_Trees), general CHAID (Chi-square Automatic Interaction Detection) models, interactive classification and regression trees (also with boosting – Boosted Trees), random forest, MARS (Multivariate Adaptive Regression Splines), artificial neural networks (ANN), other machine learning methods such as: naïve Bayes classifier (NBC), support vector machines (SVM), k-nearest neighbors (k-NN) and other regarded (or not) by different authors as data mining techniques. These methods are more and more frequently applied to various issues associated with animal breeding and husbandry.

2. Various methods used in data mining – Multivariate adaptive regression splines, naïve Bayes classifier, artificial neural networks, decision trees

2.1. Multivariate adaptive regression splines

MARS, introduced by Jerome Friedman in 1991 [1], is mainly used for solving regression-type problems. It is "a nonparametric regression method that approximates a complex non-linear relationship with a series of spline functions defined on different intervals of the independent (predictor) variable" [2]. Moreover, MARS makes it possible to fit non-linear multivariate functions. In this method, no assumptions about the analyzed functional relationship between variables are made. Instead, this relationship is determined based on regression data [3, 4]. Contrary to the global parametric models, MARS operates locally. It can be considered as a generalization of the binary recursive partitioning, in which the problem of the occurrence of the disjoint subregions and thus discontinuity of the approximating functions at the boundaries of these subregions, has been eliminated [2]. It utilizes left-sided and right-sided truncated power functions as spline functions:

$$(t-x)_+^q = \begin{cases} (t-x)^q, for\_x < l \\ 0, otherwise \end{cases},$$

$$(x-t)_+^q = \begin{cases} (x-t)^q, for\_x > t \\ 0, otherwise \end{cases},$$

where q $(q{\geq}0)$ is a power, to which the spline functions are raised to enable the adjustment of the smoothness of the obtained function estimate and t is a knot [5]. Basis functions in MARS can be a single spline function or a product of two (or more) such functions. The main idea behind MARS is the use of the combination of basis functions for the approximation of the relationship between the dependent variable and predictors:

$$\hat{y} = a_0 + \sum_{m=1}^{M} a_m B_m(\mathbf{x}),$$

where: $\hat{y}$ is a dependent variable, a_0 is a coefficient of the constant basis function, $B_m(\mathbf{x})$ is an mth basis function, a_m is a coefficient of the mth basis function and M is a number of basis functions in a model [4, 6].

An optimal MARS model is constructed in two stages. First, the model containing too many basis functions that lead to its overfitting is created. At this stage, it is also possible to take into account interactions between predictors or they can constitute only additive components [7]. At the second stage of the algorithm execution (pruning), these basis functions that contribute least to the goodness-of-fit are removed [8]. Elimination of these functions is based on the generalized cross-validation error (GCV):

$$GCV = \frac{\sum_{i=1}^{n}(y_i - \hat{y}_i)^2}{\left(1 - \frac{C}{n}\right)^2}, C = 1 + cd,$$

where: n is a number of cases in a data set, d is degrees of freedom equal to the number of independent basis functions, c is a "penalty" for the addition of the next basis function to the model, y_i is an actual value of the dependent variable, $\hat{y}_i$ is the value predicted by the model [2, 4, 9].

MARS, apart from regression tasks, can be used for classification. In the case of only two classes, dependent variable is coded as a binary one and further procedure is the same as in regression problems, whereas with more categories, the indicator variables are used and a model with a multivariate dependent variable is applied [10].

2.2. Naïve Bayes classifier

Naïve Bayes is a very simple and, at the same time, effective classifier. It can handle an arbitrary number of continuous and categorical variables [4]. It is based on the following Bayes' rule for conditional probability:

$$P(A \mid B) = P(B \mid A)\frac{P(A)}{P(B)},$$

where: $P(A)$ and $P(B)$ are probabilities of events A and B, respectively [11]. In terms of classification problems this rule can be expressed as:

$$P(y \mid \mathbf{x}) = P(y)\frac{P(\mathbf{x} \mid y)}{P(\mathbf{x})},$$

where: $\mathbf{x} = (x_1, x_2, .., x_N)$ is a feature vector and y is the class [11, 12].

In general, Bayesian classifiers determine the class to which an observation described by its feature vector belongs and the training process of such classifiers can be much simplified by assuming that the features are independent given class [4, 13]:

$$P(\mathbf{x} \mid y) = \prod_{j=1}^{N} P(x_j \mid y).$$

In practical applications, this assumption is often not fulfilled, however, it turns out that this fact does not significantly affect the quality and precision of classification [4, 11, 14]. Since $P(\mathbf{x})$ is the same for all classes, it can be omitted and thus the *a posteriori* probability according to which maximum value the observations are assigned to a given class takes the following form [12, 13]:

$$P(y \mid \mathbf{x}) = P(y)\prod_{j=1}^{N} P(x_j \mid y).$$

The main advantage of NBC is its simplicity and speed, whereas the disadvantage is the lack of any explanation of the decision made by the classifier [14].

2.3. Artificial neural networks

Artificial neural network (ANN) is an information processing system inspired by the biological systems such as the human brain. The characteristic features of the brain include incremental information processing, learning new concepts, taking decisions and drawing conclusions based on complex, sometimes irrelevant or incomplete data. The popularity of ANNs results from their ability to reproduce the processes occurring in the brain, although to a limited extent [15]. Therefore, ANNs represent different approach than traditional statistical methods in which it is necessary to define an algorithm and record it in the form of a computer program. Instead, ANNs are presented with exemplary tasks and the connections between the network elements as well as their weight coefficients are modified automatically according to the assumed training strategy. Besides the ability of self-programming, ANNs also show reduced sensitivity to the damages of their structure elements and are capable of the parallel data processing [16, 17].

The basic element of ANN is an artificial neuron, which is a very simplified model of a living nerve cell (Fig. 1) [18]. The so-called input signals (in the form of independent, explanatory variables) are sent to the inputs of an artificial neuron. They are subsequently multiplied by the corresponding weight coefficients (equivalents of synaptic potentials in the living nerve cells). The next stage of the artificial neuron functioning is obtaining an auxiliary internal signal, the so-called postsynaptic potential s [19]. This potential can be expressed using the following equation:

$$s = \sum_{j=1}^{N} w_j x_j,$$

where: x_j is a jth input signal, w_j – weight associated with a jth neuron input, N – number of neuron inputs [20].

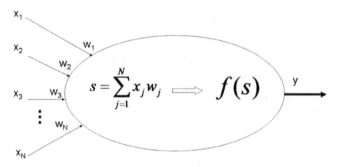

Figure 1. Schematic representation of an artificial neuron (without bias weight)

To this sum of signals, the neuron sometimes adds an additional component called bias weight, which is independent from the input signals and, if taken into account, also undergoes the learning process. Bias weight, which is associated with the constant input $x_0=1$, makes it possible to define the properties of a neuron more freely [16,18, 21]. If a neuron represents a multiple regression model, bias weight can be regarded as an intercept [22]. The weighted sum of input signals with an added (possibly) bias weight can sometimes be passed directly to the output of an artificial neuron constituting its output signal. In the more complex types of ANNs the output signal is, however, calculated using the so-called activation function [16,18]. Activation function can be a linear function – then the output signal y is calculated as: $y=bs$, where b is a given coefficient [23]. Another type of activation function is the unit step function. Then the output signal takes the following form:

$$y = \begin{cases} 0\_when\_s < 0 \\ 1\_when\_s \geq 0 \end{cases}'$$

where s - the postsynaptic potential value [20]. To describe more precisely the non-linear characteristics of the biological neuron, sigmoid functions, including logistic and hyperbolic tangent can be used. They are frequently applied, especially to solve more complex issues [15]. The logistic function can be expressed with the following formula:

$$y = \frac{1}{1+e^{(-bs)}},$$

where: b – a coefficient determining the shape of the logistic function, most often equal to 1, s – the value of the postsynaptic potential, e – base of the natural logarithm [20, 21, 24].

The algorithm used to train a single neuron (supervised method) assumes that with each input vector x_i presented to the neuron, a desired or real output value y_i corresponding to this input vector is also presented. In response to the input vector, the neuron produces the output signal $\hat{y}_i$. However, if the neuron is not fully trained, this signal differs from the desired one. Therefore, the error is calculated, which is then used to modify the weights w_j so that the neuron better approximates the relationship between input and output values [16]. This process is repeated many times until the lowest possible error is obtained. The initial weight values are usually selected at random, and they are modified in the successive iterations of the algorithm according to the gradient of an error function in the space defined by the number of neuron inputs [18].

Perceptrons are one of the ANNs types (Fig. 2). Initially, the name was reserved only for feed-forward neural networks with neurons using threshold activation function. Later, this name included also multilayer feed-forward networks with neurons having continuous activation functions [20]. In perceptrons, the signals are sent only in one direction, that is, from the network input, from which it takes the input data, to the network output, in which the network returns solution [25]. The neurons are organized in layers and the neurons of one layer are connected with all the neurons of the next layer. The neurons of the same layer cannot connect with each other and there is no feed-back to preceding layers [21, 26]. The task of the neurons of the input layer is the preprocessing of input data, which usually involves normalization or scaling. The main processing takes place, however, in the hidden and output layers [25]. The name "hidden layer" results from the fact that it does not have a direct contact with the inputs or outputs of the network [18]. The presence of the hidden layers (in the ANNs with neurons having non-linear activation functions) significantly extends the range of mapping that the network can realize. A single hidden layer is sufficient in such networks to realize any mapping relating input to output signals [21, 25].

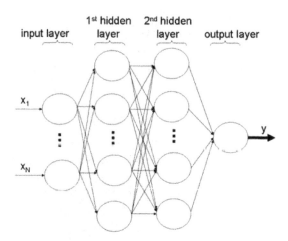

Figure 2. Schematic representation of the feed-forward artificial neural network with two hidden layers

The second frequently used ANN type is radial basis function (RBF) networks. In the case of the RBF networks, the input signals making the vector x are fed to each neuron of the hidden layer [26]. Thus, unlike in MLPs, the connections between input-layer and hidden-layer neurons are direct connections without weights [21]. In the hidden-layer, activation functions of the neurons perform the following mapping:

$$x \rightarrow \varphi(\|x - c\|), x \in R^n$$

where $(\|\cdot\|)$ most often denotes Euclidean norm and R^n is n-dimensional space [21, 26]. The functions $\varphi(\|x-c\|)$ are called radial basis functions and c denotes the center of a given radial basis function. The number of these neurons is equal to the number of cases in the training set or lower. The neuron of the output layer computes the weighted sum of the output signals from the hidden-layer neurons [20, 26]:

$$\hat{y} = \sum_i w_i \varphi(\|x - c_i\|).$$

The most frequently used basis function is the Gaussian function of the form:

$$\varphi(\|x - c_i\|) = \exp\left(-\frac{\|x - c_i\|^2}{2\sigma_i^2}\right)$$

where $\sigma > 0$ is a parameter [24].

An important issue in the practical application of the ANNs is the scaling of input signals to the range appropriate for the network with the aim of their standardization. The methods used in this case are min-max or mean-deviation. The result of the first method can be expressed with the following formula:

$$x_i^* = \frac{x_i - \min(x_i)}{range(x_i)} = \frac{x_i - \min(x_i)}{\max(x_i) - \min(x_i)},$$

where x_i^* ranges from 0 to 1 [15, 27]. The output signal from the network is also scaled appropriately. For categorical predictors, it is first necessary to convert them to the numeric form. Two methods are commonly used for this purpose: one-of-N encoding and numerical encoding. In the first method, one neuron is allocated for each possible nominal value. During the learning process, one of the neurons is on and the others are off [4]. On the other hand, in the numerical representation, numerical values that are fed to the network inputs are assigned to the consecutive categories of the nominal variable. The use of this representation causes that one neuron in the input layer corresponds to one nominal variable, however, by numbering the values of the nominal variable, the user defines its ordering, which is not always justified [18].

In the process of ANN learning, the basic role is played by weight vectors. A single weight vector determines the behavior of an artificial neuron, whereas the weight matrix – the behavior of the whole network. The main algorithm of the MLP training is an error back-propagation [28]. During the optimization process, weights are modified each time after the presentation of a given training case. The learning process is based on a training sequence consisting of the pairs $<x_i,y_i>$, where x_i is an ith vector of input values, y_i is a desired output value defined for each $i=1,..,n$, i is the number of the training vector and n is the number of training cases [16]. In the MLP functioning, the following stages can be distinguished [23]:

1. feeding the ith input vector x_i to the input layer of the network,
2. computation of the s_{ik}^h value for each neuron of the hidden layer according to the following formula:

$$s_{ik}^h = \sum_{j=0}^{N} w_{kj}^h x_{ij},$$

where: s_{ik}^h - weighted sum of the input signals for the kth neuron of the hidden layer, h – label of the hidden-layer neuron, $j=0,...,N$, N – number of input-layer neurons, w_{kj}^h - weight from jth neuron of the input layer to the kth neuron of the hidden layer, x_{ij} – jth input signal for the ith training case.

3. computation of the output value y_{ik}^h for each neuron of the hidden layer :

$$y_{ik}^h = f_k^h(s_{ik}^h),$$

where: $f_k^h(\cdot)$ is an activation function of the hidden-layer neuron.

4. computation of the s_{il}^o value for each neuron of the output layer:

$$s_{il}^o = \sum_{k=0}^{K} w_{lk}^o y_{ik}^h,$$

where: s_{il}^o is a weighted sum of signals from the hidden-layer neurons for the lth neuron of the output layer, o - the label of the output-layer neuron, $k=0,..,K$, K – the number of hidden-layer neurons, w_{lk}^o - the weight from the kth neuron of the hidden layer to the lth neuron of the output layer,

5.   calculation of the output value $\hat{y}_i$ of the output-layer neuron:

$$\hat{y}_i = f_l^o(s_{il}^o),$$

where: $f_l^o(\cdot)$ is an activation function of the output-layer neuron.

After performing all the above-mentioned phases, the network determines its output signal $\hat{y}_i$. This signal can be correct or incorrect but the role of the learning process is to make it as similar as possible (or identical in an ideal case) to the desired output signal y_i [28]. This can be achieved by appropriately modifying network weights so that the following error function E (for a single neuron in an output layer) is minimized [15, 16, 23]:

$$E = \frac{1}{2}\sum_{i=1}^{n}(y_i - \hat{y}_i)^2.$$

The optimization method used for this purpose is a gradient descent. The error function gradient is evaluated for each training case at a time and the weights are updated using the following formula [20]:

$$\Delta\mathbf{w}^{(t)} = -\eta\nabla E_i(\mathbf{w}^{(t)}),$$

where: $\Delta\mathbf{w}^{(t)}$ is a weight vector update at step t, η is a learning rate in the range [0,1], $\nabla E_i(\mathbf{w}^{(t)})$ is a gradient of the function E_i in point $w^{(t)}$, E_i is an error for the ith training case:

$$E_i = \frac{1}{2}(y_i - \hat{y}_i)^2.$$

Both the weights of the output neuron and those of the hidden-layer neurons are updated during this process. The weight modification requires the calculation of the partial derivatives of an error with respect to each weight [23, 28]:

$$\Delta w_{lk}^o = -\eta\frac{\partial E_i}{\partial w_{lk}^o}, \ \Delta w_{kj}^h = -\eta\frac{\partial E_i}{\partial w_{kj}^h}$$

In order to make the back-propagation algorithm more effective, the momentum term α is often added to the equation for the weight modification:

$$\Delta w(t+1) = -\eta\frac{\partial E_i}{\partial w(t+1)} + \alpha\Delta w(t)$$

where $\Delta w(t+1)$ is a weight update at step $t+1$ and $\Delta w(t)$ is a weight update at step t [27].

The RBF network learning algorithm consists of two stages: (1) first, the position and shape of the basis functions are determined using one of the following methods: random selection, self-organization process, error back-propagation; (2) next, the weight matrix of the output layer is obtained in one step using the pseudoinversion method [26].

An important issue in the classification and regression by means of ANNs is to establish which variables in the model contribute most to the class determination or prediction of the value of continuous variable. An ANN sensitivity analysis is used for this purpose [15]. Elimination of individual variables affects the total network error and thus it is possible to evaluate the importance of these variables. The following indices are used [4, 29]:

1. error – determines how much the network's quality deteriorates without including a given variable in the model; the larger the error, the more important the variable;
2. ratio – the ratio of the above mentioned error to an error obtained using all variables, the higher the ratio, the more important the variable; the ratio below 1 indicates the variables that should be excluded from the model to improve the network quality;
3. rank – orders the variables according to decreasing error, the higher the rank, the more important the variable.

2.4. Decision trees

In mathematical terms, decision tree can be defined as a directed, acyclic and connected graph, having only one distinguishable vertex called a root node [30]. The tree structure consists of nodes and branches connecting these nodes [4]. If a node has branches leading to other nodes, it is called a parent node and the nodes to which these branches lead are called children of this node. The terminal nodes are called leaves [30]. Classification and regression trees (CART) are one of the types of decision trees.

CART were proposed by Leo Breiman et al. in 1984 [31]. The characteristic feature of CART is that the decision trees constructed by this algorithm are strictly binary. The cases from the training set are recursively partitioned into subsets with similar values of the target variable and the tree is built through the thorough search of all available variables and all possible divisions for each decision node, and the selection of the optimal division according to a given criterion [27].

The splitting criterions have always the following form: the case is moved to the left child if the condition is met, and goes to the right child otherwise. For continuous variables the condition is defined as "explanatory variable $x_j \le C$". For the nominal variables, the condition expresses the fact that the variable takes on specific values [32]. For instance, for the variable "season" the division can be defined as follows: a case goes to the left child if "season" is in {spring, summer} and goes to the right child otherwise.

Different impurity functions $\varphi(p)$ can be used in decision nodes but the two most commonly applied for classification are Gini index and entropy:

$$\varphi(\mathbf{p}) = \sum_j p_j(1-p_j),$$

$$\varphi(\mathbf{p}) = -\sum_j p_j \log p_j,$$

where: $p=(p_1, p_2,\ldots, p_J)$ are the proportions of classes $1, 2,\ldots, J$ in a given node [33].

In order to avoid overtraining, which leads to reduced generalization ability, the CART algorithm must initiate the procedure of pruning nodes and branches. This can be done using the test set or the V-fold cross-validation [27].

3. Classification example – The use of various data mining methods for the analysis of artificial inseminations and dystocia in cattle

An example of the application of data mining methods in the animal husbandry can be the detection of dairy cows with problems at artificial insemination by means of ANNs. The effectiveness of artificial insemination depends on meeting the following conditions: cow has healthy reproductive organs and is in the appropriate phase of reproductive cycle, artificial insemination is performed within 12 – 18 hours since the occurrence of the external estrus symptoms, the bull semen has appropriate quality, artificial insemination is performed correctly [34]. The possibility of identifying cows that can have problems at artificial insemination allows the farmer to more carefully treat such animals and eliminate potential risks associated with conception. A larger number of artificial inseminations increases the costs of this process and affects various reproductive indices, which in turn reduces the effectiveness of cattle farming.

In the aforementioned work [35], the set of 10 input variables determining potential difficulties at artificial insemination was used. They included, among other things, percentage of Holstein-Friesian genes in cow genotype, lactation number, artificial insemination season, age at artificial insemination, calf sex, the length of calving interval and pregnancy, body condition score and selected production indices. The output variable was dichotomous and described the class of conception ease: (1) conception occurred after 1 - 2 services or (2) after 3 or more services (3 - 11 services). The whole set of artificial insemination records (918) was randomly divided into 3 subsets: training (618 records), validation (150 records) and test (150 records) sets. To ensure appropriate generalization abilities of ANNs, a 10-fold cross-validation was applied. ANNs were built and trained by means of Statistica® Neural Networks PL v 4.0F software. The search for the best network from among many ANN categories was performed. The best network from each category (selected on the basis of the root-mean-square error – RMS) was utilized for the detection process. An MLP with 10 and 7 neurons in the first and the second hidden layers, respectively, trained with the back-propagation method was characterized by the best results of such detection. The percentages of correct indications of cows from both distinguished categories (altogether) as well as those of the correct detection of cows with difficulties at conception and without them were similar and amounted to approx. 85%. The ANN sensitivity analysis was applied to identify the variables with the greatest influence on the value of the output variable (category of conception ease). Of the variables used, the following were the most significant: length of calving interval, lactation number, body condition score, pregnancy length and percentage of Holstein-Friesian genes in cow genotype.

Another method from the data mining field applied to the detection of cows with artificial insemination problems is MARS [35]. The effectiveness of this method was verified on the data set with analogous variables as those used for ANN analysis. From the whole set of records, two subsets were formed: training (768 records) and test (150 records) sets, without the validation set. In the model construction, up to 150 spline functions were applied, some of which were subsequently removed in the pruning process so as not to cause the overfitting of the model to the training data, which results in the loss of generalization abilities. The generalized cross-validation (GCV) error enabled the evaluation of the analyzed MARS models. The best model selected according to this criterion was used to perform the detection of cows with difficult conception. The percentages of correct detection of cows from both categories as well as percentages of correct indication of cows with difficulties at artificial insemination and those without such problems amounted to 88, 82 and 91%, respectively. Based on the number of references, it was also possible to indicate variables with the greatest contribution to the determination of conception class (length of calving interval, body condition score, pregnancy length, age at artificial insemination, milk yield, milk fat and protein content and lactation number).

Other data mining methods, CART and NBC, applied to the detection of cows with conception problems also turned out to be useful [36]. Based on the similar set of input data (the percentage of Holstein-Friesian genes in cow genotype, age at artificial insemination, length of calving-to-conception interval, calving interval and pregnancy, body condition score, milk yield, milk fat and protein content) and a similar dichotomous output variable in the form of the conception class (difficult or easy), 1006 cases were divided into training (812 records) and test (194 records) sets. Using Statistica ® Data Miner 9.0 software, the Gini index was used as an impurity measure in the construction of the CART models. The obtained models were characterized by quite a high sensitivity, specificity and accuracy of detection on the test set (0.72, 0.90, 0.85 for NBC and 0.83, 0.86, 0.90 for CART). In the case of CART, it was also possible to indicate the key variables for the determination of the conception class: the length of calving and calving-to-conception intervals and body condition score. The presented data mining methods used to support the monitoring of cows selected for artificial insemination can be an ideal tool for a farmer wishing to improve breeding and economic indices in a herd.

Another example of the application of such methods is the use of ANNs for the detection of difficult calvings (dystocia) in heifers [37]. Dystocia is an undesired phenomenon in cattle reproduction, whose consequence is, among other things, an increased risk of disease states in calves, their higher perinatal mortality, reduced fertility and milk yield in cows as well as their lower survival rate [38]. Dystocia also contributes to increased management costs, which result from the necessity of ensuring the permanent supervision of cows during parturition. Financial losses associated with dystocia can reach even 500 Euro per case [39]. According to various estimates, the frequency of dystocia in Holstein cows ranges from approx. 5% to approx. 23% depending on the level of its severity and the parity [40]. The reasons for dystocia in cattle can be divided into direct and indirect. The former include, among other things, insufficient dilation of the vulva and cervix, uterine torsion and inertia, small pelvic area, ventral hernia, too large or dead fetus, fetal malposition and malpresentation, fetal monstrosities [41,42]. These factors are difficult to account for and can occur without clear reasons. Because of that, their potential use for prediction purposes is limited. On the other hand, indirect factors such as: age and body weight of cow at calving, parity, body condition score, nutrition during gestation, cow and calf breed, calving year and season, management and diseases can be used to some extent as predictors of calving difficulty in dairy cows. Susceptibility to dystocia has also genetic background [42]. This is mainly a quantitative trait, although some major genes, which can determine calving quality and constitute additional predictors of calving difficulty class, have been identified. The limitation of the occurrence of dystocia can be achieved using various prediction models, constructed on the basis of different variables. By means of such models, it is possible to indicate in advance animals with calving difficulties, which often allows the farmer to take action against dystocia. In the cited study [37], the authors used the following input variables: percentage of Holstein-Friesian genes in heifer genotype, pregnancy length, body conditions score, calving season, age at calving and three previously selected genotypes. The dichotomous output variable was the class of calving difficulty: difficult or easy. The whole set of calving records (531) was divided into training, validation and test sets of 330, 100 and 101 records, respectively. The authors selected the best networks from among MLP and RBF network types based on the RMS error. The networks were trained and validated using Statistica ® Neural Networks PL v 4.0F software. An analysis of the results obtained on a test set including cases not previously presented to the network showed that the MLP was characterized by the highest sensitivity (83%). This network had one hidden layer with four neurons. Specificity and accuracy were similar and amounted to 82%. The ANN sensitivity analysis showed that calving ease was the most strongly affected by pregnancy length, body condition score and percentage of Holstein-Friesian genes in heifer genotype.

Besides detecting dystocia in heifers, ANNs were also successfully applied to the detection of difficult calvings in Polish Holstein-Friesian cows [43]. In this case, the following predictors were used: percentage of Holstein-Friesian genes in cow genotype, gestation length, body condition score, calving season, cow age, calving and calving-to-conception intervals, milk yield for 305-day lactation and at three different lactation stages, milk fat and protein content as well as the same three genotypes as those for heifers. The whole data set of calving records (1221) was divided into three parts of 811, 205, and 205 records for the training, validation and test sets, respectively. Using Statistica Neural Networks ® PL v 4.0F software, the best ANN from each category (MLP with one and two hidden layers, RBF networks) was searched for on the basis of its RMS error. Then the selected networks were verified on the test set. Taking into account sensitivity on this set, the MLP with one hidden layer had the best performance (80% correctly detected dystotic cows), followed by the MLP with two hidden layers (73% correctly diagnosed cows with dystocia). The ability of the RBF network to detect cows with calving difficulties was smaller (sensitivity of 67%). Sensitivity analysis showed that the most significant variables in the neural model were: calving season, one of the analyzed genotypes and gestation length.

4. Regression tasks - Milk yield prediction in cattle

The use of an important data mining method, ANN, in regression problems can be briefly presented on the basis of predicting lactation milk yield in cows. Such a prediction is significant both for farmers and milk processors. It makes it possible to appropriately plan milk production in a herd and is the basis for taking decisions on culling or retaining an animal already at an early lactation stage [44]. The commercial value of a cow is estimated by comparing its milk yield with the results of cows from the same herd, in the same lactation and calving year-season. Moreover, obtaining information on the potential course of lactation allows the farmer to appropriately select the diet, more precisely estimate production costs and profits, diagnose mastitis and ketosis [45]. Milk yield prediction is also important for breeding reasons. The selection of genetically superior bulls is, to a large extent, dependent on their ability to produce high-yielding daughters. Therefore, the sooner these bulls are identified, the sooner the collection of their semen and artificial insemination can begin. In the species like cattle, in which the generation interval is approx. 5 years, every method that can contribute to the milk yield prediction in cows before the completion of lactation will speed up the process of bull identification and increase genetic progress [46]. In the cited work [47], the input variables in the neural models were the evaluation results from the first four test-day milkings, mean milk yield of a barn, lactation length, calving month, lactation number, proportion of Holstein-Friesian genes in animal genotype. Linear networks (LNs) and MLPs were designed using Statistica ® Neural Networks PL v 4.0F software. A total set of milk yield records included 1547 cases and was appropriately divided into subsets (training, validation and test sets). The RMS errors of the models ranged between 436.5 kg and 558.2 kg. The obtained values of the correlation coefficient between the actual and predicted milk yield ranged from 0.90 to 0.96. The mean milk yield predictions generated using ANNs did not deviate significantly from those made by SYMLEK (the computer system for the comprehensive milk recording in Poland) for the analyzed herd of cows. However, the mean prediction by the one-hidden-layer MLP was closer to the values obtained from SYMLEK than those generated with the remaining models.

A similar study on the use of ANNs for regression problems concerned predictions for 305-day lactation yield in Polish Holstein-Friesian cows based on monthly test-day results [48]. The following 7 input variables were used: mean 305-day milk yield of the barns in which the cows were utilized, days in milk, mean test-day milk yield in the first, second, third and fourth month of the research period and calving month. MLP with 10 neurons in the hidden layer was designed using Statistica ® Neural Networks PL v 4.0F software. The whole data set (1390 records) was appropriately divided into training, validation and test set of 700, 345 and 345 records, respectively. However, an additional set of records from 49 cows that completed their lactation was utilized to further verify the prognostic abilities of the ANN. The RMS error calculated based on the training and validation sets was 477 and 502 kg, respectively. The mean milk yield for 305-day lactation predicted by the ANN was 13.12 kg lower than the real milk yield of the 49 cows used for verification purposes but this difference was statistically non-significant.

The next successful attempt at using ANNs for predicting milk yield in dairy cows was based on daily milk yields recorded between 5 and 305 days in milk [49]. The following predictor variables were used in the ANN model: proportion of Holstein-Friesian genes in cow genotype, age at calving, days in milk and lactation number. The dependent variable was the milk yield on a given day. Predictions made by ANNs were compared with the observed yields and those generated by the SYMLEK system. The data set (137,507 records) was divided into subsets for network training, validation (108,931 records) and testing (28,576). 25 MLPs were built and trained using Statistica ® Neural Networks PL v 4.0F software. MLP with 10 and 6 neurons in the first and second hidden layer, respectively, showed the best performance (RMS error of 3.04 kg) and was selected for further analysis. The correlation coefficients between the real yields and those predicted by the ANN ranged from 0.84 to 0.89 depending on lactation number. The correlation coefficients between the actual cumulative yields and predictions ranged between 0.94 and 0.96 depending on lactation. ANN was more effective in predicting milk yield than the SYMLEK system. The most important variables revealed by the ANN sensitivity analysis were days in milk followed by month of calving and lactation number.

Another study on milk yield prediction involved the use of ANNs to predict milk yield for complete and standard lactations in Polish Holstein-Friesian cows [29]. A total of 108,931 daily milk yield records (set A) for three lactations in cows from a particular barn as well as 38,254 test-day records (set B) for cows from 12 barns located in the West Pomeranian Province in Poland were analyzed. ANNs quality was evaluated with the coefficient of determination (R^2), relative approximation error (RAE) and root mean squared error (RMS). To verify the prognostic ability of the models, 28,576 daily milk yield records (set A') and 3,249 test-day records (set B') were randomly selected. For the cows for which these records were obtained, the predictions of the daily and lactation milk yields were generated and compared with their real milk yields and those from the official milk recording system SYMLEK. The RMS errors on sets A and B were 2.77 - 3.39 kg and 2.43 – 3.79 kg, respectively, depending on the analyzed lactation. Similarly, the RAE values ranged from 0.13 to 0.15 and from 0.11 to 0.15, whereas the R^2 values were 0.75 – 0.79 and 0.75 – 0.78 for sets A and B, respectively. The correlation coefficients between the actual (or generated by the SYMLEK system) and predicted milk yields calculated on the basis of the test sets were 0.84 - 0.89 and 0.88 – 0.90 for sets A' and B', respectively, depending on lactation. These predictions were closer to the real values than those made by the SYMLEK system. The most important variables in the model determined on the basis of sensitivity analysis were lactation day and calving month as well as lactation day and percentage of Holstein-Friesian genes for the daily milk yield and test-day records, respectively.

5. Model quality

For the evaluation of the classification and regression model quality, the indices described below, calculated on the basis of the training set or combined training and validation sets, are used.

5.1. Classification model quality

The evaluation of the classification model quality is performed using the indices such as: sensitivity, specificity, probability of false positive results $P(FP)$, probability of false negative results $P(FN)$ and accuracy. Moreover, the *a posteriori* probability of true positive results $P(PSTP)$ and *a posteriori* probability of true negative results $P(PSTN)$ are used. All the above-mentioned probabilities are calculated for the two-class classification based on the classification matrix (Table 1).

Predicted class	Actual class		Total
	Positive result	Negative result	
Positive result	A	B	A+B
Negative result	C	D	C+D
Total	A+C	B+D	A+B+C+D

Table 1. The general form of classification matrix

Sensitivity is defined as a percentage of correctly identified individuals belonging to the distinguished class (e.g. individuals with dystocia or conception difficulties):

$$Sensitivity = \frac{A}{A+C}.$$

Specificity is a percentage of correctly recognized individuals belonging to the second (undistinguished) class (e.g. individuals with easy calvings or conception):

$$Specificity = \frac{D}{B+D}.$$

The probability of false negative results $P(FN)$ defines the percentage of incorrectly classified individuals belonging to the distinguished class (e.g. indicating dystotic cow as one with an easy calving or cow with conception problems as one without such difficulties):

$$P(FN) = \frac{C}{A+C},$$

whereas the probability of false positive results $P(FP)$ corresponds to the proportion of incorrectly recognized individuals belonging to the second analyzed class (e.g. diagnosing cow with an easy calving as a dystotic one or a cow without conception problems as one with such difficulties):

$$P(FP) = \frac{B}{B+D}.$$

The *a posteriori* probabilities make it possible to answer the question about the proportion of individuals assigned by the model to a given class that really belonged to that class. They are calculated according to the following formulae:

$$P(PSTP) = \frac{A}{A+B} \text{ and } P(PSTN) = \frac{D}{C+D}.$$

In the case of some classification models it is also possible to calculate additional quality indices, such as root mean squared error RMS (for ANN and MARS):

$$RMS = \sqrt{\frac{1}{n}\sum_{i=1}^{n}\left(y_i - \hat{y}_i\right)^2},$$

where: n – the number of cases, y_i – the real value of the analyzed trait, $\hat{y}_i$ - the value of this trait predicted by a given classification model.

5.2. Regression model quality

For the evaluation of the regression model quality, the following indices are mainly used: Pearson's coefficient of correlation between the actual values and those calculated by the model (r), the ratio of standard deviation of error to the standard deviation of variable (SD_{ratio}), error standard deviation (S_E) and the mean of error moduli ($\bar{E}_{MB}$) [29].

Moreover, the relative approximation error (RAE), adjusted coefficient of determination (R_p^2) and the aforementioned root mean squared error (RMS) are used. The first two indices are calculated according to the following equations [49]:

$$RAE = \sqrt{\frac{\sum_{i=1}^{n}(y_i - \hat{y}_i)^2}{\sum_{i=1}^{n}y_i^2}} \text{ and } R_p^2 = 1 - \frac{MS_E}{MS_T},$$

where: MS_E – the estimated variance of a model error, MS_T – the estimated variance of the total variability.

In the evaluation of the regression model, special attention should be paid to two of the aforementioned parameters [17]:

1. SD_{ratio} – always takes on non-negative values and its lower value indicates a better model quality. For a very good model SD_{ratio} takes on the values in the range from 0 to 0.1. SD_{ratio} over 1 indicates very poor quality of the model.
2. Pearson's correlation coefficient – takes on the values in the range between 0 and 1. The higher the value of this coefficient, the better the model quality.

6. Prediction quality

For the evaluation of predictions made by the developed classification models, the above-mentioned probabilities calculated for the test set can be used. It is also possible to apply the receiver operating characteristic (ROC) curves, which describe the relationship between sensitivity and specificity for the models in which dependent variable has only two categories (Fig. 3).

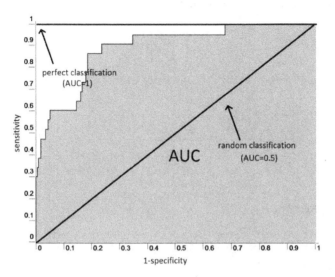

Figure 3. The receiver operating characteristic (ROC) curve and the area under curve (AUC) (from Statistica ® Neural Networks, modified)

The ROC curve is obtained in the following steps. For each value of a predictor, which can be a single variable or model result, a decision rule is created using this value as a cut-off point. Then, for each of the possible cut-off points, sensitivity and specificity are calculated and presented on the plot. In the Cartesian coordinate system, 1-specificity (equal to false positive rate) is plotted on the horizontal axis and sensitivity on the vertical axis. Next, all the points are joined. The larger the number of different values of a given parameter, the smoother the curve [50]. For the equal costs of misclassification, the ideal situation is when the ROC curve rises vertically from (0,0) to (0,1), then horizontally to (1,1). Such a curve represents perfect detection performance on the test set. On the other hand, if the curve is a diagonal line going from (0,0) to (1,1), the predictive ability of the classifier is none, and a better prediction can be obtained simply by chance [51].

The ROC curves are often used to compare the performance of different models, so it would be advantageous to represent the shape of the curve as one parameter. This parameter is called area under curve (AUC) and can be regarded as a measure of goodness-of-fit and accuracy of the model [50, 52]. AUC takes on the values in the range [0,1]. The higher the AUC, the better the model but no realistic classifier should have an AUC less than 0.5 because this corresponds to the random guessing producing the diagonal line between (0,0) and (1,1), which has an area of 0.5 [51].

For the evaluation of predictions made by regression models, the following parameters calculated for the test set can be applied [49]:

1. Pearson's coefficient of correlation between the actual values and those predicted by the model (r)
2. Mean relative prediction error Ψ calculated according to the following formula:

$$\Psi = \frac{1}{n}\sum_{i=1}^{n}\left|\frac{y_i - \hat{y}_i}{y_i}\right| \cdot 100\%$$

3. Theil's coefficient I^2 expressed by the following equation [53]:

$$I^2 = \frac{\sum_{i=1}^{n}\left(y_i - \hat{y}_i\right)^2}{\sum_{i=1}^{n}y_i^2}.$$

7. Model comparison

At least two basic criteria can be used for making comparisons between various models. These are: Akaike information criterion (*AIC*) and Bayesian information criterion (*BIC*). *AIC* can be defined as:

$$AIC = -2\ln L_{\max} + 2k,$$

where L_{max} is the maximum likelihood achievable by the model, and k is the number of free parameters in the model [54]. The term k in the above equation plays a role of the "penalty" for the inclusion of new variables in the model and serves as compensation for the obviously decreasing model deviation. The model with a minimum *AIC* is selected as the best model to fit the data [30].

Bayesian information criterion (*BIC*) is defined as [54]:

$$BIC = -2\ln L_{\max} + k\ln n,$$

where n – the number of observations (data points) used in the fit. Both criteria are used to select a "good model" but their definition of this model differs. Bayesian approach, reflected in the *BIC* formulation, aims at finding the model with the highest probabilities of being the true model for a given data set, with an assumption that one of the considered models is true. On the other hand, the approach associated with *AIC* uses the expected prediction of future data as the most important criterion of the model adequacy, denying the existence of any true model [55].

8. Summary

Data mining methods can be an economic stimulus for discovering unknown rules or associations in the object domains. No knowledge will be discovered without potential and significant economic benefits. Much acquired knowledge can be used for improving currently functioning models. These methods are capable of finding certain patterns that are rather inaccessible for conventional statistical techniques. These techniques are usually used for the verification of specific hypotheses, whereas the application of data mining methods is associated with impossibility of formulating preliminary hypotheses and the associations within data are often unexpected. Discoveries or results obtained for individual models should be an introduction to further analyzes forming the appropriate picture of the problem being explored.

Author details

Wilhelm Grzesiak* and Daniel Zaborski
Laboratory of Biostatistics, Department of Ruminant Science, West Pomeranian University of Technology, Szczecin, Poland

9. References

[1] Friedman J H (1991) Multivariate adaptive regression splines (with discussion). Annals of Statistics 19: 1-141.

[2] Zakeri I F, Adolph A L, Puyau M R, Vohra F A, Butte N F (2010) Multivariate adaptive regression splines models for the prediction of energy expenditure in children and adolescents. Journal of Applied Physiology 108: 128–136.

[3] Taylan P, Weber G-H, Yerlikaya F (2008) Continuous optimization applied in MARS for modern applications in finance, science and technology. 20th EURO Mini Conference "Continuous Optimization and Knowledge-Based Technologies" (EurOPT-2008), May 20–23, 2008, Neringa, Lithuania, pp. 317-322.

[4] StatSoft Electronic Statistics Textbook. http://www.statsoft.com/textbook/ (last accessed 14.04.2012)

[5] Xu Q-S, Massart D L, Liang Y-Z, Fang K-T (2003) Two-step multivariate adaptive regression splines for modeling a quantitative relationship between gas chromatography retention indices and molecular descriptors. Journal of Chromatography A 998: 155–167.

[6] Put R, Xu Q S, Massart D L, Vander Heyden Y (2004) Multivariate adaptive regression splines (MARS) in chromatographic quantitative structure-retention relationship studies. Journal of Chromatography A 1055: 11-19.

[7] Lee T-S, Chiu C-C, Chou Y-C, Lu C-J (2006) Mining the customer credit using classification and regression tree and multivariate adaptive regression splines. Computational Statistics and Data Analysis 50: 1113-1130.

[8] Zareipour H, Bhattacharya K, Canizares C A (2006) Forecasting the hourly Ontario energy price by multivariate adaptive regression splines. IEEE, Power Engineering Society General Meeting, pp. 1-7.

* Corresponding Author

[9] Sokołowski A, Pasztyła A (2004) Data mining in forecasting the requirement for energy carriers. StatSoft Poland, Kraków, pp. 91 – 102 [in Polish]

[10] Hastie T, Tibshirani R, Friedman J (2006) The Elements of Statistical Learning: Data Mining, Inference, and Prediction. Springer, New York, p. 328.

[11] Glick M, Klon A E, Acklin P, Davies J W (2004) Enrichment of extremely noisy high-throughput screening data using a naïve Bayes classifier. Journal of Molecular Screening 9: 32-36.

[12] Lewis D D (1998) Naïve (Bayes) at forty: The independence assumption in information retrieval. Machine Learning ECML 98. Lecture Notes in Computer Science 1398/1998: 4-15.

[13] Rish I (2001) An empirical study on the naïve Bayes classifier. The IJCAI-01 Workshop on empirical methods in artificial intelligence. August 4, 2001, Seattle, USA, pp. 41-46.

[14] Morzy M (2006) Data mining – review of methods and application domains. In: 6th Edition: Data Warehouse and Business Intelligence, CPI, Warsaw, pp. 1–10 [in Polish].

[15] Samarasinghe S (2007) Neural Networks for Applied Science and Engineering. From Fundamentals to Complex Pattern Recognition. Auerbach Neural Publications, Boca Raton, New York, pp. 2, 75, 97, 254, 311.

[16] Tadeusiewicz R (1993) Neural Networks. AOW, Warsaw, pp. 8, 19, 28, 49, 55, 56-57,59-61 [in Polish],

[17] Tadeusiewicz R, Lula P (2007) Neural Networks. StatSoft Poland, Kraków, pp. 8-20,35 [in Polish].

[18] Tadeusiewicz R, Gąciarz T, Borowik B, Leper B (2007) Discovering the Properties of Neural Networks Using C# Programs. PAU, Kraków, pp. 55, 70-72, 91-92,101 [in Polish].

[19] Tadeusiewicz R. 2000. Introduction to neural networks. In: Duch W, Korbicz J, Rutkowski L, Tadeusiewicz R (Eds.) Neural Networks, AOW Exit, Warsaw, p. 15 [in Polish] .

[20] Bishop C M (2005) Neural Networks for Pattern Recognition. Oxford University Press, Cambridge, pp. 78, 80, 82, 116, 122, 141, 165, 233, 263.

[21] Haykin S (2009) Neural Networks and Learning Machines. (3rd ed.), Pearson, Upper Saddle River, pp. 41,43-44,154,197,267.

[22] Cheng B, Titterington D M (1994) Neural networks: A review from a statistical perspective. Statistical Science 9: 2-54.

[23] Boniecki P (2008) Elements of Neural Modeling in Agriculture. University of Life Sciences in Poznań, Poznań, pp. 38, 93-96 [in Polish].

[24] Osowski S (1996) Algorithmic Approach to Neural Networks. WNT, Warsaw [in Polish].

[25] Witkowska D (2002) Artificial Neural Networks and Statistical Methods. Selected Financial Issues. C.H. Beck, Warsaw, pp. 10,11 [in Polish].

[26] Rutkowski R (2006) Artificial Intelligence Methods and Techniques. PWN, Warsaw, pp. 179-180,220,222-223 [in Polish].

[27] Larose D T (2006) Discovering Knowledge in Data. PWN, Warsaw, pp. 111-118,132,144 [in Polish].

[28] Rumelhart D E, Hinton G E, Williams R J (1986) Learning representations by back-propagating errors. Nature 323: 533-536.

[29] Grzesiak W (2004) Prediction of dairy cow milk yield based on selected regression models and artificial neural networks. Post-doctoral thesis. Agricultural University of Szczecin, Szczecin, pp. 37, 49-70 [in Polish].

[30] Koronacki J, Ćwik J (2005) Statistical Learning Systems. WNT, Warsaw, pp. 59, 122-123 [in Polish].

[31] Breiman L, Friedman J, Olshen L, Stone C (1984) Classification and Regression Trees, Chapman and Hall/CRC Press, Boca Raton

[32] Steinberg D (2009) Classification and Regression Trees. In: Wu X., Kumar V. (Eds.) The Top Ten Algorithms in Data Mining. Chapman and Hall/CRC Press, Boca Raton, London, New York, pp. 179-202.

[33] Breiman L (1996) Technical note: Some properties of splitting criteria. Machine Learning 24: 41-47.

[34] Dorynek Z (2005) Reproduction in cattle. In: Litwińczuk Z, Szulc T (Eds.) Breeding and Utilization of Cattle. PWRiL, Warsaw, p. 198 [in Polish].

[35] Grzesiak W, Zaborski D, Sablik P, Żukiewicz A, Dybus A, Szatkowska I (2010) Detection of cows with insemination problems using selected classification models. Computers and Electronics in Agriculture 74: 265-273.

[36] Grzesiak W, Zaborski D, Sablik P, Pilarczyk R (2011) Detection of difficult conceptions in dairy cows using selected data mining methods. Animal Science Papers and Reports 29: 293-302.

[37] Zaborski D, Grzesiak W (2011) Detection of heifers with dystocia using artificial neural networks with regard to $ER\alpha$-BglII, $ER\alpha$-SnaBI and $CYP19$-PvuII genotypes. Acta Scientiarum Polonorum s. Zootechnica 10: 105-116.

[38] Zaborski D, Grzesiak W, Szatkowska I, Dybus A, Muszyńska M, Jędrzejczak M (2009) Factors affecting dystocia in cattle. Reproduction in Domestic Animals 44: 540- 551.

[39] Mee J F, Berry D P, Cromie A R (2009) Risk factors for calving assistance and dystocia in pasture-based Holstein–Friesian heifers and cows in Ireland. The Veterinary Journal 187: 189-194.

[40] Johanson J M, Berger P J, Tsuruta S, Misztal I (2011) A Bayesian threshold-linear model evaluation of perinatal mortality, dystocia, birth weight, and gestation length in a Holstein herd. Journal of Dairy Science 94: 450–460.

[41] Meijering A (1984) Dystocia and stillbirth in cattle – a review of causes, relations and implications. Livestock Production Science 11: 143-177.

[42] Zaborski D (2010) Dystocia detection in cows using neural classifier. Doctoral thesis. West Pomeranian University of Technology, Szczecin, pp. 5-21 [in Polish].

[43] Zaborski D, Grzesiak W (2011) Detection of difficult calvings in dairy cows using neural classifier. Archiv Tierzucht 54: 477-489.

[44] Park B, Lee D (2006) Prediction of future milk yield with random regression model using test-day records in Holstein cows. Asian- Australian Journal of Animal Science 19: 915-921.

[45] Grzesiak W, Wójcik J, Binerowska B (2003) Prediction of 305-day first lactation milk yield in cows with selected regression models. Archiv Tierzucht 3: 215-226.

[46] Sharma A K, Sharma R K, Kasana H S (2006) Empirical comparisons of feed-forward connectionist and conventional regression models for prediction of first lactation 305-day milk yield in Karan Fries dairy cows. Neural Computing and Applications 15: 359–365.

[47] Grzesiak W (2003) Milk yield prediction in cows with artificial neural network. Prace i Materiały Zootechniczne. Monografie i Rozprawy No. 61: 71-89 [in Polish].

[48] Grzesiak W, Lacroix R, Wójcik J, Błaszczyk P (2003) A comparison of neural network and multiple regression prediction for 305-day lactation yield using partial lactation records. Canadian Journal of Animal Science 83: 307-310.

[49] Grzesiak W, Błaszczyk P, Lacroix R (2006) Methods of predicting milk yield in dairy cows – Predictive capabilities of Wood's lactation curve and artificial neural networks (ANNs). Computers and Electronics in Agriculture 54: 69-83.

[50] Harańczyk G (2010) The ROC curves – evaluation of the classifier quality and searching for the optimum cut-off point. StatSoft Poland, Kraków, pp. 79-89 [in Polish].

[51] Fawcett T (2004) ROC Graphs: Notes and Practical Considerations for Researchers. Technical Report HPL-2003-4. HP Labs, Palo Alto, CA, USA. http://www.hpl.hp.com/techreports/2003/HPL-2003-4.pdf (last accessed 14.04.2012)

[52] Bradley A P (1997) The use of the area under the ROC curve in the evaluation of the machine learning algorithms. Pattern Recognition 30: 1145-1159.

[53] Theil H (1979) World income inequality. Economic Letters 2: 99-102.

[54] Liddle A R (2007) Information criteria for astrophysical model selection. Monthly Notices of the Royal Astronomical Society: Letters 377: L74-L78.

[55] Kuha J (2004) AIC and BIC. Comparisons of assumptions and performance. Sociological Methods and Research 33: 188-229.

Chapter 13

Data Mining Techniques in Pharmacovigilance: Analysis of the Publicly Accessible FDA Adverse Event Reporting System (AERS)

Elisabetta Poluzzi, Emanuel Raschi, Carlo Piccinni and Fabrizio De Ponti

Additional information is available at the end of the chapter

1. Introduction

1.1. Data mining in a clinical pharmacology perspective

Drug use in medicine is based on a balance between expected benefits (already investigated before marketing authorization) and possible risks (i.e., adverse effects), which become fully apparent only as time goes by after marketing authorization. Clinical pharmacology deals with the risk/benefit assessment of medicines as therapeutic tools. This can be done at two levels: the individual level, which deals with appropriate drug prescription to a given patient in everyday clinical care and the population level, which takes advantage of epidemiological tools and strategies to obtain answers from previous experience. The two levels are intertwined and cover complementary functions.

Data mining has gained an important role during all stages of drug development, from drug discovery to post-marketing surveillance. Whereas drug discovery is probably the first step in drug development that resorts to data mining to exploit large chemical and biological databases to identify molecules of medical interest, in this chapter data mining will be considered within the context of long-term drug safety surveillance after marketing authorisation.

A pharmacological background is essential before considering data mining as a tool to answer questions related to the risk/benefit assessment of drugs. As a first step, it must be verified whether or not the available sources of data (e.g. spontaneous reporting systems, claim databases, electronic medical records, see below) are the most appropriate to address the research question. In other words, a prior hypothesis is required and one should consider which tool is the best option for the specific aim. In addition, the actual impact in clinical practice of any research question depends on the communication and dissemination strategies and relevant indicators to evaluate this impact should be developed as well.

The use of data mining techniques in clinical pharmacology can be broadly grouped into two main areas, each with specific aims:

1. **identification of new effects of drugs** (mostly adverse reactions, but sometimes also new therapeutic effects, and effects in special populations);
2. **appropriateness in drug use** (e.g., frequency of use in patients with contraindications, concomitant prescriptions of drugs known for the risk of clinically relevant interactions).

Both aims can be addressed using each of the three conventional sources of data listed below, although the inherent purpose for which they are created should be kept in mind when interpreting results: any secondary analysis of data collected for other purposes carries intrinsic biases.

*   **Spontaneous reporting systems** (SRS) are mostly addressed to identify adverse reactions. Virtually anywhere in the world, notification of adverse drug events is mandatory for health professionals, but also other subjects can report events to the relevant regulatory Authorities. Main Drug Agencies routinely use algorithms of data-mining to process data periodically and to find possible unknown drug-effect associations. These algorithms identify drug-reaction pairs occurring with a significant disproportion in comparison with all other pairs. Clinical pharmacology knowledge is then requested to interpret those signals and to decide if further examination is needed (either within the same source of data or by other type of data) or specific bias affects the validity of the signal. More detailed description on this specific strategy will be provided in the next paragraphs. This source of data is currently the most frequently approached with data mining in pharmacovigilance [1], because of its usefulness and the ready availability of information. In some limited cases, also aim 2 above can be addressed by this source: the detailed analysis of patient related risk factors (demographic characteristics, concomitant disorders or medications) can show *foci* of lack of appropriateness in the use of specific drugs included in adverse event reports. No inference on the incidence of the adverse event among patients exposed to a specific drug or with risk factors can be performed.
*   **Electronic medical records** (namely, patient registries) are mainly collected with the aim to assist physicians in daily appropriate prescription. For each subject, these registries usually include information on socio-demographic characteristics, diagnoses, risk factors, treatments and outcomes. Primary care is the most frequent setting for the development of this kind of registry and many authoritative examples exist: GPRD (General Practice Research Database), HEALTH SEARCH, THIN (The Health Improvement Network), IPCI (Interdisciplinary Processing of Clinical Information). Hospital examples are also important as they clearly cover complementary therapeutic areas. The high quantity of information and the high quality of data included in these

tools makes them valuable sources for data mining aimed to address clinical pharmacology questions, both in terms of new effects of drugs (especially on primary endpoints, to confirm premarketing evidence) and of assessment of appropriate drug use (closer to the main purpose of the registries).

- **Claim databases** originate for administrative purposes: for instance, in many European countries, health care costs are provided by the National Health Service to Local Health Authorities on the basis of the costs of the medical interventions provided to citizens. Claim databases include all data useful to this purpose (e.g., diagnoses of hospital admissions, reimbursed prescriptions of drugs, diagnostic procedures in ambulatory care) and, as a secondary aim, they represent an important source for epidemiological questions. These data can be equally useful for both aims (1 and 2 above), provided that their intrinsic limitations are duly acknowledged, in particular it should be recognized that information on outcomes are not strictly related to drug use (namely, adverse drug reactions) and patho-physiological plausibility supporting drug-reaction associations should be more stringently verified.

Among assessments of appropriate drug use, there is growing interest in the study of drug-drug interactions, which are usually dealt with by analyzing claim databases searching for specific drug-drug pairs known to interact with clinically relevant consequences. The final aim of this strategy is to compare the frequency of such drug-drug pairs in different settings, or in different periods of time for the same setting, to quantify the risk at population level and the impact of specific educational interventions. Also SRSs can be mined for drug-drug interactions, but in this case the aim is usually quite different: specifically assessing the actual contribution of drug-drug interaction in the occurrence of defined ADRs [2,3]. Virtually, this last step (possible association between specific drug-drug interaction and adverse events) should be performed first in the drug evaluation process; once the risk of a given drug-drug interaction is documented and the percentage of patients developing the ADR is quantified (by using causal association methodologies), the risk at the population level can be evaluated for clinical and regulatory purposes.

After identification of the most appropriate source of data to address the research question, the appropriate methodology to approach data analysis should be identified. From data cleaning (a mere data managing step, see below) to statistical methodologies (e.g., multiple regression analysis), all steps of data management are considered parts of data mining techniques. Usually, each source of data is analyzed by the own natural data mining approach (e.g., disproportion calculation for SRSs, multiple regression analysis for electronic medical records), but emergent strategies to better exploit the more accessible sources are now appearing in the biomedical literature (e.g., self-controlled time series [4]). In fact, data mining could virtually provide as many associations as possible between drug and effect, but, without a consensus among experts on the methodological steps and a confirmation of patho-physiological pathways, the association can easily conduct to interpretation errors. For instance, the risk of pancreatitis by antidiabetics is currently a matter of debate and recently Elashoff et al. [5] claimed a 6-fold increase of pancreatitis in subjects exposed to exenatide. This raised criticisms by several authors [6,7]. Elashoff et al., indeed, tried to approach SRSs by a specific strategy for analytical studies (case-control analysis), disregarding the absence of pure control subjects (see below).

Text-mining [8] and information mining [9] are also frequently used in searching possible associations between drugs and adverse events, although this is virtually ignored by regulatory agencies. Especially in this case, the source of data is a key step for a reliable result of the analysis: both free-text search into electronic patient records and text analysis of any document freely published online represent possible sources of data for these strategies. Because of the huge variety of information processed by this approach, a more strict plausibility of the associations found between drug and effect should be claimed, because of, for instance, the high risk of inverse causality.

2. Definition and objectives of data mining in pharmacovigilance

Before addressing methodological issues, we provide an overview on the potential of data mining in the field of pharmacovigilance.

2.1. The need for pharmacovigilance

Pharmacovigilance (PhV) has been defined by the World Health Organization (WHO) as "the science and activities relating to the detection, assessment, understanding and prevention of adverse effects or any other possible drug-related problems" [10]. In the past, it was regarded as being synonymous with post-marketing surveillance for adverse drug reactions. However, the concept of surveillance in pharmacovigilance and pharmacoepidemiology has evolved from the concept of surveillance in epidemiology. Surveillance and monitoring are different - surveillance involves populations, while monitoring involves individuals. Surveillance reflects real-world pharmacovigilance processes and has been recently defined "a form of non-interventional public health research, consisting of a set of processes for the continued systematic collection, compilation, interrogation, analysis, and interpretation of data on benefits and harms (including relevant spontaneous reports, electronic medical records, and experimental data)" [11].

The specific aims of pharmacovigilance are:

- the identification of previously unrecognized Adverse Drug Reactions (ADRs, novel by virtue of nature, frequency and/or severity);
- the identification of subgroups of patients at particular risk of adverse reactions;
- the continued surveillance of a product throughout the duration of its use, to ensure that the balance of its benefits and harms are and remain acceptable;
- the description of the comparative adverse reactions profile of products within the same therapeutic class;
- the detection of inappropriate prescription and administration;
- the further elucidation of a product's pharmacological and toxicological properties and the mechanism(s) by which it produces adverse effects;

- the detection of clinically important drug–drug, drug–herb/herbal medicine, drug–food, and drug–device interactions;
- the communication of appropriate information to health-care professionals;
- the confirmation or refutation of false-positive signals that arise, whether in the professional or lay media, or from spontaneous reports (see below for definition of a "signal") [12].

Therefore, PhV is becoming a holistic discipline embracing overall risk/benefit assessment, which necessarily takes place both at the individual patient level and at the population level (epidemiological perspective). It is now recognized as a key proactive approach for appropriate drug prescription and rational use of medicines, as it provides the tools to prevent, detect, monitor and counteract adverse drug reactions, by perfectly complementing the branch of pharmaco-epidemiology. A complete taxonomy of terminologies and definitions used in PhV (including medication errors) is beyond the aim of this chapter, as it has been extensively addressed by a number of Authors [10,13]. Indeed, the European Medicines Agency (EMA) has recently adopted the new **pharmacovigilance legislation (Regulation (EU) No 1235/2010** and **Directive 2010/84/EU**), approved by the European Parliament and European Council in December 2010 [14,15]. This legislation is the biggest change to the regulation of human medicines in the European Union (EU) since 1995 and is now in force as of July 2012. Great emphasis is explicitly mentioned on the role of PhV to *"promote and protect public health by reducing burden of ADRs and optimizing the use of medicines"*.

2.2. Pharmacovigilance tools: An overview

All the objective of PhV can be achieved through different types of studies, which are intended to be either "hypothesis-generating" or "hypothesis-testing" or to share these aims. The former are represented by spontaneous reporting and prescription event monitoring with the aim of identifying unexpected ADRs, whereas the latter are represented by case-control or cohort studies, which aim to prove (by risk quantification) whether any previous suspicious that has been raised is justified. Although rules and regulations governing the spontaneous reporting of ADRs vary among Countries, there are some basic commonalities: 1) with the exception of pharmaceutical companies that are legally "forced" to report ADRs to health authorities, it is an independent voluntary notification of the reporter (e.g., healthcare professional, patient); 2) it is sufficient that a suspicion arises (no certainty is required); 3) there must be an identifiable drug, patient, and event; 4) the total number of exposed to the drug and the total number that experiences/did not experience an event are unknown. In other words, the exact numerator and denominator, a pre-requisite for quantifying risk, are unavailable.

Although spontaneous reports are placed at the bottom of the hierarchy of the evidence, they represent a timely source in the early evaluation of safety issues associated with specific drugs, in particular for new compounds. Clinical trials are considered as the best source of evidence, although they suffer of several methodological issues (e.g., limited sample size, reduced follow-up, evaluation of surrogate markers) that undermine their fully external validity. By contrast, the analysis of spontaneous reports reflects the real-world scenario, in which patients experienced the primary outcome in a complex pharmacological context. This underlines the importance of a high-quality analysis according to standard procedure and strengthens the need for transparency among different data miners (i.e. independent Research Organization, Universities, Regulators, Manufacturers) to provide the best outcome for patients. It is only the convergence of proofs which allows final conclusions and decisions in pharmacovigilance. Thus, the notion of 'levels of evidence', widely used for evaluating drug efficacy, cannot be actually applied in the field of ADRs; all methods are of interest in the evaluation of ADRs [16].

Spontaneous reports are collected by drug companies and at regional, national and international level through different databases. The Eudravigilance database (European Union Drug Regulating Authorities Pharmacovigilance) is held by the European Medicines Agency and collects/exchanges electronically ADRs coming from national regulatory authorities, marketing authorization holders and sponsors of interventional clinical trials and non-interventional studies in Europe. The Uppsala Monitoring Centre in Sweden is responsible for the worldwide gathering of all serious ADRs received by regulatory authorities and companies. The FDA Adverse Event Reporting System (FDA_AERS) collects ADRs from the US as well as rare and severe events from Europe. Unfortunately, only a minority of spontaneous reporting systems offers a public access to external researchers/consumers. These include the FDA_AERS and the Canada Vigilance Adverse Reaction Online Database [17]. At national level, several regional centers support the national Agency by publicly posting a list of potential signals. For instance, the Netherlands Pharmacovigilance Centre Lareb provides a quarterly newsletter service including new emerging signals [18].

Although SRSs have been criticized due to inherent pitfalls, a recent survey found that the Population-based reporting ratio (PBRR, defined as the total number of ADR reports collected in a safety database per year per million inhabitants) revealed an increased reporting activity at national level (half of the European Countries exceed the standard threshold of 300 for PBRR, indicating a sufficient quality for signal detection), with strong correlation with the relative increase at the international level [19].

While the analysis of multiple databases has the advantage to cover a very large population and heterogeneous patterns of reporting for ADRs, it is important to note that data cannot be simply aggregated/pooled to perform DMAs for the following reasons:

- differences exists among databases, especially in terms of accessibility, drug and adverse event coding.
- overlap are likely to exist among national and international archives, especially for rare and serious ADRs. The precise extent of overlap has not been assessed yet and may vary depending on the ADR under investigation.

Therefore, combination of different databases has been proposed to achieve the highest statistical power in signal detection [20].

2.3. The term "signal" in pharmacovigilance: An evolving concept

The major aim of PhV is signal detection (i.e., the identification of potential drug-event association that may be novel by virtue of their nature, severity and/or frequency). In the literature, the term signal has been subject to debate and discussion. Some authors attempted to provide a comprehensive overview of definitions that have been proposed and implemented over the years. The WHO has defined 'signal' as "Reported information on a possible causal relationship between an adverse event and a drug, the relationship being unknown or incompletely documented." The definition is not self-contained, being followed by a qualifier that stipulates that "usually more than one case is required" [10]. This qualifier is important, because it implies that the information content of the signal must sufficiently reduce uncertainty to justify some action, and therefore partially mitigates the former limitation. This should be part of the definition. Meyboom et al. [21] stated that "*A signal in pharmacovigilance is more than just a statistical association. It consists of a hypothesis together with data and arguments, arguments in favor and against the hypothesis. These relate to numbers of cases, statistics, clinical medicine, pharmacology (kinetics, actions, previous knowledge) and epidemiology, and may also refer to findings with an experimental character.*" It is important to note that a single report or a few reports can sometimes constitute a signal of suspected causality. This is the case of well documented, high-quality reports with positive re-challenge. These so-called anecdotes provide a definitive ('between-the-eyes') drug-related reactions, which do not necessarily need further formal verification [22,23]. In PhV, anecdotes have been also technically defined as "Designated Medical Event" (DME), which is a rare but serious reactions with high drug-attributable risk (i.e., a significant proportion of the occurrences of these events are drug induced) [24]. Stevens-Johnson Syndrome/Toxic Epidermal Necrolysis (SJS/TEN) and Torsade de Pointes (TdP) are typical example of DMEs, although a formal and universally accepted list of DMEs does not exist. The most balanced way to analyze DMEs is to use disproportionality in conjunction with a case-by-case evaluation, in order to capture all possible information from spontaneous reports [25]. However, in most of the cases, information that arises from one or multiple sources (including observations and experiments) should be taken into account for causality assessment [26]. Indeed, after a suspicion has been raised (signal generation), it needs to be corroborated by the accumulation of additional data (signal strengthening). The final step involves the confirmation and quantification of the relation between drug and ADR by epidemiological methods (signal quantification). Although in every step of the process both individual case reports and analytical techniques are involved, the relative importance of these approaches differs per step [26]. Once a signal is verified, a number of regulatory actions may be considered, depending on the level of priority assigned to the signal. This prioritization process is mainly based on the assessment of public health impact, the severity of the adverse event and the strength of disproportionality. Regulatory measures may range from close monitoring of the signal over time (without practical interventions, the so-called watchful waiting) to drug withdrawal from the market due to a negative risk/benefit profile.

2.4. The need for Data Mining Algorithms (DMAs)

Currently, the "art" of signal detection can be performed on a case-by-case basis (traditional approach, especially for DMEs) or through automated procedures to support the clinical evaluation of spontaneous reports, the so-called "data mining approach". In general terms, data mining can be considered an activity related to "knowledge discovery in databases", i.e., the process of extracting information form a large database [27]. In this context, data mining is refereed to as the computer-assisted procedures, starting from processing of dataset by data "cleaning" and culminating into the application of statistical techniques, often known as data mining algorithms (DMAs). DMAs are currently and routinely used by pharmacovigilance experts for quantitative signal detection [28]. The purposes of quantitative signal detection are many-fold and may vary depending on the local habit of PhV experts. For instance, DMAs can be used as an aid to the traditional case-by-case assessment; as a screening tool to periodically generate a list of signals requiring in depth investigation (i.e., to prioritize signals); on *ad hoc* basis to detect complex data dependencies, which are difficult to be manually detected (e.g., drug-drug interactions or drug-related syndromes) [29].

2.5. The use of DMAs

Although DMAs are relatively new as compared to clinical trials and epidemiological studies, the first published attempt to assess the extent of reporting in drug safety through disproportionality, to the best of our knowledge, was by Bruno Stricker [30]. In 1997, the study by Moore et al., [31] introduced the concept of *"case/non case method"* when performing pharmacovigilance analyses. They postulated that this term was a more effective representation than case-control: controls are not actual controls since they are all exposed to at least one drug, and have at least one event (there are no untreated 'healthy' controls). They are simply not cases of the event of interest: they are cases of something else [32].

The accuracy of data mining techniques has been already tested retrospectively to determine if already known safety issues would have been detected 'earlier' [33]. However, it is generally difficult to determine when a known safety concern was first detected. Moreover, the surrogate endpoint that have been used (e.g., the date of implementation of new labeling) is unlikely to truly represent the time of first detection of a new safety signal, thus affecting the results in favor of DMAs. Overall, DMAs often provided a high level of accuracy in terms of timely prediction of risk and, therefore their use have been encouraged as an early source of information on drug safety, particularly new drugs, thus guiding the proper planning of subsequent observational studies [34].

Although the rationale and the methodology of the various approaches differ, all DMAs query databases for disproportionality and express the extent to which the reported ADR is associated with the suspected drug compared with all other drugs (or a subgroup of drugs) in the database. The reporting of ADRs related to other drugs in the database is used as a *proxy* for the background occurrence of ADRs. In other words, they assess whether statistically significant differences in the reporting exist among drugs (the so-called "unexpectedness") and provide an answer to the question: "does the number of observed cases exceed the number of expected cases?". It is important to underline that, although these approaches are known as "quantitative" signal detection methodologies, no risk quantification can be assessed. Moreover, the presence of a statistically significant result does not necessarily imply an actual causal relationship between the ADR and the drug, nor does the absence of a statistically significant result necessarily disprove the possible relationship. As a matter of fact, the term "signal of disproportionate reporting" has been suggested by Hauben & Aronson [26] to emphasize the uncertainty in causality assessment.

DMAs can be classified in frequentist and Bayesian approach. Among the former, the Reporting Odds Ratio (ROR) is applied by the Netherlands Pharmacovigilance Centre Lareb, whereas the Proportional Reporting Ratio (PRR) was first used by Evans et al. [35]. Bayesian methods such as Multi-item Gamma Poisson Shrinker (MGPS) [36] and Bayesian Confidence Propagation Neural network (BCPN) [37] are based on Bayes' law to estimate the probability (posterior probability) that the suspected event occurs given the use of suspect drug.

Frequentist or classical methods are particularly appealing and therefore widely used due to the fact that they are relatively easy to understand, interpret and compute as they are based on the same principles of calculation using the 2x2 table (see **Table 1** with **Figure 1**).

	Drug of interest	All other drugs in the database	Total
Adverse drug reaction of interest	A	B	A+B
All other adverse drug reaction	C	D	C+D
Total	A+C	B+D	A+B+C+D

A= number of reports containing both the suspect drug and the suspect adverse drug reaction
B= number of reports containing the suspect adverse drug reaction with other medications (except the drug of interest)
C= number of reports containing the suspect drug with other adverse drug reactions (except the event of interest)
D= number of reports containing other medications and other adverse drug reactions

Table 1. Formal 2x2 contingency table

The PRR involves the calculation of the rate of reporting of one specific event among all events for a given drug, the comparator being this reporting rate for all drugs present in the database (including the drug of interest). Usually, a disproportion is considered on the basis of three pieces of information: PRR≥2, $\chi 2≥4$ and at least 3 cases [35]. The ROR is the ratio of the odds of reporting of one specific event versus all other events for a given drug compared to this reporting odds for all other drugs present in the database. A signal is considered when the lower limit of the 95% confidence interval (CI) of the ROR is greater than one. Basically, the higher the value, the stronger the disproportion appears to be. In both these methods, for a given drug, the particular risk of an event being reported versus other events is compared to a reference risk: that observed for all drugs in the database for PRR and for all other drugs for ROR. This reference risk is thought to reflect the baseline risk of the reporting of an event in a subject taking a drug, provided that there is no specific association between the drug and the event of interest. The question arises as to whether this reference risk always provides an accurate estimate of the baseline risk of an event for a patient receiving any drug, since it is obtained by considering a reference group of drugs that can include drugs known to be at risk for a particular event. This aspect will be specifically addressed in the following section of the chapter. Rothman et al., [38] proposed to treat spontaneous reporting system as a data source for a case-control study, thus excluding from the control series those events that may be related to drug exposure; therefore, the ROR may theoretically offer an advantage over PRR by estimating the relative risk. However, this apparent superiority has been called into question, because both disproportionality measures do not allow risk quantification, but only offer a rough indication of the strength of the signal [39].

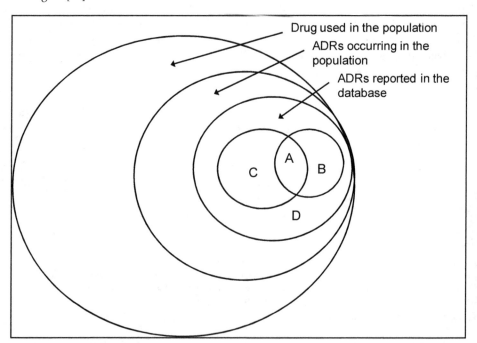

Figure 1. Relationships among patients exposed to drugs, experiencing ADRs and actual reporting (used to calculate disproportionality). Areas of circles do not necessarily reflect the precise proportion and relationships existing among circles.

As compared to the view of "frequency probability", Bayesian methods interpret the concept of probability as the degree to which a person believes a proposition. Bayesian inference starts with a pre-existing subjective personal assessment of the unknown parameter and the probability distribution (called prior distribution). They are based on the Bayes' law, assuming that there are two events of interest (D and E), which are not independent. From the basic theory of probability, it is known that the conditional probability of E given that D has occurred is represented as $P(E/D)=P(E,D)/P(D)$, where $P(D)$=probability of a suspected drug being reported in a case report;

P(E)= probability of a suspected event being reported in a case report;

P(E,D)= probability that suspected drug and event being simultaneously reported in a case report;

P(E/D)= probability that suspected event being reported given the suspected drug being reported;

Assuming that the probability that D and E simultaneously occur is the same as the probability that D and E occur and rearranging the formula, we have $P(E/D)=P(E,D)/P(D)=P(E)P(D/E)/P(D)$, which is Bayes' law.

The signal metric or signal score in BCPNN is the information component (IC) = $\log_2$ $P(E,D)/P(E)P(D)$. If drug and event are statistically independent, the ratio of the joint probability of drug and event [P(E,D)] to the product of the individual probabilities [P(E)P(D)] will equal 1 and the IC will equal zero. The use of the logarithm of the ratio is derived from information theory. The elementary properties of logarithms make them suitable for quantifying information. The IC can be conceptualized as the additional information obtained on the probability of the event (or the additional uncertainty eliminated) by specifying a drug. Separate prior probabilities are constructed to represent the possible unconditional probabilities of drug [P(D)], event [P(E)] and the joint probability of drug and event [P(E,D)]. Uninformed priors (meaning all probabilities are weighed equally in the absence of data) are used for the unconditional probabilities.

The parameters of the joint probability distribution are then selected to make the limit of the IC approach zero for very low cell counts. As data accumulate, the influence of these priors will diminish more for cells with high counts. This means that, for drugs or events for which the counts are low, the signal score is shrunk more toward the prior probabilities based on statistical independence. A signal usually requires that the lower 95% CI of the IC exceed zero [40]. A comprehensive review of the principles subtending calculation of Bayesian methods is beyond the aim of this chapter and the reader is referred to Hauben & Zhou [41] for sophisticated, yet intuitive discussion of this issue.

Although the discussion on performance, accuracy and reliability of different DMAs is fascinating, actually, there is no recognized *gold standard* methodology. Therefore, several studies have been conducted to examine and compare the performance of different DMAs, in terms of sensitivity, specificity, accuracy and early identification of safety issues. A number of investigations explored whether differences exist between frequentist and bayesian approaches and found that PRR is more sensitive than MGPS, although the estimation from the MGPS is believed to be more robust when the number of reports is small [42-45]. While, to the best of our knowledge, no studies has been conducted to compare the MGPS and BCPN, van Puijenbroek et al., [46] first attempted to compare four DMAs ROR, PRR, Yule's Q and $\chi2$ with IC. Since the IC is not the *gold standard*, these comparisons may have affected the findings, leading to an overestimation of the sensitivity. Notably, a high level of concordance was found, especially when the number of reports exceeds four. Kubota et al., [47] using a Japanese SRS, analyzed 38,731 drug-event combinations (DECs) and found a highly variable percentage of detected DEC among DMAs, ranging from 6.9% (GPS) to 54.6% (ROR). However, a misclassification bias may have affected the results. It is clear, however, that the volume of signals generated by itself is an inadequate criterion for comparison and that the clinical nature of events and differential timing of signals needs to be considered [48]. In this context, a recent pilot study by Chen et al., [49] performed on the FDA_AERS, showed a better performance of ROR in terms of timing of early signal detection as compared to other DMAs, when tested on ten confirmed DEC. The issue of timely detection is of utmost importance in PhV, because early detection of safety-related problems may trigger signal substantiation and quantification through other pharmacoepidemiological research.

Apart from sensitivity, specificity, positive and negative predictive value, the possibility for correcting for covariates should be taken into account. Due to the nature of data source (mainly focused on drug-related information rather than patient's characteristics), the reporting of specific concomitant drugs may be used as a *proxy* for underlying disease, which may act as confounder. The use of these agents may be therefore considered in the multivariate regression analysis to calculate an adjusted disproportionality [50]. The ROR is a transparent and easily applicable technique, which allows adjustment through logistic regression analysis. An additional advantage of using ROR is the fact that non-selective underreporting of a drug or ADR has no influence on the value of the ROR compared with the population of patients experiencing an ADR [51]. For these reasons, our Research Unit of Clinical and Experimental Pharmacology at the University of Bologna at present uses the ROR with 95%CI to calculate disproportionality (data provided in the following section of the chapter are presented through this DMA). An overview on the most frequently used DMAs is provided in **Table 2** to summarize operative information for the reader.

The arbitrary nature of threshold criteria for signal detection could cause the identification of potential false positive or false negative associations. A recent review of published threshold criteria for defining signals of disproportionate reporting highlighted a considerable variation in defining a significant disproportionality among practitioners of pharmacovigilance data miners. For instance, ROR-1.96 Standard Error>1 may be used instead of 95%CI. The impact of this change is actually unexplored [52]. Indeed, changing the thresholds or selecting DMAs based on sensitivity considerations alone can have major implications: a more stringent criterion increases the sensitivity of the test by lowering the number of false positives, with the risk of missing credible signals. It is necessary to find an optimum balance, not just with regard to the use of statistics (frequentist *vs* Bayesian) but also among thresholds used for signal detection. Without a clinical evaluation of the signals, it is unclear how signal volume relates to signal value – the ability to identify real and clinically important problems earlier than they would be identified using current pharmacovigilance methods. In the wake of this challenging task, data mining methods based on false discovery rates have recently been proposed with promising results [53]. In addition, novel data mining techniques are emerging, such as those based on biclustering paradigm, which is designed to identify drug groups that share a common set of adverse events in SRS [54]. Another emerging issue pertains the identification of drug-drug interaction in a pharmacovigilance database. Very recently, a new three-way disproportionality measure (Omega, based on the total number of reports on two drugs and one ADR together) was developed within the WHO_Vigibase [55,56].

DMA	Computation	Published threshold criteria	Advantage	Limitations	Regulatory Agencies
Bayesian methods					
Multi-item Gamma Poisson Shrinker (MGPS) [36]	$\dfrac{a\,(a+b+c+d)}{(a+c)\,(a+b)}$	$EBGM_{05} > 2$ N>0	Always applicable More specific as compared to frequentist method*	Relatively non-transparent for people non familiar with Bayesian statistics Lower sensitivity	FDA (AERS)
Bayesian Confidence Propagation Neural network (BCPN) [37]	$\log_2 \dfrac{a\,(a+b+c+d)}{(a+c)\,(a+b)}$	IC-2 SD>0	Always applicable More specific as compared to frequentist method* Can be used for pattern recognition in higher dimension	Relatively non-transparent for people non familiar with Bayesian statistics Lower sensitivity	UMC (WHO-Vigibase)
Frequentist methods					
Proportional Reporting Ratio (PRR) [35]	$\dfrac{a/(a+b)}{c/(c+d)}$ $95\%CI=e^{\ln(PRR)\pm1.96}\sqrt{\frac{1}{a}+\frac{1}{b}+\frac{1}{c}+\frac{1}{d}}$	PRR≥2, χ^2≥4, N≥3	Easily applicable Easily interpretable More sensitive as compared to Bayesian method*	Cannot be calculated for all drug-event combinations Lower specificity	EMA (Eudravigilance) Italian Regulatory Agency (AIFA)
Reporting Odds Ratio (ROR) [46]	$\dfrac{a/c}{b/d}$ $95\%CI=e^{\ln(ROR)\pm1.96}\sqrt{\frac{1}{a}+\frac{1}{b}+\frac{1}{c}+\frac{1}{d}}$	95%CI> 1, N≥2	Easily applicable Easily interpretable More sensitive as compared to Bayesian method* Different adjustment for covariates in logistic regression analysis	Odds ratio not calculated if denominator is zero (specific ADRs) Lower specificity	Lareb (Netherlands)

* when commonly cited thresholds are used.

χ^2= chi-squared; N= number of cases; IC= Information Component; CI=Confidence Interval; SD=Standard Deviation; EBGM=Empirical Bayesian Geometric Mean; 05=fifth percentile of the posterior distribution, i.e., there is a 95% probability that the "true" relative reporting ratio exceeds the EBGM05

Table 2. Summary of major DMAs used for signal detection.

2.6. DMAs: Current debate

In the literature, there is debate on the advantage of using the number of reports instead of sales/prescriptions as denominator for signaling approach. We believe that both methods are useful, but should be used according to the research objective. In particular, the use of drug utilization data is of utmost importance to calculate reporting rates for drugs with already known association with the event, thus estimating the lowest incidence (assuming the under-reporting is limited due to the notoriety of the ADR or at least equally distributed within the database).

Recently, the publication of PhV analyses through disproportionality measures has been subject to debate and criticism [57]. Some benefits and strengths of using DMAs are undisputed, since they are quick and inexpensive analyses routinely performed by regulators and researchers for drug safety evaluation [16]. Apart from the hypothesis-generating purpose of signal detection, other important application of this method are (a) validation of a pharmacological hypothesis about the mechanism of occurrence of ADRs [58]; (b) characterization of the safety profile of drugs [59]. Nevertheless, it is important to underline that the identification of potential safety issues does not necessarily imply the need for wider communication to healthcare professional through publication, as it may cause unnecessary alarm without a real safety alert. The number of papers on *case/non case* evaluation are increasing exponentially and calls for minimum requirements before publication in the medical literature. This would ensure dissemination of high quality studies, which offer innovative methodology or provide novel insight into drug safety. The transparency policy recently adopted by the FDA is important to share with pharmacovigilance experts current safety issues requiring close monitoring before publicly disseminating results to consumers. Likewise, disproportionality analyses submitted for publication to relevant journals should address (and optimistically try to circumvent) bias related to selective reporting, in order to provide meaningful comparison among drugs and allow provisional risk stratification.

2.7. DMAs: Caveats

When planning a pharmacovigilance analysis and discussing its results, there are a number of limitations requiring careful consideration in view of the potential clinical implications. These caveats are related both to data source, namely individual reports with relevant spontaneous reporting system, and the adopted DMA [48,60]. Underreporting is one the most important limitation on SRS as it prevents to precisely calculate the real incidence of the event in the population [61]. As a matter of fact, only a small proportion of the ADRs occurring in daily practice is reported.

Substantial deficits in data quality and data distortion occur at two levels in SRS databases: at the level of the individual case records (i.e., quality and completeness of the reported information) and at the level of the overall sample (e.g., the framework of ADRs, which may vary depending on local rules for reporting). The FDA, for example, requires the reporting of events that occur in other countries only if they are serious and unlabeled based on the

Data Mining Techniques in Pharmacovigilance: Analysis of the Publicly Accessible FDA Adverse Event
Reporting System (AERS)

301

US label. Hence a drug for which a serious adverse event has been included in the label earlier will appear to have fewer such events in the FDA AERS database than one for which the event was added later. The geographic distribution of market penetration of a new drug may also influence the apparent safety profile based on the SRS. For example, a drug whose use is predominantly in the U.S. may appear to have a very different profile than a drug whose use is predominantly in Europe, with the apparent difference potentially being due to differences in reporting expectations and behavior rather than real differences in the effects of the drugs. At present, there are also several limitations regarding the use of public-release version of the FDA_AERS. Apart from the 6-month lag time in data release through the FDA website, the most significant caveats concern the presence of duplicate reports and missing data as well as the lack of standardization in recording drug names of active substances. All these technical issues must be considered when exploring the FDA_AERS and will be specifically discussed in the following section of the chapter.

Another key danger in over-reliance on data mining may be described as "seduction bias" in which an extensive mathematical veneer of certain algorithms may seduce the safety reviewer/data miner into believing that the enormous deficiencies and distortions in the data have been neutralized [48]. Another aspect is the so called "self-deception bias", which can occur when a data miner with a strong incentive to believe in a particular outcome may consciously or subconsciously try to avoid results that contradict pre-existing expectations. In other words, the data miner may apply nonspecific case definitions of uncertain clinical relevance and/or sequential mining with different subsets of the database and/or candidate data mining parameters, until the "desired" output is achieved [48].

Concerning the overall quality of reports, there is still room for improvement due to the vast amount of missing data, especially on clinically relevant information regarding the time-to-onset of the reaction, the dechallenge/rechallenge information (an important component of the causality assessment). There should also be a commitment to improving the quality of the data, which is ultimately the rate limiting step. A recent study address some challenges and limitations of current pharmacovigilance processes in terms of data completeness and resorted to use the case of flupirtine to exemplify the need for refined ADR reporting [62].

The pattern of reporting is also widely influenced by external factors, which may affect the reliability of detected signal. Among the most important confounders, the product age (i.e., the time on the market of the compound) and stimulated reporting should be acknowledged. It is widely accepted that when a drug first receives marketing authorization, there is generally a substantial increase in the spontaneous reporting of ADRs (especially during the first two years on the market), which then plateaus and eventually declines. This epidemiological phenomenon is called "Weber effect" and was repeatedly shown for non-steroideal antinflammatory drugs [63-65]. This aspect may be related to the increased attention of clinicians towards a novel drug and may intuitively imply that the number of new signals detected reaches a peak over time with a subsequent decline. However, a new therapeutic indication or dose regimen may result in a new reporting pattern, thus one should be aware of the lifecycle status of the drug under investigation as well as significant change in its use. In addition, media attention and publicity resulting from advertising or regulatory actions (e.g., dear doctor letter or warnings against drug-related safety issues) may result in increased reporting and can generate a higher-than-expected reporting ratio, a phenomenon known as "notoriety bias" [66,67]. Notoriety bias can also affect drugs other than those directly involved in alerts, thus causing a sort of "ripple effect" [7,68]. Routine incorporation of time-trend axis should be therefore recommended when planning pharmacovigilance analysis to gain insight into the temporal appearance of the signal, especially when regulatory interventions may have affected the life cycle of drug. Even if all the studied drugs are similarly affected by notoriety at a given time, false positive signals could be generated if this notoriety effect on reporting is differentially diluted among prior reports for older drugs compared with more recently marketed drugs. This differential effect related to the time on the market was recently demonstrated by Pariente et al., [69] for five "old" antidepressants *versus* escitalopram. Finally, physicians' prescribing are affected by a number of factors, including the severity of the disease, which create the potential for confounded drug-effect associations, the so-called "channeling bias" [70].

Concerning DMAs, it should be acknowledged that disproportionality methods do not estimate reporting rates and cannot provide incidence (see **Figure 1**). No drug usage is involved in the calculation. Also while reporting rates can increase for all DEC, measures of disproportionality are interdependent: an increase in a measure of disproportionality for one combination causes a decrease for other related combinations. A similar scenario occurs when two drugs have very different reporting patterns. If one has many more reports in general than the other, but they have similar rates for a particular term, the drug with the lower overall reporting will have a disproportionality detected more easily [29].

2.8. DMAs: Current perspective in signal refinement

The issue of selecting *a priori* a reference group (among drugs or events) as control to calculate disproportionality is a matter of debate in the literature, because it can significantly impact the results and their clinical implication [5,71,72]. Indeed, this aspect represents a commendable effort towards the application and implementation of novel data mining tools for clinical application. Under certain circumstances, this approach may be of benefit to provide the clinical perspective of PhV, with the attempt to move beyond *mere* signal detection. For instance, a recent study on SJS/TEN underlined several drugs with no association, which may be considered as alternative treatment options [73]. Basically, there are four scenarios deserving mention: (a) the calculation of an intraclass ROR, (b) the selection of specific control drugs/events, (c) the removal of already known drug-event associations and (d) the removal of non serious ADRs such as nausea, vomiting, abdominal pain, which are highly likely to be reported and may mask serious ADRs.

a.   The calculation of an intraclass ROR is based on the only analysis of reports recording drugs of interest instead of the entire database (e.g., calculate the ROR of pancreatitis for the antidiabetic drug exenatide by using ADRs reported with all antidiabetic agents) [7]. This would allow to assess the disproportionate reporting of a given compounds in comparison with other agents within the same therapeutic class, and may therefore be viewed as a secondary sensitivity analysis to provide provisional risk stratification. Indeed, one of the most important aspect and a compelling need for a clinician is to identify safer molecules within therapeutic classes. Moreover, this strategy helps to mitigate the so-called "confounding by indication bias" [74], by limiting the analysis to a population of patients that presumably share at least a set of common risk factors and diseases. Nonetheless, the so-called "channeling bias" (i.e., the possibility that drugs may be differently prescribed in relation to the severity of disease) still remains.

b. The selection of specific control group of events or drugs is currently perceived as an attractive strategy for signal detection, and consists in the identification and exclusion of a cluster of events with no proved relation with the drug of interest. From one side, this approach may be of benefit to detect the hidden signals, which may escape from identification when the standard approach including all events is employed [71]. The most important limitations are related to the fact that the identification of control events/drugs is based on the expert opinion and therefore cannot be automatically implemented for all ADRs. Most remarkably, the risk is to select controls on the basis of the lack of evidence on possible association, which does not necessarily mean evidence of no association.

c. A different approach for selecting group is based on the removal of already known drug-event association, which are usually over-reported in a pharmacovigilance database and may therefore mask possible novel associations. This bias is defined in the literature as the "competition bias" [72]. Indeed, if the event is significantly associated with other drugs, this will modify the denominator by increasing the background reporting rate, thereby possibly decreasing the sensitivity of the signal detection process. However, this *ad hoc* strategy precludes its automated application signal detection. Notably, the relevance of competition bias may depend on the nature and severity of the ADR, as it may have significant impact for clinically serious and relatively common adverse events.

d. Another approach is based on the so-called "masking" or "cloaking" effect, which has been largely recognized, but only recently has its impact been explored in the FDA_AERS [75]. One simple application could be to exclude from the analysis all non serious ADRs, which are often submitted by relevant manufacturers. Notably, the FDA_AERS database offers the possibility to identify these reports, which are categorized as: 15-day reports, serious periodic reports, or non serious periodic reports for new molecular entity within the first 3 years following FDA approval.

While one is particularly stimulated to publish and disseminate results on positive associations (i.e., statistically significant disproportionality), it is very important to report also negative findings, i.e., the lack of drug-event association, which may be of benefit especially for prescribers [73,76].

In the light of the inherent limitations affecting pharmacovigilance analyses, the most important step in data mining approach is related to the *a priori* management of database before the application of DMAs (i.e., the definition and processing of the initial raw dataset). Therefore, the following section will describe key issues before applying statistical analysis to spontaneous reports and explore how they can impact results. We will provide insight into the FDA_AERS and address major methodological issues encountered when approaching data mining. This choice is mainly based on the fact that the FDA_AERS is a worldwide publicly available pharmacovigilance archive and, therefore, we believe that transparency may improve accuracy, allow comparison of results among researchers and foster implementation. By virtue of its large population coverage and free availability, the FDA_AERS is emerging as a cornerstone for signal detection in PhV and is progressively being exploited by US and European researchers [25,73,77,78]. In addition, a number of commercial tools, namely query engines are now available. For instance, the FDAble [79] and OpenVigil [80], which is a free search query available through the University of Kiel. Another public source on drug-induced adverse reactions is represented by the DrugCite [81], which allows a number of tools, such as mobile applications to describe the primary safety profile of drugs or calculator to assess the probability of an adverse event being associated with a drug. It also allows searching the FDA_AERS database by providing easily interpretable graphics for the adverse events reported over time, stratified by relevant category, ages and gender, thus offering a quick check for clinicians on safety information. This would be of benefit for the entire drug safety assessment.

3. Methodological issues: the need for a pre-specified dataset

According to the Medwatch Program [82] founded in 1993, the US Food and Drug Administration (FDA) collects spontaneous reports on adverse reactions of drug, biologic, medical device, dietary supplement or cosmetic. In addition to reports coming from products' manufacturer, as required by regulation, FDA receives adverse event reports directly from healthcare professionals (such as physicians, pharmacists, nurses and others) and consumers (such as patients, family members, lawyers and others). Healthcare professionals and consumers may also report these events to the products' manufacturers, which are required to send the report to FDA as specified by regulations.

Raw data from the MedWatch system, together with ADR reports from manufacturers, are part of a public computerized information database called AERS (Adverse Event Reporting System) [83].

The FDA_AERS database contains over 4 million reports of adverse events of worldwide human drugs and biological products (concerning about 3 million of patients) and reflects data from 1997 to the present.

In this section we describe the anatomy of the FDA_AERS database and analytically illustrate dictionaries and coding systems used by this database. Furthermore, we describe our method to perform a systematic mapping of information originally not-codified. Subsequently, we discuss two important limitations that affect this dataset, duplicates and missing data, and we suggest a strategy for their detection and handling.

3.1. Anatomy of the FDA_AERS database

FDA_AERS is a relational databases structured in compliance with the international safety reporting guidance (ICH E2B) [84] issued by the International Conference on Harmonization. FDA_AERS includes different file-organized tables linkable through specific items and grouped in quarterly periods. Data from first quarter of 2004 to present are freely available into FDA website and can be easily downloaded [85], whereas previous data can be purchased from NTIS (National Technical Information Service) website [86]. Each file-package covers reports within one quarter of year, with the exception of the first available year (1997) where file-package covered the November-December 1997 period.

All data are provided in two distinct formats: SGML and ASCII. Although the first format conforms to the guidelines of the ICH E2b/M2 concerning transmission of individual Case safety reports [84], the ASCII data files are more useable. Indeed, these files can be imported into all popular applications for relational database such as ORACLE®, Microsoft Office Access, MySQL® and IBM DB2®.

Each quarterly file package includes, besides a text file containing a comprehensive description, the following 7 data files:

- DEMO file (demographic characteristics), including information on "event date", patient "age" and "gender", "reporter country" and "reporter's type of occupation".
- DRUG file (information for reported medications), including role codes assigned to each drug: "primary suspect drug" (PS), "secondary suspect drug" (SS), "interacting" (I) or "concomitant" (C).
- REACTION file, including all adverse drug reactions coded by MedDRA terminology [87] (for an overview of this tool see below);
- OUTCOME file (type of outcome, such as death, life-threatening, hospitalization);
- RPSR file, with information on the source of the reports (i.e. company, literature);
- THERAPY file, containing drug therapy start dates and end dates for the reported drugs (0 or more per drug per event).
- INDICATIONS file, containing all MedDRA terms coded for the indications of use (diagnoses) for the reported drugs;

Each file will generate a specific table that is linkable to each other using "ISR number" (Individual Safety Report) as primary key field. The ISR is a seven digit number that uniquely identifies an AERS report and allows linking all data files (see **Figure 2**).

Another important field is the "CASE Number" identifying an AERS case, which can include one or more reports (ISRs) due to possible follow-up of the same drug-reaction pair. If correctly linked, Case number allows identifying all ISRs of the same reports. It is though important to introduce this concept since this field is crucial in de-duplication process. Indeed "duplicate" ISRs (multiple reports of the same event) will normally have the same CASE number (but different ISR numbers).

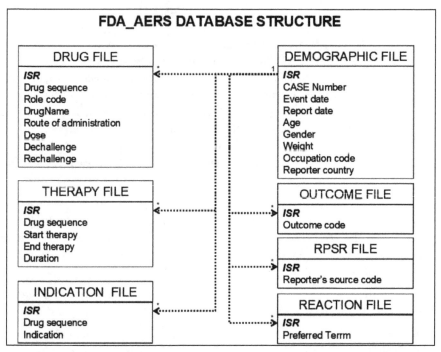

Figure 2. FDA_AERS database structure pictured according the Unified Modeling Language (UML) standardization. In each object, major fields of interest are reported in the FDA_AERS data files.

After downloading and assembling database, to proceed with pharmacovigilance data-mining, data management is essential for specific fields reporting (i) the adverse drug reaction ("PT-Preferred Term" in the REACTION file) and (ii) the suspected drug ("DrugName" in DRUG file). Unlike the adverse event, which is coded using the Medical Dictionary for Regulatory Activities (MedDRA) terminology [87], drugs are entered as textual terms and therefore an internal mapping procedure is required.

3.2. Adverse drug reaction identification: The multi-axial MedDRA hierarchy

In FDA_AERS, adverse events are coded according the Medical Dictionary for Regulatory Activities (MedDRA) terminology, which allows to classify adverse event information associated with the use of pharmaceutical and other medical products (e.g., medical devices and vaccines). This terminology is clinically validated, developed and maintained by international medical experts.

The dictionary was designed in the early 1990s for the use in the pharmaceutical industry and regulatory environment, to support all stages of the regulatory process concerning human medicines. It is owned by the International Federation of Pharmaceutical Manufacturers and Associations (IFPMA) and it was approved by the International Conference on Harmonisation (ICH) [88,89]. MedDRA is maintained by MSSO (MedDRA

Maintenance and Support Service Organization) [87] and JMO (Japanese Maintenance Organization) [90], which are independent organizations with missions to provide international support and continued development of terminology and to foster use of this tool. Access rights to MedDRA ASCII files are free for non-profit organizations (i.e. regulatory authorities, academic institutions, patients care providers and non-profit medical libraries), while a purchase subscription is required to business companies (i.e. pharmaceutical industries, contract research organizations, software developers).

The MedDRA terminology contains more than 60,000 terms for medical conditions, syndromes, diagnosis, clinical signs, laboratory and clinical investigations and social circumstances. These are organized within 5 hierarchical levels that help to bring together similar medical conditions. The structural elements of the MedDRA terminology are:

- SOC (System Organ Class) - Highest level of the terminology, and distinguished by anatomical or physiological system, etiology, or purpose
- HLGT (High Level Group Term) – Subordinate to SOC, superordinate descriptor for one or more HLTs
- HLT (High Level Term) – Subordinate to HLGT, superordinate descriptor for one or more PTs
- PT (Preferred Term) – Represents a single medical concept
- LLT (Lowest Level Term) – Lowest level of the terminology, related to a single PT as a synonym, lexical variant, or quasi-synonym

Although LLTs represent the bottom of the hierarchy, they consist of synonymous, lexical variants and representations of similar conditions; therefore PT level is generally considered the favourite for use in pharmacovigilance analysis, because it coresponds to a unique medical concept.

Since a PT (with its subordinate LLTs) may be represented in more than one of the superordinate levels, the MedDRA hierarchy is multi-axial. When a PT is included in two o more axes, a single SOC is designed as "primary" and others as "secondary" locations. This feature provides more flexibility in choosing and retrieving conditions to investigate. An example of the multi-axial hierarchical structure of MedDRA is shown in **Figure 3**.

To assist terminology searches and data retrieval, especially when MedDRA is used in post-marketing surveillance, utilities, called Standardised Medical Query (SMQs), were built and continually updated in a cooperative effort between the ICH and the Council for the International Organization of Medical Sciences (CIOMS). SMQs are groups of PTs and HLTs (with all their subordinate PTs) related to a defined medical condition or area of interest. SMQs may include very specific as well as less specific terms. The term lists are tested to verify their sensitivity and to avoid "noise" presence. SMQs may have certain specific design features: narrow and broad scope, algorithmic approach and hierarchical structure. "Narrow and broad searches" allow to identify cases that are highly likely to represent the condition of interest (a "narrow" scope) or to identify all possible cases, including some that may prove to be of little or no interest on closer inspection (a "broad" scope). In addition, for some SMQs a combination of search terms from various sub-categories of the broad search terms is available (algorithmic search approach). This strategy is able to further refine the identification of cases of interest compared to the broad search category, therefore it yields greater sensitivity compared to the narrow search and greater specificity compared to the broad search. Moreover, in order to create more inclusive queries, some SMQs are a series of queries related to each other in a hierarchical relationship [91].

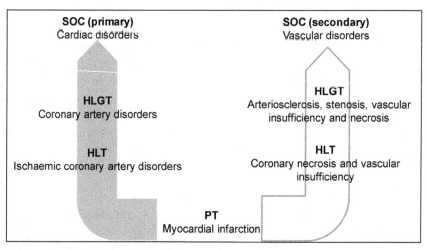

Figure 3. Example of MedDRA multi-axial structure from preferred term (PT) to system organ class (SOC), through high level term (HLT) and high level group term (HLGT).

Concerning the analysis of FDA_AERS, a specific knowledge of MedDRA terminology is essential in order to link "PT" field of REACTION table of FDA_AERS with this terminology. This represents the basis for different data-mining approaches to detect pharmacovigilance signals. Indeed, whereas an approach based on PT level is useful to investigate a particular DEC, it is unfeasible for large-scale screening of all possible DEC [92]. Furthermore, as demonstrated by Pearson et al. [93] the performance of a disproportionality detection improved from PT level to HLT level and to SMQ. However, a broader-level terms might generate false signals because it contains disparate PTs, not all clinically relevant.

3.3. Drug mapping: From free text to the ATC code

In FDA_AERS, the drug(s) used by the patient are reported in the "DRUGNAME" field as free text: either brand name or generic name can be reported, but also a combination of both, and misspellings can be present because of the lack of drug codification. This issue represents an important limitation of FDA_AERS data mining, as recognized by various authors [54,94]. To address this aspect, an *a priori* mapping process to analyse the possible association between drug and adverse reaction is necessary. Therefore, we created an *ad hoc* drug-name archive, including all generic and trade names of drugs marketed in US and in most European Countries by using public lists freely available on authoritative websites and public accessible drug dictionaries. In particular we used the following lists:

- **Drugs@FDA Data Files** [95]: the freely downloadable version of the Drugs@FDA online version. It contains information about FDA-approved brand name and generic prescription and over-the-counter human drugs and biological therapeutic products. It comprises drug products approved since 1998 to present. This list supplies drug name, as brand or generic, with the relevant active ingredient and other information (e.g. dosage form, route of administration, approval date). While the online application is updated daily, downloadable data files are updated once per week. Data files consist in 9 text tables, which can be imported into a database or spreadsheet.

- **WHO Drug Dictionary** [96]: a computer registry containing information on all drugs mentioned on adverse reaction reports submitted by 70 countries participating in the WHO International Drug Monitoring Programme from 1968 onwards. This registry provides proprietary drug names together with all active ingredients and the chemical substances. Drugs are classified according to the Anatomical-Therapeutic-Chemical classification (ATC) [97] (for more details on this classification see below). Drugs recorded are those which have occurred in adverse reaction reports, and therefore the database covers most drugs used in countries involved in the WHO Programme. In collaboration with IMS Health, the WHO Drug Dictionary has been enhanced to include commonly used herbal and traditional medicines [96]. The registry is property of the Uppsala Monitoring Centre (UMC) and can be used by WHO collaborative centres or under license subscription. The Dictionary is available in different formats as data-files, with pre-defined relationships between the tables: a sample of registry and its technical description is freely available [98]. Our research group used this tool through the collaboration with the Pharmacology Unit of University of Verona as Reference Centre for Education and Communication within the WHO Programme for International Drug Monitoring.

- **EUROMEDSTAT** (European Medicines Statistics) Project [99]: a collaborative project promoted by the Italian National Research Council and funded by the European Commission. It started in 2002 and involved academics and government agencies from most European Union Member States, representatives of the WHO and the Council of Europe. Among aims of the project there was to build a European database of licensed medicines in order to perform comparison of drug utilization and drug expenditure among European countries. This database covers only a two-year period (2002-2003) and includes trade names of licensed medicines with relevant active ingredients and ATC codes, in addition to other information (e.g. price, reimbursement rules and licensed country).

The three lists are separately used to map "DrugName" reported in FDA_AERS into the corresponding active substance. This mapping approach allowed allocating a substance name to about 90% of all records in the entire database. Then, substance names have been indexed according to the Anatomical Therapeutic Chemical (ATC) classification [97]. This task was performed to facilitate data elaboration and allow analysis of database at different level (from specific active substance to the broad therapeutic group). Indeed, in the ATC classification, the active substances are divided into different groups according to the organ or system on which they act and their therapeutic, pharmacological and chemical properties. This international classification is developed and maintained by the WHO Collaborating Centre for Drug Statistics Methodology (WHOCC), and was recommended as a standardized nomenclature since 1981. The WHOCC releases a new issue of the complete ATC index annually.

In the ATC classification, drugs are divided into different groups according to the organ or system on which they act and/or their therapeutic and chemical characteristics. The classification assigns to each substance one (or more) 7-digit alphanumeric code (ATC code), where it can recognize 5 different levels (**Table 3**):

- 1st level indicates the anatomical main group and consists of one letter (there are 14 main groups);
- 2nd level indicates the therapeutic main group and consists of two digits;
- 3rd level indicates the therapeutic/pharmacological subgroup and consists of one letter;
- 4th level indicates the chemical/therapeutic/pharmacological subgroup and consists of one letter;
- 5th level indicates the chemical substance and consists of two digits.

Level	ATC Code	Description
1st	A	ALIMENTARY TRACT AND METABOLISM
2nd	A10	DRUGS USED IN DIABETES
3rd	A10B	BLOOD GLUCOSE LOWERING DRUGS, EXCL. INSULINS
4th	A10BA	Biguanides
5th	A10BA02	Metformin

Table 3. Example of ATC codification for the antidiabetic metformin

Therefore, each bottom-level ATC code stands for a specific substance in a single indication (or use). This means that one drug, with more therapeutic uses, can have more than one ATC code. On the other hand, several different trade names share the same code if they have the same active substance and indications.

Although the ATC classification has a particular codification for combination products, in our methodology we decided to split the single active substances of the combination. This allows to analyse risk profile of a given substance and not of a particular product.

The drug mapping strategy described above is not the only possible to manage DrugName field of FDA_AERS. Indeed, other researchers used different methods and tools to index drugs and analyse the same database. For example, a research group of the Columbia University [54] first recognised drug name by using MedLEE, a text processor that translates clinical information from textual to vocabularies of the Unified Medical Language System (UMLS); afterwards they mapped drug names to generic name using RxNorm, a tool linking substance names (normalized names) of drugs with many drug names commonly used. A

Japanese research team [94] attempted to unify all drug names into generic names by detecting spelling errors through GNU Aspell, an open source spell checker.

3.4. How to handle missing data

As expected in large medical databases, also FDA_AERS is troubled by missing data, especially in old case reports. The fraction of missing data varies strongly with the variable considered and with the file analyzed. For example, in cumulative quarter DEMO files of 2004 – 2010 period, gender is 8% missing, age is 34% missing and event_date is 34% missing. These percentages are higher in corresponding THERAPY files, where end_therapy_date is not-filled in 64% of records. Reasons for the different fractions of missing data are still unclear and could be related to the reporter type, as argued by Pearson [100]. Pearson reported a difference of 10% in completeness of age field between reports coming from manufacturers (21.3% of missing age data) and those directly from patients or health professionals (31.1%).

Missing data is a well-recognized problem in large databases and widely discussed in the literature [101,102]. Various approaches have been used to deal with it with different consequences. Generally, these strategies fall into three classes: omission of incomplete records (deletion of records), imputation of missing values (single imputation) and computational modifications of missing fields (multiple imputation). The first approach (deletion of records) reduces the sample size and the subsequent statistical efficiency; it should be used only for small fractions of missing data. For large fractions of missing data one alternative is represented by single imputation of missing data on the basis of those available, but also this approach could modify the dataset. Another approach is the multiple imputation strategy, that allows to complete automatically missing information creating several different plausible imputed datasets and appropriately combining their results. It is obvious that neither this latter is free from drawbacks.

In our studies on FDA_AERS, we preferred the single imputation approach to manage missing data. We applied it only to demographic data (DEMO file) in order to improve quality and completeness of information for each case and, subsequently, to identify and remove duplicates (for details see below). To this purpose, we chose the following 4 key-fields, essential to characterize a single case: event_date, age, gender, reporter_country. Since each case, identified by a "CASE number", consists of one or more reports (ISRs), ideally representing the follow-up reports, we firstly linked each case with owner ISRs. Then, when a high level of similarity was present between two records (at least 3 on 4 of considered key-fields), we filled missing data. On the contrary, records with more missed key-fields were deleted. We acknowledge that this missing data handling could generate some biases, but, in the intent of our analyses, we consider these possible biases less hazardous than the deletion of a high number of records.

Noteworthy that FDA_AERS files different from DEMO could require other missing data handlings. Therefore, we advise to choose the appropriate methodology on the basis of both type of field and the magnitude of missing data.

3.5. Detection and removal of duplicates

A major problem in spontaneous reporting data is the presence of duplicates (i.e. the same report submitted by different reporters) and multiple reports (i.e. a follow-up of the same case with additional and updated information). Unfortunately, the exact extent of duplication present in FDA_AERS, and in other similar databases, is unknown. As a matter of fact, although this form of data corruption and its distortion in disproportionality analysis are well-recognized by researchers, only a few of studies examined the issue [103]. There are two major reasons for duplicate generation: different sources (e.g. health professionals, patients and manufacturers providing separate case reports related to the same event) and failure in linking of follow-up case reports to first event records. Some circumstances could generate extreme duplication [104]. For example, the reporting of the same event related to various concomitant drugs by manufacturers of each suspected drug (manufacturers have a statutory obligation to report the adverse event to FDA and to forward it to other involved manufacturers). Another possible source of duplication can be retrieved in the transfer of reports from national centers to the FDA.

Since in FDA_AERS the drawback of duplication is still unsolved and it can distort the final results, it becomes essential to mitigate this phenomenon before initiating the actual data mining process. To this aim, we performed a deduplication procedure firstly linking CASE number with relevant ISRs, secondly through the 4-key fields used in missing data handling (event_date, age, gender, reporter_country) and thirdly revising drug and event reported.

CASE	EVENT_DT	AGE	GNDR_COD	REPORTER_COUNTRY	Substance_Name	PT
6112494	20060624	59		UNITED STATES	AZITHROMYCIN	SYNCOPE
6112494	20060624	59	M	UNITED STATES	DELAVIRDINE	SYNCOPE
6112494	20060624	59	M	UNITED STATES	LAMIVUDINE	SYNCOPE
6112494	20060624	59	M	UNITED STATES	RITONAVIR	SYNCOPE
6112494	20060624	59	M	UNITED STATES	SAQUINAVIR	SYNCOPE
6112494	20060624	59	M	UNITED STATES	sulfamethoxazole and trimethoprim	SYNCOPE
6112494	20060624	59	M	UNITED STATES	ZIDOVUDINE	SYNCOPE
6112494	20060624	59	M	UNITED STATES	ABACAVIR	SYNCOPE
6120628	20060624	59	M	UNITED STATES	SAQUINAVIR	SYNCOPE
6120628	20060624	59	M	UNITED STATES	ABACAVIR	SYNCOPE
6120628	20060624	59	M	UNITED STATES	AZITHROMYCIN	SYNCOPE
6120628	20060624	59	M	UNITED STATES	DELAVIRDINE	SYNCOPE
6120628	20060624	59	M	UNITED STATES	RITONAVIR	SYNCOPE
6120628	20060624	59	M	UNITED STATES	SULFAMETHOXAZOLE	SYNCOPE
6120628	20060624	59	M	UNITED STATES	TRIMETHOPRIM	SYNCOPE
6120628	20060624	59	M	UNITED STATES	ZIDOVUDINE	SYNCOPE
6120628	20060624	59	M	UNITED STATES	LAMIVUDINE	SYNCOPE
6139100	20060624	59	M	UNITED STATES	ZIDOVUDINE	SYNCOPE
6139100	20060624	59	M	UNITED STATES	ABACAVIR	SYNCOPE
6139100	20060624	59	M	UNITED STATES	AZITHROMYCIN	SYNCOPE
6139100	20060624	59	M	UNITED STATES	DELAVIRDINE	SYNCOPE
6139100	20060624	59	M	UNITED STATES	LAMIVUDINE	SYNCOPE
6139100	20060624	59	M	UNITED STATES	RITONAVIR	SYNCOPE
6139100	20060624	59	M	UNITED STATES	SAQUINAVIR	SYNCOPE
6139100	20060624	59	M	UNITED STATES	SULFAMETHOXAZOLE	SYNCOPE
6139100	20060624	59	M	UNITED STATES	TRIMETHOPRIM	SYNCOPE

Record: I◄ ◄ [1 ► ►I ►*] di 26 (Filtrati)

Figure 4. Example of duplicates in FDA_AERS for the 3 same reports of syncope

As advised by the FDA, we link the Case number with (ISRs) because of a "case" consists of one or more reports (ISRs) and if correctly linked, a follow-up report will have the same CASE number as the initial report (but a different ISR number). Then we grouped all records of a given case number and we associated the demographic information (event_date, age, gender, reporter country) the suspected drug/s and the reported event/s. Starting from this dataset, we performed a semi-automated de-duplication procedure in order to delete reports with different case number but reporting the same event. This procedure is based on the assumption that two or more apparently identical events are unlikely to be different events if the following conditions are fulfilled: they occurred in the same data with the same drugs, they were reported for same patients coming from the same country (**Figure 4** shows an example of duplication in FDA_AERS).

The following scheme (**Figure 5**) summarizes all the illustrated steps of our datamining strategy in analyzing the FDA_AERS.

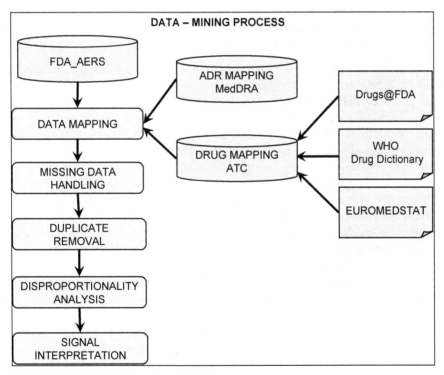

Figure 5. Steps of FDA_AERS data-mining process

4. Results of FDA_AERS data mining: some examples

Once the dataset has been processed for duplicates and missing data, there are some issues requiring further considerations to perform the complete analysis.

First, the analysis is usually conducted in terms of drug-event pairs, where every event is considered as many times as the reported drugs. Each of these drug-event pairs will be classified as cases or non cases, depending on the event of interest.

Second, the disproportionality can be performed at each level of MedDRA terminology (i.e., SOC, HLGT, HLT, PT) and the level of specificity of terms could be best defined by case-specific clinical judgment, rather than by rigid use of one level of terminology [105]. The importance of the choice of the level is well represented by a study aimed to investigate the safety profile of thiazolidinediones by using FDA_AERS [34]: while the disproportionality analysis at SOC level "injuries, poisoning, ..." did not find any statistically significance for "injury", the analysis of immediately lower level HLGT "Bone and joint injuries" showed a disproportionality signal for both thiazolidinediones.

Third, disproportionality can be referred to all drugs included in the entire database or to a specific therapeutic class (see also reference group issues, above), isolated through the ATC code. The latter approach is needed to avoid the confounding by indication that occurs when a given class of drugs is preferentially used in subjects who have *a priori* higher or lower risk of presenting the event under investigation [74].

Fourth, disproportionality can be calculated by using two different approaches: a sequential cumulative strategy or a quarter-by-quarter approach. The cumulative analysis is the most adopted technique, both by regulators, academic researchers and manufacturers: it consists in the identification of a precise time point and a retrospective evaluation of reports, which are cumulatively considered. Indeed, several published papers on disproportionality cover a time period encompassing a number of years. Notably, this time period can be also split in different "time windows" (e.g., years, months), which can be analyzed for instance on a quarter-by-quarter basis (i.e., by calculating the ROR independently for a given window). While this approach may be useful to evaluate the behavior of the disproportionality over time and check whether the signal appears or disappears, it should be acknowledged that this strategy is highly influenced by fluctuations of the reporting, caused by seasonal changes in reporting and mostly by the typical attitude of recording the submitted reports and entering the database in January. This may cause an erroneous peak in reporting, which does not reflect the actual occurrence of the ADR. As an explanatory example, **Figure 6** compares results from the cumulative *versus* quarter-by-quarter analysis, performed on the association between exenatide and pancreatitis. Notably, the quarter-by-quarter analysis found a striking correspondence between the relevant FDA warning and the appearance of disproportionality (which, by contrast was found in the subsequent quarter in the cumulative analysis), but is characterized by large fluctuations of ROR (with very broad confidence intervals). The cumulative approach is therefore usually recommended as the most balanced and accurate approach for the analysis. Finally, an important aspect that should be kept in mind regards the selection of the time period of the analysis on the basis of the marketing authorization of the primary suspect drug. In **Figure 6**, only the period starting from the second quarter was described because exenatide received marketing approval in April 2005.

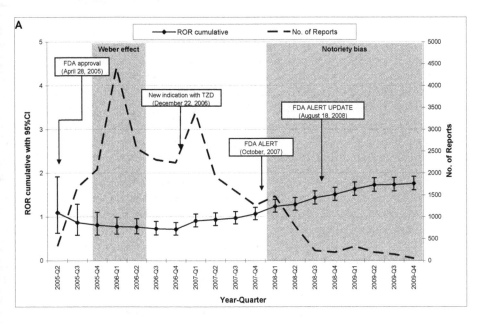

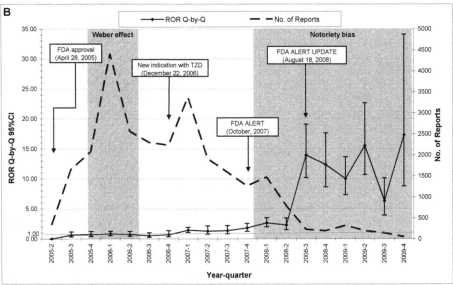

Figure 6. Comparison between cumulative (panel A, reprinted from [7], with permission of the copyright holder: Springer) and a quarter-by-quarter approach (panel B). Time trends of ROR with corresponding 95%CI of pancreatitis associated with exenatide use (full line) and relevant total number of spontaneous reports (dotted line). Boxes with relevant arrows indicate major regulatory measures in exenatide marketing history. Grey areas indicate the underlying epidemiological phenomena that may explain the observed peaks (see text for details).

5. Conclusions

On the basis of our experience, we have provided insight into the FDA_AERS to exemplify how to address major methodological issues discussed in the first part of the chapter. Because the FDA_AERS is a worldwide publicly available pharmacovigilance archive, we believe that fostering discussion among researchers will increase transparency and facilitate definition of the most reliable approaches. By virtue of its large population coverage and free availability, the FDA_AERS has the potential to pave the way to a new way of looking to signal detection in PhV. The existence of private societies developing and marketing software to analyze FDA_AERS data calls for the need to agree on data mining approaches.

PhV is a clinically oriented discipline, which may guide appropriate drug use through a balanced assessment of drug safety. Although much has been done in recent years, efforts are needed to expand the border of pharmacovigilance. For instance, although patients are important stakeholders in pharmacovigilance, little formal evaluation has been undertaken of existing patient reporting schemes. Notwithstanding some differences in the way various countries handle patient reports of ADRs, patient reporting has the potential to add value to pharmacovigilance by: reporting types of drugs and reactions different from those reported by clinicians; generating new potential signals; describing suspected ADRs in enough detail to provide useful information on likely causality and impact on patients' lives [106].

Registries (and their linkage to other data sources) have become increasingly appealing in postmarketing surveillance of medications, but their role is still very variable among countries. Notwithstanding significant limitations due to the lack of a control group and the need for complete case ascertainment to maintain data integrity, they are of utmost value for providing drug safety data through monitoring the incidence of rare adverse events particularly for highly specialized medications with significant financial cost [107]. Indeed, one of the most important aim of disease-based or drug-based registries is to promote appropriate use and guarantee access to innovative drugs.

One of the most important aspects to improve accuracy of signal detection in pharmacovigilance is to combine multiple methods, each in a distinct perspective (e.g., healthcare databases, spontaneous reporting systems), to increase the precision and sensitivity of the approach and complement limitations of each method [108]. In this context, the EU-ADR [109] and ARITMO projects [110] represent examples of multidisciplinary consortia aiming to create a federation of databases, namely healthcare databases and spontaneous reporting systems, to address drug-related safety issues.

In conclusion, our key messages are: (1) before applying statistical tools (i.e., DMAs) to pharmacovigilance database for signal detection, all aspects related to data quality should be considered (e.g., drug mapping, missing data and duplicates); (2) at present, the choice of a given DMA mostly relies on local habits, expertise and attitude and there is room for improvement in this area; (3) DMA performance may be highly situation dependent; (4) over-reliance on these methods may have deleterious consequences, especially with the so-called "designated medical events", for which a case-by-case analysis is mandatory and complements disproportionality; and (5) the most appropriate selection of pharmacovigilance tools needs to be tailored to each situation, being mindful of the numerous biases and confounders that may influence performance and incremental utility of DMAs.

We support the implementation of DMAs, although one should not automatically assume that greater complexity is synonymous of greater precision and accuracy. Overall, data derived from DMAs should be considered with caution and guided by appropriate clinical evaluation. This clinical perspective should always be considered to support really appropriate drug use, balancing drug effectiveness, safety and, above all, actual patients' needs.

Author details

Elisabetta Poluzzi, Emanuel Raschi, Carlo Piccinni and Fabrizio De Ponti*
Department of Medical and Surgical Sciences, University of Bologna, Bologna, Italy

Acknowledgments

We thank Ariola Koci, statistician working at the Department of Medical and Surgical Sciences, University of Bologna for assistance in data management. She was supported by a Scholarship granted by the University of Bologna.
This chapter was supported by funds from the University of Bologna.

6. References

[1]   Edwards IR (2012) An agenda for UK clinical pharmacology. Pharmacovigilance. Br. J Clin Pharmacol 73: 979-982.

[2]   Leone R, Magro L, Moretti U, Cutroneo P, Moschini M, Motola D, Tuccori M, Conforti A (2010) Identifying adverse drug reactions associated with drug-drug interactions: data mining of a spontaneous reporting database in Italy. Drug Saf 33: 667-675.

[3]   Tatonetti NP, Denny JC, Murphy SN, Fernald GH, Krishnan G, Castro V, Yue P, Tsao PS, Kohane I, Roden DM, Altman RB (2011) Detecting drug interactions from adverse-event reports: interaction between paroxetine and pravastatin increases blood glucose levels. Clin Pharmacol Ther 90: 133-142.

[4]   Maclure M, Fireman B, Nelson JC, Hua W, Shoaibi A, Paredes A, Madigan D (2012) When should case-only designs be used for safety monitoring of medical products? Pharmacoepidemiol. Drug Saf 21 Suppl 1: 50-61.

[5]   Elashoff M, Matveyenko AV, Gier B, Elashoff R, Butler PC (2011) Pancreatitis, pancreatic, and thyroid cancer with glucagon-like peptide-1-based therapies. Gastroenterology 141: 150-156.

[6]   Moore N (2011) Journal's withdrawal of article. Paper OK, title wrong. BMJ 342: d2732-

---

* Corresponding Author

[7] Raschi E, Piccinni C, Poluzzi E, Marchesini G, De Ponti F. (2011) The association of pancreatitis with antidiabetic drug use: gaining insight through the FDA pharmacovigilance database. Acta Diabetol [in press].

[8] Warrer P, Hansen EH, Juhl-Jensen L, Aagaard L (2012) Using text-mining techniques in electronic patient records to identify ADRs from medicine use. Br. J Clin Pharmacol 73: 674-684.

[9] Shetty KD, Dalal SR (2011) Using information mining of the medical literature to improve drug safety. J Am Med Inform. Assoc. 18: 668-674.

[10] Edwards IR, Aronson JK (2000) Adverse drug reactions: definitions, diagnosis, and management. Lancet 356: 1255-1259.

[11] Aronson JK, Hauben M, Bate A (2012) Defining 'surveillance' in drug safety. Drug Saf 35: 347-357.

[12] Aronson JK (2012) Adverse Drug Reactions: History, Terminology, Classification, Causality, Frequency, Preventability. In: John Talbot JKA, editors. Stephens' Detection and Evaluation of Adverse Drug Reactions: Principles and Practice. Chichester, UK: John Wiley & Sons, Ltd. pp. 1-119.

[13] Aronson JK (2009) Medication errors: definitions and classification. Br. J Clin Pharmacol 67: 599-604.

[14] (2010) Regulation (EU) No 1235/2010. Available: http://eur-lex.europa.eu/LexUriServ/LexUriServ.do?uri=OJ:L:2010:348:0001: 0016:EN:PDF. Accessed 2012 Apr 27.

[15] (2010) Directive 2010/84/EU. Available: http://eur-lex.europa.eu/LexUriServ/LexUriServ.do?uri=OJ:L:2010:348:0074: 0099:EN:PDF. Accessed 2012 Apr 27.

[16] Montastruc JL, Sommet A, Bagheri H, Lapeyre-Mestre M (2011) Benefits and strengths of the disproportionality analysis for identification of adverse drug reactions in a pharmacovigilance database. Br. J Clin Pharmacol 72: 905-908.

[17] (2012) Canada Vigilance Adverse Reaction Online Database. Available: http://www.hc-sc.gc.ca/dhp-mps/medeff/databasdon/index-eng.php.   Accessed   2012 Apr 30.

[18] (2012) Netherlands Pharmacovigilance Centre Lareb. Available: http://www.lareb.nl/default.aspx. Accessed 2012 Apr 30.

[19] Srba J, Descikova V, Vlcek J (2012) Adverse drug reactions: Analysis of spontaneous reporting system in Europe in 2007-2009. Eur. J Clin Pharmacol [in press].

[20] Hammond IW, Gibbs TG, Seifert HA, Rich DS (2007) Database size and power to detect safety signals in pharmacovigilance. Expert Opin Drug Saf 6: 713-721.

[21] Meyboom RH, Hekster YA, Egberts AC, Gribnau FW, Edwards IR (1997) Causal or casual? The role of causality assessment in pharmacovigilance. Drug Saf 17: 374-389.

[22] Aronson JK, Hauben M (2006) Anecdotes that provide definitive evidence. BMJ 333: 1267-1269.

[23] Hauben M, Aronson JK (2007) Gold standards in pharmacovigilance: the use of definitive anecdotal reports of adverse drug reactions as pure gold and high-grade ore. Drug Saf 30: 645-655.

[24] Hauben M, Reich L (2004) Drug-induced pancreatitis: lessons in data mining. Br. J Clin Pharmacol 58: 560-562.

[25] Poluzzi E, Raschi E, Motola D, Moretti U, De Ponti F. (2010) Antimicrobials and the risk of torsades de pointes: the contribution from data mining of the US FDA Adverse Event Reporting System. Drug Saf 33: 303-314.

[26] Hauben M, Aronson JK (2009) Defining 'signal' and its subtypes in pharmacovigilance based on a systematic review of previous definitions. Drug Saf 32: 99-110.

[27] Bate A, Lindquist M, Edwards IR (2008) The application of knowledge discovery in databases to post-marketing drug safety: example of the WHO database. Fundam. Clin Pharmacol 22: 127-140.

[28] Balakin KV, Hauben M, Bate A (2009) Data Mining in Pharmacovigilance. In: Balakin KV, editors. Pharmaceutical Data Mining: Approaches and Applications for Drug Discovery. Hoboken, NJ, USA: John Wiley & Sons, Ltd. pp. 341-378.

[29] Bate A, Evans SJ (2009) Quantitative signal detection using spontaneous ADR reporting. Pharmacoepidemiol. Drug Saf 18: 427-436.

[30] Stricker BH, Tijssen JG (1992) Serum sickness-like reactions to cefaclor. J Clin Epidemiol. 45: 1177-1184.

[31] Moore N, Kreft-Jais C, Haramburu F, Noblet C, Andrejak M, Ollagnier M, Begaud B (1997) Reports of hypoglycaemia associated with the use of ACE inhibitors and other drugs: a case/non-case study in the French pharmacovigilance system database. Br. J Clin Pharmacol 44: 513-518.

[32] Moore N, Thiessard F, Begaud B (2005) The history of disproportionality measures (reporting odds ratio, proportional reporting rates) in spontaneous reporting of adverse drug reactions. Pharmacoepidemiol. Drug Saf 14: 285-286.

[33] Hauben M, Reich L (2005) Potential utility of data-mining algorithms for early detection of potentially fatal/disabling adverse drug reactions: a retrospective evaluation. J Clin Pharmacol 45: 378-384.

[34] Motola D, Piccinni C, Biagi C, Raschi E, Marra A, Marchesini G, Poluzzi E (2012) Cardiovascular, ocular and bone adverse reactions associated with thiazolidinediones: a disproportionality analysis of the US FDA adverse event reporting system database. Drug Saf 35: 315-323.

[35] Evans SJ, Waller PC, Davis S (2001) Use of proportional reporting ratios (PRRs) for signal generation from spontaneous adverse drug reaction reports. Pharmacoepidemiol. Drug Saf 10: 483-486.

[36] DuMouchel W. (1999) Bayesian data mining in large frequency tables, with an application to the FDA spontaneous reporting. Am Stat 53: 177-201.

[37] Bate A, Lindquist M, Edwards IR, Olsson S, Orre R, Lansner A, De Freitas RM (1998) A Bayesian neural network method for adverse drug reaction signal generation. Eur J Clin Pharmacol 54: 315-321.

[38] Rothman KJ, Lanes S, Sacks ST (2004) The reporting odds ratio and its advantages over the proportional reporting ratio. Pharmacoepidemiol. Drug Saf 13: 519-523.

[39] Waller P, van PE, Egberts A, Evans S (2004) The reporting odds ratio versus the proportional reporting ratio: 'deuce'. Pharmacoepidemiol. Drug Saf 13: 525-526.

[40] Hauben M (2003) A brief primer on automated signal detection. Ann. Pharmacother. 37: 1117-1123.

[41] Hauben M, Zhou X (2003) Quantitative methods in pharmacovigilance: focus on signal detection. Drug Saf 26: 159-186.

[42] Hauben M, Reich L (2004) Safety related drug-labelling changes: findings from two data mining algorithms. Drug Saf 27: 735-744.

[43] Almenoff JS, LaCroix KK, Yuen NA, Fram D, DuMouchel W (2006) Comparative performance of two quantitative safety signalling methods: implications for use in a pharmacovigilance department. Drug Saf 29: 875-887.

[44] Li C, Xia J, Deng J, Jiang J (2008) A comparison of measures of disproportionality for signal detection on adverse drug reaction spontaneous reporting database of Guangdong province in China. Pharmacoepidemiol. Drug Saf 17: 593-600.

[45] Chen Y, Guo JJ, Healy DP, Lin X, Patel NC (2008) Risk of hepatotoxicity associated with the use of telithromycin: a signal detection using data mining algorithms. Ann. Pharmacother. 42: 1791-1796.

[46] Van Puijenbroek EP, Bate A, Leufkens HG, Lindquist M, Orre R, Egberts AC (2002) A comparison of measures of disproportionality for signal detection in spontaneous reporting systems for adverse drug reactions. Pharmacoepidemiol. Drug Saf 11: 3-10.

[47] Kubota K, Koide D, Hirai T (2004) Comparison of data mining methodologies using Japanese spontaneous reports. Pharmacoepidemiol. Drug Saf 13: 387-394.

[48] Hauben M, Patadia V, Gerrits C, Walsh L, Reich L (2005) Data mining in pharmacovigilance: the need for a balanced perspective. Drug Saf 28: 835-842.

[49] Chen Y, Guo JJ, Steinbuch M, Lin X, Buncher CR, Patel NC (2008) Comparison of Sensitivity and Timing of Early Signal Detection of Four Frequently Used Signal Detection Methods. An Empirical Study Based on the US FDA Adverse Event Reporting System Database. Pharm Med 22: 359-365.

[50] Poluzzi E, Raschi E, Moretti U, De Ponti F. (2009) Drug-induced torsades de pointes: data mining of the public version of the FDA Adverse Event Reporting System (AERS). Pharmacoepidemiol. Drug Saf 18: 512-518.

[51] van der Heijden PG, Van Puijenbroek EP, van BS, van der Hofstede JW (2002) On the assessment of adverse drug reactions from spontaneous reporting systems: the influence of under-reporting on odds ratios. Stat. Med 21: 2027-2044.

[52] Deshpande G, Gogolak V, Smith SW (2010) Data Mining in Drug Safety. Review of Published Threshold Criteria for Defining Signals of Disproportionate Reporting. Pharm Med 24: 37-43.

[53] Ahmed I, Thiessard F, Miremont-Salame G, Begaud B, Tubert-Bitter P (2010) Pharmacovigilance data mining with methods based on false discovery rates: a comparative simulation study. Clin Pharmacol Ther 88: 492-498.

[54] Harpaz R, Perez H, Chase HS, Rabadan R, Hripcsak G, Friedman C (2011) Biclustering of adverse drug events in the FDA's spontaneous reporting system. Clin Pharmacol Ther 89: 243-250.

[55] Strandell J, Bate A, Hagg S, Edwards IR (2009) Rhabdomyolysis a result of azithromycin and statins: an unrecognized interaction. Br. J Clin Pharmacol 68: 427-434.

[56] Strandell J, Caster O, Bate A, Noren N, Edwards IR (2011) Reporting patterns indicative of adverse drug interactions: a systematic evaluation in VigiBase. Drug Saf 34: 253-266.

[57] de Boer A. (2011) When to publish measures of disproportionality derived from spontaneous reporting databases? Br. J Clin Pharmacol 72: 909-911.

[58] De Bruin ML, Pettersson M, Meyboom RH, Hoes AW, Leufkens HG (2005) Anti-HERG activity and the risk of drug-induced arrhythmias and sudden death. Eur Heart J 26: 590-597.

[59] Giezen TJ, Mantel-Teeuwisse AK, Meyboom RH, Straus SM, Leufkens HG, Egberts TC (2010) Mapping the safety profile of biologicals: a disproportionality analysis using the WHO adverse drug reaction database, VigiBase. Drug Saf 33: 865-878.

[60] Stephenson WP, Hauben M (2007) Data mining for signals in spontaneous reporting databases: proceed with caution. Pharmacoepidemiol. Drug Saf 16: 359-365.

[61] Hazell L, Shakir SA (2006) Under-reporting of adverse drug reactions : a systematic review. Drug Saf 29: 385-396.

[62] Anderson N, Borlak J (2011) Correlation versus causation? Pharmacovigilance of the analgesic flupirtine exemplifies the need for refined spontaneous ADR reporting. PLoS One 6: e25221-

[63] Wallenstein EJ, Fife D (2001) Temporal patterns of NSAID spontaneous adverse event reports: the Weber effect revisited. Drug Saf 24: 233-237.

[64] Hartnell NR, Wilson JP (2004) Replication of the Weber effect using postmarketing adverse event reports voluntarily submitted to the United States Food and Drug Administration. Pharmacotherapy 24: 743-749.

[65] McAdams MA, Governale LA, Swartz L, Hammad TA, Dal Pan GJ (2008) Identifying patterns of adverse event reporting for four members of the angiotensin II receptor blockers class of drugs: revisiting the Weber effect. Pharmacoepidemiol. Drug Saf 17: 882-889.

[66] De Bruin ML, Van Puijenbroek EP, Egberts AC, Hoes AW, Leufkens HG (2002) Non-sedating antihistamine drugs and cardiac arrhythmias -- biased risk estimates from spontaneous reporting systems? Br. J Clin Pharmacol 53: 370-374.

[67] Motola D, Vargiu A, Leone R, Conforti A, Moretti U, Vaccheri A, Velo G, Montanaro N (2008) Influence of regulatory measures on the rate of spontaneous adverse drug reaction reporting in Italy. Drug Saf 31: 609-616.

[68] Pariente A, Gregoire F, Fourrier-Reglat A, Haramburu F, Moore N (2007) Impact of safety alerts on measures of disproportionality in spontaneous reporting databases: the notoriety bias. Drug Saf 30: 891-898.

[69] Pariente A, Daveluy A, Laribiere-Benard A, Miremont-Salame G, Begaud B, Moore N (2009) Effect of date of drug marketing on disproportionality measures in pharmacovigilance: the example of suicide with SSRIs using data from the UK MHRA. Drug Saf 32: 441-447.

[70] Petri H, Urquhart J (1991) Channeling bias in the interpretation of drug effects. Stat. Med 10: 577-581.

[71] Ooba N, Kubota K (2010) Selected control events and reporting odds ratio in signal detection methodology. Pharmacoepidemiol. Drug Saf 19: 1159-1165.

[72] Pariente A, Didailler M, Avillach P, Miremont-Salame G, Fourrier-Reglat A, Haramburu F, Moore N (2010) A potential competition bias in the detection of safety signals from spontaneous reporting databases. Pharmacoepidemiol. Drug Saf 19: 1166-1171.

[73] Papay J, Yuen N, Powell G, Mockenhaupt M, Bogenrieder T (2012) Spontaneous adverse event reports of Stevens-Johnson syndrome/toxic epidermal necrolysis: detecting associations with medications. Pharmacoepidemiol. Drug Saf 21: 289-296.

[74] Gregoire F, Pariente A, Fourrier-Reglat A, Haramburu F, Begaud B, Moore N (2008) A signal of increased risk of hypoglycaemia with angiotensin receptor blockers caused by confounding. Br. J Clin Pharmacol 66: 142-145.

[75] Wang HW, Hochberg AM, Pearson RK, Hauben M (2010) An experimental investigation of masking in the US FDA adverse event reporting system database. Drug Saf 33: 1117-1133.

[76] Hauben M, Hochberg A (2008) The Importance of Reporting Negative Findings in Data Mining. The Example of Exenatide and Pancreatitis. Pharm Med 22: 215-219.

[77] Jones SC, Sorbello A, Boucher RM (2011) Fluoroquinolone-associated myasthenia gravis exacerbation: evaluation of postmarketing reports from the US FDA adverse event reporting system and a literature review. Drug Saf 34: 839-847.

[78] Piccinni C, Motola D, Marchesini G, Poluzzi E (2011) Assessing the association of pioglitazone use and bladder cancer through drug adverse event reporting. Diabetes Care 34: 1369-1371.

[79] (2012) FDAble. Available: http://www.fdable.com/. Accessed 2012 Apr 30.

[80] (2012) OpenVigil. Available:
http://webcl3top.rz.uni-kiel.de/pharmacology/pvt/queryaers.php. Accessed 2012 Apr 30.

[81] (2012) DrugCite. Available: http://www.drugcite.com/. Accessed 2012 Apr 30.

[82] (2012) MedWatch: The FDA Safety Information and Adverse Event Reporting Program. Available: http://www.fda.gov/Safety/MedWatch/default.htm. Accessed 2012 Apr 30.

[83] (2012) Adverse Event Reporting System (AERS). Available:
http://www.fda.gov/drugs/guidancecomplianceregulatoryinformation/surveillance/adversedrugeffects/default.htm. Accessed 2012 Apr 30.

[84] (2012) International Conference on Harmonisation of Technical Requirements for Registration of Pharmaceuticals for Human Use. Available:
http://www.ich.org/. Accessed 2012 Apr 30.

[85] (2012) The Adverse Event Reporting System (AERS): Quarterly Data Files. Available:
http://www.fda.gov/Drugs/GuidanceComplianceRegulatoryInformation/Surveillance/AdverseDrugEffects/ucm082193.htm. Accessed 2012 Apr 30.

[86] (2012) National Technical Information Service. Available:
http://www.ntis.gov/about/index.aspx. Accessed 2012 Apr 30.

[87] (2012) MedDRA - the Medical Dictionary for Regulatory Activities. Available:
http://www.meddramsso.com/. Accessed 2012 Apr 30.

[88] Brown E (2007) Medical Dictionary for Regulatory Activities (MedDRA). In: Mann R, Andrews E, editors. Pharmacovigilance. Chichester, UK: John Wiley & Sons, Ltd. pp. 167-186.

[89] Mozzicato P (2009) MedDRA. An Overview of the Medical Dictionary for Regulatory Activities. Pharm Med 23: 65-75.

[90] (2012) Japanese Maintenance Organization (JMO). Available: http://www.pmrj.jp/jmo/php/indexe.php. Accessed 2012 Apr 30.

[91] (2012) Introductory Guide for Standardised MedDRA Queries (SMQs). Version 15.0. Available: http://www.meddramsso.com/files_acrobat/SMQ_intguide_15_0_English_update.pdf. Accessed 2012 Apr 30.

[92] Bate A, Brown EG, Goldman SA, Hauben M (2012) Terminological challenges in safety surveillance. Drug Saf 35: 79-84.

[93] Pearson RK, Hauben M, Goldsmith DI, Gould AL, Madigan D, O'Hara DJ, Reisinger SJ, Hochberg AM (2009) Influence of the MedDRA hierarchy on pharmacovigilance data mining results. Int. J Med Inform. 78: e97-e103.

[94] Kadoyama K, Miki I, Tamura T, Brown JB, Sakaeda T, Okuno Y (2012) Adverse event profiles of 5-fluorouracil and capecitabine: data mining of the public version of the FDA Adverse Event Reporting System, AERS, and reproducibility of clinical observations. Int. J Med Sci. 9: 33-39.

[95] (2012) Drugs@FDA Data Files. Available: http://www.fda.gov/Drugs/InformationOnDrugs/ucm079750.htm. Accessed 2012 Apr 30.

[96] (2012) The WHO Drug Dictionary Enhanced. Available: http://www.umc-products.com/DynPage.aspx?id=73588&mn1=1107&mn2=1139. Accessed 2012 Apr 30.

[97] (2011) ATC/DDD Index 2012. Available: http://www.whocc.no/atc_ddd_index/. Accessed 2012 Apr 30.

[98] (2012) WHO Drug Dictionary Samples & Documents. Available: http://www.umc-products.com/DynPage.aspx?id=73551&mn1=1107&mn2=1139&mn3=6040. Accessed 2012 Apr 30.

[99] (2002) EURO-MED-STAT (European Medicines Statistics). Available: http://ec.europa.eu/health/ph_projects/2001/monitoring/fp_monitoring_2001_exs_12_en.pdf. Accessed 2012 Apr 30.

[100] Pearson R (2006) The Problem of Disguised Missing Data. Available: http://www.sigkdd.org/explorations/issues/8-1-2006-06/12-Pearson.pdf. Accessed 2012 Apr 30.

[101] Sterne JA, White IR, Carlin JB, Spratt M, Royston P, Kenward MG, Wood AM, Carpenter JR (2009) Multiple imputation for missing data in epidemiological and clinical research: potential and pitfalls. BMJ 338: b2393-

[102] Marston L, Carpenter JR, Walters KR, Morris RW, Nazareth I, Petersen I (2010) Issues in multiple imputation of missing data for large general practice clinical databases. Pharmacoepidemiol. Drug Saf 19: 618-626.

[103] Norèn GN, Orre R, Bate A, Edwards IR (2007) Duplicate detection in adverse drug reaction surveillance. Data Min Knowl Disc 14: 305-328.

[104] Hauben M, Reich L, DeMicco J, Kim K (2007) 'Extreme duplication' in the US FDA Adverse Events Reporting System database. Drug Saf 30: 551-554.

[105] Bate A, Lindquist M, Orre R, Edwards IR, Meyboom RH (2002) Data-mining analyses of pharmacovigilance signals in relation to relevant comparison drugs. Eur J Clin Pharmacol 58: 483-490.

[106] Avery AJ, Anderson C, Bond CM, Fortnum H, Gifford A, Hannaford PC, Hazell L, Krska J, Lee AJ, McLernon DJ, Murphy E, Shakir S, Watson MC (2011) Evaluation of patient reporting of adverse drug reactions to the UK 'Yellow Card Scheme': literature review, descriptive and qualitative analyses, and questionnaire surveys. Health Technol. Assess. 15: 1-iv.

[107] Willis CD, McNeil JJ, Cameron PA, Phillips LE (2012) Monitoring drug safety with registries: useful components of postmarketing pharmacovigilance systems. J Clin Epidemiol. 65: 121-125.

[108] Trifirò G, Patadia V, Schuemie MJ, Coloma PM, Gini R, Herings R, Hippisley-Cox J, Mazzaglia G, Giaquinto C, Scotti L, Pedersen L, Avillach P, Sturkenboom MC, van der LJ, Eu-Adr Group (2011) EU-ADR healthcare database network vs. spontaneous reporting system database: preliminary comparison of signal detection. Stud. Health Technol. Inform. 166: 25-30.

[109] EU-ADR project (2012). Available: http://www.alert-project.org/. Accessed 2012 Apr 30.

[110] ARITMO project (2012). Available: http://www.aritmo-project.org/. Accessed 2012 Apr 30.

Permissions

The contributors of this book come from diverse backgrounds, making this book a truly international effort. This book will bring forth new frontiers with its revolutionizing research information and detailed analysis of the nascent developments around the world.

We would like to thank Dr. Adem Karahoca, for lending his expertise to make the book truly unique. He has played a crucial role in the development of this book. Without his invaluable contribution this book wouldn't have been possible. He has made vital efforts to compile up to date information on the varied aspects of this subject to make this book a valuable addition to the collection of many professionals and students.

This book was conceptualized with the vision of imparting up-to-date information and advanced data in this field. To ensure the same, a matchless editorial board was set up. Every individual on the board went through rigorous rounds of assessment to prove their worth. After which they invested a large part of their time researching and compiling the most relevant data for our readers. Conferences and sessions were held from time to time between the editorial board and the contributing authors to present the data in the most comprehensible form. The editorial team has worked tirelessly to provide valuable and valid information to help people across the globe.

Every chapter published in this book has been scrutinized by our experts. Their significance has been extensively debated. The topics covered herein carry significant findings which will fuel the growth of the discipline. They may even be implemented as practical applications or may be referred to as a beginning point for another development. Chapters in this book were first published by InTech; hereby published with permission under the Creative Commons Attribution License or equivalent.

The editorial board has been involved in producing this book since its inception. They have spent rigorous hours researching and exploring the diverse topics which have resulted in the successful publishing of this book. They have passed on their knowledge of decades through this book. To expedite this challenging task, the publisher supported the team at every step. A small team of assistant editors was also appointed to further simplify the editing procedure and attain best results for the readers.

Our editorial team has been hand-picked from every corner of the world. Their multi-ethnicity adds dynamic inputs to the discussions which result in innovative outcomes. These outcomes are then further discussed with the researchers and contributors who give their valuable feedback and opinion regarding the same. The feedback is then collaborated with the researches and they are edited in a comprehensive manner to aid the understanding of the subject.

Apart from the editorial board, the designing team has also invested a significant amount of their time in understanding the subject and creating the most relevant covers. They scrutinized every image to scout for the most suitable representation of the subject and create an appropriate cover for the book.

The publishing team has been involved in this book since its early stages. They were actively engaged in every process, be it collecting the data, connecting with the contributors or procuring relevant information. The team has been an ardent support to the editorial, designing and production team. Their endless efforts to recruit the best for this project, has resulted in the accomplishment of this book. They are a veteran in the field of academics and their pool of knowledge is as vast as their experience in printing. Their expertise and guidance has proved useful at every step. Their uncompromising quality standards have made this book an exceptional effort. Their encouragement from time to time has been an inspiration for everyone.

The publisher and the editorial board hope that this book will prove to be a valuable piece of knowledge for researchers, students, practitioners and scholars across the globe.

List of Contributors

Adem Karahoca
Bahçeşehir University Software Engineering Department, Turkey

Dilek Karahoca
Bahçeşehir University Software Engineering Department, Turkey
Near East University Computer Technology and Instructional Design PhD Program Department, TRNC

Mert Şanver
Google USA, USA

Joaquin Villanueva Balsera, Vicente Rodriguez Montequin, Francisco Ortega Fernandez and Carlos Alba González-Fanjul
Project Engineering Area, University of Oviedo, Spain

Alberto Ochoa, Daniel Azpeitia, Petra Salazar, Emmanuel García and Miguel Maldonado
Juarez City University, México

Rubén Jaramillo and Jöns Sánchez
LAPEM, México

Javier González and Claudia Gómez
ITCM, México

Julio Ponce, Sayuri Quezada, Francisco Ornelas and Arturo Elías
UAA, México

Edgar Conde and Víctor Cruz
Veracruzana University, México

Lourdes Margain
Universidad Politécnica de Aguascalientes, México

Bin Li, Lihong Shi, Jiping Liu and Liang Wang
Chinese Academy of Surveying and Mapping, Beijing, China

Branko Markoski, Zdravko Ivankovic and Miodrag Ivkovic
University of Novi Sad, Technical Faculty "Mihajlo Pupin", Zrenjanin, Serbia

J. Indumathi
Department of Information Science and Technology, College of Engineering, Anna University,
Chennai, Tamilnadu, India

Haiwei Pan
College of Computer Science and Technology, Harbin Engineering University, Harbin, Heilongjiang, China

Ahmed Al-Jedai
Pharmacy Services Division, King Faisal Specialist Hospital and Research Centre, Riyadh, Saudi Arabia
Alfaisal University, College of Medicine, Riyadh, Saudi Arabia

Zubelr A. Nurgal
King Faisal Specialist Hospital and Research Centre, Riyadh, Saudi Arabia

Frans Coenen
Department of Computer Science, The University of Liverpool, UK

Marta García-Fiñana
Department of Health Sciences, The University of Liverpool, UK

Vanessa Sluming
Institute of Translational Medicine, The University of Liverpool, UK

Ashraf Elsayed
Department of Mathematics and Computer Science, The University of Alexandria, Egypt

Seow-Ling Teh and Janna Ong Abdullah
Department of Microbiology, Faculty of Biotechnology and Biomolecular Sciences, Malaysia

Parameswari Namasivayam
Department of Cell and Molecular Biology, Faculty of Biotechnology and Biomolecular Sciences, Malaysia

Rusea Go
Biology Department, Faculty of Science, Universiti Putra Malaysia, Malaysia

Jerzy Korczak
University of Economics, Wrocław, Poland

Wilhelm Grzesiak and Daniel Zaborski
Laboratory of Biostatistics, Department of Ruminant Science, West Pomeranian University of Technology, Szczecin, Poland

Elisabetta Poluzzi, Emanuel Raschi, Carlo Piccinni and Fabrizio De Ponti
Department of Medical and Surgical Sciences, University of Bologna, Bologna, Italy